PRELUDE TO MAGDALA

PRELUDE TO MAGDALA

Emperor Theodore of Ethiopia and British Diplomacy

Percy Arnold

Edited by Richard Pankhurst

BELLEW PUBLISHING
London

First published in Great Britain in 1991
by Bellew Publishing Company Limited
7 Southampton Place, London WC1A 2DR

ISBN 0 947792 53 8

Printed in Great Britain by
Billing & Sons Ltd, Worcester

CONTENTS

PREFACE

The author, the late Percy Arnold, was a scholarly British journalist who in the 1960s spent some two years in Addis Ababa, acting as researcher for Emperor Haile Selassie's autobiography. At this time he acquired a deep interest in Ethiopian affairs, and was particularly fascinated with the history of nineteenth-century Anglo-Ethiopian relations.

On returning to Britain he spent many years studying the dispute between the British Government and Emperor Theodore II (reigned 1855–68) – a notable Ethiopian protagonist of reform and reunification of the then divided country – which led to the detention of a British consul. This remarkable event was followed, with the inevitability of a Greek tragedy, by others no less remarkable: the imprisonment of three other British officials and several German and other European missionaries at that monarch's mountain fortress of Magdala; the British Government's decision, after seemingly interminable debate, on military intervention; the despatch of Sir Robert Napier's expedition of 1867–8 which crossed the greater part of northern Ethiopia without encountering any significant opposition, and was much acclaimed in Britain where a number of roads and two public houses were named in his and its honour; the destruction of Theodore's army as a result of Britain's superiority in modern weapons; Theodore's dramatic suicide at Magdala on Easter Sunday, 1868; the collapse of the government Theodore had forged; the looting of manuscripts, crowns, crosses and other artifacts (largely to the benefit of the British Library); a bitter power struggle among Ethiopian chiefs to decide who should inherit his crown; and, eventually, the reunification and modernisation of Ethiopia which Theodore had envisaged, but which he failed to achieve, and never lived to see.

Arnold's object in carrying out extensive research, in the British Public Record Office, the British Library and elsewhere, was not to retell the so often told story of the Magdala campaign, but to examine the events – in both Ethiopia and Britain – which served as its Prelude. His book is thus in its way a history of Britain in the 1860s – and of policy-making in Downing Street – as much as of Emperor Theodore and Ethiopia; the work is interesting moreover for its insights into some of the personalities involved, not least Walter Plowden, Britain's first Consul in Ethiopia, a great admirer of Theodore; and the author's particular *bête-noir* – the 'pushful' Dr Charles T. Beke.

By the time of his death in 1980 the author had virtually completed an extensive study of events and policies leading up to the Magdala campaign, but did not live to edit it or to write the concluding chapter on the battle and its aftermath. The editor was moreover confronted with several different versions of the manuscript which required considerable editing, as well as the addition of a final chapter. The work, it soon transpired, was also too long to satisfy today's publishing requirements, and had therefore to be pruned, as the author would undoubtedly himself have done had he lived. It is, however, hoped that Percy Arnold's inimitable style and humour, as well as all the principal events in his story, have been faithfully retained. Specialists wishing to consult the original unabridged text will find copies at the Royal Geographical Society in London and the Institute of Ethiopian Studies in Addis Ababa.

Differences in the spelling of Ethiopian names found in this book are due to the absence in mid nineteenth century Britain of any generally accepted system for their transliteration into English. The country then, as for many centuries, was known abroad by the two terms Abyssinia and Ethiopia, both of which therefore appear almost interchangeably in the text. The author, writing in the 1960s and dealing with nineteenth century material, refers to the people now widely known as Oromo by the then current term Galla.

RICHARD PANKHURST
Addis Ababa and London

ACKNOWLEDGEMENTS

Acknowledgements are due to the author's sister, Roxane Arnold, without whose devotion this work would not have been published, to Sheila Saville for typing successive drafts with great dedication; to Olive Chandler for helping with checking references and quotations; to Denis Gerard for his kindness in photographing the engravings; to Nigel Britten for valuable guidance and to our publishing friends Rex Collings and Ib Bellew for their advice and co-operation.

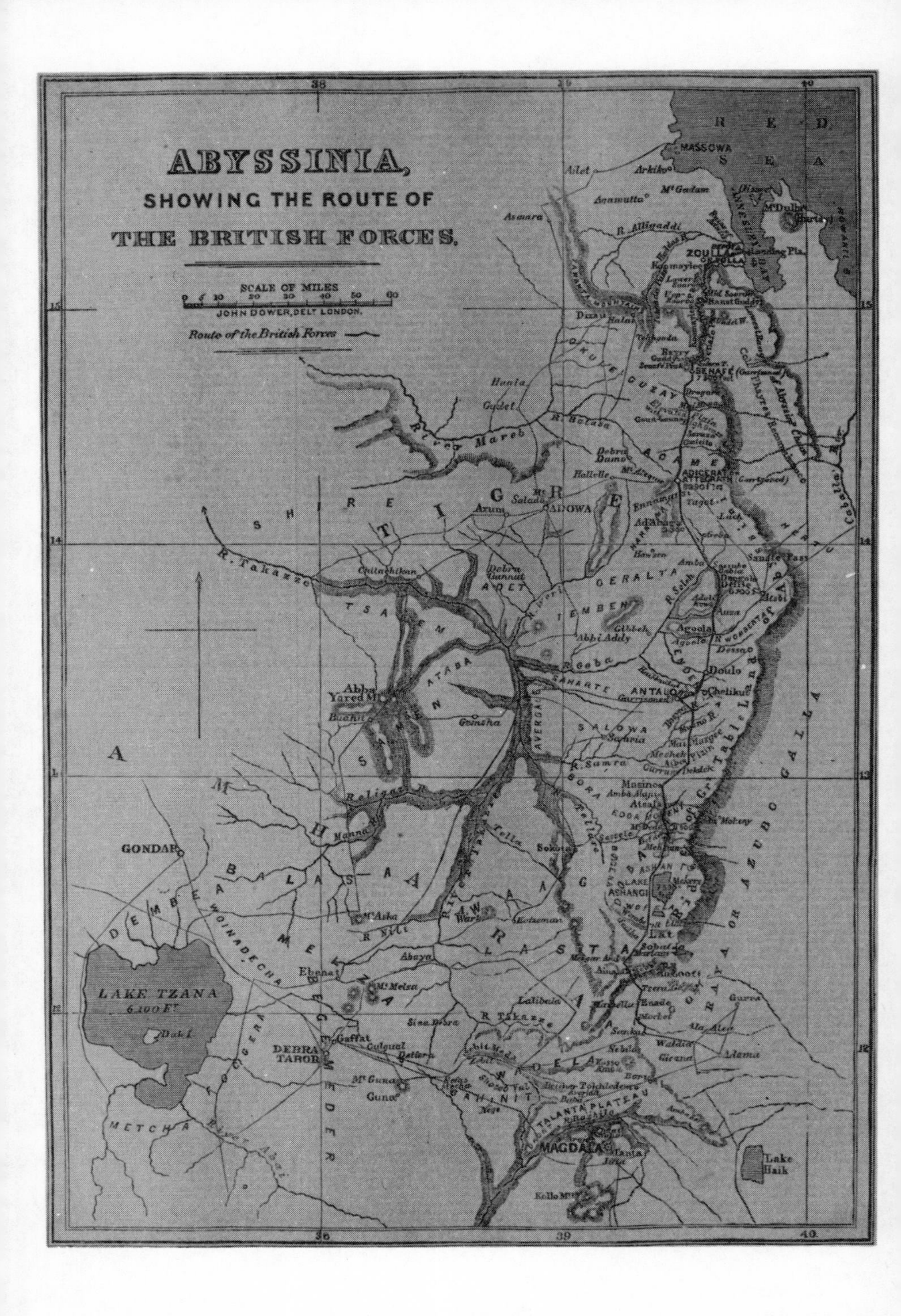
ABYSSINIA,
SHOWING THE ROUTE OF
THE BRITISH FORCES.
SCALE OF MILES
0 5 10 20 30 40 50 60
JOHN DOWER, DELT LONDON.
Route of the British Forces
RED SEA
MASSOWA
ZOULLA
SENAFE
ADIGERAT
ADOWA
ANTALO
TIGRE
GONDAR
LAKE TZANA
6,100 FT
DEBRA TABOR
MAGDALA
TALANTA PLATEAU
Lake Haik
River Mareb
R. Takazze
LASTA
ASHANGI

IMPERATIVE NECESSITY

I

PARLIAMENT IS SUMMONED
(1867)

It was the middle of the night when Disraeli, the Chancellor of the Exchequer, walked slowly down a corridor of the Houses of Parliament after the critical debate which he had opened in the afternoon, and now, not a little tired, he was homeward bound. With him was a somewhat younger man, the Secretary of State for Foreign Affairs, Lord Stanley, heir to a great title and vast estates, whom the Chancellor had but recently called 'a comrade in arms, and friend of my public life'.

The two members of the Government, as they walked away from the debating chamber that Wednesday, 27 November, could be well pleased with the night's debate, as also with the course of business, both in the House of Commons and in the House of Lords, since the special summoning of Parliament only nine days previously. It was unusual, in those days, for Parliament to be meeting at that time of year. Parliament had not met since it was prorogued on 21 August, and would not have met again until February in the following year, but exciting events had taken place since the summer, and the Chancellor of the Exchequer had urged upon the Prime Minister the need to summon Parliament without waiting for next February: approval of Parliament was needed on constitutional matters, and for raising further money before the end of the financial year.

Problems had become pressing, and on 8 September the Chancellor had written to the Prime Minister:

> I must call your consideration to the difficult and dangerous position to which, it seems to me, your Government is drifting . . . I see only one mode of extricating ourselves from the impending peril, and that is a very disagreeable one. Parliament ought, in my opinion, to be called together as soon as practicable.

The Prime Minister agreed, but in September he was a sick man and away from London at his home at Knowsley in Lancashire.

Arrangements for a November meeting of both Houses of Parliament therefore fell mainly upon the ever-industrious Chancellor.

So Parliament met on Tuesday, 19 November: the Queen, then at Windsor, did not attend the opening, and her Speech was read by the Lord High Chancellor (not to be confused with the Chancellor of the Exchequer – the two ancient offices had been separated since the thirteenth century). This office was held by Frederick Thesiger, first Baron Chelmsford; he had in his youth served as a naval officer, but subsequently turned to the profession of law with success, and at the early age of 40, had achieved the highest office of the English judiciary, and which, curiously, also gave its holder a seat in the Government.

According to custom for the reading of the Queen's Speech in the House of Lords, not only were there present the peers of the realm, but also members of the House of Commons summoned by the Yeoman Usher of the Black Rod.

The Lord High Chancellor read aloud:

> My Lords, Gentlemen of the House of Commons, Her Majesty not thinking fit to be present here this day in Her Royal Person, hath been pleased . . . to cause Letters Patent to be issued under Her Great Seal, constituting us and several other Lords herein named Her Commissioners to do all things in Her Majesty's name, on her part necessary to be performed in this Parliament.

The Letters Patent then being read by the Clerk of the House, the Lord Chancellor again rose and read the Queen's Speech which began:

> 'My Lords and Gentlemen, in again applying to you for your Advice and Assistance, I regret that I have found it necessary to call your attendance at an unusual, and probably for many of you an inconvenient Season.
>
> The Sovereign of Abyssinia, in violation of all international law, continues to hold in captivity several of My Subjects, some of whom have been especially accredited to him by Myself, and his persistent disregard of friendly representations has left Me no Alternative but that of making a peremptory demand for the liberation of My Subjects . . . '

When the Lord Chancellor had concluded, the Gentlemen returned to the House of Commons, and after a brief adjournment, both Houses entered upon their debates. The procedure, similar in both Houses, was for a member propose that an Address be presented to the Queen, thanking her for her gracious Speech, which was of course a statement of Government policy discussed on the proposal for the Address of thanks.

The Government could have arranged for Parliament to meet to consider only the urgent Ethiopian question, but, on the advice of the Chancellor, it had been decided to make the opening of Parliament the beginning of the new session, with a full Government programme.

So the Queen's Speech had contained some twelve subjects in addition to that of Ethiopia. They included the occupation of Rome by troops of the French Emperor Napoleon III; the alteration of borough boundaries; the prevention of cattle plague; and the recent Irish disturbance.

On the opening day of Parliament the debates went well for the Government. It seemed clear that, despite cautious reservations by the Opposition, both in Lords and Commons, the Government would carry Parliament with them on their Ethiopian policy.

True, in the Commons in the first day's debate the Chancellor of the Exchequer's formidable opponent, the Leader of the Opposition, had been deliberately restrained in his comments on the Government in view of the anxiety the Chancellor was suffering on account of his wife's very grave illness. The sympathetic reference by Mr Gladstone to this domestic tribulation brought tears to Disraeli's eyes.

Encouraged though the Government were by the favourable reception of their policy during the first few days of the assembly, they still needed a supply of money to carry out the venture they had embarked upon, and this it was that had brought the Chancellor of the Exchequer, as finance minister, to the House of Commons again on Tuesday, 26 November. He was now less anxious about his wife, whose health was slowly improving, but still he had to force himself to attend the House because he was himself a sick and tired man.

It was late afternoon when the ailing Chancellor rose in the House, sitting as a Committee of Supply, to ask for a Vote of Credit of £2,000,000. He was presenting them, he said, with 'rough Estimates, but not careless Estimates' of Government requirements to meet the situation in Ethiopia. The £2,000,000 would be money enough, he assured the House, until the end of the financial year. In the following year a further £1,500,000 might be required. Who could tell how short or how long this adventure in a little-known land, of which we heard such diverse reports, would last?

The Chancellor reminded the House that the problem which the Government confronted was one they had inherited from the previous Government, whose members and supporters now formed the Opposition.

Members of both Houses were by now familiar with, and becoming increasingly knowledgeable about, the whole sad affair of the Ethiopian dispute: many had improved their knowledge of African geography, like the Member for Nottingham (Mr Osborne), who confessed: 'When the subject was first brought before Parliament I was in the state of ignorance of many Foreign Secretaries, and I did not know where Massowah was.'

It was more than three years since the matter had first been raised in Parliament by a Question in the Commons, and two years since it had first been debated in the Lords. Many members had even earlier known about events which were the origin of the dispute, and outside Parliament there was, as the Chancellor said, 'the general interest which for a long time the subject has commanded throughout the country . . . '

Many members regarded the almost mysterious Ethiopian monarch as responsible for the present difficulties. An opinion of him widely shared was expressed by one Member as 'the somewhat eccentric King Theodore'; Lord Stanley, who had not mentioned the Ethiopian affair on the opening day, now spoke at length, and said that when the British Government first appointed a British Consul to the court of the Ethiopian monarch, 'King Theodore was . . . known to be an able and ambitious sovereign, somewhat unscrupulous, perhaps, and careless of life – but that apparently insane mixture of suspicion and violence which now characterised his disposition had not then developed itself, and could not have been foreseen.'

Lord Stanley, it should be explained, sat in the Commons for he was not a peer of the realm but enjoyed his title of Viscount by established courtesy as first son and heir of an Earl, the renowned Lord Derby, then Prime Minister.

The debate which ensued ranged far and wide, questions were asked about Britons and other Europeans then in Ethiopia, including the devoted German protestant missionary Mr Flad who two years earlier had brought a message from Emperor Theodore to the Queen of England. For the present difficulties some blamed particular individuals, others blamed British policy. The member for Nottingham did both. He said:

> This is one of the mischievous legacies that have been left to us by former Governments. I may say it is a Palmerstonian legacy. For the last twenty years we have been thrusting our intervention everywhere in every quarter of the globe, under the pretence of advancing what is called British influence and prestige and our commercial interests.

The Chancellor, however, knew the outcome of his request for funds, when Mr Gladstone, Leader of the Opposition making his weighty contribution to the debate, said of the Government's proposals, 'I am wholly unprepared to censure or condemn the policy which the Government have pursued.'

But the debate continued, and it was only after 1 a.m. that the weary Chancellor had the satisfaction of witnessing the House approve his Vote of Credit for £2,000,000. He could be particularly pleased because the Government did not command a majority in the Commons, and the Government's Ethiopian policy was admittedly a gamble.

No one in Parliament felt happy about the dispute. Many felt relief that at last a decisive step had been taken, but more regretted that such action had proved necessary. In explaining to the Commons the Government's reluctance to embark on drastic action, Lord Stanley used words the Prime Minister had employed. At the opening of Parliament on 19 November, Lord Derby had said in the Lords: 'no Government came to a decision with more reluctance, or with a stronger sense of the imperative necessity which would alone justify such a decision'. And now Lord Stanley, justifying the Government's venture, said in the Commons that it was: 'an undertaking which nothing could have induced the present Government – or I suppose any Government – to engage in except the conviction of an imperative necessity'. How this situation had arisen will be explained in the chapters that follow.

How the money just voted was to be raised would be a matter for further debate. But for now the Chancellor and his friend could be reasonably content. When they reached the courtyard of the Houses of Parliament, the Foreign Secretary had to help the Chancellor into a horse cab for the quarter of an hour's drive home. Although the Prime Minister and the Chancellor used houses in Downing Street as offices and as a place for Cabinet meetings, neither resided there, but lived at their private London houses. So the cab drove the Chancellor to Grosvenor Gate in Park Lane. On arrival the puzzled driver waited in vain for his passenger to get out, and may well have thought that the elegant MP was drunk. In fact the Chancellor was too ill to move and had to be assisted into his house. He went to bed and stayed there for the next ten days, leaving his deputy to conduct the next financial steps for raising the required money for this Ethiopian venture.

Part I

WALTER PLOWDEN

2

MR PLOWDEN: BASHA BULAD
(1846–7)

Late in 1846 a young Englishman was at the Red Sea island port of Massawa. That in itself was unusual. He had come down to the coast from the interior of Ethiopia, and was now preparing for his homeward journey to England which he had not seen for eight years.

The young traveller had descended from the massive highlands to the hot coastal plain by a route well known to African and Arab traders, and to many captured slaves. He was not the first European to travel that ancient route, but it was indeed rare for an Englishman to make that journey. The route was not without peril to life, limb and property; nor when he at last arrived safely there did the authorities at Massawa look upon him with favour; for the Turkish Governor was prejudiced, not to say hostile, towards Christians, whether European or Ethiopian.

The stranger's presence was soon known to the suspicious Governor and authorities of Massawa, whose revenues came mainly from the tolls, always vexatious and often exorbitant, levied on goods and chattels of merchants trading with Ethiopia; moreover the authorities had little love for the English, who could not mind their own business and must everlastingly be interfering with the slave trade. Massawa was not the only, but it was certainly the main gateway to the highlands of Ethiopia, and this coral island port had the best harbour for miles along the coast. The authorities were not backward in exploiting this advantage.

The presence of any Frank was in those days quickly observed in that little town which consisted mainly of mud huts and a few stone buildings; but the Englishman who had just been ferried over from the mainland was thin and strikingly tall, which attracted special attention. Not only his outstanding physique, however, made his presence notable; news and gossip and the reports of spies travelled quickly, and it was known that despite his youth and his small retinue this Englishman was the friend of the great Ras Ali, the powerful prince who ruled over Ethiopia in the name of an Emperor of ancient lineage but whose power had long been subjugated. Over many provinces of the Empire Ras Ali's rule was only nominal, but his authority was absolute in those parts of central Ethiopia where his army could make his will prevail over ever-recalcitrant, war-loving and often too ambitious chiefs.

Few princes in Ethiopia maintained their throne and their rule, except by the power of the sword. Ras Ali claimed special authority, but there were many provincial rulers ready to defy it. There were three Christian princes of whom Ali had specially to beware. To the south-east, the King of Shoa where a stable, inherited kingship had, in contrast to other parts of Ethiopia, prevailed for six generations; to the south, Dejazmatch Goshu, ruler of Gojjam; and to the north, Dejazmatch Wubie, ruler of Tigré.

The lone Englishman in Massawa was making his arrangements with special care, for he was not merely homeward bound, he was also on an important mission, largely of his own devising, and he was planning to return. Walter Plowden, for that was his name, had made his mark in Ethiopia, or at least in one of the great provinces of that much divided Empire – divided by high mountains and deep, precipitous ravines, and divided more cruelly by continuous and devastating civil wars. He was also by now an experienced and knowledgeable traveller over provinces seldom visited by Europeans; but for the rest this young man of 26 was of no particular consequence. Yet as he made his plans he was aware of his achievements and the possibilities which they held out for himself – and for England – and had consequently a modest sense of his own importance. He was the bearer of gifts and a letter to the Queen of Great Britain, the young Queen Victoria, from the mighty Ethiopian ruler, Ras Ali, whose friendship and esteem he had won, and whose Ethiopian envoy was now to accompany him to England, visiting foreign lands for the first time.

From Massawa, when he could get a ship to take him, the rest of the journey would be not at all unusual for an Englishman. It was part of a familiar route to and from England and India. The journey would be up the Red Sea to Suez, with maybe a stop on the Arabian shore at the pilgrim port of Jeddah. Then from Suez overland to Cairo and on to Alexandria. (The Suez Canal was not built until 27 years later.) From Alexandria once again by sea either to Marseilles and across France, or more likely all the way by sea through the Straits of Gibraltar to England. The hazard was the Red Sea if the traveller was in a small craft, as many a traveller and more than one Christian missionary had discovered.

Plans had to be made, but the hazards ahead would have to be met as they arose; Mr Plowden, with the confidence of youth, could reflect that so far fortune had favoured him.

It was very much by chance that Plowden had gone to Ethiopia and entered upon his remarkable life there. He was known to the Ethiopians as Basha Bulad. He was addressed by courtesy as Basha, a military term of Turkish origin; Bulad was as near Plowden as the Ethiopian tongue could get.

Walter Chichele Plowden was born in England and had his early education there, but had gone out to India where his parents lived and for a time worked with merchants in Calcutta. Tiring of this, in 1843 he had taken ship to return to England, via the Red Sea route. Arriving at Suez, he had met another Englishman, John G. Bell, who had suggested he should join him on a journey to Ethiopia to discover the source of the White Nile and possibly to trade. Not averse to adventure, Plowden had agreed and soon the two Englishmen were sailing down the Red Sea to Massawa, and through this gateway entered Ethiopia. The unexpected attractions of the country and of its peoples had soon seduced Bell and Plowden from their original plan. Instead of crossing through Ethiopia they had stayed in it to become the trusted friends and counsellors of Ethiopian princes.

Now, back in Massawa, Plowden was thinking of the future. He penned a letter on 15 October 1846, to the British Foreign Secretary, Lord Palmerston. The essential part read:

> Having spent nearly four years in the interior of Abyssinia [Ethiopia], on my return I was pressed by the principal Chief in this part of the country, Ras Ali, to undertake the conveyance of a few presents to Her Majesty, the fame of whose greatness had reached his ears . . . if these presents are now refused, and I am consequently obliged to return them to their donor, it will be perhaps hereafter a source of regret . . . should the advances of the Ras be now rejected, the access to this magnificent and almost unknown region will probably be rendered difficult for years, if not closed, to the man of science or the zealous missionary . . .

Hopefully, Plowden despatched his letter to England, and waited for the answer. He had thus started a chain of events that no one could foresee.

3

LORD PALMERSTON

(1846–7)

In 1846 a Whig Government was in office in England. This was the period of 'the hungry forties', when there was widespread distress resulting from bad wheat harvests, the crops having been spoilt by rain, and especially in Ireland where disease had ruined the potatoes, the main diet of the poor. In consequence there were in both countries alarming riots and arson, the more menacing in Ireland.

The Prime Minister was Lord Russell, then aged 54, and the Foreign Secretary was Lord Palmerston, aged 62. These two aristocrats, both of keen intellect, were very different in temperament and appearance, but for the past 16 years their careers had run parallel. Both had established their reputation and popularity among their supporters in the great Whig Government of Lord Grey which came into office in 1830 and brought about fundamental reforms, of which the most important were the momentous step of extending the parliamentary franchise in 1832, and abolishing slavery in all British territories in 1833. Both aristocrats, notwithstanding their titles, sat in the Commons, which Palmerston did to the end of his long life. Both entered Parliament in their early twenties and both represented 'rotten' English boroughs.

The studious and outwardly cold John Russell, little John or Johnny as he was often called on account of his small build and frail appearance, enjoyed his title of Lord by courtesy as a younger son of the sixth Duke of Bedford.

Lord Palmerston has been aptly called the Most English Minister. His viscountcy was, however, of the Irish Peerage, and this enabled him to sit in the Commons. Tall and robust, expansive by temperament, elegant in dress, he was soon very much a man about town. He had won lasting fame as the skilled and forceful, if at times seemingly reckless, champion of British interests abroad; and also as a champion of governments under a constitution rather than under individual autocrats. Every country in Europe was aware of his power and influence. But at home he was less of a democrat and more of a Tory than a Whig. The Foreign Secretary to whom Walter Plowden wrote was thus not only a renowned elder statesman in his own country, but also in the councils of Europe.

Walter Plowden's letter reached the Foreign Office in London on 2 December 1846, about six weeks after it was written, not a very long time for those days. A communication from Massawa about Ethiopia was interesting if only because of its rarity, but it did not of itself appear to be very important. Yet to the imaginative mind of Lord Palmerston every new subject, if of any possible substance at all, was worth examination. Of course, by the end of 1846 more pressing subjects had been and were engaging the attention of the British Foreign Secretary and the Government.

At home there was still the unhappy situation of hunger, arson and riots in England and Ireland, and as a conscientious owner of land in Ireland, Palmerston felt personally involved. Overseas, as always, important events had been or were engaging the Foreign Secretary's attention. There had been civil war in Switzerland; Anglo-French diplomatic rivalry in Athens; less dramatic, but requiring careful attention, were the new diplomatic relations with the Vatican, where Britain had recently for the first time appointed an ambassador, and where a new Pope, Pius IX, had just created the illusion that a liberal pontiff was now the father of the Roman Catholic Church and ruler of the Papal States in the Italian peninsula where political restlessness was growing. It was soon after Pius IX came to his high office that he personally gave his blessing to a Piedmontese Capuchin missionary who would soon be facing the storms of the Red Sea on his way to Massawa and Ethiopia.

Walter Plowden had great faith in his luck. Although he could not have known it when he wrote to Lord Palmerston his luck was in; he could hardly have chosen a better moment to write. Lord Palmerston was just having his attention drawn to Ethiopia in general, and to Massawa in particular, thanks largely to the scholarly, enterprising and ever importuning Dr Charles Beke who had travelled to Ethiopia where he had spent some three years. Englishmen in 1846, including the Foreign Secretary, were in their varying degrees suspicious of the foreign policy of France, then ruled by Louis Philippe, and Dr Beke was among the more suspicious. So when he read in the *Morning Herald* that Monsieur Rochet d' Héricourt was about to pay another visit to the Kingdom of Shoa, he cut the passage out and sent it to Lord Palmerston on 9 November. Moreover, Dr Beke had been active elsewhere and before the end of that month the Foreign Secretary was to hear of him again, and of Ethiopia. It came about in this way.

The sugar-growing, French-speaking island of Mauritius in the Indian Ocean was already then an English colony, having been captured from Napoleonic France in 1810. In Dr Beke's time there was in the City of London a Mauritius Association, and Dr Beke (at his own instigation one suspects) was taken along to meet members of the Association and spoke to them about Ethiopia. He took the occasion to air two of his pet notions: first, that Christian Ethiopians of very industrious habits could be induced to go to work on the sugar plantations of Mauritius for little more than the few shillings a year they were obtaining in their own country, and second, that a British consulate should be established in Massawa to assist the passage of these ideal immigrants. Massawa might even 'be purchased from the Ottoman Government for a mere trifle'. The Association was much impressed by Dr Beke's ideas, and Mauritius, being a colony, sent a report of his speech to the Secretary of State for the Colonies in Downing Street.

Ethiopia being an independent country, and Massawa not a British colony, the Colonial Secretary sent the report of Dr Beke's speech across the road to the Foreign Secretary, whose office was also in Downing Street, on 27 November for his comments.

Five days later, on 2 December, there arrived at the Foreign Office out of the blue a letter from an Englishman actually in Massawa. This letter from Plowden immediately received favourable consideration – thanks largely to the interest that Dr Beke had stimulated – and it had come into the hands of intelligent and perceptive people. In those days it was the custom at the Foreign Office to write on the back of letters they received a brief summary of their contents and sometimes a brief comment. On this letter – perhaps in view of all that followed an historic one in Anglo-Ethiopian relations – a Foreign Office official wrote: 'Mr W. Plowden. Has arrived from the interior of Abyssinia with an Envoy and Presents to the Queen from Ras Ali. Is in want of means to come on to England.' Clearly the observation of a perceptive official.

Lord Palmerston acted quickly: on 10 December a letter was

despatched by the Foreign Office to Plowden, telling him that money would be made available for him and the Ethiopian Envoy to travel to England. The next day Lord Palmerston wrote a minute to his officials as follows:

1. Where exactly is Massowah?
2. Who and what is Dr Beke?

The matter of the Englishman waiting in Massawa was still receiving attention, but on 18 December Lord Palmerston himself signed the letter of instruction to Mr Murray, British Consul-General in Alexandria, to make the necessary money available to Plowden.

The mails, usually going by steamer, taking the time they did, it was mid January 1847 when Murray, having received the instructions from London, passed them on to Captain Haines in Aden and also to Mr Ogilvie, British Consul at Jeddah, as possibly being a quicker way of messages reaching the not too accessible Massawa.

Meanwhile the constant reader of the *Morning Herald* had remained active. In January 1847 he sent Lord Palmerston an extract from that paper to show that the French were at it again, for it reported that 'Oubie, King of Tigré', had given the French Consular Agent a letter and presents for the King of France. Dr Beke in his covering letter again took the opportunity to draw attention to the importance of Massawa. That Dr Charles Beke was knowledgeable about Ethiopia was now known, that he was mindful of British interests seemed obvious, that he would like to be British Consul in Massawa seemed not improbable.

That Dr Beke continued to bombard the Foreign Office with his epistles which he did at the rate of about one a month throughout 1847, may have had some use in not letting the Foreign Office forget the subject. For from Plowden there was no further news.

In due course the Foreign Office received from Aden, via Cairo, the routine confirmation that arrangements had been made to despatch money to Massawa, but of what Plowden was doing about his journey there was no mention. It was not until June 1847 that news of Plowden reached Lord Palmerston.

A despatch from Consul-General Murray in Alexandria dated 18 June 1847 read:

I have the honour to inform your Lordship that Mr Walter Plowden

> has just arrived here from Abyssinia, having been shipwrecked in the Red Sea.
>
> He narrowly escaped with his life, and all the presents destined by the Chief, Ras Ali, for Her Majesty were either lost or spoilt. The Abyssinian Envoy sent by the Ras to accompany him was so frightened by this, his first voyage, that he absolutely refused to attempt a second, and Mr Plowden was accordingly obliged to leave him in Cairo.

Walter Plowden had a tale to tell.

After leaving the Dahlak islands, where after only a short day's sail from Massawa, his small sailing ship had been forced to take shelter, worse storms were encountered. More than once all aboard thought their last hour had come and fervent were the calls of the ship's Ethiopian and Arab passengers and crew to Holy Mary or to Allah; their faith in the Virgin Mary and the Prophet seemed steadily to increase, while Plowden's in the captain steadily decreased, and he continued to take what solace he could from his tobacco pipe. As the days went by, the frequent storms alternated with exasperating calm, and when the weather was moderate much time was lost tacking against the wind. After this always trying and often fearful voyage it was a joy to all on the eighteenth day out of Massawa to see on the horizon the white walls of the city of Jeddah on the Arabian shore, and presently the not too brave or competent captain brought the little ship safely into the crowded harbour. Plowden was delighted to see so many ships flying the British flag, but a little disappointed when closer in to see they all had Arab captains and crews, mostly from Aden.

The Englishman and his two Ethiopian companions spent some days in the bustling town of Jeddah, and, with the useful help of a resourceful man of all trades who attached himself to the little party, bought new clothes and provisions and hired a ship, for 35 Maria Theresa dollars, with a captain who seemed as he proved, brave and skilled, for the second half of the Red Sea journey – from Jeddah to Suez, which might take fifteen days, if the weather held good.

Soon after leaving Jeddah the ship ran into more bad weather. While crossing the Gulf of Akaba, Plowden experienced the worst storm he had ever known, and the not distant coast seemed terribly threatening, but the able *rais* brought his ship safely to the coastal village of Tor and, drab as it was, it was a welcome haven. Once again the little ship put to sea, and they were now in the narrower Gulf of Suez. After more days of bad weather and now more than

30 days since leaving Massawa, Plowden felt heartily sick of the whole voyage and envied the passengers on the occasional steamer to be seen farther out at sea, making the Red Sea journey so much more comfortably.

Some 10 days after leaving Jeddah the little ship took shelter and not for the first time in a nook of a coastal reef. At nightfall a favourable wind blew up and the captain took the ship out to sea again. All being well and not having had any good sleep for some days he presently handed over the helm to a sailor and went to rest, and the vessel made progress despite rough weather. Then suddenly in the night a sailor's wild cry rang out 'Shap!' – reef. The captain sprang to the helm and shouted orders, but for once the little ship did not respond. To the accompaniment of a great cry of despair from the crew she struck heavily. Very quickly the *rais* and his crew scrambled into the water, and, standing on the reef, tried to lift the ship clear, but she was stuck fast and was soon filling with water. Efforts to refloat her were all to no avail. At last one sailor offered to take Plowden to the dimly visible shore some four miles off in the ship's tiny canoe. No one else would risk the journey through the rough sea so Plowden accepted the offer, gave his money to his Ethiopian servant to look after, and set off; if the journey proved possible, the sailor would return and one at a time bring everyone ashore. The Arab paddled with skill the half swamped canoe, the Englishman with unceasing efforts bailed out the water and the shore was reached despite reefs and rough waves. Plowden landed and the canoe went back to the ship for one more of the others.

The storm grew worse and a thick haze settled over the sea and hid the ship from view. Plowden waited some hours on the shore, but no one appeared and he then feared that the ship had broken up and all were lost. There in the night, in the storm, cold and drenched, he thought that his young Ethiopian servant who had for so long served him so well and so loyally was now dead, and at the thought of it the lone Englishman wept aloud. Recovering himself, he took stock of what he should do; he reckoned that the village of Tor, some 40 miles away across desert and sandy hills, was his only hope, and he set off in that direction. Tired and often stumbling he walked till it was what he guessed must be three in the afternoon, to reach a hill summit which he reckoned must be more than a 1,000 feet above the shore. The view ahead showed him how difficult was the distance still to be covered, but looking back there was a sight to give him a moment of joy. Far away, off the coast in the now bright afternoon light he saw just a speck, but clear enough to show it was the ship, still intact. Thus encouraged he struggled on through the rest of the day and right through the night, with only snatches of rest and a short sleep before the dawn. When he awoke in the morning he saw Mount Sinai before him revealing how far he had gone off course during the night, and now a landmark to steer him aright.

By now weak with hunger, and exhausted by the heat of the day and in pain with thirst, he struggled on, slithering in the sand each time he came to a hillock; at last, almost out of his mind with these torments and above all with thirst he threw himself on the ground and wished only to die. But the thought of the men on the little ship to whom he must send help brought him to his senses and made him force himself to stagger on to Tor. After another night and day, he met a villager who helped him, now half dead and half mad, into Tor where a poor old Greek gave him shelter. Plowden got villagers to go along the coast to the ship; a couple of days later they returned to say that they had met his fellow travellers who had got ashore, bringing very little with them; they had seen their ship plundered by one passing ship, but had been rescued by another and taken on board for Suez; they would not believe that the Englishman for whom they had searched could be still alive.

Plowden contrived to hire a dromedary and six days after arriving in Tor he set off on the animal, with the owner sitting behind him, sometimes chanting, sometimes asleep, and so after four nights of travel in this fashion reached Suez.

In Suez Plowden met his two Ethiopians who had thought him dead, and great was the rejoicing. So, on 23 May 1847, he wrote to Mr Murray in Alexandria as follows, without overstatement:

> I regret to inform you that I have been shipwrecked in the Straits of Suez and after some suffering have arrived here with the Envoy of Ras Ali.

– and he then went on to explain that he would stay a while in Suez to try and recover the presents sent by the Ras.

With the help of the Governor of Suez and the British Agent in the town some of the presents were recovered from the plunderers, but in very poor condition, and no longer fit to offer to the Queen.

Mr Murray arranged for Plowden to sail from Alexandria by steamer and on 5 August, just about a year after he had arrived at Massawa from the interior of Ethiopia, Plowden landed at Southampton.

On duly reaching London, Plowden put up at the Tavistock Hotel in Covent Garden and lost little time in getting in touch with the Foreign Office in Downing Street, not fifteen minutes' walk away for a long-legged man.

4

OUR CONSUL IN ABYSSINIA
(1847–8)

Lord Palmerston's main interest in Ethiopia was, it seems, the prospect of increasing British trade with that little known country, and it was for this reason that he wanted to see the young Englishman recently from those parts. This view harmonised with Plowden's, and within a week of his arrival he sat down in his little London hotel to write a statement on his 'Mission and the Prospects of Trade with Ethiopia'. This document was dated 13 August 1847.

The Foreign Secretary, who, amid his other preoccupations, had been giving thought to the question of Ethiopia, had before him the report for which he had asked on the regular reader of the *Morning Herald*. This brief report spoke favourably of Dr Charles Beke, mentioning that he had been a professor of English in Leipzig (in the then kingdom of Saxony), had usefully assisted the British Consul there, and had acted for him when the Consul was absent; later Dr Beke had travelled in Ethiopia at the expense of some society in London. The report concluded 'Dr Beke is a clever man but "pushing".' At the foot of this report Lord Palmerston minuted: 'I am inclined to think it would be a good thing to appoint a Consul at Massowah and perhaps Dr Beke would be a good man for it.' The minute was dated 15 August. Walter Plowden had sent his memorandum to Lord Palmerston perhaps just in time.

A few days later Plowden received a written request from A. V. Addington of the Foreign Office, saying his Lordship would be glad to have more information regarding prospects of trade with Ethiopia and adjoining countries and was there any port beside Massawa suitable for commerce? The young man promptly set about writing out what was asked of him. With a note saying he hoped that what he now submitted would be useful notwithstanding that he had not travelled in Ethiopia with any intention of collecting commercial information, he sent Addington a very informative 'Memorandum on Trade with Abyssinia', eight foolscap pages in neat handwriting, dated 20 August. Plowden's two reports gave Lord Palmerston most of what he might want to know, and they also incidentally confirmed the relevant facts and some opinions about trade prospects given by Dr Beke to the Mauritius Association.

Plowden's reports stated that he thought Ethiopia could absorb a considerable amount of English manufactures and a demand for them already existed. He thought British trade with Ethiopia could be quadrupled. He added his view that the Ethiopians were shrewd enough to understand the value of a trade treaty, and that chiefs and merchants had told him that they wished for British protection when they reached Massawa. The country had, however, a feudal system of government, rending the people's ideas 'of the value of commerce limited and careless'.

The Foreign Secretary had asked his Office for information about Plowden, and this was sent to him with a minute dated 18 August. Its author, whose identity remains hidden under the initials 'E.H.', was probably a Mr Hammond. He concluded with these words: 'His uncle, if I remember rightly, said he was a high spirited and enterprising youth, though without steadiness for a mercantile life. I think he might well be employed in Abyssinia.'

The 'enterprising youth' did not let the grass grow under his feet in London. Eight days after sending in his second report, and a couple of days after the Foreign Secretary had seen the minute about him, he sent Addington a third memorandum containing further useful information, about the Powers in possession of Massawa and related matters.

A few days later Lord Palmerston had made up his mind. He gave his opinion, and instructions, in a brief memorandum, written in his own bold hand, dated 22 August 1847: 'I will appoint Mr Plowden Consul at Massowah . . . I do not think it expedient to endeavour to obtain possession of any Territory in that Quarter. Our object ought rather to be to encourage and secure the independence of the Native Rulers.' He also proposed that Ras Ali should be invited to enter into a Trade Treaty with England, and that a draft should be prepared by the Foreign Office. He concluded in words that were to have special significance later: 'Mr Plowden's residence should be Massowah but he should go up from time to time to Gondar to keep up personal Relations with the Ras and settle with him any questions which may arise.' So the first definite decision was that day taken to establish official representation of England in Ethiopia. The seed thus sown was to grow into a plant that would bear bitter fruit.

Britain was not then pursuing a policy of territorial expansion. The scramble for Africa had not yet begun, and Cobden and other radical Members of Parliament were arguing that British colonies were more trouble than they were worth. At that time, with the Industrial Revolution in full swing and production of manufactured goods steadily increasing, Britain's imperialism took instead the form of protecting and expanding her trade abroad, and capturing new overseas markets.

Plowden's salary was fixed at £500 a year, to start ten days before embarkation, and he was given permission to engage in mercantile pursuits, but would not be entitled to any pension. Addington and his assistants at the Foreign Office busied themselves with the necessary arrangements, and several departments were formally notified that Her Majesty had been graciously pleased to appoint Mr Walter Plowden her Consul in Abyssinia.

There were to be presents from the Queen to Ras Ali. It was agreed that the best plan would be to give Plowden the money and he would know best what to buy. Plowden pointed out that gifts would not be greatly appreciated unless they included some muskets, and the much coveted matchlocks might only be obtainable in Egypt. All this was agreed to: the Foreign Office suggested £500 for all the presents; Lord Palmerston cut it to £400.

There was also a letter to prepare to send to Ras Ali by Command of the Queen which Lord Palmerston would sign. Officials at the Foreign Office were not quite sure to whom the letter should be addressed. The first draft was written out to 'The Ras of . . . ', and later in another hand the name 'Abyssinia' was inserted. The second draft was to 'His Highness the Ras of Tigré, Abyssinia'. By a stretch of courtesy Ras Ali might have been described as the Ras of Abyssinia, but he was certainly not the Ras of Tigré – Dejazmatch Wubie, ruler of Tigré, would have called him to book had he used that title!

Lord Palmerston's letter expressed the British Government's 'true feeling of friendship for the illustrious Ruler' of Abyssinia, and Lord Palmerston doubted not that:

> the desire of the British Government to enter into a Treaty with

> Abyssinia will be highly satisfactory to your Highness . . . who will clearly perceive the great advantage which Abyssinia will derive from intimate connection with the Sovereign of the British Empire, whose dominions extend from the rising to the setting sun, and whose fleets are to be met with in every part of the seas which encompass the earth.

The Queen's Commission appointing Plowden was dated Buckingham Palace, 21 November 1847, and was countersigned by Lord Palmerston. Plowden was appointed 'to be Our Consul in Abyssinia', and the commission desired 'the Emperor of Abyssinia to receive and admit' Walter Plowden, 'Our Consul as aforesaid . . .'

At last, all the arrangements completed, the cases of presents on board, and carrying the letter for Ras Ali and the proud possessor of the Queen's Commission, Consul Walter Plowden sailed from Southampton on 3 February 1848, on board a steamship bound for Alexandria. He had been in England six months.

Stopping for a short time at Alexandria and Cairo, he duly sailed from Suez, down the Red Sea, to Aden where, an East India Company ship of war being eventually ready, he sailed on 19 July. The ship cruised along the African coast which the Consul thus had an opportunity to observe, before reaching Massawa. It was a happy Walter Plowden who disembarked from the Brigantine *Tigris* on the sweltering hot day of 5 August 1848, Her Britannic Majesty's Consul to Abyssinia. It was exactly a year after he had so hopefully landed in Southampton. He would go on trusting his luck.

Consul Plowden now had before him two clear duties: first, to establish his Consulate, and, second, to go up into the interior to present to Ras Ali his credentials, the letter from Lord Palmerston written by command of the Queen, and Her Majesty's presents.

The first thing Plowden did was to secure a building, perhaps it should be called a large hut, to be his house on the island, which was very hot at that time of the year. Next, he secured a plot of land and a straw hut in the village of Monculo, some three miles inland on the somewhat cooler mainland.

He also attended to his second duty, and made enquiries and plans to go up to Gondar. He sent a message and the present of a carpet to Dejazmatch Wubie, with a request for permission to go through Tigré into the interior of Ethiopia. In due course he made his way towards Adowa. Situated on one of the great routes between Massawa and the interior, it was an important market town, where wares from distant lands were bought and sold; a great meeting place for merchants from many places.

Dejazmatch Wubie was then living some seven days' journey away at Maitalo to the south-west, in the fastness of the high mountains of Semien, his native province, whence 12 years earlier he had sallied forth to usurp the throne of Tigré.

Before leaving Adowa the British Consul had with his usual diligence sent despatches to the Foreign Office. He reported with satisfaction the welcome he had received from the ruler of Tigré, who controlled the roads into the interior. Some little time afterwards he sent Lord Palmerston, with the translation, two letters from Wubie. The first asked Plowden to find in Massawa, or if not there perhaps in his own country, builders or masons; he would give them wages or land and take care of them. The second letter read in part:

> Formerly my ancestors were in possession of, and governed all the coast of the Red Sea and Massowah; recently when we quarrelled among ourselves, the Turks took possession of Massowah. After this, two years back, they also sent troops to the mainland, and occupied Moncouloo and Arkeeko. The Naib of Arkeeko being thus prevented from paying my usual tribute, I this year sent down my forces and drove the Turks back into the Island of Massowah. You are a Christian Queen, and the friend of Christians; you are powerful, and I now request your assistance and friendship, that you will not permit Mohammadan forces to ravage and occupy my territories, but will insist on their remaining content with the possession of the Island of Massowah (though that even they have no right to), without setting foot on the mainland, or interfering with the Naib that I appoint at Arkeeko and the coast . . . I wish much for the friendship of the English, and trust that you will now show the sincerity of your good-will towards Abyssinia.

Plowden now set off to join Ras Ali at Debra Tabor.

5

CAMP AND TREATY
(1849)

On nearing Debra Tabor, Plowden's caravan was met by a messenger and a guide sent by Ras Ali, and on entering the town Plowden's friend, John Bell, greeted him. John Bell, called Yohannes by the Ethiopians, was now a general in Ras Ali's army, the chief of a nearby district which the Ras had given him, and was married to an Ethiopian lady of rank.

Debra Tabor was cool and healthy, but with no stone building other than that of the Ras it was more like a camp than a town. Bell led Plowden to the stone residence. After passing through the bustling courtyards, with many people waiting for an audience they were shown into the inner hall, where the silence contrasted sharply with the constant clamour outside. Ras Ali was delighted to see Plowden back from England after his long absence, and invited him to lodge within the grounds of the palace, but the Englishman preferred a quieter place, so the Ras had him lodged at the house of a Muslim chief on a hill, some two hundred yards from the hubbub of the main camp and the inquisitiveness of its frequenters.

The next day the Consul again had an audience with the Ras and presented Palmerston's letter which he, standing, read out in translation; the Ras could not understand the point of it. Next the Consul produced the Queen's gifts; these dazzled Ras Ali and he made no attempt to conceal his delight. The Consul wisely thought that success sufficient for the moment.

Over the next few days he from time to time raised the matter of the Commercial Treaty, but the Ras kept on putting off the matter. Plowden wrote of Ras Ali that he had 'a supercilious indifference of anything that does not immediately concern himself' – and consequently anything regarding Europe. Moreover, the Ethiopian ruler had then more pressing matters on his mind.

As everyone throughout the length and breadth of the land

knew, the Ras would one day, sooner rather than later, and before the rains began, march southwards into Gojjam to subdue Dejazmatch Birru Goshu; but precisely when his drummers and heralds would announce the order to the chiefs to march with him (and woe betide those who did not) would until the last minute remain, according to Ethiopian custom, the secret of the great chief himself.

While Ras Ali thought much about war and little about the English Treaty, the Consul made the best of it – for, as he had written, 'Those who have no patience should not come to Abyssinia.' He travelled to the shores of Lake Tana and grazed his animals. Then, learning that Ras Ali was on the march to Gojjam, he hurried back to Debra Tabor and prepared a caravan and considerable provisions, for on a campaign of this sort food for at least a month had to be carried. When all was ready, General Bell and Consul Plowden (with his two copies of the Trade Treaty) set off for the wars. The Englishmen's personal party consisted of about a hundred people, servants and guards. On the way they came upon other chiefs with their soldiery hastening to join up with the army of their overlord, Ras Ali, in feudal obedience to his summons. At the Blue Nile they camped for a while, and then crossed to Gojjam by way of a bridge built centuries earlier by the Portuguese, with the river some 30 feet below. Plowden and his entourage remained attached to Ras Ali's army for three months, first at one encampment and then at another.

At last the Consul ventured to raise the question of the Treaty, but without meeting any favourable response. At this time a chief who enjoyed the title of Wagshum and was a brother-in-law of the Ras had obtained leave to return to his district where a revolt had broken out during his absence. Plowden now told the Ras that this would be a good occasion to sign the Treaty, so that he could leave the camp with the signed copy for despatch to England and travel under the escort of the Wagshum for the first part of his way. Ras Ali remained indifferent to the Treaty, until suddenly one morning he sent word to Plowden that he would sign it. Plowden has himself told the story:

> I went into his inner tent, and had the Treaty read to him by my scribe. After the Abyssinian manner, he kept talking . . . On his asking me some trifling question, in answer, I begged his attention to what was being read, to which he assented, and yawned exceedingly; however, it was got through, some points being explained and dwelt on by me. Whereupon, the Ras said he saw no harm whatever in the document;

> on the contrary, that it was excellent, but appeared to him exceedingly useless, inasmuch as he did not suppose, as Abyssinia was then constituted, that one English merchant would or could enter it in ten years. He then sealed the two copies, and gave his own to a favourite *deftera* [scribe], with orders to take it to Debra Ṭabor, and lock it up there . . .

Thus at last and with due protocol the Anglo-Ethiopian Commercial Treaty was signed for the Empire of Ethiopia by its Chief Minister, Ras Ali, and for Britain by Consul Walter Plowden, during the campaign in Gojjam at the Ras's camp in the highlands at Ermowga, at the end of the rains in 1849. The British Consul eventually departed from Ras Ali's camp with his precious copy of the Treaty.

The lanky, lone Englishman had achieved something: subject to eventual ratification, he had established treaty relationship between Britain and Ethiopia. This he had done mainly by his own skill, determination and courage, but perhaps too soon. Over the next ten years Ethiopia really had little to do with Britain, as wise Ras Ali had well foreseen, and the Trade Treaty never did bring any increase in trade; nor was it Britain's influence that increased in Ethiopia, but Plowden's in the course of strange events; and a certain Dejazmatch Kassa's.

6

DARING AND SKILFUL ADVERSARY

(1849–54)

After sending Lord Palmerston the signed copy of the Anglo-Ethiopian Treaty from Massawa in April 1849, Walter Plowden spent another six years as Consul based at Massawa before he asked for leave to revisit England. He spent those years actively, often up in the interior, at times with Ras Ali and General Bell at Gondar or elsewhere, at other times visiting that other great chief Dejazmatch Wubie, wherever he might be found. When Plowden was in Massawa he stayed usually at the village of Monculo, turning its dry sandy soil into a good vegetable garden; but Massawa itself was an endurance, with successive Turkish Governors always hostile to him and to all Europeans, doing all they could to make life difficult, and hoping to make it impossible, so that all Europeans would leave, with none to bear witness to slaving and other malpractices.

Often Plowden was for long periods without news, despatches or instructions from England, and at one time he observed that the Foreign Office might have sent replies to his despatches, but he had not for some while received any, no boat from Aden having come into Massawa for eight months. This isolation notwithstanding, Plowden sent despatches to the Foreign Office fairly frequently, dutifully reporting on trade and politics, and occasionally giving a general picture of social conditions in Ethiopia.

During Plowden's Consulship six gentlemen of the English or Irish nobility (and no others) held in turn the high office of Her Majesty's Secretary of State for Foreign Affairs. With all of them the Consul exchanged despatches, so for a number of years there were British Ministers and former Ministers who knew something of the Consulate to Ethiopia and its affairs.

When Plowden was appointed to Massawa at the end of 1847

and for two years more, Lord Palmerston was the Foreign Secretary. But in 1851 the ever-independent Lord had too enthusiastically expressed congratulations to the French Ambassador in London upon the *coup d'état* by which Louis Napoleon (nephew of Napoleon I) had made himself dictator of France. Neither Queen Victoria, enraged not for the first time at Palmerston's self-assertion, nor the Cabinet, had yet expressed an opinion on Louis Napoleon's revolutionary way of becoming the head of a country. My Lord Palmerston was now being too independent once too often; the Queen and her beloved German husband were utterly against him, the Cabinet was not for him, and so the Prime Minister, Lord Russell, who had also been somewhat affronted, decided to dismiss his old colleague, although he took the opportunity to impress upon the Queen that it was not she but the Government which really decided on foreign policy. Palmerston, with some dignified protest, walked out of the Foreign Office. He was replaced by a younger peer, the second Earl of Granville. But Lord Russell's Government lasted only another two months, after which the Tories came in with the Earl of Derby as Prime Minister, the Earl of Malmesbury as Foreign Secretary, and Benjamin Disraeli as Chancellor of the Exchequer, all of whom held their offices for the first time.

Thus it was to Lord Malmesbury, newly in office, that in 1852 the British Consul gave news that a rebel, Dejazmatch Kassa, was then emerging on the Ethiopian stage. On 24 January 1853 he wrote:

> One of the great vassals of Ras Ali, named Dejajmatch Kasai, possessing large provinces between Gondar and Sennaar, has rebelled and . . . pillaged Gondar and the adjoining provinces.
>
> The Ras has ordered several large bodies of troops to be put in motion from Tigré and Godjam, but the final result of these matters is still very uncertain. Much must depend upon the continued fidelity or neutrality of the Dejajmatch Oobeay, who, whilst tributary, is nearly the equal of the Ras himself.
>
> As long as the feudal system prevails in Abyssinia, it is hopeless to expect tranquillity; I trust, however, that at present the position and power of the Ras will be in no wise endangered.

When writing this despatch the Consul did not know that a month earlier there had been another change of Government in England. Prime Minister Lord Derby was out and a coalition had been formed under the Tory Earl of Aberdeen. The Whig Lord

Russell came in as Foreign Secretary, but only for a few months, to be followed by an able Whig diplomat, the Earl of Clarendon, who was to stay at the head of the Foreign Office for five years without interruption.

Continuing his reports of Kassa's activities, the Consul, now up in Tigré, wrote on 24 May:

> This rebel Chief has gained another decisive victory over the combined forces of Ras Ali and Dejajmatch Oobeay. He has since ravaged Begemder in various directions, and even as far as Debra Tabor, the residence of the Ras . . . The Ras will now, therefore, probably return to Begemder, to check in person the formidable revolt of Dejajmatch Kasai, who has shown himself a daring and skilful adversary.

In a later despatch, of 25 July, Plowden wrote more favourably of the rebel:

> Dejajmatch Kasai is increasing in force, and having, with the assistance of some Turks, in a degree disciplined his army, it is even thought by some that the Ras is in danger . . . Dejajmatch Kasai has shown on several occasions a more enlarged and generous disposition than is usually found in an Abyssinian Chief, and appears disposed to encourage strangers.

Three days later Plowden reported the dramatic rout of his old friend, Ras Ali, but spoke yet more favourably of the victor. Nothing succeeds like success. Writing on 28 July he observed:

> Dejajmatch Kasai has completely defeated Ras Ali . . . there is some probability that Dejajmatch Kasai may become master of Abyssinia, and . . . he appears to be a man of sufficient capacity to civilize and improve this distracted country.
>
> He has already, in his camp and territory, put a stop to several barbarous and disgusting practices, and in his reception of Europeans has shown that he values them and their arts far more highly than any other Abyssinian Chief has lately been disposed to do.

A month later, on 29 August, Plowden confirmed the important turn of events. The conflict was now much more than a provincial rebellion, it was a war to determine who should rule Ethiopia; but the issue was still in the balance:

> . . . The whole country beyond Gondar is in arms, and at least a dozen great Chiefs have all secret intentions of aiming at power.
>
> How it will end none can say, but in the meantime there is a scene of wonderful confusion; not only affairs are embarrassed but legislation

is almost suspended, and each man's person and property is in imminent peril . . . Till, by the fortune of arms, some order be restored under some one Chief, further negotiations with the Ras must be useless.

The Consul's ensuing reports continued to tell of Kassa's successes. On 28 September he wrote:

. . . the troops of the Ras Ali have been again defeated by Dejajmatch Kasai . . . If Dejajmatch Kasai obtain a complete mastery over the whole country, as he is a man of talent, there will be some prospect of increasing our intercourse with Abyssinia.

About a fortnight later, on 15 October, he informed the Foreign Secretary, Lord Clarendon, that:

There appears to be but little chance for the Ras Ali; in the meantime it remains so uncertain who will finally prevail in the struggle, if any does so entirely, that it must be useless at present to risk any negotiation.

A few months will probably decide all, and if then Dejajmatch Kasai shall be powerful enough to unite the whole country under a vigorous Government, his character will be favourable to our views.

If, on the contrary, he fails, there will be little prospect of doing any good for some time in the interior of the country, which will then present a scene of terrible confusion.

While the Consul was concerned with keeping the Foreign Secretary informed about the desperate civil war, the Minister had been considering Plowden's earlier despatches touching upon the value, if any, of having a British Consularship to Ethiopia. At this time, the end of 1853, the Foreign Secretary was much occupied with a graver question. Russia, after having invaded the Balkan provinces of Turkey, had declared war on the Ottoman Empire, and it was expected that the latter would declare war on Russia. The danger was growing almost daily that other European states would become involved in the war, in order to stop Russia advancing on Constantinople, Europe's most strategic gateway. Despite the anxiety of this crisis, Lord Clarendon found time to write to Plowden about the Consulate at Massawa. In a letter of 3 October he observed:

Her Majesty's Government have had under their consideration the observations respecting your position in Abyssinia and the difficulties in regard to opening a commerce with that country, contained in your despatches . . .

Her Majesty's Government were led by the representations formerly made by you to expect that advantage would result to British interests from the conclusion of a Treaty with the Rulers of Abyssinia and from the establishment of a British Consulate in that country. It appears, however, from your reports now before me, that there is little reason to expect that such will be the case.

Nevertheless, Her Majesty's Government having concluded the Treaty and established the Consulate, are reluctant to renounce all hope of benefit from those measures; but their means of obtaining in this country information on which to act are necessarily very limited; and I must have recourse to you for a report as to the possibility of your establishing yourself either at Massowah or any other place on the sea-coast where you may retain an influence on the Rulers of Abyssinia, and facilitate communication with the provinces under their Government.

... it is obvious from your despatches that the difficulty of dealing with Abyssinia results, in a great measure, from the absence of any place on the coast with which a safe communication can be kept up: and it is to the discovery of such a place at which you may fix your residence that I would particularly direct your attention.

The Foreign Office had now (thanks to Plowden's own elucidation) at last realised the difficulties of a British Consul to Ethiopia. As to where the Consulate Office should be, the sad truth was that there was then no good 'place on the sea-coast where you may retain an influence on the Rulers of Abyssinia, and facilitate communication with the provinces under their Government'. That Plowden at Massawa was so active in Ethiopia amounted to a near miracle. He made not Massawa but his saddle his Consulate.

While the civil war in Ethiopia remained undecided Plowden had no wish to lose his friendly relations with Dejazmatch Wubie of Tigré, still one of the most powerful chiefs, and he maintained contact with him. The Consul revealed something of the thoughts of an Ethiopian chief in his despatch to Lord Clarendon, dated Massawa, 20 October 1853. At this time Wubie was still supreme in Tigré and felt all the more so with the overthrow of Ras Ali, until recently his overlord, and even ventured to call himself King of Ethiopia; he might as well make his claim when there appeared to be a crown for the taking.

The Chief of Tigré has several times pressed me to assist him in buying with his own money some muskets and rifles, and that I have as often refused.

I have often pointed out to Her Majesty's Government that it is not

> reasonable to expect anything for nothing from an Abyssinian Chief; nor can Dejaj Oobeay understand how on the one hand I request, and even obtain his friendship, and on the other refuse him so slight a request.

With this letter Plowden sent a message from 'Dejaj Oobeay, King of Ethiopia', which declared:

> What were the terms of our friendship? That I should do what you demand of me, and that you should do what I ask you.
>
> Now, if it be possible, do you go for me to your country; if not, some person in your confidence, who understands guns, should go . . . I wish to buy guns and pistols of different kinds and of good quality, and rely upon you.

Wubie, however, was perhaps counting his crown before the coronation, or so the British Consul's next communication, of 21 December, seemed to show:

> Dejaj Kasai has . . . made an irruption into the dominions of Dejaj Oobeay, near Gondar; and without encountering the latter chief, marched hurriedly towards Godjam, where, Dejaj Birro having assembled a large army, threatened his rear.
>
> Dejaj Oobeay by this movement having been obliged to withdraw his whole army from Tigré, that province is left without any government for the present.
>
> As a natural consequence, all have taken up arms, and the law of the strongest is the only one now in force throughout Abyssinia.

Early in the following year, Consul Plowden reported from Massawa on 25 January:

> Ras Ali is still holding out in Edjow, and Dejaj Kasai, in possession of Begemder, Gondar, etc. He continues to increase his forces, and it is uncertain in what quarter he will strike the next blow.
>
> Dejaj Oobeay has been obliged for the present to abandon Tigré, which province is much distracted . . .

Thus the opening of 1854, in the Englishman's reckoning, saw the civil war in Ethiopia still in full swing, with Dejazmatch Kassa increasing his advantage, but still without signs of a lasting settlement. At the end of February Plowden reported that 'peace has been patched up' between Kassa and Wubie, and 'except just now in Tigré, no one in Abyssinia knows whom to call master, and I can only hope that one or two more decisive battles will end this confusion and uncertainty'.

In a despatch to Lord Clarendon a little later, Plowden stated, 'it is reported to me that Dejaj Kasai still makes progress . . . and it is said that the Ras Ali, harassed even in his Galla provinces, has been obliged to take refuge in a sanctuary'. Plowden wrote this despatch from Massawa on 14 March 1854. He was unaware of the Foreign Secretary's greater preoccupations; two days earlier Britain and France had entered into an alliance with Turkey, and before the end of the month they had declared war on Russia in defence of Turkey. The unnecessary Crimean War had begun.

While the European powers were concerned with the conflict which could determine whether Turkey or Russia should control Europe's most strategic gateway, Constantinople, Consul Plowden, still unaware of that war, continued to concern himself with his own parish. Plowden, practical perforce, but at heart always a knight errant, went up into Northern Ethiopia on a self-appointed mission.

7

HAZARDOUS ENCOUNTERS
(1854–60)

Plowden, while following the struggle for power in Ethiopia with increasingly partisan feelings, was careful not to get involved in it. He was, however, not unheedful of a call now made upon him by a Christian community in distress. He set off to Bogos, now better known as Keren, which the Egyptians had then recently overrun. He did so in response to a call to bring peace to that troubled area by the exercise of his authority as a Consul of a great nation, Britain. He reported his errand to Lord Clarendon on 15 March 1854:

> I have the honour to inform you that the Bey of Taka, an Egyptian military post, has ravaged a district called Senhait, or Bogos . . . and has carried into slavery . . . about 300 of the inhabitants.
>
> The principal people of that country have represented to me that they are professing Christians, have always been so, and have never paid tribute to the Egyptian Governor; that they owe allegiance to Dejajmatch Oobeay, but that the confusion of affairs in Abyssinia prevents his affording them protection.
>
> It appears that the Bey . . . thought it a favourable opportunity to extend the faith of his Prophet, and increase the revenue of his Master; and has accordingly threatened to repeat his invasions constantly until they shall adopt the Mahometan creed and submit to his sway . . .
>
> The whole population has now fled to the mountains, and the Chiefs have sent to inform me that if within a certain time I can procure them an assurance of peace and protection they will receive it with joy, and act in all matters by my counsel; otherwise they have no alternative but to submit to the demands of the Bey in every respect.

Plowden met the people of Bogos, went over the border to Kassala to visit their enemies, and brought some peace to the troubled people. Lord Clarendon supported the Consul's action, for he replied to Plowden, on 6 July, saying:

> I approve of the conduct which you have pursued . . . and I have given such instructions to Her Majesty's Agent . . . Consul-General in Cairo . . . to induce the Pasha of Egypt to put a stop to those proceedings and prevent their further recurrence.

The Consul's mission had met with some immediate success, and more success came later when, supporting his Consul, Lord Clarendon made effective representation to the Pasha of Egypt to bring about the restitution of the people of Bogos taken off into slavery and to stop further raiding. The Foreign Secretary also told the Pasha that Britain could not approve of any Egyptian invasion of Ethiopia.

Plowden was soon back in Massawa and resumed his despatches about the still undecided civil war in Ethiopia, and gave this summary on 29 June:

> The Ras Ali has entirely abandoned the contest, and is living in a sanctuary by permission of Dejaj Kasai.
>
> Dejaj Kasai is in Godjam, where Birru Gosho still holds out, but without daring to risk a battle.
>
> Dejaj Oobeay is in Tigré, but through fear has sent a large sum to Dejaj Kasai as tribute.
>
> The country is tolerably quiet . . .

General John Bell supported Ras Ali in battle, but eventually Bell too had to seek sanctuary. Kassa sought him out, and soon after Bell threw in his lot with Kassa.

On 10 July Plowden was able to announce another major victory for Kassa, and in concluding his despatch he offered the Foreign Secretary an opinion more as an Ambassador than as a Consul:

> If Dejaj Kasai succeeds in his bold attempt to destroy the military oligarchy and to restore the deposed monarchs of Gondar, there will still be some hope for Abyssinia . . .
>
> Still, however he may improve the internal condition of the country and re-organize its Government, a hazardous and doubtful attempt, the main difficulty of the want of a sea-port will remain insurmountable by any Abyssinian Ruler; and, unless that want is supplied by us, Abyssinia will ever remain isolated from the rest of the world, nor will any Embassy or Consulate produce any profitable or lasting effect.

Plowden had written of Ethiopia's need of a port – which would be gained in the fullness of time, but he was anticipating history by nearly a hundred years, and the road Ethiopia had first to travel was not easy.

As the conflict for power in Ethiopia took its still undecided course, the Consul thought it wise to maintain friendly relations with that formidable prince, Dejazmatch Wubie, who might yet become the ruler of all Ethiopia. So, leaving Massawa, he climbed up to Tigré where he reported to the Foreign Secretary from Adowa on 25 September:

> Dejajmatch Oobeay . . . is now preparing all his resources for a final struggle with Dejaj Kasai . . . a pitched battle will decide early in November between the rivals for supremacy.
>
> The contest is important. Should Kasai be the victor, from his vigorous character, and the bent he has taken towards reform and discipline, I shall then hope that something may be effected for Abyssinia, even in its internal administration by the destruction of the feudal system, the introduction of paid Governors and Judges, the organization of the army, and the disarming of the people; if, on the contrary, Oobeay wins the day, his pride, that will not permit him to listen to the counsel of Europeans, will be an effectual barrier to improvement.

Plowden spoke as though he himself were one of the Ethiopian patriots hoping for the country's salvation. He continued to send Lord Clarendon reports of history in the making, and his own involvement. On 6 November, for example, he wrote from Massawa:

> Dejajmatch Kasai has written to me a letter full of esteem for me and respect for the English nation, and stating that he has by proclamation forbidden, under severe penalties, the exportation of slaves.
>
> The struggle between him and Dejajmatch Oobeay will be decided in a few weeks, and if, as I hope, Kasai becomes master of Abyssinia, further reforms may be expected from the only man in the country who has ever shown originality of thought or desire for improvement.
>
> It remains for Her Majesty's Government to consider whether it will assist him in his views should he succeed in the present contest, and in establishing on a firm basis the Government that he will have created by a series of hazardous battles.

The conflict which the Consul expected did not take place, but the next news he gave of the rebel Kassa, on 28 November, was sufficiently dramatic:

> I have the honour to inform you that Dejajmatch Kasai is to be styled King of Abyssinia . . . A peace with Dejajmatch Oobeay is on the *tapis* on the conditions that he acknowledge Kasai as his liege lord and pay him yearly tribute . . . The Ras Ali is finally taken prisoner . . . Kasai has forbidden the exportation of slaves under the severest penalties, and proposes to exclude Mahometans from high dignities or emoluments.

> He is disposed, I think, to listen to advice, and I hope to be able to visit him when the terms of the accord with Oobeay shall be well defined; nor am I without hope that my counsels . . . may produce some good effect in urging reforms in the interior.

Once again the Consul concluded his despatch as though he were an Ambassador or Political Resident in Ethiopia.

Up in the highlands the political manoeuvring and intrigue was continuing, with Kassa and Wubie each hoping to secure the imperial crown. Kassa eventually decided to march north and challenge Wubie who had withdrawn his army to his native mountainous district of Semien. By forced marches through difficult country Kassa and his troops came upon Wubie's army encamped at a great plain amidst the mountains at Deraskie. Kassa's weary warriors were near to revolt, but by a short but great harangue he inspired them to attack.

The battle of Deraskie proved decisive. In the fierce, long-drawn-out battle fought from early morn to dusk, victory swayed in the balance, with Wubie having advantage in musketry and cavalry. However, towards evening he went to rest a while, was surprised by one of Kassa's patrols, and taken prisoner. With Ethiopian soldiers the death or capture of their chief means defeat; soon Wubie's dismayed army was overwhelmed. Once again the intrepid Dejazmatch Kassa was victorious.

Two days later, on 7 February 1855, there took place at Deraskie a grand and historic ceremony. With the impressive pomp and ritual that had gone down through custom and tradition, perhaps for more than 2,000 years, and was older than the Christian Church itself, Abun (or Bishop) Salama, in the Church of Our Lady, crowned and anointed – and in the fields and meadows around, the vast multitude of clergy, army, camp followers and peasantry acclaimed – Kassa as Theodorus the new Negusa Negast – King of Kings – of Ethiopia, a worthy successor in the long continuous line of Ethiopia's Kings since that first King of Kings to worship the true God, Menelik the First, son of King Solomon, the son of King David. The new Emperor's wife and loyal ally, the beautiful Tewabetch, became Iteghe, or Empress. Great was the rejoicing and long the revelry.

So it came to pass that a boy, dispossessed of his heritage, in Qwara fleeing from the burning monastery, more than once a fugitive, was now King of Kings; and barely 37 years old. Three days before no one could have said for certain who would be the new Emperor, but none was greatly surprised at the outcome of the long rivalry, least of all Kassa, now Theodore, for from his early youth it had been his secret that this was his destiny.

Kassa, who could be ascetic, could also love revelry, but he loved conquest more. He soon had his army on the march again to capture the *amba* (a flat-topped mountain with precipitous sides), held by two of Wubie's young sons, where the deposed Dejazmatch's treasury was kept. It was taken by a ruse, and seldom have victors seen such a store of spoils, of muskets and other arms, of coins and other precious things. Theodore was now well equipped for more than one campaign.

Emperor Theodore – as Kassa must now be called – had he wished to press his army to forced marches, could have plunged down from the Ethiopian ramparts and reached Massawa in a few days and captured the coveted seaport. Had he done so he would have been careless of strategy and politics, so he contented himself with saying 'My Empire now reaches to the Sea.'

To be King of Kings of all Ethiopia, Theodore still had to exact submission from the Negus of Shoa. There were doctrinal differences within the Ethiopian church, between the Abun and the priests in the south, so the Bishop said to the victorious Emperor, 'Let us go into Shoa and re-establish the faith.' Theodore appointed a governor for Tigré in place of Dejazmatch Wubie.

The great army, numbering some 150,000 men, mounted and on foot, with camp followers and turbaned priests with drums and cymbals and the holy wooden symbol of the Covenant of the Ark, led by Theodore and the Abun, turned south, more of a migration than a column of march. The army which had hurried north led by an adventurous Dejazmatch, marched south in triumph, led by a great Emperor.

It was February 1855. In England there had been important political changes. Palmerston had become Prime Minister. The war in the Crimea had been going badly for Britain and her allies. The British Parliament, and even more the British public, were growing concerned at the incompetence of the generals and the suffering of the troops; all this they were learning by letters home from the soldiers, but also from that innovation, the war correspondent. For the first time newspaper correspondents had accompanied a British army and military censorship was still an undeveloped craft, so the public had learnt of appalling administrative follies and of the suffering of their soldiers in the Crimea. The Government was held largely to blame, and the Earl of Aberdeen, the Prime Minister, and his coalition Government were forced to resign. One member of the Government, the Home Secretary, had stood out as the one person who could put matters right, and that was Lord Palmerston. So while Kassa, little known to the world, was fighting for the victory which made him Emperor Theodore, in England Palmerston, whose name was known in most countries of the world, now rather deaf but otherwise strong and energetic in mind and body, became at the age of 71 Prime Minister for the first time.

Not long after this Plowden received an invitation from the new Emperor to come up to the highlands to discuss various matters, including the acquisition of mechanics from England. So at the end of March he left Massawa to seek, wherever he might be, the Emperor in whom he placed such great hopes for Ethiopia, and en route to Tigré he wrote to Lord Clarendon on 7 April;

> Dejajmatch Kasai has taken, since his coronation, the name and style of 'Theodorus, King of Ethiopia', there being an ancient prophecy that a King of this name should reform Abyssinia, restore the Christian faith, and become master of the world.
>
> He is now persuaded, I hear, that he is this destined Monarch, and his new seal bears the motto of 'King of Kings'. He has ordered the Mahometans in his dominions to become Christians within the year, and has driven out the Roman Catholics.
>
> He has 50,000 men, and has ordered a part of them to march against the Mahometan Gallas, who have assembled in great force in the Province of Worrahaimano in defence of their faith. Next year he will reduce Shoa to obedience, and probably most of the Pagan Galla tribes.
>
> His other ideas of conquest I will recount when I have seen him . . . So strong is his crusading spirit that a Syrian has persuaded him to send a message to the Emperor of Russia, as the defender of the Cross against the Crescent . . .
>
> The King is capable of great things, good or evil. He wishes to discipline his army, and has in part already succeeded; to abolish the feudal system; to have paid Governors and Judges; and to disarm the people.
>
> He is just, hearing in person the poorest peasant; he has stopped the system of bribes; he has, by his own example, and by giving dowries and rewards to those who marry, discouraged polygamy and concubinage; he has forbidden the Slave Trade, and has tranquillized the whole country, no one daring to dispute his pleasure.

> His fanatical zeal, his vehement character, and the pride engendered by his wonderful success – armies and strongholds defeated or taken almost by the terror of his name – render it hard to foresee how he will receive European advances; and our relations with Turkey and Egypt will complicate every difficulty.

Some time was to pass before Plowden could meet the newly crowned monarch. When Plowden reached Gondar, the Emperor had gone off to subdue the restless and turbulent Wollo Gallas, who had been ravaging villages and burning churches while he was in the north. Plowden reconciled himself to waiting for the Emperor's return.

Theodore, as he had planned, accompanied by the Abun, then marched on into Shoa. The Negus, chiefs and armies of that province prepared to resist the advancing Emperor, but the night before the battle, the Negus died and was spared seeing the defeat of his army. Faithful Shoan chiefs fled with Menilek, the son of the Negus, and acknowledged the young prince as their lawful king. Theodore, however, succeeded in capturing young Menilek whom, after appointing his own Governor of Shoa, he carried off with him, but he treated him with the respect due to his princely rank, and took a liking to the intelligent child.

On his return march Theodore passed through Wollo, where he captured the *amba* of a Galla chief who had not previously submitted to him. This *amba*, to the east of Debra Tabor, was called Magdala. Theodore was attracted to this imposing *amba* and, deciding to make it his armoury and treasury, he rebuilt two of its churches, and fortified it and two nearby hills as much to keep the local population in subjection as to give added protection to Amba Magdala.

After the victories in Shoa and Wollo, Theodore went triumphantly into Gojjam and established his camp there. Plowden all the while had been waiting in Gondar, with the town always threatened by a rebel called Negussie who on one occasion actually forced it to pay ransom to avoid pillage and destruction. Then, at long last, after seven months of waiting, the British Consul received a summons from Theodore to come to his camp in Gojjam.

In the ensuing days, there in the heart of Ethiopia, Consul Plowden wrote an informative Report to the Foreign Secretary on the Ethiopia of his time for which students of that country's affairs must be grateful to this day. That Report, dated 25 June, contained the following passages:

King Theodorus is young in years, vigorous in all manly exercises, of a striking countenance, peculiarly polite and engaging when pleased, and mostly displaying great tact and delicacy. He is persuaded that he is destined to restore the glories of Ethiopian Empire, and to achieve great conquests; of untiring energy, both mental and bodily, his personal and moral daring are boundless . . .

When aroused his wrath is terrible, and all tremble; but at all moments he possesses perfect self-command. Indefatigable in business, he takes little repose night or day; his ideas and language are clear and precise; hesitation is not known to him; and he has neither councillors nor go-betweens. He is fond of splendour, and receives in state even on a campaign. He is unsparing in punishment – very necessary to restrain disorder, and to restore order in such a wilderness as Abyssinia. He salutes his meanest subject with courtesy; is sincerely though often mistakenly religious, and will acknowledge a fault committed toward his poorest follower in a moment of passion with sincerity and grace.

He is generous to excess, and free from all cupidity, regarding nothing with pleasure or desire but munitions of war for his soldiers. He has hitherto exercised the utmost clemency towards the vanquished, treating them rather as his friends than his enemies. His faith is signal; without Christ, he says, I am nothing; if he has destined me to purify and reform this distracted kingdom, with His aid who shall stay me; nay, sometimes he is on the point of not caring for human assistance at all . . .

The worst points in his character are, his violent anger at times, his unyielding pride as regards his kingly and divine right, and his fanatical religious zeal.

He has begun to reform even the dress of Abyssinia, all about his person wearing loose flowing trousers, and upper and under vests . . . Married himself at the altar, and, strictly continent, he has ordered or persuaded all who love him to follow his example, and exacts the greatest decency of manners and conversation . . .

He has suppressed the Slave Trade in all its phases, save that the slaves already bought may be sold to such Christians as shall buy them for charity: setting the example, he pays to the Mussulman dealers what price they please to ask for the slaves they bring to him and then baptizes them.

He has abolished the barbarous practice of delivering over murderers to the relatives of the deceased, handing over offenders, in public, to his own executioners to be shot or decapitated.

The arduous task of breaking the power of the great feudal Chiefs – a task achieved in Europe only during the reigns of many consecutive Kings – he has commenced by chaining almost all who were dangerous, avowing his intention of liberating them when his power shall be consolidated. He has placed the soldiers of the different provinces under the command of his own trusty followers, to whom he has given high titles, but no power to judge or punish; thus, in fact, creating generals in place of feudal Chieftains more proud of their birth than of their monarch, and organising a new nobility, a legion of honour dependent on himself, and chosen specially for their daring and fidelity.

To these he gives sums of money from time to time, accustoming them to his intention of establishing a regular pay; his matchlock-men are numbered under officers commanding from 100 to 1,000, and the King drills them in person. In the common soldiers he has effected a great reform, by paying them, and ordering them to purchase their food, but in no way to harass and plunder the peasant as before; the peasantry he is gradually accustoming to live quiet under the village Judge, and to look no more to military rule. As regards commerce, he has put an end to a number of vexatious exactions, and has ordered that duties shall be levied only at three places in his dominions. All these matters cannot yet be perfected, but he intends also to disarm the people, and to establish a regular standing army, armed with muskets only, having declared that he will convert swords and lances into ploughshares and reaping-hooks, and cause a plough-ox to be sold dearer than the noblest war horse . . .

He is peculiarly jealous, as may be expected, of his sovereign rights, and of anything that appears to trench on them; he wishes, in a short time, to send embassies to the Great European Powers to treat with them on equal terms. The most difficult trait in his character is this jealousy and the pride that, fed by ignorance, renders it impossible for him yet to believe that so great a Monarch as himself exists in the world.

In his present campaign he proposes to subdue or exterminate the Mahometan Gallas, and perhaps Shoa. Next year he will devote to the settlement of Tigré, including the tribes along the coast, and meditates the occupation of Massowah. After that he wishes to reclaim all the provinces lately conquered by Egypt along his northern frontier . . . nor does his military ardour hesitate to dream of the conquest of Egypt, and a triumphant march to the Holy Sepulchre.

Some of his ideas may be imperfect, others impracticable; but a man who, rising from the clouds of Abyssinian ignorance and childishness without assistance and without advice, has done so much and contemplates such large designs, cannot be regarded as of an ordinary stamp . . .

Turning to his own meeting with this remarkable man, Plowden added:

The evening before the day fixed for my departure the King sent to me to know the object of my coming. I replied that I had not come on the part of the Government or in any official capacity; but that as I was about to visit England, it was important that I should know and report His Majesty's disposition respecting the establishment of a Consulate, and friendly relations generally; I hinted also at what had been arranged with the Ras Ali. The King said, 'I know nothing of what Ras Ali may have done; I am young and inexperienced in public affairs; I have never heard of a Consulate under the former Kings of Abyssinia, and this matter must be referred to my Council and the principal people of my Court' . . .

The next morning . . . he spoke to me in the most affectionate manner, gave orders for my honourable reception everywhere as far as Massowah, and said, 'In refusing your request for a Consulate, my only reason is that it appears an innovation, but do you not forget my friendship for you, and cause your Queen also to regard me as a friend. After the rains I shall send to Her Majesty an Embassy and letters, and when these wars are finished I will give every favour and protection to Englishmen who may visit my country: do you also visit me and write to me' . . .

I see much to hope for in these conversations. It is well to find a King in Abyssinia proud of his dignity, alive to his responsibility, capable of considering grave matters, and of replying with decision, not lightly giving assent to a thing he does not understand, and yet seeking for our friendship in all ways that he can understand.

As a result of Plowden's reports the British Government duly recognised Theodore as the supreme ruler of Ethiopia. Such recognition was, however, bedevilled by a fear that was long to trouble Britain's attitude to Ethiopia; fear that there might be war between Egypt, which had recently seized much territory in the area, and Ethiopia which hoped to regain its lost territories. Such a conflict seemed undesirable to Britain, for Egypt was still part of the empire of the Sultan of Turkey who was an ally of Britain. This was apparent in a letter which the Earl of Clarendon despatched to Consul Plowden on 27 November:

Her Majesty's Government are convinced that the establishment of friendly and intimate relations between Great Britain and Abyssinia would be attended with many advantages to both countries; and you will accordingly inform the King that the Queen, our gracious Sovereign, will have much pleasure in receiving, and treating with due honour, the Ambassadors whom His Majesty may send to her Court.

This must, however, depend upon your receiving from the King a distinct assurance that he renounces all idea of conquest in Egypt and at Massowah . . .

> Should you receive a complete and satisfactory assurance on this subject, and should the King of Abyssinia determine to send Ambassadors to Her Majesty's Court, it will be your duty to accompany them, and you are hereby authorized to defray the expenses of their journey to England, respecting which you will be careful to observe all reasonable economy.

Plowden spent about a fortnight at Theodore's camp. The two men had met before during a period when Theodore, then Dejazmatch Kassa, was on friendly relations with his father-in-law, Ras Ali. Now began the close understanding between the zealous reforming Emperor and the zealous, forward-looking Consul. There also began the discussions that were to go on interminably about Theodore's desire to send an Embassy to England to confirm his friendship towards the Queen of that country and if possible to secure the aid of that Christian monarch.

Theodore's ambition, which he did not conceal, was to extend his power over the old Ethiopia of the north, now in the hands of the infidel, in particular Massawa on the coast and inland towards Sennar, on the border of which he retained vivid memories of his early youthful exploits. But he also had greater ambitions in which he hoped the Christian princes of Europe would help him: He would conquer the Mohammedan lands, Sudan, Egypt, and go on and liberate Jerusalem from the Turks. Wild dreams? But wild only perhaps because he had not the army to accomplish the crusade. They were dreams no more wild than that of the Balkan farmer's son, Mohomed Ali, who had become ruler of Egypt, and master of Mecca, Medina and even Jerusalem, and had sent his army to the outposts of Constantinople. Such were Theodore's hopes. Plowden's hopes were to persuade the Emperor to recognise the Trade Treaty which the Ras had signed, under whatever name and form might be agreeable to Theodore, and this British representative would help and guide Theodore in the reform of the Empire.

The remarkable Walter Plowden did in fact establish very nearly that position for himself in practice. But the expedition of the Embassy which Plowden was ready to accompany to England was always postponed, for Theodore said he must establish his authority beyond question throughout Ethiopia, and eventually that meant the complete reduction of Tigré, where the French were intriguing, before he would make any formal approach to establish closer relations with any European power.

So time passed. Besides the reasons of policy which made Theodore reluctant to let Plowden depart, alone or with an Embassy, there were always the real dangers of civil war which might make it impossible for Plowden to reach Massawa, or Khartoum, alive. In these long-lasting proceedings Consul Plowden more than once received the written approval of the Foreign Secretary, Lord Clarendon.

On one occasion Plowden wrote to the Foreign Secretary that Theodore desired British assistance to discipline his army and introduce reforms into his government, and then added in regard to Theodore: 'I have cast my lot with his, and his very respect and affection for me have created numerous enemies among those who have long flourished on disorder.' And still Lord Clarendon wrote back to Plowden approving his conduct.

Theodore, however, was not succeeding in establishing his rule over the whole Empire; when he went to subdue a rebel in the south, rebellion broke out in the north; victorious in the south, he would turn north, and rebellion would again break out behind him. So the difficulties within the realm continued, and from without danger continued of attack by Egypt, as reported by travellers and spies. Early in 1857 the Christian Patriarch of Alexandria came to Ethiopia on a peace mission from the ruler of Egypt, Pasha Seyd. At first all went well, but before long Theodore suspected that the Patriarch, acting for a Mohammedan ruler, aimed at trapping him into tokens of submission to Egypt, and he had both the Patriarch and the Abun placed under house arrest; when it suited him or he was in a mood, Theodore had scant regard for the immunity of priest or envoy. Only Plowden's intercession saved the two prelates from being treated worse, and eventually he helped to secure permission for the aged Patriarch to depart with presents for the Pasha of Egypt. A year later, the Pasha, hoping a different ambassador might have better success, sent one of his Beys to Theodore's court, but with no better result, and the disappointed Bey, fearing the consequences of his failure, on reaching Khartoum on the return journey poisoned himself. It seemed impossible to remove Theodore's distrust, dating from the days of his youth, of the Turks and Egyptians. Nor were his doubts by any means groundless, for, as Plowden himself wrote to the Foreign Office: 'Egyptian designs on Abyssinia are as constant, however veiled, as those of Russia on Constantinople.'

Theodore now suffered a loss at one of his camps, worse than a battle lost. Tewabetch the beautiful died; her father, Ras Ali, and Theodore composed songs of lament for her. Those close to Theodore claim they saw a slow change come over him. She had exercised a finely balanced influence over the husband she loved, steadying, restraining, encouraging as the occasion required. After her death his best qualities sometimes flagged, and his worst grew; but he still had, besides good Ethiopian counsellors, two wise and loyal English friends, Walter Plowden, and John Bell (whom the Ethiopians called Yohannes), who had chosen to dwell among his people.

Three years passed, and the Emperor was still unable fully to assert his rule over the whole of the Empire. Plowden, however, thought it his duty to remain with or near the Emperor, and writing to the Earl of Clarendon on 5 June 1858, he gave his reasons:

> The King always talks with increasing pleasure and eagerness of his intended Embassy to England, and has even several times spoken of sending his only son.
>
> It is evident that our future relations depend upon the life and fortunes of one man, and are therefore precarious . . . but, unless I receive orders to the contrary, I must still consider it my duty to remain at all hazards, at any rate till the end of the rainy season in November.

When November came, Plowden was still in central Ethiopia, but now he was no longer writing to Lord Clarendon. Lord Palmerston and his Whig Government had been defeated, and Lord Derby, the Tory leader, had become Prime Minister for the second time, and had called on his close friend Lord Malmesbury to be Foreign Secretary, likewise for the second time. During the short time he and his party were in office, the Tory Lord Malmesbury continued to approve Plowden's conduct, as Whig Lord Clarendon had done.

Despite the end of the rains in November, Plowden continued to stay on, well into the following year, either at Gondar or with the Emperor in his wars, mainly against insubordinate Gallas, but he had now told the Emperor that he wished to go to Massawa, from which he had been absent now four years, and there he would await events. On 27 May 1859, he reported that he had taken leave of Theodore, but had been attacked by a violent fever, obliging him to remain in Ethiopia for a further rainy season. And he added:

> The King was very kind to me during my illness, and as I shall, I trust, leave him on the most friendly terms, I cannot, I think, do better than to wait in England the issue of these struggles for power, when our negotiations can be resumed with more certainty and on more precise terms.

In a despatch of 20 September of the same year, Plowden reported that the Emperor had been once again successful in a campaign in the south, but, to the north,

> The troops of his adversary in Tigré, Dejajmatch Negoosee [a protégé of the French], have pushed on to the neighbourhood of Gondar, and even further, and the war has become more envenomed and complicated.
>
> It is impossible to say what an hour or a day may bring forth in these countries, but I see in these events only an additional reason for leaving the country until the struggle shall be decided, as until that I can be of no practical use here.

The day was seemingly drawing nearer for Plowden to make his longed-for journey to England, where, meanwhile, there had been another change of government. The Tories were out, Palmerston was again Prime Minister and Lord Russell was once more at the Foreign Office. But in the New Year Plowden was still in central Ethiopia, whence he wrote to the Foreign Secretary with something of the old eager admiration for his hero, Emperor Theodore. A despatch of 3 February 1860, read:

> The King, having marched six weeks upward of 600 miles over a country without roads, and presenting great natural difficulties, has entered Tigré with 60,000 men, leaving about 15,000 on the Galla frontier, to make head till his return.
>
> His adversary Dejaj Nagoosee has retreated without firing a shot, and the King has been received with songs of triumph by the whole population of Tigré.
>
> The dénouement remains to be seen.

With Tigré again subjugated by Theodore, its great trade route to Massawa would once more be open; Plowden could proceed there and sail for England and his knowledgeable Italian assistant Signor Baroni would then write the consular report for him, and, in his slightly imperfect English, keep the Foreign Secretary informed of events in troubled Ethiopia.

Lord Russell, the Foreign Secretary, did not share his Consul's enthusiasm for Theodore's efforts to unify Ethiopia (almost fanatical though Russell was in his support for Italian Unity, then beginning to seem possible). Already on 18 January 1860, some six weeks before the Consul penned his last-mentioned despatch, Russell, replying to an earlier report from him, had written:

> I have received your despatch of 20th September last . . . , respecting the operations of the King of Abyssinia against hostile tribes by whom he is harassed, and in connection with this subject, I have to observe to you that Her Majesty's Government do not consider that any special advantage is derived from your repeated visits into the interior. You will therefore return to Massowah, which is your proper residence, and you will not leave it, unless under very exceptional circumstances, without orders or permission from the Secretary of State . . .
>
> The interests of the port are intimately connected with British interests in India, and, with judicious care and encouragement, it may become the outlet of a large trade between Abyssinia and Her Majesty's dominions.

Well, Mr Consul, put that in your pipe and smoke it; and so much for the unity of Ethiopia. Russell spoke of tribes, yes, but some of them occupying territories twice the size of his beloved Kingdom of Piedmont in the still-divided Italian peninsula. It was understandable that the Foreign Secretary should wish the Consul to confine himself to consular and trade duties at the seaport and keep out of the civil wars of Ethiopia, in which France was suspected of having more than a finger, but Russell's polite but cold reprimand had limited relation to realities in Ethiopia. Plowden could well have replied that without order and a united government trade could not flourish, and that in assisting Theodore to bring about such a desirable condition he was doing more for a large trade between Ethiopia and Her Majesty's dominions than by dealing with the complaints and frustrations of Indian traders in Massawa. It is a safe guess that if Russell – plucky Little Johnny – had been British Consul to Abyssinia, he would have been seldom seen in Massawa, but would have been most of his time in the interior of Ethiopia deeply involved in the political battles of the day.

By the end of February Plowden had left Debra Tabor and was on his way to Gondar, beginning his journey to England. A conversation at the Foreign Office in London between two such able servants of the Queen as her Foreign Secretary and her well-beloved Consul Walter Plowden would surely produce a clarification and understanding of what Britain's attitude to emergent

Ethiopia and what the Consul's duties, in the circumstances, should be. It is idle to speculate what Plowden might have replied to the Foreign Secretary by despatch from Ethiopia or in conversation in Downing Street. He never received the reprimanding despatch nor did he meet Lord Russell.

Effective arrangements at Massawa having been made in advance, it was in March, as anticipated, that the Italian gentleman then in charge at the British Consulate, sent his despatch, addressing it to Mr Colquhoun, the British Consul-General in Egypt. The opening despatch marked the end of a chapter. In his slightly imperfect English the man from Bologna wrote from Massawa on 30 March:

> I have the painful task of reporting a melancholy event. Mr Plowden . . . has been assassinated. On arriving close to the town of Gondar, and while crossing the River Kaha, he was suddenly attacked by 400 men, headed by Garred (a Chief under the orders of the rebel Dejaj Negoosie), and in the skirmish he received a mortal wound in his breast . . .
>
> Please to inform Her Majesty's Government of this lamentable occurrence . . .

Emperor Theodore of Ethiopia had around him to the day of his death faithful and devoted Ethiopian followers, but during an important part of his life and reign he had three especial people who greatly influenced him for his good and the good of his country and on whom he knowingly relied; two of these, his beloved wife Tewabetch and his loyal friend Walter Plowden were now dead. Theodore's victories and conquests had been considerable, but his great reforms were scarcely begun; and of his three especial companions only John Bell now remained. And as Plowden had truly written not long since, 'It is impossible to say what an hour or a day may bring forth in these countries . . . '

Part II

DUNCAN CAMERON

8

'FOR THE BETTER PROTECTION OF OUR SUBJECTS'

(1860–2)

News of the death of Consul Plowden in Ethiopia in February reached the Foreign Office on 11 May 1860. Lord Russell lost little time in appointing a successor.

Information on the death of the Consul also came in a despatch from the British Consul-General in Egypt, Mr Colquhoun, who ventured 'respectfully to suggest no time should be lost in replacing Mr Plowden, and that we should also have an efficient Agent, whether Consul or Vice-Consul, at Massowah'. It is clear from Colquhoun's despatch that he thought it advisable that there should be two British agents, one to replace Plowden in Ethiopia itself, and another to be an efficient agent at Massawa.

Russell was concerned only with sending out one Consul, but in so doing he needed little prompting. By the Queen's Commission dated 30 June, only seven weeks after Russell first heard of the death of Plowden, Captain Cameron, an experienced soldier, at that time British Vice-Consul at Poti, a Russian port on the Black Sea, was appointed British Consul to reside at Massawa. Captain Cameron's Commission of Appointment read in part as follows:

> Victoria, by the Grace of God, Queen of the United Kingdom and Ireland, Defender of the Faith . . . To all and singular to whom these Presents shall come, Greeting:
>
> Whereas We have thought it necessary for the encouragement of Our subjects trading to the Dominions of the Emperor of Abyssinia, to appoint a Consul to reside at Massowah, to take care of the affairs of Our said subjects, and to aid and assist them in all their lawful and

> mercantile concerns: Now Know ye that We, reposing especial trust and confidence in the discretion and faithfulness of Our trusty and well-beloved Charles Duncan Cameron, Esquire . . . have nominated, constituted, and appointed, as We do by these Presents nominate, constitute, and appoint him the said Charles Duncan Cameron, to be Our Consul in Abyssinia.

It may be noted here that by the Queen's Command, which Lord Russell countersigned, Captain Cameron was thus appointed to be 'Our Consul in Abyssinia', but 'to reside in Massowah', which was Turkish territory.

In contrast with the promptness of the appointment, Captain Cameron himself showed no impatience to proceed to his new post. Besides dutifully studying the despatches between his predecessor and a series of Foreign Secretaries, Captain Cameron was engaged in writing a history of the famous defence of Kars in the Crimean War; he also found time to attend the Annual Meeting of the learned British Association held in Manchester. Thus, appointed in June 1860, Cameron was still in England at the beginning of the following year. No one seems to have complained about this delay, and now the Foreign Secretary set out in a letter to the new Consul the general line of policy he was to pursue. This letter of guidance did not greatly differ from that given by Lord Palmerston to Plowden, except that Russell, having had enough of Plowden's travelling around Ethiopia and supporting Emperor Theodore, dwelt on these matters at the outset. Russell wrote on 2 February 1861:

> Your first duty on arriving in Massowah, which you will consider as the headquarters of your Consulate, will be to make yourself acquainted with the general state of political affairs in Abyssinia . . .
>
> It seems to Her Majesty's Government undesirable that you should avow yourself the partizan of either of the Contending Parties if the contest is still going on. Whatever interest Her Majesty's Government may have in Abyssinia can best be advanced by the tranquillity of the country; but if the British Agent becomes the partizan of one side, the rivalry of European interests which, however disavowed by the Governments of Europe, is almost invariably found to exist on the part of their Agents in such countries as Abyssinia, will stimulate foreign Agents to declare a partizanship for the other, and thus a civil contest will be promoted and encouraged which would otherwise die out of itself, or very shortly be brought to a conclusion by the decided preponderance of a victorious party.

> But although it is not desirable that you should engage in a contest with the Agent of any other Power for superiority of influence, or that you should openly exhibit suspicion or jealousy of his proceedings or of the influence which he may be supposed to have acquired, it will be your duty closely to watch any proceedings which may tend to alter the state of possession either on the sea-coast or in the interior of the country, and you will keep Her Majesty's Government . . . fully informed of all matters of interest which may come under your observation . . .
>
> In addition to matters of a political or commercial nature, you will pay particular attention to any Traffic in Slaves which may be carried on within your district, and report fully upon the same . . .

Correspondence relating to Ethiopia continued to reach the Foreign Office. On 18 March despatches from the Consul-General in Alexandria arrived with a letter from the Emperor to Signor Baroni which read in translation:

> I have the pleasure to inform you that all those who murdered . . . our friend, Plowden, and killed Bell (Yohannes), have been exterminated by me, not one excepted . . . You must come to Adowah as soon as possible, being anxious to despatch to our beloved and gracious Majesty the Queen of England some of my servants, to inform Her Majesty of all that has occurred here.

So now both the two friends who had gone up from Massawa in 1843 to search for the source of the White Nile but had stayed in Ethiopia, were dead. Had Theodore now – in 1861 – been proffered the helping hand from Britain that he had sought, he might have retained his sobriety, and his greatness. But what did Lord Russell, or those at the Foreign Office, know of this, or understand how much it meant to Theodore to 'despatch to our beloved and gracious Majesty the Queen of England servants to tell Her Majesty of all that had occurred here'?

Despite the passing months the new Consul, Cameron, had still not left England, and Signor Baroni was still the Acting Consul in Massawa; and up in Ethiopia Emperor Theodore was still concerned about establishing or maintaining contact with Britain. In the autumn of 1861 Baroni again wrote to Lord Russell about King Theodore's proposed mission to London. James Murray, a senior Foreign Office official, wrote to Consul Cameron that Baroni had asked for instructions about this mission, but that Lord Russell 'cannot give any instructions until he receives further information as to such mission'. Lord Russell had chosen to be cautious: after all he was thinking not only of Ethiopia, but of her neighbours Egypt and Turkey, and also of France. Theodore could wait.

On another matter the Foreign Secretary himself wrote directly, on 13 November, to Cameron, who was still in England:

> The Queen having learnt that the King of Abyssinia paid a ransom for the late Mr Consul Plowden, and Her Majesty being desirous of making some acknowledgement for the kindness shown by the King to one of her officers, she has directed that a suitable present should be presented through you to the King: and I therefore transmit to you a rifle and a pair of revolver pistols, which you will deliver to the King as soon after your arrival in Abyssinia as you have an opportunity of doing so.

At last Consul Cameron packed his numerous bags, the rifle and the two pistols, and left England on 19 November. He travelled to Trieste where he took ship for Alexandria, reaching it on 3 December, and waited there till his heavy luggage caught up with him, and then set off for Cairo, and, overland, on to Suez whence he sailed for Aden. On 13 January 1862, he arrived at that port where he stayed three weeks. He then sailed from Aden on the schooner *Mahe* of Her Majesty's Indian Navy, and arrived at his post, Massawa, on 9 February. Cameron reported his safe arrival to Lord Russell and in a separate despatch reported that Signor Baroni had resigned. Shortly after his arrival he seems to have employed a Frenchman, named Bardel.

A few days later Cameron reported to Lord Russell that he had written to King Theodore, 'stating that I am charged with presents for him, which I have been ordered to deliver in person'. Cameron told Lord Russell he proposed to start at the end of March.

Some three months after Cameron had left London, Lord Russell had further thoughts, and considered that not only should presents be given to King Theodore for ransoming, as Russell thought, 'the remains of the late Mr Plowden', but that he should also address a letter to the King. This he did on 20 February, and despatched it to the Consul at Massawa. The letter addressed to 'King Theodore of Abyssinia' began:

> The Queen my Sovereign has been informed by her servants in the East of the exertions which your Highness kindly made to recover the remains of her late Consul Mr Plowden, and of your generosity in declining to accept re-payment of the sum of money which you paid

> for that purpose. Her Majesty commands me to assure your Highness that she views your conduct in regard to this affair as proof of friendship towards herself and the British nation, of which she is duly sensible.

The letter then referred to the gift of a rifle and the pair of pistols as a present from the Queen herself; and spoke of 'Captain Duncan Cameron, whom she has appointed as Consul in Abyssinia'. The letter concluded by expressing the Minister's 'best wishes' for the Emperor's 'uninterrupted health and happiness', and recommended him to 'the protection of the Almighty'.

There is some confusion about the ransom. The French traveller, Guillaume Lejean, who arrived in Ethiopia as his country's Consul not long after Cameron, later gave a somewhat Gallic account, stating that the demand for ransom was made to Plowden's Ethiopian mistress. If Walter Plowden had an Ethiopian mistress, the Foreign Office documents are silent on the matter; so one can only hope it is true.

Eventually, towards the end of March 1862, Cameron and his caravan set off with his gifts and letters from the hot plain of the Red Sea shore to scale the hills and mountains of the interior, as Plowden had set off, with letters and gifts, 15 years earlier, at the start of his consulship. Cameron had every reason to set off as hopefully to Emperor Theodore at Gondar as Plowden had to Ras Ali at Debra Tabor. The second Consul's route would be much the same as that of the first, except for the final part. Plowden on the last part of his southward journey had struck off to the east, to avoid the rebel Chief Kassa. For Cameron there was no question of avoiding Kassa; he was in fact going to meet the erstwhile rebel Kassa, now Theodore, Emperor of Ethiopia.

9

A LETTER TO QUEEN VICTORIA
(1862–3)

In a despatch to Lord Russell written from Gojjam on 31 October 1862, Captain Duncan Cameron recorded the auspicious welcome he received at Theodore's camp.

It had long been the custom, as for a number of years it was to continue to be, for the ruler of the Ethiopian Empire to make his capital wherever he might pitch his camp. This would be arranged systematically, each chief with his army, and the ruler's counsellors and the clergy, all with their own tents, nearest to him. A great tent with the holy replica of the Ark of the Covenant within it served as church. Rulers of the greater provinces also camped in a similar fashion. The camp might be at a town, or some distance from one; grazing land and considerations of defence usually determined where the Emperor or prince would decide to halt.

Thus the Consul's despatch from the Emperor's camp bore no place name other than that of the province, Gojjam. But a messenger seeking the camp would have no difficulty in finding it; days before nearing the place, officers at customs houses or mountain passes, villagers, peasants and priests, would tell him where the great encampment was, and also where the prince's enemies were encamped, and where ambushes might be expected.

As Captain Cameron drew near to the royal encampment of Theodore, King of Kings of Ethiopia, a great brigade came out to meet and escort him into the camp. Cameron relates:

> King Theodore having sent for me at the close of the rainy season, I joined him at his camp . . . I was received with a salute of twelve guns, and 6,000 cavalry, infantry and matchlock men, were marched out to escort me to the camp.
>
> My reception, as regards this point, was the best His Majesty has yet accorded to any Envoy.
>
> On my arrival I was conducted to the King, who awaited me in a large apartment entirely covered and carpeted with silk.

He received me in a reclining posture, with a double-barrelled gun and two loaded pistols by his side. His Ministers and his General stood around in their robes of state. I was allowed to be seated.

After a few compliments, mead and broiled meat were brought in, and the interview became public.

It lasted many hours, during which His Majesty gave me a detailed account of his last campaign against Negoosee. This he did with much apparent modesty. He dwelt with graphic clearness on the death scene of his late Grand Chamberlain, the Englishman Bell, in which our countryman singled out the Chief Garred, to whom Mr Plowden owed his death, and killed him on the battle-field, while the King similarly dispatched the same rebel's brother. Both the slain were His Majesty's cousins. He spoke of his further revenge for Mr Plowden's death, when he executed 1,500 of Garred's followers on the same day. He did this, he said, to win the friendship of Her Majesty.

He afterwards broke out into invectives against the Turks; said they were encroaching on him on every side; spoke of the seven flags, as he expressed it, that they had planted on the sea-coast, and dwelt much upon alleged advances from the Egyptian quarter. He announced his intentions of fighting with them, and sending Ambassadors to the European nations to justify his conduct.

There for the moment the Consul's audience with the Emperor ended. Theodore's forceful, warlike tone against Egypt and Turkey seems to have somewhat surprised the Consul. As the representative of the then pro-Ottoman British Government he failed to appreciate the extent of Egyptian incursions into Ethiopia or the bitterness with which Theodore regarded them.

Captain Cameron then pitched a tent, and prepared for a long stay, but how long it would be he could not guess. Two days after his first interview he received a message from the Emperor to put down in writing the purpose of his visit. This he did, stating that he was deputed to present to the Emperor the gifts and the Foreign Secretary's letter introducing him to the Emperor, and also to discuss with him future Anglo-Ethiopian relations. The Consul pointed out that when Walter Plowden was killed two matters were outstanding, namely a Treaty and the sending of an Embassy to England, and he now offered to take up these matters where Plowden had left them.

The following day Captain Cameron was summoned to deliver the gifts and Lord Russell's letter. The gifts (though much smaller than those sent by the British to King Sahle Selassie of Shoa a generation earlier) are said to have given the Emperor some pleasure, especially the inscription on the gun to the effect that it was given by Her Majesty, in return for the King's kindness to Mr Plowden. On this occasion the King spoke of his goodwill towards Britain and the great things he expected from the friendship of the Queen, and declared that he was anxious to purchase ammunition and fire-arms in Britain. He railed against the Turks, and spoke of the great things he could do if assured of British support on the coast.

When Sunday came round, the Consul was again summoned to the Emperor, to an audience with courtiers present; Captain Cameron reported:

> The tone of the King had become bolder regarding Turkey. He spoke of the poverty of his country . . . and vaunted more boastfully than before of the achievements he would perform if England would prevent any interference by France on the sea-coast, and keep off a Turkish fleet.

The British Consul, in view of his Government's pro-Turkish policy, was disturbed by the warlike prospects held out by the Ethiopian monarch; Lord Russell, or indeed any British Foreign Secretary, he knew, would be very reluctant to get involved in any pact, and perhaps war, against Egypt, Turkey and even France! Well aware of this, the Consul stated in the same despatch:

> Feeling convinced that, however strong may be the wish of England to befriend Abyssinia, this was not the temper I was sent to encourage, I waited till an opportunity should occur of correcting His Majesty with regard to what I felt to be the sentiments of my Government.
>
> This soon offered, by His Majesty asking me whether England would not force his Ambassador through Massowah and Egypt . . .
>
> I replied that if there were war, England could not take his Ambassadors through Egypt without the consent of that Government; if there was peace, that I could see no obstacle. He repeated the question in another form, wishing that I should leave him an opening for skirmishes on the frontier, as apart from actual war . . . I gave the same reply.
>
> His Majesty then said that his empire and religion were in danger of being crushed, and that *he* would fight to death in their defence; but he made this important addition, that he would not make or bring on war until he had made an appeal to all Christendom. I told him that I was glad to hear this and that I would write it to my Government.

Over the next few days Cameron was to learn more about the ways and customs of Theodore's court. He waited several days expecting to have a private audience of the Emperor, but received no invitation. Instead, as he reported:

> My food became scant and bad, and I detected a disposition among the spies who had been attached to me, according to the custom of the country, under pretence of rendering me service, to turn matters in such a way that at last I should solicit the King to leave.
>
> I was hourly asked when I was going, which I settled one morning by replying to the usual question, to one who I knew would carry it to the King, that I might stay six months, if my business was not finished.
>
> An hour after, I received a peremptory message from His Majesty to leave for the sea at once, and send him an answer whether my Government would receive his Embassy or not.

Oh, if only Cameron had packed his bags and hied him to Massawa, how different so many things might have been! Unfortunately, the Consul did not do so, for he wrote:

> I considered . . . as I had been sent to His Majesty at a considerable expense, and on a mission of pure courtesy, it was his duty at least to give me some reply to the question of a Treaty, which had been so long pending, including the other important point as to his admitting a Representative of Great Britain to reside in his country if such were our wish.
>
> I thought too that unless I had clear details with regard to his projected Embassy, much embarrassment might ensue to us hereafter, while at the same time I had wished to know His Majesty's intentions regarding the slave trade, and to elicit information from him regarding an intercourse with his new kingdom of Shoa, and his hold on the tribes to the side of Zeyla.

And the Consul therefore wrote to the Emperor a letter setting out these matters.

It is difficult for anyone writing long after these events to rid his mind of the knowledge of the tragedy which followed, and difficult not to be wise as to what should have been done; but those who lived in that day and hour had to make decisions in the circumstances in which they found themselves, and they could not foresee the strange turn of events soon to take place. Was it wrong of Cameron to stay on, after the Emperor had bade him leave for Massawa, and to write his letter to the Emperor, setting out other matters to be discussed?

Meanwhile, from other sources Theodore had received information which disturbed him: that the ruler of Egypt was in France, and the Sultan of Turkey was in Egypt. Theodore concluded that his enemies around him were strengthening. He sent Consul Cameron a message, thanking him for his letter, pointing out the peril in which he stood from two powerful enemies without, and begging the Consul to act sincerely by him.

The Emperor had already told him that at Matemma near his native province of Qwara on the north-western border, the Turks had been collecting tribute unjustly. So now Cameron sent Theodore a note saying he would be willing to return to Massawa by way of Matemma, and stop the Turks in their activities, or at least find out the facts. Further, he informed the Emperor that he had written to the British Consul at Khartoum in the Sudan, asking him to do his utmost to preserve peace on the frontier between Egypt and Ethiopia, and to report to the British Consul-General at Alexandria any aggression against Ethiopia; Cameron also reassured the Emperor about his Embassy to Britain.

Together with his report of 31 October Cameron forwarded an important letter from Emperor Theodore. It was addressed to Queen Victoria, and the British Government's reaction, or rather absence of reaction to it, was to have dire consequences. The translation which was prepared by Theodore's own interpreters, read as follows:

> In the name of the Father, of the Son, and of the Holy Ghost, one God in Trinity, chosen by God, King of Kings, Theodoros of Ethiopia, to Her Majesty Victoria, Queen of England. I hope your Majesty is in good health. By the power of God I am well. My fathers the Emperors having forgotten our Creator, he handed over their kingdom to the Gallas [a reference to Ras Ali's Galla dynasty] and Turks. But God created me, lifted me out of the dust, and restored this Empire to my rule. He endowed me with power, and enabled me to stand in the place of my fathers. By his power I drove away the Gallas. But for the Turks, I have told them to leave the land of my ancestors. They refuse. I am now going to wrestle with them. Mr Plowden, and my late Great Chamberlain, the Englishman Bell, used to tell me that there is a great Christian Queen, who loves all Christians. When they said to me this, 'We are able to make you known to her, and to establish friendship between you', then in those times I was very glad. I gave them my love, thinking that I had found your Majesty's goodwill. All men are subject to death, and my enemies, thinking to injure me, killed these my friends. But by the power of God I have exterminated these enemies, not leaving one alive, though they were of my own family, that I may get, by the power of God, your friendship.
>
> I was prevented by the Turks occupying the sea-coast from sending

> you an Embassy when I was in difficulty. Consul Cameron arrived with a letter and presents of friendship. By the power of God I was very glad hearing of your welfare, and being assured of your amity. I have received your presents, and thank you much.
>
> I fear that if I send Ambassadors with presents of amity by Consul Cameron, they may be arrested by the Turks.
>
> And now I wish that you may arrange for the safe passage of my Ambassadors everywhere on the road.
>
> I wish to have an answer to this letter by Consul Cameron, and that he may conduct my Embassy to England. See how the Islam oppress the Christian!

The day after his despatch to Lord Russell, Captain Cameron addressed him several other letters. In one he anticipated what would now be called Aid to Developing Countries. He noted that the French had already taken such action in relation to Ethiopia, but their scheme was 'interrupted by the last revolution'. The British Consul wrote: 'I would venture most respectfully to suggest whether it would not be desirable to ask King Theodore to intrust our Government with a fixed number of lads who might receive a certain education, and be afterwards instructed in some useful trade.' And the gallant Captain added: 'It might also be well if His Majesty were invited to send to England with his Embassy a few young officers, who might be put in a position to carry back with them some notions of gunnery and engineering.'

In another despatch the Consul asked Lord Russell whether he should press the Emperor regarding a Trade Treaty with England. Alas, Consul Plowden first, and after him Consul Cameron, were obsessed with this ridiculous and useless notion of the Trade Treaty. Ethiopia had been carrying on trade for centuries, and many merchants, Arab, Armenian, and Indian, as well as Ethiopian, had grown rich without any Trade Treaty at all; the main thing was to trade.

In concluding this despatch, Cameron made this important observation regarding the proposed Embassy:

> I would beg to state that unless answers to my despatches of today and yesterday are forwarded soon, next rainy season, which begins in April, may arrest the projected Embassy, and put off everything for another eighteen months – which time may be profitably employed by others.

And then the Consul made a suggestion that was at the heart of the matter of any close and effective diplomatic relationship between Britain and Ethiopia. Like Plowden before him, he came, travelled and understood, and so made a suggestion much as Plowden had done: 'It might be worthy of your Lordship's consideration whether a Resident Envoy would not be better than a Consul.'

His diplomatic discussions being completed, the British Consul, as he prepared for his long journey northward, could feel well pleased with what he had done. He had learnt a good deal about Theodore and his policies; he had met and established friendly relations with him; and he had carried out the main instructions of his mission. Moreover, he had gone so far in re-establishing relations between Ethiopia and Britain, which had diminished since Consul Plowden's death, that the Emperor had given him a signed and sealed letter to Queen Victoria. What more could a British Foreign Secretary expect of a Consul on his first two-month visit to the court of an African potentate? Lord Russell was presently to tell him just how well pleased he was.

When Cameron took leave of Theodore in November 1862 there seemed a fair prospect of good relations developing between Ethiopia and Britain. The most important matter was whether Theodore's Embassy would be received in London, and also whether Britain would arrange for the safe conduct of that Embassy beyond the Ethiopian frontier. Until a reply came on that important issue there was not much more Cameron could do. He had an assistant representing him in Massawa, so he might as well spend the intervening time as usefully as possible, and one thing he could do was to go and give comfort, and perhaps protection, to the Christian Ethiopians in the northernmost province of Bogos, who were again lamenting raiding and slaving by their Muslim neighbours. Nearly eight years earlier Plowden had brought them a welcome respite from such torments. Cameron had three good reasons for following the precedent set by Plowden: first, he could bring some immediate peace to the troubled Christian tribe; second, he might do something to reduce the border tension which might cause a war between Ethiopia and Egypt, and thereby endanger friendly relations between Britain and Ethiopia; and third, his efforts would show the Emperor that Britain cared for his endangered Christian subjects. The journey to the north was clearly well worthwhile, so Cameron thought.

Before parting from Theodore, Cameron told him of his intention to visit the northern frontier; the Emperor was reluctant that

Cameron should go to the frontier town of Matemma; he said he had already lost Plowden, and he did not now wish to lose Cameron in a similar way, but Cameron must decide for himself what he did. After Cameron had told him of these contemplated journeys, the Emperor continued to show him kindness and friendship, and apart from the danger made no objection to the Consul's plans.

Leaving Gojjam in November, Cameron, although not in too good health, made easy progress northwards by way of Gondar, and then, still northwards through more rugged country, until he came to gentler hills and plains and reached busy Adowa in December.

Plowden, on his first journey as Consul on his way up to Ras Ali, had been forced to act with dexterity to avoid capture and robbery by a rebel. Captain Cameron on his journey back from visiting Emperor Theodore had his adventures also. Cameron related his contretemps in a despatch of 1 January 1863:

> I have been intercepted in my journey coastward, by the sudden rising of a rebel on my road . . . Intelligence of this having reached me, I remained on my guard at Adowa . . . I was hurried away by officials, barely carrying with me my money, ammunition, some clothes and writing materials.
>
> I am now lodged at Axum, whose church enjoys privileges of sanctuary, similar to those of mediaeval Europe . . . My person is, therefore, safe. My property left behind is, I trust, equally so, being deposited in the church at Adowa.

When Theodore learnt that Cameron had been prevented from going to Massawa by rebel bands he had at once sent one of his generals to disperse the brigands. The Consul had meanwhile written to the Pashas of Kassala and Matemma in the then but recently occupied Egyptian Sudan requesting them to keep their frontier tribes from raiding into Ethiopia; he also offered to go to Bogos, as had Plowden before him, to ensure the safety of the Christians there. He thereupon made his way northwards to Bogos.

He had meanwhile twice despatched messages to the Emperor. In the first he told him what he had written to the Pasha of Kassala, and in the second, written from Bogos, he urged that the Emperor should endeavour to establish a regular government of some kind in that area.

Cameron's actions were intended to preserve peace, for the sake of the people, and to remove dangers which might prevent Britain from agreeing to receive an Embassy from the Emperor. That Embassy remained very much in Cameron's mind, as it did in that of Theodore. So Cameron concluded his despatch to Lord Russell: 'I shall proceed to Casalla as soon as I receive answers to my despatches.' But Cameron, receiving no answers, decided to proceed on his mission without them.

While in Bogos, until the end of March, the Consul was still on Ethiopian soil, but now the gallant Christian knight-errant set off across the border into another country, the Egyptian-occupied Sudan. Ought Cameron never to have left Ethiopia; was this the fatal step? He went to the town of Gedaref in Kassala province. From there on 20 May, he sent a despatch to Lord Russell:

> My object in coming to the Soudan was to visit Kassala, about cattle stolen from Abyssinians at Bogos . . . you are aware that, during the late troubles in Abyssinia, Mr Plowden assumed the protection of the tribes of Bogos and others in the neighbourhood. A step which, though I cannot refer to archives, I suppose was known to, and not disapproved by, Her Majesty's Government.
>
> I do not feel justified, without further instructions, in relinquishing an influence which has already done much to prevent the absorption of these friendless people into Islam.

Cameron was right; the archives showed that in 1854 the Foreign Secretary, the Whig Lord Clarendon, had approved Plowden's action; Cameron might indeed have added that at the time he was writing – 1863 – Lord Clarendon was a Cabinet colleague of Lord Russell.

In Gedaref Cameron exacted what promises he could that restitution should be made to the Ethiopian people of Bogos.

At about this time a despatch from Russell caught up with Cameron. It made no mention of Cameron's despatches from Gojjam or of Theodore's letter, but this was understandable, as Russell's despatch was dated 8 January 1863, and the Gojjam despatches had not as yet reached him. Russell asked about the Egyptian Red Sea port of Suakin, and the advisability of opening a British vice-consulate there. This request made it seem to Cameron all the more important that he should pursue his investigations in the Egyptian Sudan, since he was actually in the district. Cameron provided what information he could, and gave the name of a Greek merchant who he thought might be suitable as a British vice-consul.

Still without any reply from Russell to his Gojjam despatches or to Theodore's letter to Queen Victoria, Cameron, in June, left Gedaref, where he had suffered from fever, and began his journey southwards into the cool highlands of Ethiopia. He headed for the imperial capital, Gondar, and could reasonably expect that there, or on the way, he would receive the British Government's reply which he could give to the Emperor. Meanwhile, he could feel pleased that he had not wasted his time.

By now, however, Lord Russell's long-awaited reply to Cameron's long and thoughtful despatches of the previous autumn was on its way to Ethiopia. The reply was rather terse. Dated 22 April it declared:

> With reference to your despatch of the 31st October last, I have to state to you that it is not desirable for Her Majesty's Agent to meddle in the affairs of Abyssinia and you would have done better if you had returned to your post at Massowah when the King told you to do so. This it will be right that you should do at once, and you will remain at Massowah until further orders.

Unaware that this reprimand was on its way, and quite unaware of the mischief it was to cause, Captain Cameron innocently proceeded back to Gondar. There it was his duty to report to the Foreign Secretary the misfortune that had befallen another Consul, little aware of the far greater tribulation that soon would fall on himself.

10

IRON CHAINS
(1863)

The direct journey from Gedaref to Gondar takes about 14 days, travelling first by camel and later by mule. After arriving at the Ethiopian capital, Captain Cameron took up residence at the village of Jenda to the south of the town.

In that year, 1863, Cameron was in Jenda during July and August and in Gondar in September and October, and from these places he wrote despatches to Lord Russell. During that time and also later Russell and at least one other Foreign Office official wrote letters to Cameron, never knowing quite where he might be, but addressing them to him at Massawa, where Cameron had made arrangements for them to be sent on by messenger. But for some considerable time after Cameron took up residence at Jenda neither received the messages of the other, which was puzzling, accustomed though both the Foreign Secretary and the Consul were to the long time communications sometimes took to travel. Thus each was writing into the void, not knowing what the other might have written or might have done in the meanwhile.

On arriving at Jenda, Cameron made it one of his first duties to report to the Foreign Secretary about the French Consul affair. He related how the French Consul for Massawa (so he described him), Monsieur Guillaume Lejean, had arrived in Ethiopia the previous December, and travelled to Gojjam, where Theodore was encamped, and presented a letter from Emperor Napoleon III offering the friendship of France. Theodore then invited M. Lejean to follow him on his campaign, and the French Consul accepted, but subsequently changed his mind, presented himself in uniform before the Emperor and demanded permission to go to Massawa; this the Emperor refused because of rebels on the route (which was true, commented Cameron). Nevertheless Lejean attempted to leave, but the Emperor had him fastened with an iron chain for a day, and later ordered him to Gafat, near Debra Tabor, where there were Protestant missionaries; Lejean was free to explore the surrounding country, but was forbidden to leave until an answer arrived from Napoleon to the letter Theodore had sent him.

A fortnight later Cameron wrote again to London, reporting that the Pasha of Sudan had a force of 14,000 men on the frontier, hoping to provoke the Emperor to attack him; Theodore, however, did not fall into the trap. While dutifully sending this report, Cameron was waiting for a response to his earlier despatches from Gojjam and to Theodore's letter to Queen Victoria; he therefore concluded his second despatch from Jenda, dated 15 August 1863: 'I am here, awaiting replies to my despatches of 31 October last, so that I may communicate them to the King at once, and leave.'

A good nine months seemed a long time to wait for a reply to important communications. Not that Cameron's despatches had been entirely ignored at the Foreign Office, though when they arrived a number of things were occupying the attention of that Office and London in general. There was all the excitement about the marriage of the Queen's eldest son, the Prince of Wales, to the beautiful Princess Alexandra of Denmark, and Society was all agog as to who would get invitations to the wedding. Ethiopia was a long way from a London *en fête*, where but a handful knew or cared about its existence or its woes. And there were some things Cameron did not and could not know.

First, he was still unaware that a reply to him from Lord Russell was on its way, telling him not to get himself or England involved in trying to put right Ethiopia's political problems, and to get himself down to Massawa, as quickly as mules' legs could move. Second, he did not know that a letter had passed from James Murray at the Foreign Office, to a Mr Merrivale, at the India Office, on 5 May. It stated that he was 'directed by Lord Russell' to transmit a despatch and its enclosures 'from Her Majesty's Consul in Abyssinia', and added: 'The enclosed papers being sent in original, I am to request that they may be returned to this office when done with.'

Although Russell was so eager for Cameron to leave Ethiopia, one of his principal officers continued to refer to Cameron as Her Majesty's Consul in Abyssinia, a description which most people, unless put on their guard, would regard as one of protocol no less than one of topography. But more relevant to British policy in relation to Ethiopia at that moment was the final phrase of the letter requesting that the documents 'be returned to this office when done with'. Had Consul Cameron, waiting for an answer, known of that letter, he might well have exclaimed: 'When done with, indeed!', and he might well have asked: 'When done what with?'

Third, the British Consul was unaware that another despatch clipping his wings was on its way to him from James Murray containing this admonition written on 13 August: 'I am . . . to remind you with reference to the expression "Envoy" and "Mission" which repeatedly occur in your despatch, that, as Her Majesty's Consul at Massowah, you have no representative character in Abyssinia.' So much for the Queen's Commission declaring that Our beloved James Duncan Cameron was Our Consul in Abyssinia! It would seem that Her Britannic Majesty's Consul and Her Britannic Majesty's Secretary of State for Foreign Affairs were not seeing eye to eye.

Meanwhile Cameron's despatches, written in his blissful ignorance of the effect they were having on arrival, continued to reach, and, one may presume, increasingly irritate, the gentlemen at the Foreign Office. Russell himself answered Cameron's despatch of 20 May from Gedaref (explaining why he was in the Sudan), and his Lordship, writing on 8 September, observed:

> I have to state to you that Her Majesty's Government do not approve of your proceedings in Abyssinia nor your suggestions founded upon them.
>
> I have only to desire that you will abstain from all interference in the internal affairs of that country, and that you will remain at your post at Massowah, whither you were ordered by my despatch of 22nd of April last to return and reside.

Clarifications, admonitions, reprimands. They were all now too late. Cameron's despatches, fulsome and hopeful; Lord Russell's, restrictive and cold, were all beside the point. Duncan Cameron and John Russell might propose, but in Ethiopia it was Emperor Theodore who disposed.

Russell heard the disturbing news about the French Consul from various sources in October 1863, and Cameron's apparent silence on the matter therefore added to the mystery, as it seemed to the Foreign Office, of the British Consul's actions and unknown whereabouts. By some strange mischance Cameron's despatch of

July about the arrest of the French Consul reached the Foreign Office only in April of the following year, 1864.

Russell may well have reflected that if only Consuls posted to Massawa would stay there, or get back there the soonest possible, Foreign Secretaries would have a little less to worry about. But *l'affaire* Lejean was as nothing compared to *l'affaire* Cameron which was soon to plague British Foreign Secretaries.

Serenely innocent of the fact that his minister had ordered him back to Massawa, Cameron at Jenda continued to concern himself with the affairs of Ethiopia.

The Captain's quarterly statement of 1 October indicates that he was confident that he had been executing his duties in and around Abyssinia thoroughly; the impious thought may even have passed through his mind that if anyone was not doing his duty it was the Foreign Secretary and others at the Foreign Office, who had not yet, as far as he knew, sent a reply to the Emperor of Ethiopia's request that the Queen of Great Britain should receive an Embassy from him.

But Cameron's quarterly statement did not reach Lord Russell until four months later, on 6 February 1864, with a whole packet of other despatches. From them Russell learnt something of what was going on in Ethiopia and what could happen in that country. He also learnt that the Consul was still in Ethiopia, and still dutifully meddling in Ethiopian affairs, for he received a letter from his Consul-General in Egypt sending the unwelcome news that: 'Captain Cameron would appear not to have received the despatch of your Lordship, transmitted by me to him some time ago, requiring him to quit the interior of Abyssinia, and take up his residence at or near Massowah.'

But that was not all for Lord Russell to read about this tiresome business of the Consul who ought to be in Massawa. Still by the same mail, in a later despatch, dated 23 January, the Consul-General in Egypt reported:

> I have conversed with a French gentleman who has been with M. Lejean, the French Consul in Abyssinia. He informs me that, in the last days of September, Captain Cameron was still in Gondar, he could not say a prisoner of King Theodore, but that His Majesty declined to allow him to quit Gondar.

The despatch concluded:

> I have written to the person in charge at Massowah to send at once to Captain Cameron, and I have impressed upon him the urgent necessity that he should use every endeavour to quit the interior and repair to the coast.

This was now pious advice. If only someone at the Foreign Office had replied to his despatch, and to Theodore's letter to Queen Victoria, which had now been in the hands of the Foreign Office for nearly a year, Captain Cameron could have left Ethiopia, and done so while the Emperor was in a happier mood. But now on 6 February the Frenchman's reported statement gave Lord Russell his first warning of Captain Cameron's possible danger. The actual alarm sounded a month later and Lord Russell acted swiftly.

11

MISSIONARIES IN PERIL
(1863–4)

The Reverend Henry Stern, accompanied by his lay colleague, Mr Cornelius, made his missionary journey among the Falashas, or Judaic Ethiopians, north-west of Lake Tana, in September 1863, and returned to his mission station at Jenda by the end of the month. His report of this journey, among 'the mystical Jews of Ethiopia', appeared in the *Jewish Intelligence* in England in May 1864.

The well-sited mission station of the London Society for Promoting Christianity among the Jews at Jenda consisted of seven thatched conical huts, including the chapel and the school house. The Protestant community living there was both small and international. There was Mr Stern, the head of the mission, and Mr Cornelius; Mrs Flad who, like her lay missionary husband, Flad, was German, and she had her young children with her; and there were the Ethiopian converts and followers. In addition there was Consul Cameron, who had struck up a friendship with Mr Stern.

Charming, restful Jenda was a good place to recover from a bout of fever, and, if not quite the strategic place to further British commerce, was as good a place as any, and better than many, to await the all important reply to Theodore's letter; it was certainly a much healthier place than Massawa; and now there did not appear to be much the Consul could do about Anglo-Ethiopian relations until that reply arrived. And there were servants of various Middle East and Oriental nationalities.

To this simple, serene place, in beautiful hilly country, the home from home for the handful of Europeans, Henry Stern came back after his journey among the Falashas, 'delighted with all that I had witnessed and experienced'. Almost immediately Mrs Flad told Mr Stern that he had come back in the nick of time, for that very day she had received a letter from her husband requesting him to come to Gondar because Theodore wanted to communicate to all

Europeans in or near the capital the answer from the Emperor of the French to his letter which he had sent about the same time as he had sent letters to Queen Victoria, the Emperor of Russia and other European monarchs. Consul Cameron had received a similar summons from the Emperor himself.

When these summons arrived it was eleven months since Theodore had sent his letters to the European monarchs; Cameron had carried the letter addressed to Queen Victoria as far as Axum, where he had entrusted it to an Ethiopian messenger to take to Massawa, and that letter had then gone to Aden and thence to London. About the same time a Frenchman, Monsieur Bardel, set off with a letter to Napoleon III, but, in this case Bardel himself carried it to Paris. There was still no answer from Queen Victoria, which was disturbing. But now Bardel was back with the reply from the French Government; and this, the first reply from one of the European sovereigns, was unfortunate.

Emperor Theodore was not amused. As for the representatives of two of those countries, their behaviour had been strange indeed. The British Consul had behaved incomprehensibly; instead of taking the royal letter to London, or at least to Massawa, to ensure its safe despatch from there, he had gone off not merely to Bogos where there were afflicted Ethiopian Christians, but into Egyptian territory, where he had been feasted by Theodore's enemies, and had thereafter failed to produce any reply from London.

Then there was the French Consul, M. Lejean: he too had behaved in a strange way for the representative of an allegedly friendly state. After expressing willingness to follow Theodore on one of his campaigns, he had abruptly decided that he wanted to leave the court, and had said so in a most offensive manner. And now the other Frenchman, M. Bardel, while showing loyalty to Theodore, had brought back a strange tale from Paris. It seemed that the foreign representatives were pursuing a most objectionable course in their relations with Theodore. The fact that Bardel was a sycophant and liar was not apparent to Theodore, or he chose not to be aware of it.

The diplomatic malodour was known to both Mr Stern and Captain Cameron. So when they received their summons to Gondar they both knew that all was not well. They set off with some misgivings on the day after Stern's return from his happy missionary tour. They found the Emperor's great camp and the city itself, as Stern relates, 'plunged in merriment and gaiety'.

They made their way into the town, and, as convention required when nearing the Palace, they dismounted and proceeded on foot. In the merry confusion they could find no official to announce them, so they made their way instead through the throng to the house of a *debtera*, a lay cleric, where they knew they would find hospitality.

On the way they met the hero of the moment, M. Bardel, and Cameron entered into conversation with him. In the press of people the Frenchman did not at first notice Stern and thus spoke more freely than he might otherwise have done. But Stern overheard one remark in particular: 'I shall crush them all.' This could have referred to the Protestant missionaries, the European craftsmen, or M. Lejean, the French Consul. Whoever it might have been, the words startled missionary Stern.

At last, safely housed with their *debtera* friend, the Consul and missionary spent the next day, Sunday, undisturbed. The royal business for which all the Europeans had been summoned began the following day, Monday, and early that morning all were summoned to the Palace. Stern and Cameron went along together and found on a grassy lawn two gorgeous tents, indicating that some important business was about to be transacted. Among those in one of the tents was the French Consul, M. Lejean. Stern and Cameron were directed to the other tent, where already there were the European craftsmen, in their Ethiopian clothes.

Soon half-a-dozen officials of the Palace came and led the Europeans up the broad steps of the Palace to a vestibule, and they were led to the audience hall which still retained some of the odour of the previous days' feasting. In a recess of one of the large glassless windows Theodore was seated, surrounded by books and papers. When all those summoned were seated in front of the Emperor an order was given for Bardel to rise, and he did so with an air of importance. Then began one of those solemn performances intended to impress the Europeans even more than the Ethiopians, but which the Europeans regarded as theatrical, and always, even when touched with tragedy, somewhat farcical.

Pursuing the pattern of these sessions, Theodore put questions to Bardel who gave the required, if not pre-arranged answers. In the course of this dialogue Bardel told his story. He had arrived at the court of the Emperor of the French in Paris; he had met with a most discourteous reception; he was provided with neither a house nor food, nor money to supply his daily wants. Bardel said he had eventually presented Theodore's letter to Napoleon III who had thereupon asked him a number of questions about Ethiopia. By this time most of the Europeans were convinced that Bardel was making up the whole story. Continuing, Bardel said Napoleon III had then turned to the well-known traveller d'Abbadie and consulted him about Theodore's letter. M. d'Abbadie's observation immediately, said Bardel, produced a change in Napoleon's attitude, and he dismissed Bardel with the words, 'I will have no direct intercourse with a sovereign who cuts off the hands and feet of his subjects.'

That was Bardel's story. Stern, who had been listening carefully, did not believe a word of it, but it was obviously the story which Theodore accepted; and Stern felt he would have risked his life had he challenged it.

Bardel continued his essay in high diplomacy, and said that although Napoleon did not wish to have direct relations with the court of Ethiopia, he did not wish to end relations between the two Empires and so he ordered one of his ministers to reply to Theodore's letter. This diplomatic document was now handed round for the Europeans to inspect, and it was then passed to Cameron to read aloud in French. When the British Consul came to the end, Theodore snatched the paper from him, flung it to the ground and said bitterly, perhaps with a tone of wounded pride: 'Is this an answer to my letter? Napoleon may think himself great, but I am greater still; his genealogy is only of yesterday; mine, on the contrary, I trace back to David and Solomon. True he is rich, and I am poor; he is powerful and I am weak; he has fine palaces and I only poor ruins, but' – and here Theodore paused and turned his eyes heavenwards, and continued – 'glory, wealth and renown will yet be my portion!'

The Emperor then turned to Lejean, who was in disgrace. The Consul pleaded, through interpreters, that Theodore was misconstruing the letter, and asked for permission to present despatches he had received from France, stating that an Ethiopian embassy would be accepted as soon as permission for it to travel through Egypt had been arranged.

Theodore would have none of this, and he was minded to put both the French Consul and his travelling companion Dr Legarde, in chains. Fortunately for them Abuna Salama had already interceded with Theodore on their behalf, and the Emperor contented himself with ordering the deportation of the two Frenchmen.

Later Stern wrote down his reflections on Theodore and that day's events:

> The departure of the French Consul, the doubts and suspicions about an answer to his letter from the British Government; the report that a strong Turkish [Egyptian] force had taken their position at Matemma, on the north-western border; the consciousness that he could not cope with a foe [Egypt] whom he had insolently challenged to combat; together with a fading vision of ever obtaining by diplomacy the coveted possession of Senaar to the north-west and the isle of Massowah to the north-east, soured his temper . . . Ominous indications of coming events henceforth cast their dismal shadow athwart our serene and hitherto unclouded horizon. No one, of course, had the remotest idea in what shape or form the impending crisis would develop itself. I believed the royal indignation would burst on the missionaries in an order for their expulsion, and on the British Consul in a mandate for a forcible unfettered detention.

Stern had already come to the conclusion that he had attained the object of his sojourn in Ethiopia; he felt he had securely established the mission at Jenda, in so far as he could, and he could now return to Europe. What he had seen at the Court at Gondar determined him to hasten his departure, before events not yet clearly foreseeable might delay it. He intended to go and pay his respects to the Emperor in his nearby camp two days later, but by then Theodore with part of his army had, unexpectedly, departed on an expedition against a rebel to the north.

On St George's Day, 13 October 1863, Stern left Gondar on his homeward journey to Massawa and Europe. The hour of his departure was somewhat delayed by going to bid farewell to Abuna Salama, who that morning rose late, but nevertheless the missionary took a substantial breakfast with the prelate. These pleasurable formalities completed, Stern mounted his mule and went to bid farewell to Cameron. He found the British Consul waiting and ready to accompany him part of the way, and with his mule already saddled.

To avoid the heat of the day Stern and Cameron, with his retinue, soon trotted off, taking the path towards the foaming and gushing river Kaha, where they were joined by Bardel, also with a retinue, so the party was now quite a cavalcade. But the Europeans were not the only travellers on that route, for the Emperor was on the march and masses of soldiers with their ill-clad followers were, as Stern relates, 'forcing their course in the same direction, in order to join their respective chiefs'. Although the rabble was tolerably civil to the Europeans who overtook them, they showed an unwonted disdain that renewed Stern's misgivings. These fears had been confirmed when he learned that some of Cameron's servants and two representatives of the Scottish Church Mission, Mr Staiger and Mr Brandeis, bearing letters from their masters to Massawa, had been plundered and maltreated.

For two hours Stern and his companions rode on in pleasant conversation, after which they bade one another farewell. Stern was not sorry to be leaving Ethiopia.

Followed by a faithful servant, the departing missionary sped on through an ever increasing crowd heading towards the imperial camp, until, about midday, he reached the verdant plateau of Wagara, where he caught up with his servants and followers who had gone ahead with the baggage. But here a disagreeable surprise confronted him: he saw, about ten minutes' ride away, the imperial camp.

Stern consulted with his people whether they should make camp forthwith, but all told him he must first go and pay his respects to the Emperor, lest failure to adhere to this customary courtesy might be taken as rudeness. The missionary had hoped he had seen the last of Theodore, but reluctantly accepted this advice. But first his party alighted in a pleasant green spot and rested a while under shady trees and amidst fragrant shrubs. In his tent the missionary took a welcome noon-day rest, but the thought of visiting the camp depressed his spirits; so he tried jotting down some notes to dispel the gloom, but this proved a poor solace, so he resolved to get the unpleasant business over. Throwing his *shamma*, or toga, around him with determination, he set off, accompanied by two servants, towards the hill on whose summit the imperial tent stood out conspicuously. He described the ensuing events as follows:

> As I approached, all previous surmises and misgivings vanished, and, confiding in the consciousness of my integrity, which I thought would be a shield strong enough to guard me against the machinations and malice of insidious foes . . . I boldly advanced till I stood within a respectful and becoming distance of the never-to-be-forgotten spot.
>
> Whilst waiting for the approach of an officer or domestic of the royal household who would announce my visit, groups of drunken military chiefs and district governors came staggering, in most unseemly attitudes, out of the royal banqueting tent. Many gazed at me in stupid

bewilderment; others, with heavy tongues, bawled forth a compliment or abuse on the white men. I felt disposed to retreat, but to this, for sapient reasons, my companions justly objected. I then suggested that we should seek the shelter of a shady tree or bush till the banquet was over and his Majesty visible. This proposal was equally rejected as incompatible with Abyssinian rule. The last jar of hydromel had at last, as a royal page, *en passant*, assured me, been quaffed, the last reeking joint had been devoured, the last batch of rioters had at last vanished, when the folds of the tent were thrown aside, and his Majesty, surrounded by half-a-dozen officers and several pages, strutted into the open air. My companions quickly prostrated themselves into the dust; whilst I, without imitating their servile obeisance, made a humble and deferential bow. 'Come nearer,' shouted the attendants. I obeyed, and advanced a few steps. 'Still nearer,' reiterated several stentorian voices. I complied, and made another forward movement. 'What do you want?' sharply demanded the flushed and drink-excited Negoos. 'I saw your Majesty's tent,' was the response, 'and came hither to offer my humble salutations and respects to your Majesty.' 'Where are you going?' 'I am, with your Majesty's sanction, about to proceed to Massowah.' 'And why did you come to Abyssinia?' 'A desire to circulate the Word of God among your Majesty's subjects prompted the enterprise,' I rejoined. 'Can you make cannons?' 'No,' was the reply. 'You lie,' was the laconic retort; and then, turning . . . towards Negusee, one of my companions, a servant of Consul Cameron, he imperatively demanded to know the name of his province. 'I am from Tigré,' tremulously responded the poor man. 'And you are the servant or interpreter of this white man?' 'No, your Majesty; I am in the employ of Consul Cameron, and only accompany him down to Adowa, whither I am bound to see my family.' 'You vile carcass! . . . you dare to bandy words with your king. Down with the villain, and *bemouti* [by my death], beat him till there is not a breath in his worthless carcass.' The order was promptly obeyed, and the poor, inoffensive man . . . was dashed on to the ground, where . . . the animated and robust frame was, in less than a minute, a torn and mangled corpse. 'There's another man yonder,' vociferated the savage king; 'kill him also.' The poor fellow . . . was immediately dragged to the side of his motionless companion, and . . . doomed to share the same unhappy fate. I was amazed, bewildered and surprised. In my agitation I might, unconsciously, have put my hand or finger to my lips. This the cruel tyrant construed into an act of defiance, and, without one warning or reproof, he rushed upon me with a drawn pistol, like a lion balked of his prey. For an instant I saw the glittering weapon sparkling in the rays of the sinking sun, and then, as if checked in his fell design by an invisible power, it disappeared again in the case suspended round his waist. 'Knock him down! Kill him!' were the words which rung appallingly on my ear. In the twinkle of an eye I was stripped, on the ground, and insensible. Stunned, unconscious, and almost lifeless, with the blood oozing out of scores of gashes, I was dragged into the camp, not, as my guards were commanded, to bind me in fetters, but, as they thought – and I heard it from their own lips – to bury me.

A stifling sensation . . . roused me to something approaching consciousness. I tried to speak, but my throat and mouth, full of clotted blood, forbade the attempt. I sought to look around me, but my eyes were glued, and I did not dare to open them. I endeavoured to recollect the events of the last few hours, but my swimming and giddy head rendered the effort abortive. Rousing myself from this state of painful lassitude and stupefaction, my mind, though sadly confused, retained some faint recollection of the last hour's terrible scene. The soldier to whom I was fastened, and whose *shamma* my bleeding wounds had thoroughly saturated, noticed that I was in great agony and distress. The gentle touch with which he lifted the chain convinced me that he was not one of Theodore's hardened ruffians. 'What do you want?' he kindly inquired. I pointed to my parched and feverish lips. 'Woha' [water]. 'Tenisu' [get up], 'and you shall have some.' With difficulty I raised my cold, shivering, and stiff limbs, and, together with my kind guardian, crept to a watch-fire, where there was a party who had a skin full of water. 'Hit' [go], 'Turk,' they shouted, 'for our Christian cups shall not touch a Moslem's lips.' 'I am not a Mahomedan,' I mournfully sighed, 'but a Christian, and a believer in a blessed Trinity.' These faintly-breathed words acted like a galvanic battery on their insensible hearts. Promptly the water cup was raised to my quivering lips, and a place vacated for me near the fire. A good, cold draught roused me to a knowledge of my misery and wretchedness, loneliness and desolation . . . The world around me was dead to a white man's anguish, and indifferent to his woes: but though far removed from the sight of those whose words might have soothed the aching, lacerated, and bleeding missionary, whose hands might have bathed his throbbing temples, staunched his bleeding wounds . . . there was One present who, in the utter despondency and despair of the storm-tossed heart, could point to His own solemn and touching words: 'Fear not, for I am with thee; be not dismayed, for I am thy God. I will strengthen thee . . . yea, I will uphold thee with the right hand of My righteousness.'

Stern went on to recall that the 'long interminable night of suffering and trial, with its dew and cold and darkness, at length drew to a close'. He adds that his suffering:

. . . during the cold and damp of night and inflammation, if not subdued, was at least checked, but the wind and sun, acting on the

> unswathed and exposed gashes, produced the most exquisite and indescribable torture. Death... would then to me have been an angel of mercy; but though I yearned most impatiently for his visit, he would not come. The fetters fastened around my native companion's wrist were unriveted, and my swollen, palsied arms, instead of being held in irons, were pitilessly grasped by two savage ruffians in the service of a notorious villain, Ali Woobeshat, the governor of Woggera. Excited to a pitch almost verging on frenzy, I tried to shake off the dastardly poltroons, but the exertion exceeded my energy, and I sank prostrate at their feet. Forced to get up, I was partly carried and partly dragged out of the detested camp. The physical effort was too much for my failing strength, so that, despite the goading of the zealous myrmidons of Ali Woobeshat, I had to rest again and again. Water! Water! was my entreaty. This mournful cry several parties of soldiers who passed by heard; but although they cast many a pitiful glance on the disfigured and woe-begone stranger, not one had compassion enough to allay the maddening thirst of my burning tongue . . . Pushed on by the cowardly savages, who imagined that a man who could not stand might yet be able to run, I crawled forward, and at length, to the satisfaction of the custodians, was safely housed in a peasant's reed-built cabin. Two chiefs, Hassan Ali, the nominal governor of Yedshou, and Basha Medeka, a noble of Woggera, who had the previous evening broken their sticks on my head, received me. Whether my wretched and almost dying condition moved their pity, or whether they thought that my decease might draw upon them the wrath of their master, I cannot positively assert. I know that they were attentive to my wants, and, together with the villagers, did everything in their power to mitigate my sufferings . . .

At the next sunrise soldiers came into Stern's hut, with orders from Theodore that the missionary should go along with them. This was a great blow to him, but he resigned himself. Still quivering with pain and shock, and still in his bloodstained garments, he was lifted on to a mule. The Emperor was moving his camp back to Gondar, and the captive missionary had to go too.

Some of his guards showed him compassion and whispered to him: 'The King will have mercy on you. It is your intimacy with the Aboona that brought you into trouble; but he is powerful and will satisfactorily arrange the unfortunate misunderstanding.' Stern enquired whether he had done wrong in calling on the Emperor at the camp late at noon. The reply was: 'Wrong! Why, if you had not called, we had orders to arrest you, and who knows whether the stick alone would have been the penalty you would have incurred!'

On nearing Gondar the party made a brief halt and the guards, who, with some consideration had left Stern unfettered, then tied a strong belt round one arm and waist, in preparation for entering the camp, and the party moved on again. The missionary told his remaining servants that they could profit little by staying with him and they would do well to escape, but they refused to do so. However, as they drew nearer to Gondar the guards noticed that one of Stern's servants had disappeared, and with a shrewd guess as to where he had gone, two chiefs rode off smartly to find him. Their guess was right, and they found him with the Abun. Showing great respect for the high priest they nevertheless apprehended the servant and brought him back; the missionary noticed a twinkle in the eye of his servant who presently slipped two pieces of paper into his hand. Pulling his *shamma* loosely round him to conceal the papers, he found he had two letters, both expressing sympathy: one from Cameron, the other from the Abun who also said he would do what he could to secure his release.

It was late in the afternoon when the party entered the camp and halted just outside the royal enclosure. The bound and aching missionary was lifted from his mule, and placed on the ground, with his head on a stone, to find what rest he could. It was after sunset when word went round that the Emperor had re-entered the camp, and soon the weary prisoner heard the shout *Tenisu* – get up – and almost simultaneously he was lifted to his feet and hustled before the Emperor. On reaching the royal presence Stern saw his servants were all under arrest.

Theodore immediately began to interrogate the missionary: 'Who gave you permission to take my people to your country?' The missionary replied: 'Your Majesty is misinformed, I never intended to take a single Abyssinian to Europe.' 'Why did you insult me when I punished two of my subjects who did not conduct themselves with becoming propriety in my presence?' Stern answered: 'Your Majesty, there is a God above and He knows that courtesy prompted me to approach your Majesty's tent.' After a pause Theodore exclaimed: 'You white men hate me, and I hate you. I allow you to come and stay in my country merely because I want to get some of your *belhad* [arts]. England and France boast of power and riches; I defy them both.'

Theodore then turned to Stern's servants and interrogated them, beginning by asking why they accompanied the missionary. Their simple answer was: 'Because he pays us.' 'And where are you going?' he then asked. Several replied simultaneously: 'To our home at Adowa.' Theodore retorted angrily: 'And cannot I pay you more, you vile peasants' sons!' and then: 'Guards, seize them.' This order was instantly obeyed, and the unlucky servants were seized, stripped of their clothes and cuffed and buffeted. Theodore then turned to the missionary's guards and ordered: 'Watch him well, and do not allow anyone without my sanction to approach him.'

Promptly half-a-dozen officers seized Stern and led him off. Manacled at ankles and wrists, chained to a guard, sometimes so fettered that he could neither stand upright nor stretch out to full length, his possessions – his Bible, his papers, his collection of butterflies, his camera, his single copy of his own book, *Wanderings among Falashas in Abyssinia* – were all confiscated. He was made to subsist on a diet of *teff*, or millet, bread, baked by a servant of one of the jailers, and a little pepper paste. His European friends and the Abun all interceded with the Emperor for his release: but in vain. Stern's hopes were sometimes raised and as often dashed. He learnt that the Emperor had said that he was to be confronted openly with all his sins. In his distress and sorrow he threw himself 'on the bosom of a sympathetic Saviour'.

Then one day things really looked brighter: the missionary's foot chains were removed. The following morning the guards were reduced to two; but this relief was presently marred by the tramp of feet, the hum of voices and rattle of shields and spears. At noon the chief jailer, Jaques Obey, came into the tent with a number of guards who seized him and hustled him in the direction of the noise. Here to his surprise he beheld the élite of the army drawn up in a large square formation and at the far end on a throne sat, dignified and proud, the dreaded Emperor, shaded by two gigantic silk umbrellas. The monarch in a shrill voice gave the order: 'Bring the Falasha forward' – an allusion to the fact that the missionary was a Jew. The crowd of soldiers made way and the worn, ill-kempt, manacled prisoner advanced. Stern gazed at the throng of soldiers; many a chief there was well-known to him, but not one gave him any sign of recognition.

To the left of the throne were M. Bardel and a German, Herr Zander, seemingly as counsellors to the Emperor; to the right were Ethiopian church dignitaries. Some way in front of the throne and seated on carpets were Consul Cameron in his uniform, the lay missionaries Josephson, Staiger and Brandeis, all in their European clothes, but with a white *shamma* over them, by way of court dress, and near them, the European artisans.

A new shock awaited Stern. As he looked around he saw that he was not the only captive missionary; a hundred steps away stood his colleague Rosenthal – in chains. This quite shook Stern. How widespread, he wondered, had Theodore's persecution become? Then Stern also saw Mrs Flad; she appeared also a prisoner, though not in chains. It was apparent that this ceremony was to be a trial, and the accused were those three so recently respected members of the mission at Jenda.

At the command of the Emperor, a court official read out from the *Fetha Negast* – the Law of the Kings – the ordinances considered relevant concerning those who spoke in a manner offensive to the *Negusa Negast*, the King of Kings, and these were crimes punishable by death. These then being the crimes of which the three Europeans were accused, the death sentence was pronounced upon them. The prisoners were then told the actual accusations against them. The charges were, seemingly, all based on papers seized from them.

The principal charges against Stern were ten. He was accused of making disparaging remarks about Theodore by saying that (1) the Emperor had no good counsellors, (2) he had plundered various districts of Ethiopia, including the Abun's domains at Jenda, (3) he was no friend of the Mission to the Jews, (4) he had provoked the hostility of France and the aggression of Egypt, (5) he had murdered in cold blood 700 to 800 people, (6) his mother had sold *kosso* (medicinal flowers); furthermore (7) Stern had said that Mrs Flad had acted dishonestly (over certain money matters), (8) he had said that there were no legal marriages among the Ethiopians, (9) he had been in communication with the Abun, and finally, (10) he was guilty of the sin of pride.

Missionary Rosenthal stood charged on two counts. First, in a letter to his brother-in-law in London, he had cast aspersions on the Emperor's domestic life; and second, he had remarked that Ethiopia would probably enjoy greater security under Egypt than under her native sovereign.

Mrs Flad was charged that in a letter she had made disparaging remarks about the Emperor; fortunately for her, she had also written disparaging remarks about his enemies the Turks. She was pardoned. Stern and Rosenthal were far less fortunate.

Stern was permitted to speak. He repudiated all the accusations.

As for the passages from his papers, he claimed that the Amharic translations had distorted what he had written; and as for his book the passage quoted had been mutilated to misrepresent him; in fact the book, he contended, unequivocally demonstrated his regard and esteem for the Emperor.

One of the strangest episodes in the trial was when Theodore called upon some of the military chiefs and priests to recite his royal genealogy. From Adam to Solomon and on to the great Ethiopian Emperor Fasilidas, founder of Gondar, the line was correctly recited, but after that there were some confusions. Theodore was furious, and berated his chiefs and priests. In his rage he at one point challenged Stern to choose weapons and fight a duel with him. Stern's reply was that he was a priest and did not fight.

All was in vain. The Ethiopian scribe asked the assembled Europeans for their opinions. They replied that Stern and Rosenthal were guilty. There is some mystery as to why the Europeans confirmed the guilt which carried the death penalty. Did they think, perhaps with good reason, that it was useless to oppose the Emperor and that it was better to humour him and place their hopes on his granting the two missionaries pardon? Or were they merely concerned with keeping in favour with him and saving their own skins? Perhaps each of those Europeans was, in varying degrees, actuated by both motives.

When, seemingly, the Europeans turned against him, Stern felt utterly deserted and quite shattered; he knew well enough that for him and Rosenthal it was a confirmation of the death sentence. Stern in desperation now turned to one of the Emperor's interpreters, Ato Samuel, though he suspected him of being one who had brought him all his troubles, and entreated him to solicit the royal pardon. Displeased, Samuel at first ignored him, but after repeated entreaty, retorted angrily: 'Tomorrow, tomorrow.' The trial had now lasted three hours, the pleadings were over, Theodore waved his hand, the two condemned prisoners were seized by guards and almost carried through the assembled throng to the prison tent which they were then to share and once again chains were fastened upon their wrists and ankles. Stern was utterly weary in body and depressed in mind; he sought comfort in his Christian faith, but hoped that no new torments would be inflicted upon him and his fellow prisoner before the execution of the death sentence. And would poor Rosenthal see again his anguished wife and his children?

At sunrise on Monday morning some of the men of Agha Faree Meshed (the military commander who was the Royal Gatekeeper and Chief Executioner) came and seized all the prisoners' baggage and took it to the Emperor. The rest of the day passed quietly, but that evening Jaques Obey entered the tent, half drunk, eyed Stern, then, cursing him, examined his chains and began hammering them tighter. This jailer then examined Rosenthal's chains, but considered them tight enough.

The next morning Samuel and an officer appeared and in the name of the Emperor promised Stern free pardon if he would confess that it was through the family of Ras Wubie's wife that he had obtained the information regarding Theodore's family and descent. Stern replied that he had no acquaintance direct or indirect with that lady or her family. The inquisitors went away in a bad humour.

More anxious days of waiting followed, but an atmosphere of calm before the storm crept into the prison tent and the two prisoners began to think that the impatiently awaited letter from the Queen of Great Britain must have arrived.

It was now December, and at noon on the fourth of that month the prisoners, who had had no previous hint of any pending amelioration, were surprised when guards entered their tent, removed the leg chains, and led them to the royal enclosure. They found Theodore holding a trial in which about a dozen peasants lodged complaints that they had been despoiled by some pillaging soldiers. The two missionaries bowed in the direction of the monarch who, however, ignored them, so they waited and looked on at the trial. The Emperor gave judgement against the peasants and condemned them to the cruel penalty of the *giraff* or whip. It took about two hours to flog all the peasants, and these men, who had stood before the Emperor stalwart and robust, now lay before him, lacerated, faint, and dying.

The only woman suppliant among the peasants the Emperor pardoned. Her pardon was hardly fulsome, as her husband, brother and neighbours lay dying about her.

The two missionaries soon realised that they had been brought to the royal enclosure specially to witness the scene. So that they might the better appreciate the significance of the penalty the executioners occasionally flicked some of the blood on the whips on to the faces of the two Europeans. Stern and Rosenthal could not help but think this was a prelude for their own subjection to the same torture. Somewhat stupefied by the spectacle, Stern could only wonder how much of the penalty his enfeebled body could stand when his turn came. Standing thus half dazed, he then became aware that Ato Samuel had approached, and ordered the guard to lead the two Europeans before the Emperor.

Theodore, with apparent relish, then asked Stern: 'Are you afraid now?' The missionary made no reply, even when Theodore repeated the question. The monarch thereupon asked: 'Why did you insult me?' Stern now thought it wisest to reply, and said, as before, that neither he nor Rosenthal had ever had any thought of insulting His Majesty, but if they had done any wrong, they craved pardon. Before Samuel could complete the translation of these words, Theodore angrily ordered the guards to tear off the Europeans' *shammas* and shirts, and thus, half stripped, the two prisoners were led back to their prison tent. They devoted themselves to prayer and meditation, during what they believed to be their last night.

However on the following morning, in a strangely kindlier mood, the crude master jailer, Jaques Obey, came with some clothes for the two prisoners and said that the Emperor's anger had relented and probably they would soon receive a complete pardon. The guards became more friendly and once again spoke to them without reserve; they stated that Theodore, the day before, had intended to kill them both, but they had been spared through the intervention of the venerable Echege, the head of the Ethiopian monks. The missionaries knew full well that they were not popular with the Ethiopian clergy, and had never expected help from that quarter; this unexpected act greatly comforted them; they felt there might yet be hope. Thus the prisoners passed some 15 days, untormented, but still scarcely daring to hope.

During this waiting and uncertainty, one fine morning in December there was a surprise visit from Mr Flad and Ato Samuel, accompanied by servants of the Emperor and the Archbishop. Samuel said that it had been Theodore's intention to kill the missionary, and he would have done so, had God permitted it; but now the Emperor wished to give him a chance to regain the royal favour and this he could do by helping to obtain from Europe one or two gunpowder-makers and the requisite machinery, which was to be done through Mr Flad whom the Emperor was sending to

Europe. If Flad was successful, on his return Stern would be liberated and honoured and rewarded and become famous in Africa and Europe; meanwhile, during Flad's visit to Europe, he was to accompany the Emperor on his campaigns and take photos of the districts visited. The unbending missionary had no inclination to meet these wishes; he had no enthusiasm to become one of the world's earliest army press photographers. Flad and the others, however, warned him not to oppose the monarch. Reluctantly Stern gave his acquiescence; there were soon signs of reward for both the prisoners.

Next day guards came to remove the two missionaries' fetters. The prisoners were allowed some new clothing. Most prized of all was the arrival of two Bibles. A few days later Flad, with Samuel, came again to the prison tent and asked Stern to write letters to help procure munitions in Europe. Wrily Stern penned the required letters.

Pleased with his plans, Theodore sent word about them to the European artisans at Gafat. They took the occasion to send a petition to the Emperor politely remonstrating about Stern and Rosenthal's continued captivity, suggesting that they could be liberated, and undertaking that they would provide the machinery and make the gunpowder. The artisans may have been moved by pity for the suffering fellow Europeans; or they may also have had no wish for more Europeans to come to earn dollars which they would quite like to earn themselves. Soon after this Samuel, on a visit to the prison tent, said to the two captive missionaries: 'Be of good cheer, your liberation is not far distant.'

Theodore saw sense in the artisans' proposal and sent word to them to come to his camp at Gondar, and bring about a reconciliation between him and the two European prisoners.

Just at this critical moment Consul Cameron thought it appropriate to carry out the instructions of the Foreign Secretary, brought to him four weeks previously. He applied to the Emperor for permission to leave his court and proceed to the coast. This was unfortunate. It was now about three months since the Emperor had received the reply from the French Government which he had found so unsatisfactory. It was about a month since Cameron had received the despatches from the British Government, but *without* the long-awaited reply from the Queen. Now, the British Consul had received orders from his Government to leave Theodore's court. The inference was obvious: the British Government had no intention of replying to his letter, and no intention of receiving an Embassy from him – the Embassy which had been under discussion since the time of Plowden. Theodore's conclusion was perfectly correct. In December 1863, the British Government (and certainly the Foreign Office) had no thought of replying to the letter from the Emperor of Ethiopia to the Queen, and no intention of receiving his Embassy. All this was offensive, and an insult which Theodore was not disposed to accept quietly.

At this time also, a priest arrived from the Ethiopian church at Jerusalem, who came with a tale of woe against the Turk – and the British. For many years the British Consul in Jerusalem had exercised some protection over the Ethiopian church and clergy there. The Church consisted of a chapel at the Holy Sepulchre. Recently the Coptic Church of Egypt had, not for the first time, laid claim to that chapel, and, with the approval of the Turkish Government, the Christian clerics of Egypt had driven out the Ethiopian monks and seized their venerated chapel. The Ethiopian monks appealed for the intervention of the British Consul in Jerusalem. On the former occasion the Consul, Mr Finn, had successfully protected the Ethiopians; but the new Consul, Mr Moore, acting on instructions from the Foreign Secretary, Lord Russell, had told the Ethiopians that he had no right to interfere in matters which were the responsibility of the Turkish Government, and so he left the Ethiopians, as it seemed to them (and indeed to the unhappy British Consul) in the lurch.

Where now were the friendly English and the friendly British Government of Plowden's day? To Theodore it appeared clear enough that the British and their Government, and perhaps all Europeans, had turned against him. He had done nothing to offend them. He had held out the hand of friendship, but they had turned against him. Why this should be so he could not understand, but that they scorned him was obvious enough. He had a few months earlier expelled the French Consul, Lejean, and his companion Dr Legarde. Now he would teach the British – and all Europeans – a sterner lesson. He ordered the arrest of the British Consul, the remaining missionaries, and some other Europeans – but not his Frenchman, Bardel, or the European artisans.

News of this new turn of affairs, that was to dash their newly-aroused hopes, did not immediately reach the two missionaries in their prison tent, so they passed the Christmas of 1863 and the ensuing New Year not unhopefully.

The morning of Sunday, 3 January 1864, brought a glimmer of hope to the chained missionaries; their guards told them that the Negus was exchanging messages with the *Faranji*, or Europeans, and that they would probably be liberated soon. Vain hope. In the early afternoon the jailer came back and ordered the two missionaries to follow him to the Emperor. Rosenthal asked his fellow prisoner what he thought this summons might signify, and Stern answered him, 'On a Sunday, both whips and sticks are in abeyance; we have no cause to apprehend anything inauspicious.' So they followed Jaques Obey, without too much anxiety; but a new surprise awaited them.

They were led to a white tent in front of which were spread out a number of carpets, and this rare display of royal pomp roused hopes in the two prisoners of some favourable outcome. But they were soon perplexed, for there they found most of their European friends, and asking them what was the meaning of this, they received the reply: 'We are all prisoners and about to be chained.'

Cameron's untimely obedience to the order contained in Lord Russell's instruction to return to Massawa had exhausted Emperor Theodore's much strained patience. The Emperor had accordingly ordered the arrest of all the Europeans in and around Gondar not actually in his employment, and that Sunday morning they had been rounded up, their property seized. Most of the Ethiopian servants of the Europeans other than those of Cameron, had managed to slip off to avoid arrest.

The European men had accepted arrest peacefully, perforce, but the seizure of their belongings roused the fury of the two European women. Mrs Flad, who spoke Amharic fluently, gave the soldiers a piece of her mind; she told them: 'Go, tell your king that we are weak oppressed women; yet if he wishes to kill us, we, together with our infants, would deem it a mercy to be despatched at once, rather than be subject to a slow and lingering torture.' The message was later conveyed to Theodore, who commented: 'These white women compared to ours are perfect devils.' Mrs Rosenthal, who spoke only a little Amharic, nevertheless let fly with it, especially when she pursued a soldier through the compound who had stolen some lumps of sugar. She got the sugar back. One little lady also took the arrest badly. Mrs Flad's eldest daughter, aged about four, was particularly upset when a soldier came across her rag doll; little Miss Flad cried, and gave forth in her best Amharic to recover the doll, and her tearful protestation ended in success after about half an hour.

The Europeans newly brought to the royal camp knew full well the custom of the country. After Stern and Rosenthal joined them they had not long to wait before manacles were brought and hammered on to their wrists.

All the prisoners were then led off to the prison tent. As the captives settled down to rest as best they could, Samuel came to make a camp inspection, particularly to see that Consul Cameron had a bed. To Stern he remarked: 'I hope you are happier now, in the company of your friends, than in your former isolation.' The next day servants of the newly arrested Europeans came drifting back and some found their way into the camp and rejoined their imprisoned masters.

Theodore, employing messengers and notably Ato Samuel, then posed a number of questions to some of his European prisoners. These covered the absence of a reply from Queen Victoria, explanation of passages in Stern's writings, and interpretation of passages in the Bible.

There followed more days of tedium for the prisoners, with occasional anxiety. Relief to the monotony was provided on some evenings by a quarrel among the guards, and on some days by unclear messages from Theodore or the gift from him of a cow or a few sheep; also, Theodore sometimes sent copies of English journals purloined from the Consul's house with a request for the meaning of a picture or cartoon, or a passage from the Bible. Thus into the prison tent came pictures taken from the *Illustrated London News* and *Punch*, enjoying a circulation and a readership the London managers of those periodicals could hardly have contemplated.

Ato Samuel was the messenger on these quite frequent biblical or journalistic errands, and his arrival in the prison tent now became a cause for amusement and light relief for the chained inmates. One day, however, Samuel entered the tent with a fierce scowl, and handed Cameron a large, fully-written sheet of paper which turned out to be a formal protest from M. Lejean, the expelled French Consul, about the treatment he had received during his stay at Theodore's court. After glancing over the document, Cameron exclaimed: 'Samuel, Samuel, this is a sad business!' The royal messenger demanded that the document be expounded to him, and Stern undertook to do this. There were some 18 specific complaints in M. Lejean's letter, all criticising the Emperor's conduct in biting phrases. Stern found some satisfaction in punctiliously translating the offensive accusations, Samuel almost exploded with indignation, and at the end he did explode, and said what he thought of the departed French Envoy.

Having enjoyed this little treat, the prisoners were nevertheless fully aware that as the only Europeans on whom Theodore could lay his hands, they might have to suffer for the safely distant Frenchman's vitriolic epistle. But no new blow fell on them, and the steady flow continued of *Punch*, the *Illustrated London News*, and miscellaneous advertisements therefrom, requiring elucidation, the flow being occasionally enlivened by the picture of an amply dressed beauty taken from the glossy French *Le Follet*, though how this lively, competitive periodical entered the otherwise monopolistic circulation area of the two English magazines, the prisoners never discovered.

In the round-up of the Europeans it was conspicuous that Bardel was not among them. Rumour had it that he had gone off on a reconnoitring mission for the Emperor to Kassala, to see what the Egyptians might be up to. By the end of January rumours were afloat that he would soon be back, and then the European artisans at Gafat would be summoned to attend a special council. For once rumours proved true.

On 3 February Bardel returned from his secret mission. Two days later the Europeans from Gafat arrived and went straight to the royal tent, and stayed for a long interview and when it was over they proceeded to the prison tent of their fellow Europeans. The artisans brought with them orders for the release of some of the Europeans. Flad, Staiger, Brandeis, Josephson, Joseph and Schiller, were immediately freed. Cameron, Stern and Rosenthal were still detained, but the artisans gave them a little hope, for they told the Consul that if he pledged himself that the British Government would not insist on satisfaction for all that had passed, the artisans could bring about his release and that of the two still-captive missionaries, and they might even obtain the Emperor's permission that they should leave the country.

Thereafter the artisans had a number of interviews with Theodore, some of them of long duration. The discussions, however, were not about the three captives, but about their own affairs; and the casting of cannon, on which the Emperor set so much store.

12

NO GUNBOAT AT ADEN

(1864)

In March 1864 Europe was much concerned about the German invasion of the Danish provinces of Schleswig and Holstein. In Britain it preoccupied the whole Government, and not least the Prime Minister, Lord Palmerston, still vigorous in his eightieth year, and the Foreign Secretary, Lord Russell, still alert at 71. For a while Queen Victoria was anxious, as were some members of the Government, lest her Prime Minister, at times bellicose, and her Foreign Secretary, not infrequently hasty, might lead the country into war against Prussia and Austria. There was a good deal of popular sympathy in Britain for little Denmark, standing up to the big German bullies. And also because it was but a year since the Prince of Wales had married Princess Alexandra of Denmark; the nation was still rejoicing in the birth of their first child in January, only two months before the Germans forced their war on Denmark. More realistically, the Government was concerned about the Germanic powers extending their territorial sovereignty along the North Sea coast. Soon, however, the Cabinet took the line that Britain could not, or should not, enter alone into a war against Prussia and the other German states.

These were particularly anxious days for the Foreign Secretary. Some of his anxieties were reflected in the Queen's Speech (read in Her Majesty's absence by the Lord Chancellor) when Parliament had reassembled in February after the winter recess. The Speech began by recording the happy event of January, telling Lords and Commons that: 'Her Majesty is confident that you will share Her Feeling of Gratitude to Almighty God.' The Speech then plunged into troublesome foreign affairs: 'The State of Affairs on the Continent of Europe has been the Cause of great Anxiety to Her Majesty.' Then followed a reference to an affront for which Britain had demanded and obtained satisfaction: 'The barbarous Murders and cruel Assaults committed in Japan upon Subjects of

Her Majesty rendered it necessary that Demands should be made upon the Japanese Government . . . '

These events, which resulted 'incidentally' in the British destruction of Kagoshima, the capital of a powerful Japanese chief, arose out of a tragic contretemps. Three Englishmen had unwisely tried to force their way through a cortège of the great chief Satsuma as it passed along a highway near Yokohama. The impudent foreigners were promptly dealt with as any Japanese would have been who had acted in a similarly offensive manner; they were attacked, one was killed and two were wounded. The British Government called for punishment of the Japanese assailants. The prince refused to comply. Britain sent a naval squadron to Kagoshima, and bombarded it. This resulted, as the Speech said, in 'the Destruction of a considerable Portion of the Town'. It is perhaps a disadvantage for a weak maritime power to have its capital, or a large town, on the coast, if it quarrels with a powerful maritime power. In such cases inland states are less vulnerable.

In the midst of these and other preoccupations came unexpected and dramatic news from Ethiopia. On 8 March 1864, there arrived at the Foreign Office a despatch from the British Consul-General at Cairo, Mr Colquhoun, revealing for the first time the plight in which Captain Cameron found himself. The strange news came from the Sudan.

On the last day of 1863 a Swiss Protestant missionary had arrived at Khartoum, after a visit to Ethiopia, bringing information which he set down on 4 January 1864, in a letter to the British Consul, John Petherick. The latter, the very same day, sent the letter on to the British Consul-General in Cairo, with a covering letter saying: 'Mr Haussmann, a missionary direct from the camp of King Theodore of Abyssinia, arrived at this place on the 31st ultimo. The enclosed letter just received from him I consider of so important a nature, that with this day's post I forward it to you.' The Consul-General in his turn thought he should send the information to the Foreign Secretary, and he thus wrote to Lord Russell on 24 February: 'I received some days ago, a packet of letters from Mr Petherick . . . One of these contains a letter of some interest, and I think it right to send it *in extenso* to your Lordship, with its German idioms such as it reached me.' The letter 'of some interest' said:

Coming direct from Abyssinia . . . and having witnessed there some very important events which regard Europeans and English subjects, I have the honour of laying before you a brief report thereof . . .

Captain Cameron lived at Gondar since the beginning of September 1863, waiting for the answer of the English Government to a letter of King Theodore, which letter had been sent about nine months before. Before, however, this answer, which was said to be on the road, arrived, some very tragical events happened. The Rev. H. A. Stern . . . in September 1863, left Djenda . . . in order to go back to Europe by way of Gondar and Massowah. Having stayed at Gondar for some time, he started for Massowah. At Woggere . . . he passed the King's camp and went to pay the latter a parting visit, the time for which, however, was unhappily chosen, it being evening, and the King having given a great dinner that day.

Mr Stern had with him two servants, one of whom was to serve him as interpreter. As the servant, however, understood his business very badly, the King got angry, and ordered the servants to be beaten, which was done immediately. Mr Stern not being able to endure this sight, turned round and bit his finger, not knowing that this meant vengeance in Abyssinia. On this the King ordered him to be beaten too. The servants died of their ill-treatment, whilst Mr Stern, though severely wounded, survived . . . The King went back to Gondar, where he took Mr Stern and all his servants, all chained. At Gondar, he had Mr Stern's papers visited, in which nothing, however, offensive was found. The King had hitherto not been Mr Stern's friend, though he had always treated him well, as the Europeans in general. It is however, doubtless, that his suspicions had by somebody been aroused against Mr Stern having not only but by words, but by writing, insulted him.

Captain Cameron immediately applied to the King, but could not get an interview, and having in a letter to the King alluded to the friendship which had hitherto existed between Abyssinia and England, got only as an answer, the question – Where are the proofs of that friendship? (meaning thereby the answer to his letters to the English Government). Henceforth the King cut off any direct intervention of the Consul . . .

Some days afterwards, a second visitation of Mr Stern's papers was made, and, at that time, several remarks were found against the King, by which the latter was highly offended . . . The consequences of this was, that Mr Stern's feet were put in chains, and the King's suspicions were aroused against the other Europeans at Djenda. Some days afterwards, November 11, a considerable military force appeared at Djenda and made all the Europeans prisoners, amongst whom I was myself. We were brought to Gondar with all our property. The King ordered immediately Mr Rosenthal to be put in heavy chains, whilst he set us at liberty the following day, keeping, however, back our papers. Some

> days afterwards a Council took place, the King having summoned all Europeans present in Abyssinia, and having promised that they should be judges. This promise was, however, not fulfilled; and thus no result was attained by the Council. The only hope was put in the arrival of the long-expected English letters, which arrived the day after the Council; but as these letters did not contain any answer for the King, not only the fate of the prisoners was not changed, but the Consul himself put in a very awkward position to the King, which was enhanced still more by the rumours generally spread then, that two Egyptian armies were approaching to the Abyssinian frontiers.

Turning to the future the missionary continued:

> It is not at all likely that the King will set the prisoners free, nor let the English Consul go, until the answer of the English Government to the letters of the King will have arrived. Further, I allow myself the remark that any forcible means to get the liberty of the prisoners, the missionaries, and the Consul, for even the latter is scarcely better than the prisoners, will, in my opinion, and in that of every European in Abyssinia, the Consul included, prove highly dangerous for the surety and even lives of them. The King will prove desperate, and, as he is the absolute Ruler of his country, and the Europeans there actually in his power, peaceable means will, no doubt, prove more successful. For the present, the King will not likely go to the utmost, but he may do anything. I am not sure, but it is probable, that by some rich presents given to the King, and accompanied with friendly words, this awkward affair might be turned to a good end.

The Rev. Haussmann's letter gave the Foreign Secretary the first definite news of the imprisonment of Consul Cameron and other Europeans. The reply to Mr Colquhoun which Lord Russell wrote the very next day, 9 March, was the opening of a battle of wits between the British Government and Theodore, whose policy, tactics and reasoning it was to find for so long so difficult to measure. Russell observed:

> I have to instruct you to communicate as soon as possible with the Resident at Aden . . . and to request him to apply to King Theodore for the immediate release of Mr Cameron, and of any other British subjects whom he may hold under restraint, and for permission for their immediate departure . . .
>
> The Resident should plainly intimate to the King that, if he hesitates to comply with this demand, he will incur the very serious displeasure of the British Government, the consequences of which may involve him in great embarrassment, and shake the authority which he at present exercises in Abyssinia.

> Although I can only instruct you to demand as of right the release of British subjects, yet the Resident in Aden should use his best exertions to induce the King to set at liberty any other Europeans who may be detained in his dominions against their will.

Thus on 9 March 1864, with Lord Russell's precise despatch, the struggle for the release of Captain Cameron and other Europeans had begun. The setbacks were to be innumerable, the sufferings of the captives prolonged; but the one who suffered least, in the end suffered most.

The first setback was a comparatively minor one, and it did not come from Theodore. Lord Russell would have been the first to assert that British representatives abroad must remain at their posts, unless expressly ordered elsewhere, and should not interfere with the affairs of other countries. He could hardly complain, therefore, at the reply that came back from Brigadier Merewether. The Brigadier, who was in the service of the Government of Bombay, wrote from Aden, on 31 March:

> I am utterly unable to do anything in the case you mention; there is no Government steam-vessel in the harbour and no man-of-war on the Station . . .
>
> I would beg to point out that I have, properly speaking, nothing whatever to do with Abyssinia, though always ready to afford every assistance in my power to Her Majesty's Consul there when it is asked for. It would only be in a very extreme case, even if the means were at my disposal, that I should be justified in interfering in the affairs of that country, without first seeking instructions from the Government under which I am serving.

In Cairo, meanwhile, Consul-General Colquhoun was regretting that two good men were not available to go to Gondar, and he wrote to Lord Russell that Mr Petherick, recently Consul at Khartoum, would by then already be near Cairo on his way home, 'or he would, under other circumstances, and when wearing an official character, have been the person to have been charged with the matter'. And, continued the Consul-General, 'I do not know where Mr White Baker is at present; I suspect far to the south-west. He would have been well suited to such a Mission.' So those two gentlemen were not to add this exploit at the source of the Blue Nile to their adventures at or near the source of the White Nile, and their reputation, as that of their wives, has rested with their White Nile explorations, White Baker becoming better remembered as Sir Samuel Baker.

Some time later the Consul-General was to lament that another person who would have been helpful, Consul Plowden's old friend, the gentleman from Bologna, was no longer available: 'Old Mr Baroni, formerly Acting Consul at Massowah, whose knowledge of the country and persons in Abyssinia would have been most valuable, died about four months ago.'

In Aden meanwhile Brigadier Merewether, while waiting for instructions from Bombay, received confirmation of the imprisonment of Cameron and the others. In mid-April the schooner *Fanny* of the Indian Navy had been at Massawa, and there her Captain, Commander Thynne, learnt that the arrest of the British Consul and the other Europeans was common knowledge, to be spread to every port on the Red Sea, and beyond; every dhow and schooner sailing from the harbour would carry the news, for gossip in the bazaars and at the shrines, near and far. Besides reporting the gossip, Commander Thynne brought back proof positive: a note written in pencil by Cameron himself, bearing his initials:

> Myself, Stern, Rosenthal, Cairnes, Bardel, McCravie and McKilvie are all chained here.
>
> Flad, Staiger, Brandeis, and Cornelius sent to Gaffat to work for the King. No release until civil answer to King's letter arrives.

There was some irony in the date, 14 February 1864, [Cameron in error had actually written 1863] for although did not know it: it was just a year plus two days since the 'King's letter', still awaiting a 'civil answer' had reached the Foreign Office.

Haussmann's letter had arrived at the Foreign Office on 8 March, and Lord Russell took action on it on 9 March, but the general public knew nothing about the imprisonment of a British Consul and two members of a London missionary society until over a fortnight later. When the news did reach the public the emphasis was on the plight of the missionaries, who for the Foreign Secretary were of only secondary concern.

All the best people who paid their ninepence (including tax) for *The Times* on 25 March, got their money's worth of reading matter, including advertisements; and for good measure they also found, at the bottom of a page, an item tinged with tragedy. Under the simple heading 'MISSIONARIES IN ABYSSINIA' the newspaper reported that 'Painful intelligence has been received from Abyssinia of the cruel treatment which the Rev. Mr Stern and his colleague, Mr Rosenthal, agents of the London Society for the Promotion of

Christianity among the Jews, have suffered from King Theodore.' Not so top people also learned much the same news, though not quite so fully, from other London papers, including the *Daily News*, *Standard* and *Globe*, but they learned it a day earlier, for those papers published their briefer summaries on 24 March.

The British public at that time was hardly aware of the existence of Europeans in Ethiopia, and it was thanks to the Swiss missionary, Haussmann, that they now heard, almost by chance, of the predicament of two representatives of a London missionary society and of a British Consul. But after this there was for some time no further mention of the captives. The British public, with no more news about Ethiopia to remind them of the captives, could well have forgotten about them. And soon, early in April, there was an event providing much more interest, the arrival in England of the great popular hero of the day, the Italian patriot Garibaldi, who had already made his contribution to the unification of Italy. The enthusiasm with which the visitor was welcomed by the populace, and also by an influential section of the aristocracy, among them two staunch friends of Italian independence, Lords Palmerston and Russell, and also Lord Shaftesbury, evoked alarm in Queen Victoria, who thought Garibaldi too much of a revolutionary, and the scorn of Karl Marx (then just completing *Das Kapital*) who thought him not a revolutionary at all. The builder of Italian unity, and challenger of ancient monarchies, was avoided by Mr Disraeli, on this occasion playing safe.

While there was nothing to remind the British public of the captives in Ethiopia, there were people deeply concerned who could not let the matter rest. Most of these were connected with missionary societies, some being also relatives of the captives. And there was, of course, the irrepressible Dr Beke.

If there were any members or friends of the Jews' mission who had not already learned about the captives from the Press, they were told about them in their magazine *Jewish Intelligence*, the 'monthly register of the proceedings of the London Society for Promoting Christianity amongst the Jews'. The issue dated 1 April 1864, had an article headed 'Recent Distressing News' which began:

> Our readers will learn with extreme regret that our latest advices from Abyssinia . . . convey the sad news that our missionary brethren, the Rev. H. A. Stern and Mr Rosenthal, were in a situation of extreme

> peril, having from some untoward circumstances incurred the displeasure of King Theodorus.

The article then continued in true missionary vein:

> If ever there was an occasion for prayer, in connection with our Mission, this is undoubtedly one . . . We may humbly hope that He who has guided and guarded our brother Stern through many a peril hitherto, will in His great mercy have protected him this time also. Meanwhile prayers ought daily to be made for him and his companions; and we would suggest that morning and evening at the family altar, he and they should be specially remembered at the throne of grace . . .

In learning about the distress of the two missionaries, the readers of the *Jewish Intelligence* learned also that Lord Russell had promptly sent an instruction to the British Government's representative in Egypt to take some steps on behalf of the captives, a piece of information which Lord Russell did not impart to the general public; but the London Society had a very important and influential president.

In one of the last pages of the April issue in the section headed *Births*, there was the item: 'Abyssinia. At Genda. June 26th, 1863, the wife of Mr H. Rosenthal, a son.' Thus in June 1863, all still seemed bright and hopeful at the mission station.

Also deeply interested in events in far-off Ethiopia was Mrs Charlotte Stern, the English wife of the missionary, who did not for one minute forget her husband. Mrs Stern, who lived near the Seven Sisters Road in Holloway, north London, had learned with consternation of her husband's plight, cruel news for a wife to receive. After waiting in vain for further news, she wrote to Queen Victoria, petitioning her to intercede with Emperor Theodore. Mrs Stern's letter went to the Foreign Secretary, for transmission to the Queen, while Mrs Stern, with her children, waited anxiously for the outcome of her endeavour.

In the 1860s a number of missionary and other benevolent societies used to hold their Annual Meetings in May, and many of them did so at the now demolished Exeter Hall, in the Strand, in the centre of London, a great meeting place for religious bodies and reformists' organisations. The London Society followed this custom, but also had two other pleasant, well supported customs: one was to hold a church service on the evening before the Annual Meeting, and the other to have a breakfast on the day itself.

In that year, 1864, the service was held on Thursday evening, 5 May, at St Marylebone Church, the sermon being delivered by Rev. Fielding Ould, Rector of Tattenhall, Cheshire, who, however, made no reference to the misfortune in Ethiopia. The breakfast, attended by a number of clerical and other friends of the Society, was followed by a sermon given by the Rev. W. Cadman, Rector of Holy Trinity, Marylebone. Later that day the Annual Meeting was attended by 63 clergymen, but of the many Bishops who gave their support to the Society not one attended.

The stalwart joint-secretary of the Society, the Rev. Charles Goodhart, ecclesiastical incumbent of Park Chapel, Chelsea, a well-known Evangelical clergyman, began by reading a summary of the annual report, with an account of the Society's widespread activities in England, and at its 30 or so stations abroad. Then the chairman, the Society's President for the past 16 years, rose to address the meeting. The Society was fortunate to have such a distinguished President, for he was none other than the famous philanthropist and social reformer, the Right Honourable the Earl of Shaftesbury, now in his sixty-second year.

Lord Shaftesbury embarked on two tirades: he castigated first the 'iniquitous purpose' of a recently published book, *The Life of Christ*, already enjoying a wide circulation, by a French philosopher, Ernest Renan, and, secondly, the Bishops, a few of whom, at least, he felt, might have attended that Annual Meeting. Then, later in his address, Lord Shaftesbury told the meeting:

> Another event to which I must call your attention is that unhappy catastrophe which has befallen our friend Mr Stern. God grant that it may be better than we expect. God grant that it may be better than our fears . . . We are now full of distress and alarm, because he has fallen into the hands of that barbarian Philistine, and we know not what may have happened to him.

Lord Shaftesbury was not a man just to talk; he had already taken some action on behalf of Mr Stern, and, as he said:

> Every effort has been made that could be made in his favour, both by private individual and the Government. I can answer for it that they have been most anxious on the subject. They have communicated with all their officers. They have sent messages to the King of Abyssinia, and instructed their Consuls and diplomatic agents to do all in their power with a view to effecting the liberation of Mr Stern; and a few

> days ago I transmitted to Lord Russell – and I have no doubt he will be attending to – a letter from Mrs Stern, addressed to Her Majesty, praying – and I joined in the prayer to Lord Russell – that Her Majesty might be induced, by a letter under the sign manual, written by the Queen herself, to intercede with the King of Abyssinia to have mercy upon him. I trust that by the blessing of God, that may be effective.

These proceedings passed practically unnoticed by the newspapers, even though the great Lord Shaftesbury had presided. The conversion of the Jews to Christianity, although the first activity of its founders, had lost news value. Nevertheless, a number of people had now had their attention again drawn to the plight of two missionaries. The clergymen and others who attended the Exeter Hall meeting could not, as they dispersed to their parishes, be unaware of the tribulation of their two brethren in Ethiopia. Moreover, a month later the June issue of *Jewish Intelligence* carried the words of Lord Shaftesbury to a much greater number of people, in many walks of life, for the Friends of the Society comprised 990 Life Members, as well as 900 annual subscribers, and the report reached even more people, for each month 73,000 copies of this journal were printed.

Lord Shaftesbury had, however, been too optimistic about Mrs Stern establishing communication with Queen Victoria. A few days after receiving Mrs Stern's letter Lord Russell returned it to Lord Shaftesbury on the grounds that Her Majesty's Government were doing all that could be done, and that it therefore seemed unnecessary to trouble Her Majesty just then. But Mrs Stern was not one to be defeated and ere May was out this housewife of Holloway was, with the Earl of Shaftesbury's help, to tip the balance of immediate events.

And now, still early in May 1864, while Lord Russell wished to leave Queen Victoria's mind undisturbed, had some minds in Whitehall been disturbed? Perhaps not; yet it was now, and only now, that Theodore's letter, still awaiting a civil answer, together with Consul Cameron's despatches of October and November 1862, which had accompanied it, and which had all been sent from the Foreign Office to the India Office on 5 May 1863, emerged from the files of that Department. The official at the India Office to whom the documents had been sent, now sent them across to the Foreign Office, where they properly belonged, and where they arrived the same day, with this note:

India Office, May 11, 1864

Mr Merivale presents his compliments to Mr Hammond, and begs to return the enclosed papers relating to the affairs of Abyssinia, which were sent to this Office for perusal.

Theodore's letter, and Cameron's accompanying despatches, had been at the India Office for just over a year; and during that time no one there or at the Foreign Office seems to have noticed them. Perhaps the papers had been perused, at some time, but the India Office offered no comment on them.

Mr Merivale's note, on India Office notepaper, was, in the style of those days, handwritten in ink. There were later added to it in pencil several comments, all presumably written at the Foreign Office. Under Merivale's words 'sent to this Office for perusal', is the pencilled comment, 'i.e. 5th May, 1863'. In the margin, in pencil, is a cross-reference: 'Consul Cameron No. 18 Oct. 31/62 enclosing letter from King Theodore to the Queen.' And on the back of Merivale's note are the pencilled words: ' . . . Mr Murray says nothing to be done on this.'

Thus up to 11 May 1864, by which time the relevant documents were again with them, the Foreign Office, who were now also aware of the detention of the Consul and the missionaries and were concerned about their liberation, were nevertheless still abiding by their decision, taken a year earlier, to ignore Theodore's letter, written 18 months previously. But the Foreign Office were reckoning without the housewife in Holloway.

It was a Wednesday when the Foreign Office received Theodore's unanswered letter back from the India Office, and determined once again to do nothing about it. Then over the next few days various things happened. On Friday Mrs Stern received a letter from Aden. By then she already knew that her own letter had not reached Queen Victoria, and she saw in the letter from Aden a new opportunity to make an effort on behalf of her husband. On Saturday she wrote, in her clear, elegant handwriting, to Lord Shaftesbury as follows:

Yesterday I received a letter direct from Aden giving me a copy of the slip of paper written by Captain Cameron . . . with the addition of a few words omitted in my letter, but as they seem to me so very important, nay the very thing on which the release of the unfortunate prisoners depends, I take the liberty of sending them to your Lordship, they are as follows: 'No release until civil answer to King's letter arrives.'

On Sunday, Lord Shaftesbury, having received Mrs Stern's letter, sent it on to the Foreign Secretary. That day, or perhaps on Monday, Lord Russell, on receiving Mrs Stern's letter, wrote his comment on the back of it, and sent it to one of his senior officials at the Foreign Office for his attention. Russell wrote on the back of the letter, 'Is there any letter of the King of Abyssinia unanswered?'

On Monday, at the Foreign Office two memoranda were written to answer the Foreign Secretary's question. For over a year British diplomacy had treated Emperor Theodore's letter as good as buried. Charlotte Stern, wife of the missionary last heard of in chains in Gondar, had resurrected it. She gave the diplomats something to think about. They now had a new look at the Ethiopian monarch's long-neglected letter.

All this was to have its repercussions in Parliament a fortnight or so later. The detention of European missionaries and the British Consul was raised in the House of Commons on Friday, 3 June, by a question put by Henry Seymour, the Liberal Member for Poole. He asked for information on the ill-treatment of missionaries and on the imprisonment of Her Majesty's Consul, and what steps Her Majesty's Government had taken. It fell to the Under-Secretary for Foreign Affairs, since the Foreign Secretary, Lord Russell, sat in the House of Lords, to answer the question. The Under-Secretary was the Whig Member for Southwark, (just across the river from Westminster), Austen Henry Layard, the venturesome explorer of Asia Minor who had found the site of Nineveh. It fell to him to deal with the legacy of that other venturesome Englishman in far-off lands, who also had received encouragement from Lord Palmerston, that great and imaginative Foreign Secretary – Walter Plowden.

In his reply Mr Layard said the Government had received indirect information that the 'King of Abyssinia' had placed in confinement Her Majesty's Consul and several missionaries, and also the French Consul, but the French Consul had been released. This news, however, might be incorrect, as the King took care that no information should leave the country, and the facts were difficult to get at, but Her Majesty's Government would do all in their power to obtain the release of Captain Cameron and the missionaries. The most natural step would be to send some person there to demand their release, but Her Majesty's Government were rather afraid that he would share the same fate as the Consul and the missionaries. The question was how to reach the King without endangering the liberty of others. He trusted, however, that some means would soon be found of communicating with the King, and the subject was under serious consideration by the noble Lord, the Head of the Foreign Office. Henry Layard spoke truly when he said the matter was under the serious consideration of Lord Russell, but, on that Friday afternoon he apparently thought it appropriate to say no more, and not to give the additional information that the Foreign Secretary had in fact already instructed the Consul-General in Egypt to request the British Political Resident in Aden to make approaches to Theodore for the release of the prisoners, probably because no action had yet resulted from that request.

The following day, Layard's reply was reported in the Press, several papers giving the statement at some length. Mr Seymour had put his question in the House of Commons in good time, for about a month later Parliament adjourned for the Summer Recess and was not due to meet again until the following October.

The Saturday papers had given the public something to think about over the weekend. Monday brought a further item of news, this time about the British Consul. *The Times* published one of its periodic columns of news from India, culled from newspapers in that country, under the heading 'Bombay Mail', which quoted the *Bombay Gazette*, which stated that: 'intelligence has reached Aden of the imprisonment of Captain Cameron, the British Consul, and other British subjects at Gondar by the Abyssinian authorities. The reason for this has not transpired.'

Russell, now that he had decided to secure the release of Cameron and his companions, was not neglecting the task. He placed his hopes on action taken through the British Resident at Aden, and his own best means of communication continued to be by mail addressed to the British representative in Egypt. (There was still no Suez Canal, though talks for its construction were then going on.) So it was to the Consul-General that the Foreign Secretary, on 16 June, explained a new development and sent further instructions.

In this despatch the Foreign Secretary explained that the cause of the action Theodore had taken might have been the failure to answer his letter. Her Majesty had therefore now addressed a letter to him. Moreover, people who knew the country advised that a 'properly qualified person' should take this message to him. These knowledgeable people had also advised that such a mission would be aided if it also carried a letter from the Coptic Patriarch Qerelos in Alexandria to Theodore and one to the Abun of the Ethiopian Church. It was also advised that a correct translation 'into the language of Abyssinia, should if possible accompany the Queen's letter', and a copy had been sent to the Consul-General so that he could obtain such a translation in Egypt. All documents were then to be despatched to the Political Agent at Aden.

How many people in England were at that time knowledgeable about Ethiopia, apart from Dr Beke? Whosoever they might have been, they advised wisely in some matters, but they could not know everything about the ever-changing situation in Ethiopia, and they were wrong in assuming that at that time the Emperor would look with favour at the Patriarch or the Abun meddling in his policy. The Emperor might well regard the Patriarch in Alexandria as a puppet of his sworn enemies the Egyptians; and the Abun be regarded as an interfering prelate, and in this he was not the first Christian monarch so to regard the head of his Church.

His first instructions regarding a mission to Theodore having been despatched, the Foreign Secretary was now engaged in selecting the 'properly qualified person' to deliver Queen Victoria's letter. Who was that person to be? In England the choice struck not a few people as strange, considering the number of well-tried generals, brigadiers and colonels available. And there was always Dr Beke who called on Lord Russell at the Foreign Office and had written more than once to say that he was really the best qualified person for such a delicate mission. Nor were other volunteers lacking, for by now the subject of the captives had been widely reported.

The Foreign Secretary was of course employing his own department's Consular and Diplomatic Service and also the service of the India Office and the Bombay Government in the person of Brigadier Merewether; now he had a further request to make of the India Office. Lord Russell's choice of the 'person best qualified' had fallen upon Hormuzd Rassam, an assistant at Aden of Brigadier Merewether, and at Russell's request the India Office agreed to release him for this purpose. The Foreign Secretary also required the help of another department, the Navy.

On the same day that Russell sent his instructions to Aden together with the Queen's letter, one of his senior officials, James Murray, accordingly wrote to the Secretary of the Admiralty on what he described as a 'matter of great importance'. Explaining the intention of sending a properly qualified person to present the Queen's letter to the Emperor, Murray continued:

> Lord Russell has been advised, on the best authority, that unless this gentleman is conveyed in some state to Massowah, the main object of saving the lives and securing the liberty of the captives will be defeated; and as there are no means at the Queen's disposal of coercing a Ruler in the interior of Africa, Lord Russell does not doubt that the Lords of the Admiralty will concur with him in the expediency of adopting whatever other steps may conduce to the end in view. This, Lord Russell has been informed, may probably be secured by sending the bearer of the Queen's letter from Aden to Massowah in a ship of war, and his Lordship trusts that the exigencies of the service will permit of a ship being placed accordingly at the disposal of the Political Agent at Aden.

The Secretary of State for India duly gave his approval to the arrangements.

The Admiralty, although equally willing to assist in the enterprise, had their difficulties. The Secretary of the Admiralty replied promptly to the Foreign Office on 17 June: 'I am commanded by my Lords Commissioners of the Admiralty to request you will state to Earl Russell that there is no vessel of war at present in the Red Sea or in the neighbourhood of Aden . . . '

But the next day came a letter from the India Office to say that the steamer *Dalhousie* might be, or soon might be, at Aden. Within 24 hours it was agreed that the *Dalhousie* should be detained at Aden, if she should appear in that neighbourhood, but as there was still some doubt about her movements the Admiralty would send orders to the Senior Officer of Her Majesty's ships at Bombay as well as Trincomalee in Ceylon to send a ship of war to Aden should he be unable to use the *Dalhousie*. These arrangements being agreed, Lord Wodehouse, Under-Secretary at the India Office, wrote to Lord Russell on 22 June that necessary instructions would be sent to Aden by the mail leaving England in five days' time.

A month later the India Office was able to inform the Foreign Office that Brigadier Merewether had detained the *Dalhousie* at Aden and she was being prepared for her journey to Massawa. In his despatch dated 4 July Brigadier Merewether said that it would take a month for a vessel of war to reach Aden from Trincomalee, and added: 'The "Dalhousie" is a large steam transport but not a man-of-war; but she has two small cannonade of her own, and I am having four field pieces made suitable for ship-board use, which will be put on board and give her some appearance of armed equipment.'

In England meanwhile offers to help liberate the captives were by then reaching Russell from various parts of the country. Among the first to want to help was, of course, Dr Beke, writing from 11 Austin Friars, London. Also in London, from 5 West Road Terrace, Forest Hill, Major Edmund Plowden, formerly of Her Majesty's Indian Forces, offered his help, and stated that he was a first cousin of the former Consul Walter Plowden and a relative of the present Consul Cameron. To the many volunteers Lord Russell or his Parliamentary Under-Secretary, A. H. Layard, M.P., or one of their deputies, replied that the help was not required and other arrangements had been made. And in Aden the properly qualified person was preparing to embark on the *Dalhousie* with her brave show of cannon, to proceed to Massawa on his unexpected and difficult mission.

13

NOT SO MERRY MAY

(1864)

The Ethiopian Christian Church observes a large number of fast days. A few weeks before Easter the captives had another occasion for alarm. Emperor Theodore sent a messenger to the prisoners' compound to ask Mr Stern to prove from the Bible that fasting was not a Divine injunction, and not necessary for Salvation, and on this subject a number of messages passed between the prison enclosure and the royal pavilion. Eventually a message from Stern referred to the Book of Isaiah, Chapter 58, which reproves hypocritical fasting, whereupon Theodore took this as a reflection upon his own actions, and soon the ominous cry echoed across the camp, 'Bring Cocab', the latter being an Amharic translation of Stern's name, soon to be followed by the shout 'Tow' – stop. For a while the prisoners waited anxiously, but that day nothing further happened.

Soon the Ethiopian unloved Lent, as Stern called it, and then Easter, passed away, and the unwelcome season of May, the beginning of the Ethiopian winter, stole upon the captives. In some parts of the globe May brings with it the blooming of flowers and sunshine after cold and storms, but May – and June – in the Ethiopian highlands herald the end of sunny weather, and the beginning of the rainy season, when roads will soon become muddy, almost impassable, and many long-dry river beds racing torrents; army marches become difficult if not almost impossible and many soldiers are disbanded to return to their villages. May and June were to be far from merry for the captives.

The seasonal downpours began to keep the prisoners in their tents, but the captives continued to spend their time in more or less the pattern which they had evolved, though now a little more gloomily. The daytime routine usually began at dawn when they each had a small tin of black, bitter coffee and a piece of wheaten bread; Cameron, who did not enjoy too good health, rose later. At ten in the morning the Europeans held divine worship, including the reading of the Bible, with an exposition and an extemporary prayer. The prisoners had a woman cook, a Shangalla called Mystoura, who had been in service with Consul Plowden; she was of a gloomy disposition. At noon a *masob*, or high basket, which serves Ethiopians as a table, was brought into the tent, and on it five or six pieces of bread made of *teff* or *mashilla* grain, and soon after in came a saucepan containing boiled lentils. Mystoura scooped out the lentils from the pan with her hand and placed them on the basket; occasionally she provided sun-dried meat called *qwanta*, and at other times a small quantity of fresh meat stews; on rare occasions she provided a kind of macaroni. The prisoners ate squatting round the basket. Cameron and the Rosenthals fared better. They each had separate tents and dined in private more comfortably. After the midday meal the prisoners pottered about their daily chores, or passed the time in conversation with one another or their guards. Sometimes they spent a while in private prayer. Towards sunset they gathered for evening prayer. Then came the evening meal. It being soon dark they retired to bed. Thus the prisoners spent their monotonous days in chains, with little joy and little hope; thus they entered upon their first Ethiopian winter as prisoners in the land they all once loved.

There was a prospect of famine during the rains of 1864. This did not improve the mood of the royal camp, and there was simmering discontent among the soldiers which also did not improve the humour of the restless monarch. When this happened someone often had to pay dearly. One day, indeed, within sight of the European captives' enclosure, 40 convicted Ethiopians had their hands and feet amputated, and were left to die, while others perished under the whip. Witnessing these events, the European prisoners' gloom deepened; and then came a day to remember.

Early on 12 May Theodore interviewed the Abun in public outside the royal pavilion, in full view of the army and other people of the camp. Their talk soon became a noisy discussion in which they hurled insults at each other. The fierce exchange could be heard by the European captives, and at one stage Stern was alarmed to hear his name mentioned. All the while the army and people, watching the heated and unseemly dispute between the Head of the State and the Head of the Church, maintained a marked silence. After an hour the Emperor, tired of the quarrel, mounted his horse and dashed furiously across the nearby plain, followed by a horde of his courtiers and soldiers.

Always anxious when his wrath was roused, the captives were relieved at his sudden departure; they thought this storm had passed them by. They were mistaken. Not long afterwards they heard the tramp of feet, and suddenly into their compound rushed a number of soldiers and after them the Abun, clad in simple Egyptian garb, with a black silk scarf thrown over his face, followed by a procession of turbaned priests, chiefs and court officials. From the assembly came the cry, 'Cocab' and 'Ferengoch' – or Europeans. The chained Europeans, seeing such an array of dignitaries of church and state, confronted them deferentially, but quite mystified.

When the assembly were all in the compound, the Abun seated himself. There was a brief pause, then the royal notary stepped forward, opened a small parcel, took from among several papers a document, and read from it the charges that had already been brought against Stern and Rosenthal, made up from Stern's notes and book and Rosenthal's letter. There was deadly silence while the notary recited the accusations.

This done, Samuel took over the proceedings and asked Stern and Rosenthal, almost entreatingly, from whom they had obtained the information concerning Theodore. Rosenthal easily gave his answers and said that he had never had any communication with the Abun. Samuel was soon satisfied with Rosenthal's answers. The inquisitor then turned, less affably, to Stern and asked him the same question: who had supplied him with the information concerning the Emperor contained in his book and papers. All the captives meanwhile anxiously tried to guess what this raking up of charges was leading to; Stern, knowing the Emperor as well as he did, was quite sure that the ceremony was a serious matter. He turned to the Frenchman Bardel, who had fallen from the Emperor's favour and was now chained too, and asked if he would object if he, Stern, denied the correctness of the translations. The Frenchman replied: 'No, I only read the English; Birru and Samuel and the *debteras* are responsible for the Amharic.' Then the missionary faced Samuel, and, addressing him with severity, deprecated the malice of those who had sought his destruction by attributing to him words not found in his papers.

Having spoken directly thus to Samuel, Stern now addressed the whole assembly, according to his own account, as follows:

> What offence have I committed? That I said the King had pillaged certain provinces was no libel, for I saw it myself. That I stated a number of people had been executed at Dubark – the skulls attest the fact. That I was informed about his Majesty's descent, I must blame the late Mr Bell and the Negus's own speech . . . That I was not impelled by any ill-feeling towards the Negus, my book incontestably proved, for the very mistake about his origin was an honour in Europe, since beyond the waters, not a man's glorious ancestry, but his own deeds, shed lustre around his name. The bishop I honour as a friend, and were he even my enemy, neither diversity in our religious sentiments nor the dread of danger, nor the hope of favour should make me swerve from the truth.

Samuel, speaking gently but somewhat ironically, observed: 'We do not wish that you should utter a falsehood – but there are different ideas in Europe, America, Asia – and this, you know, is Africa!'

All this time the Abun had sat aside on the ground, but now he started up and poured forth abuse on the Emperor. But Samuel already knew his orders, and, not put off by the outburst, called out: 'Guards, seize your prisoners', and the Europeans were driven to their tents. The Abun then led the Ethiopian cortège away. The Europeans were now left alone with only their guards around them.

It was about sunset when Theodore and his followers at last came back at a gallop. He raced up to his pavilion, asked some questions, and then came across to the prisoners' compound, his voice ringing out: 'Dog! Falasha! Scoundrel! Tell me the name of the man who reviled my ancestors – or I'll tear the secret out of your *hailanya* [stout heart]!' To the guards around him, Stern began to reiterate what he had already told the assembly, but before he could say more than a few words, the guards began hitting him, with blinding blows, seized his hands and tied ropes round his arms. Rosenthal was treated in the same way. Mrs Rosenthal thought the end had come and in despair ran into Cameron's arms. Cameron also thought they were about to be killed and called out: 'Stern, we shall soon be in heaven!' The guards then drove Mrs Rosenthal out of the tent.

Then Cameron and all the other European prisoners were thrown to the ground and had ropes tied about them. It was the usual custom to tie the ropes round the victim's upper arm only, but in the case of the Europeans they were tied round their arms from the shoulder right down to the wrists; nor was this considered enough, for their arms were tied behind their backs, and ropes were wound round their chests. When the prisoners, except Mrs Rosenthal, had been tied, Theodore left them lying on the ground.

As the prisoners lay thus, some prayed, some groaned and sighed, and one banged his head on a stone. It was now night; the guards were silent awaiting the Emperor's orders, while from outside the compound came the howl of wild dogs careering around the camp in search of food. Overhead a bright, beautiful crescent moon shone through a white canopy of clouds.

Now every few minutes Samuel appeared within the compound with messages from Theodore. His recurring question was whether Stern would confess; and each time, not receiving a satisfactory answer, he whispered to the guards: 'Give him another rope round his chest.' Still the missionary gave no satisfactory answer, so the guards poured cold water down the prisoners' backs, and the ropes slowly tightened.

Samuel appeared yet once more, and said to Stern, 'Speak,' and Cameron, subjected to the torture like the others, called out: 'Stern, Stern, say what you know!' The torturings had now lasted about three-quarters of an hour, and Stern prayed that he might die. But now Theodore ordered the ropes to be removed. This caused bitter pain, for the taut cords snapped, tearing with them the flesh in which they had been embedded. Stern, at his fellow sufferers' request, poured forth a prayer, but it was one of despair. However, the guards now became gentle and rendered the prisoners what aid they could, helping them to their couches to settle down to sleep. And so 12 May came to an end; a day to remember.

In fitful sleep the prisoners found some relief, but in the morning woke to await nervously for some new harrowing message from Theodore. But to their great relief the Emperor rode out early, and the rest of the morning was passed silently and in grim apathy. It was almost noon when they had their next alarm. The chief of the guards came to the prisoners' tents and urged them to satisfy the Emperor's demands. Stern's answer was: 'Tell those who sent you that I have spoken the truth; and if the King does not believe me, I can swear on this book', and Stern raised aloft the Bible, 'that the bishop never spoke to me about his descent.' The chief retorted: 'Well, you will get the ropes again, and that, too, much severer than last night.' With this prospect the prisoners were left in suspense. By evening Samuel made his disturbing appearance, but went over to Cameron and tended his wounds.

Stern made bold to ask why the Emperor, having pardoned him, again revived the affair. Samuel turned and abused the missionary, declaring: 'Villain! How dare you criticise the King's actions and defy his authority? Look here and behold the suffering you have inflicted on your brethren.' He then went over to him and bending down whispered, 'Come out, I want to speak to you.' Stern got up and went out of the tent, where Samuel said to him: 'Don't think I am angry with you . . . but what possesses you for the sake of the bishop, who is neither your countryman nor of your belief, to incur the wrath of the King, and expose your person to suffering? He is my Abun but you are my friend; and I don't care what happens to him if you only (whose money I have eaten) by obliging the Negus, win honour and favours.' Stern shook his head, and Samuel walked away, cursing him.

It was dark as Stern re-entered his tent. The guards took up their positions for the night. The prisoners said their prayers and prepared for sleep. They had hardly settled down before several voices outside roared: 'Cocab! Rosenthal! Makerer!' They dragged themselves out of their tents to see what was happening. In an instant guards seized Stern and stunned him with heavy blows, and at the same time bound ropes around him. Rosenthal and Makerer were likewise beaten and bound. The Emperor's voice was heard clearly: 'Tie his legs too, if he does not confess.' Samuel came and stood over the prisoners and three other people were stationed to pass the royal commands. Stern felt his eyes almost start from their sockets, and his veins swell and throb; he raised his eyes to heaven and prayed that he might die. In a few minutes he became dizzy, his eyes dimmed, his mind confused, and he shrieked: 'Samuel, Samuel! What do you want?' Calmly Samuel replied: 'Tell Janhoi all you have been told by the Abun.' In his mind Stern was saying: 'Oh my God, my God, have I still longer to endure this martyrdom?' Then he cried out, in a hoarse suffocating voice: 'Yes, the Abun often told me that the King was more dreaded and possessed more power than any of the former sovereigns of Ethiopia, but that his ambition and cruelty had depopulated the country.'

The Emperor's loud command came clearly across the cool night air: 'Untie the ropes, untie his ropes and ask him if he is not a merchant of insects.' The ropes were loosened. Stern was a collector of insects, but he hesitated to say he was a merchant of insects, but this was not a time for logical niceties. Samuel muttered: 'Do you want a fresh trial of the ropes?' Voices coming from the royal tent now called out: 'Ask him whether ladies in England do not eat rabbits and mice?' As Stern made no answer, the chief jailer hit him. Samuel, who seemed to pity him, called out a reply for him: 'Yes.'

Again the King's voice was heard: 'Ask him whether the Queen of England does not sell thread, needles and tobacco at Massawa?' After this question there came a chuckle from some of Theodore's ladies. Then came another question: 'Ask him whether it is loyal for the Abun to commit . . . ?' (In his published record the missionary did not disclose the offence, whatever it was.) Stern, now frantic in his continuing pain, roared: 'No, no!' The ropes were entirely removed. One of the other tied prisoners, Makerer, was then questioned about things he had said, or was supposed to have said, in Massawa about Theodore. His answers seemed satisfactory, and he too was untied. Rosenthal was never questioned: the guards in their enthusiasm had tied him up by mistake, without ever having had any orders to do so. So he too was untied. Theodore was apparently satisfied with the 'confessions', or maybe satisfied with having extracted answers, for he ordered the prisoners an ample supper of bread, arak and hydromel (a drink made from honey and water).

About half an hour later Samuel stumbled into Stern's tent, somewhat drunk, followed by a young slave boy, bearing a horn full of arak. The interior of the tent then presented a strange scene. Standing or seated were the Ethiopian guards; lying huddled on the floor, the captives, forlorn, and sorrowing; in the centre several Ethiopians squatted around a flickering taper, watching the lad pour out arak from a gigantic horn. The prisoners now and then painfully raised their arms to receive the drink. Stern was unable to move, so Samuel raised a cup to his lips. Eventually when all the arak had been drunk, the prisoners fell wearily to sleep.

The next morning, it was hardly dawn before Samuel appeared at the door of the tent, and addressed Stern: 'Cocab, his Majesty does not intend to kill you – he knows you are not afraid to die, on the contrary he will preserve your life and torture you till your flesh rots on your bones. Now satisfy the Negus – or ropes will extort what you deny as a favour.' Stern could see the ropes lying in the tent, and they added force to Samuel's words. At the thought of renewed torture, he replied: 'Samuel, I told you last night my conversation with the bishop, and if that does not satisfy you, God's will be done. I will not tell a lie.' Persisting in his interrogation Samuel said: 'If the statement of the King's lineage did not emanate from the bishop, it emanated from someone of his priests or domestics – and the King has proofs that would never let him believe otherwise.'

Stern now remembered that one of the Abun's men, who was then safe from the King's power, had often told him, in the presence of others, about various episodes of Theodore's life, and some people might have related this to the monarch, so he replied: 'Yes, Gebra Egziabeher often spoke to me about the exploits of the King, and at my request also gave me details about his birth and education, but never did he utter a word derogatory to his Majesty.' Samuel said he would report this to the Negus and left.

Not only the missionary, who was the main object of Theodore's venom, but all the European prisoners wondered what would be the outcome of the interrogation. Their customary morning prayer gave them some comfort, but it was with dread that they faced the new day. They wondered if anyone in Britain had heard of their plight. Was anyone there doing anything to succour them? Help seemed far away; torture close to hand. More than once during the day, together or alone, they prayed; but they scarcely dared to hope.

Part III

HORMUZD RASSAM

14

THE QUEEN'S LETTER

(1864)

In the late spring and early summer of 1864 the Foreign Office had been busy drafting a letter from Queen Victoria to Emperor Theodore. It was decided that it should be despatched to Aden and thence taken to Ethiopia. This epistle, which was written as from Balmoral on 26 May, declared:

> Victoria, by the grace of God, Queen of the United Kingdom and Ireland, Defender of the Faith . . . to Theodore, King of Abyssinia . . .
>
> We have duly received the letter which your Majesty delivered to our servant Cameron, and we have read with pleasure the friendly expressions which it conveys. We learn with satisfaction that your Majesty has successfully established your authority in the country over which you rule, and We trust that you may long continue to administer its affairs in peace and prosperity. We do not require from your Majesty the further evidence of your regard for ourselves which you propose to afford by sending a special Embassy to our Court. The distance which separates Abyssinia from England is great; the difficulties and delays which would attend the journey of your Ambassadors might be hard to overcome; and much unavailing disappointment and regret might result from any accident which might befall your Ambassadors on the road. Our servant Cameron will convey to us your wishes, and he will assure you of our friendship and good-will . . .
>
> Accounts have, indeed, reached us of late that your Majesty had withdrawn your favour from our servant, and had subjected him and many others in whom we feel an interest to treatment which is inconsistent with your professions. We trust that these accounts have originated in false representations on the part of persons ill-disposed to you. But your Majesty can give no better proof of the sincerity of the sentiments which you profess towards us, nor ensure more effectually a continuance of our friendship and good-will, than by dismissing our servant, and any other Europeans who may desire it, from your Court, and by affording them every assistance and protection on their journey to the destination to which they desire to proceed. Our servant Cameron will

then be able personally to explain to us your wishes in regard to any matters which you may desire to represent to us.

The letter was signed: 'Your good friend, Victoria R,' and bore the counter-signature: 'Russell'. It was duly sent to Egypt, on 16 June, for transmission to Aden.

By mid-June Lord Russell, Mr Layard and the officials at the Foreign Office could therefore feel satisfied that the Queen's letter to the troublesome Ethiopian Emperor had been finally despatched. Whatever its consequences it was now off their hands; so they thought.

When the letter and accompanying instructions reached Alexandria, the British Consul-General, Mr Colquhoun, had only a little earlier gone on leave, and acting in his stead was Mr Reade, recently appointed Consul in Cairo, but now temporarily transferred to Alexandria. So it fell to Reade to inform Lord Russell, on 30 June, that there was no one in Alexandria who could translate the Queen's letter into 'the Abyssinian language', and that it was therefore being sent to Cairo for translation. Soon, however, he had to send a further despatch to say that no translator could be found in Cairo either, and consequently the letter was being translated into Arabic, which 'will be well understood at the Court of Abyssinia'. Since the translation was to be in Arabic, it could well have been done in London where scholars in the language were not lacking. As it turned out, even in Cairo, where the language of the country was Arabic, it was an Englishman, assisted by two Egyptians, who translated the Queen's letter – the acting British Consul Frederick Ayrton, who had lived in Egypt for several years, and had made a special study of Ethiopian affairs.

The translation presented no difficulty, but to the surprise of the British Consular officials they did find difficulty in obtaining the two letters they wanted from the Coptic Patriarch in Egypt. In a despatch to Lord Russell, Acting Consul-General Reade stated that Mr Ayrton was encountering 'a very strange and inexplicable reluctance on the part of the Copts to accede to our request for their friendly offices. Till now, all applications made to them, in conformity with your Lordship's instructions, have been met with futile and unfriendly excuses, which, though not expressed in plain terms, can only imply a negative signification. I hope, however, that the scruples of the Patriarch may be overcome through the good offices of the Viceroy, to whom I shall at once make representation on the subject.' The diplomatic manoeuvre succeeded, and, under the pressure of Khedive Ismail, Patriarch Qerelos reluctantly let the British have the letters. Despite their considerable knowledge, the British Consular officials seemed unaware of the old feud between Theodore and a former Coptic Patriarch, or of the more recent quarrel in Jerusalem between the Ethiopians and the Egyptian Copts.

The British Consuls in Egypt, even if not sufficiently acquainted with the animosity among Christians, were fairly knowledgeable about the more definitely political affairs of Ethiopia. They were certainly nearer to Ethiopia and its way of thinking than were the politicians and officials in Downing Street. Reade in Alexandria and Ayrton in Cairo gave thought to the Queen's letter and consulted with one another, and were in agreement that the letter, drafted with so much care by their masters at the Foreign Office, was quite the wrong epistle to address to a ruler of Ethiopia. In a cypher telegram to Lord Russell, dated Alexandria, 2 July, the Acting Consul-General discreetly pointed this out, stating:

> If not too presumptuous in me . . . I would suggest alteration of the Royal Letter. Well informed persons here think discouragement of Embassy would give offence to Theodore and would be otherwise objectionable . . . I await your reply which if telegraphed immediately may reach me before the departure of the China mail.

Russell, if given to acting impetuously (and too often without consulting his colleagues) was also quick to grasp any essential point in a despatch, and now he himself drafted a reply to Reade which went off by telegram on 6 July, and later his despatch in confirmation strangely stated: 'The Queen's Letter must be delivered, but the bearer may explain that Her Majesty will be happy to receive King Theodore's Mission if the King himself has no objection on account of difficulties.'

Almost in an instant Russell had altered British policy towards Ethiopia. From the time of the arrival at the Foreign Office of Theodore's letter to Queen Victoria in February 1863, until 5 July 1864, it had been British policy not to receive an Embassy from Ethiopia, partly because such a mission did not seem very useful, but more particularly to avoid offending Egypt. Now, on the instant, Russell reversed that policy, or at least gave the appearance of reversing it. Theodore had made Ethiopia appear more important to Russell in July 1864 than it had appeared in February 1863.

Reade promptly telegraphed his acknowledgement of Russell's telegram, and passed on to Aden the instruction that an Ethiopian Embassy would be welcomed.

But now it was the turn of the knowledgeable Mr Ayrton, Acting British Consul in Cairo, to have a hand in shaping British policy. When Lord Russell received Ayrton's complete memorandum, which arrived a week or so after the telegram, he found it interesting and persuasive. The document ran to 13 pages of foolscap, in neat, clear handwriting. In it Ayrton sent a draft for a suggested new letter from the Queen to the Ethiopian Emperor. Russell's comment was brief and as usual to the point. At the foot of Ayrton's draft letter he wrote: 'I agree with Mr Ayrton, but his proposed letter must be re-modelled. July 14. R.' Officials at the Foreign Office promptly went into action to draft a new royal letter.

Russell had shifted his ground still further. The civil answer was to be yet more civil, and Theodore's suggestion to send an Embassy to England was to be formally accepted in the letter from the Queen. The idea of receiving an Embassy, which went back to Plowden's days, was thus now accepted, belatedly.

A rapid exchange of telegrams between Downing Street and Alexandria now ensued. On 19 July James Murray telegraphed Reade asking whether the first version had already been sent to Aden or whether there was time to send an amended letter. At 6.30 p.m. on the following evening Reade's reply arrived. The Queen's letter had already been forwarded by the Bombay mail boat which had left Suez on 12 July, and Reade ended his message: 'afraid too late communicate with Aden before Rassam's departure thence. I shall write, however, to Political Resident at once to detain letter until further orders, if he has power to do so.'

In his eagerness to detain the Queen's letter, which he and his colleague so much feared might have unfortunate consequences, Reade had exceeded his instructions, something always displeasing to the Foreign Office and to Russell in particular. Without delay Murray, staying on late at his office, sent the following telegram (which was, as usual, in the Foreign Secretary's name): 'You must not desire Resident at Aden to detain Queen's letter. Let it go.' This telegram left the Foreign Office at 1 a.m. on 21 July. A day later, Reade telegraphed: 'Have received your Lordship's telegram of yesterday and have intercepted at Suez the letter I had written to Aden.' All's well that ends well, but the Foreign Office could not overlook that Reade had acted beyond his instructions, and at the foot of the decyphered copy of Reade's offending telegram, Murray made a note: 'Caution Mr Reade against excess of zeal.' Not a reprimand, but at least a rebuke seemed necessary, and not to offend the zealous Acting-Consul, it was sent in a personal letter from Murray, discreetly marked 'private', which ended 'allow me to remind you that you were not instructed by my telegram to go so far, and it might have produced inconvenience if the Political Resident had detained the Queen's Letter. I would therefore give you a private hint to avoid excess of zeal.'

On 29 July Parliament rose for the summer recess in a calmer atmosphere than had prevailed earlier in the year. The Danish question had resolved itself, with Bismarck having it all his own way, but Palmerston's Government had survived the severe attacks over its handling of the dispute; and now Government ministers could enjoy the easing of political pressure, and could, without misgivings, go on their holidays. Queen Victoria too was at last relieved of the double fear that had caused her anxiety and unhappiness for the past six months: that Lords Palmerston and Russell would lead her country into war, and that it would be a war against her beloved Germany and her royal relatives there.

Meanwhile, in Aden duty was taking its steady course. On 21 July Lt-Col. Merewether, the Resident there, addressed a despatch to his Government in Bombay, with copy to London, which stated: 'Translation of Queen's Letter with letters of Patriarch to King Theodore and the Abun came by Jedda last night from H. M. Consul in Egypt. Mr Rassam will leave this evening in the *Dalhousie* for Massowah.' The Queen's letter, however inappropriate, was on its intended way.

15

THE MAN FROM NINEVEH
(1864)

After the startling news reached Aden in April 1864 that Emperor Theodore had imprisoned the British Consul, Protestant missionaries and other Europeans, there was much gossip and discussion on what means the British Government would adopt to liberate them. But when Lt-Col. Merewether, the Political Resident in Aden, told his First Assistant, Hormuzd Rassam, that he had received a telegram from the Secretary of State for India stating that he, Rassam, had been chosen by the British Government to convey Queen Victoria's letter to the Emperor, Rassam was very surprised, and felt highly honoured.

Wisely, Rassam sought and obtained permission for Dr Henri Blanc, a Frenchman, formerly a surgeon in the Indian Army and then employed in Government service in Aden, to accompany him. The little mission was soon ready to depart but was delayed for a while, awaiting the Amharic translation, as they thought, of the Queen's message which was to bring about the release of the captives. Some three weeks after being told of his appointment the impatiently expected translation arrived, and it turned out to be in Arabic. On 20 July Rassam and his little party boarded the waiting steamer *Dalhousie*, commanded by Lieutenant Morland, of the former East India Company's Navy, to sail for Massawa, which it reached three days later.

When the Kayim-Makam, or Lieutenant-Governor of the port, learned that the English mission intended to proceed into Ethiopia he protested that, as a friend of the English and an admirer of the British Government, he deemed it his duty to prevent the mission doing any such thing. He thought Theodore was mad; he had ill-treated foreign representatives for years past and after an initial show of good treatment this mission would fare no better than the others. He told Rassam that if the British Government 'intend to adopt coercive measures for your liberation in the event of your incarceration, they had better begin to make preparations at once'. Rassam, however, replied that he would have to proceed into the interior as ordered, and that neither he nor Dr Blanc had any anxiety about the result.

The Turkish Governor of the port, Purtoo Effendi, thereupon said that 'as an official of the Sublime Porte, the ally of the British Government', he would be happy to render 'every assistance' in his power. And so he did, all the time he was in charge at Massawa, both to the members of the mission and in facilitating provisioning of the British ship. Different indeed was this helpfulness compared with the hostile attitude of the Turks at Massawa in the days of Consul Plowden.

The mission made the *Dalhousie* their home and headquarters. The urgent matter was to obtain messengers to go up into the interior to inform Theodore that a mission had arrived at Massawa with a message from the Queen of Great Britain. The Lieutenant-Governor promised to assist in this, but, Rassam states:

> He sent word the day after, that, although he had offered handsome rewards for the service, he could find none willing to undertake it. I had also commissioned two other influential persons to aid me in this matter; but it was not till the evening of the 24th that two Mohammedan Abyssinians engaged to convey a letter to the dreaded monarch. They, however, insisted on my assurance beforehand that the epistle contained nothing which would in any way compromise them. They undertook to go up to Góndar, and return with an answer in the course of a month, if the rise in the Tākkāzê river did not impede their progress.

Rassam was not doing badly in obtaining his two messengers only two days after his arrival. Had he known how long it would take before he received an answer, a day more or less in getting his messengers might have troubled him less; but he always had in mind that not only the freedom but perhaps the lives of the captives depended on what he did and how quickly. Not to compromise his relationship with the Emperor, he did not then send any message to Consul Cameron or any of the other European captives; he also instructed the messengers not to take any written word from the prisoners, unless given to them by the Emperor; but they were to find out all they could about their condition. Rassam was much influenced by Cameron's original pencilled note: 'No release until civil answer to King's letter arrives.' He was now preparing to deliver that vital 'civil answer' and was determined that everything he did in relation to the Emperor should also be civil, so as not to endanger the object of the Queen's letter and his mission – the release of the captives.

It was with such considerations in mind that he wrote his first letter to the Emperor, on 24 July, and he did so in Arabic because, as he has said, 'I had heard that he understood that language; besides it was known that he had several Egyptian writers at his Court.' The letter read:

> I have the honour to inform your Majesty that I arrived at this port yesterday, bearing a letter to your address from Her Majesty our British Queen (may God protect her!), and, as I am desirous to deliver the letter into your hands, I shall await your answer here.
>
> Should your Majesty acquiesce in my coming to your parts for the purpose of consigning the letter to you, personally, my desire would be fulfilled, as I am most anxious for the honour of seeing you, and of enjoying the gratification of being at your happy Court . . .
>
> But should you not deem it advisable for me to come to you at present, owing to the rains and the consequent difficulty of travelling, I hope that you will oblige me by releasing Cameron and his imprisoned companions . . .
>
> Will you be pleased, further, to send a trustworthy person, with the Consul, to whom I may deliver the Queen's letter . . .
>
> I am directed to acquaint you that in the event of your wishing to send an embassy to England, as you intimated in your letter addressed to our Queen, Her Majesty will be glad to receive it. If you are able to send the Mission down before my return to Aden, I will take care that it is forwarded to England in safety.
>
> I enclose herewith three letters – one addressed to your Majesty from the Patriarch of the Copts in Egypt, and two to the address of Abun Salama, the Metropolitan of Abyssinia; one of these is from the aforesaid and the other from myself. If you send the replies to me, I will transmit them to their destination.

And so the two Ethiopian messengers went off with Rassam's civil letter on which so much depended. Rassam had made one serious mistake, but this he only subsequently discovered. He should not have made any mention of the Patriarch or the Abun. Much later he was to learn that Theodore said of him when he received the letter: 'So he has already made friends with my enemies, the priests.' Fortunately, Rassam had taken the precaution of sending the letters to the Emperor and not direct to the Abun.

On his arrival at Massawa several important merchants, and other worthies whom Rassam consulted on local affairs, told him that the Emperor did not permit foreign officials to enter his territory without his permission, also that no messenger could be found to take messages to the prisoners. With this inability to make contact with the captives the great mystery still remained, for most people outside Ethiopia and some within, as to why the Europeans had been imprisoned. While waiting for the return of his two messengers Rassam tried to probe the mystery, as well as to find out as much as he could of the country through which he might soon have to travel. To this end he sent a messenger up to an Ethiopian living at Adowa, Ato Mircha Warkee, who had been recommended to him: Ato Mircha had been educated at an English mission school in Bombay. On his return the messenger said that the arrival at his house of someone from 'the English' had frightened Ato Mircha out of his wits and he forbade a second attempt on the plea that he would surely suffer if it were discovered that he was in correspondence with Europeans.

About this time Rassam, finding the heat in Massawa unbearable, sent word to Monsignor Biancheri, Italian Bishop of Eastern Abyssinia, who was spending the summer months up on the hills where a Roman Catholic mission had been established, to ask if he and his friends might pass some days there. But, Rassam records, 'it appears that my letter so terrified the venerable prelate, that he forthwith despatched his deputy Padre Delmonte, to dissuade me from penetrating into Abyssinia, intimating that, as the English were at present under the King's displeasure, some of his soldiers might seize and detain us until they consulted his Majesty about our disposal.' Some days later the Indian merchants in Massawa came to call on Rassam, and later the local merchants. All spoke strongly against Theodore, and advised Rassam not to place himself in his clutches.

The little British mission was certainly learning while waiting. Besides discovering how the once great pioneer of reform was now widely feared and hated, the mission received reports, often contradictory, of continuing rebellion against Theodore, and one of the most powerful rebels was a prince of Tigré, the country through which the mission would have to travel to reach Gondar. Rassam and his companion Dr Blanc nevertheless remained confident that the two messengers who had gone up to the Emperor would return safely and bring his invitation for them to come up to his court; they cherished the conviction that Queen Victoria's 'civil answer' would bring about the liberation of the captives and ensure happy and friendly relations between their two countries.

The callers on Rassam were many. They included notables of the town and nearby mainland and merchants from the interior. Very few took an optimistic view. One who was less pessimistic was an Armenian merchant named Khoja Beros who said he would not advise the mission to go up into Ethiopia for pleasure, 'but as your sole object is to obtain the release of your Consul and others whose lives are in danger . . . do not hesitate to proceed after receiving a safe-conduct from the King. Trust in God and he will deliver you.' Another person even spoke almost optimistically. The latter, Rassam recalls:

> was the first to give me authentic information about the captives, who, he said, were still in chains. His impression was that the King would release them, on hearing that I had brought a letter for him from Her Majesty. He was not so severe upon the King as others; on the contrary, he was of opinion that his Majesty had not been treated with due respect and consideration by the Europeans generally.

On 15 August there was entertainment which was a change from the ordinary daily life at Massawa. Early in the day the Turkish fort fired a royal salute; later there was a high mass at the Roman Catholic Church; the good ship *Dalhousie* was dressed with every available flag, and in the evening Lieutenant Morland gave a sumptuous dinner at which claret and champagne flowed, so that 'his guests must have forgotten that they were at such an outlandish place as Massowah'. All this was to honour the birthday of the Emperor of the French, Napoleon III. Meanwhile, reports trickled in of the progress of the two messengers who had now been gone from Massawa 15 days: they were said to be still in Tigré. This was a little disheartening.

With guides and sometimes an armed escort provided by the obliging Lieutenant-Governor, Rassam and Dr Blanc and their servants explored the adjoining mainland and its hills, to find somewhere cooler than the *Dalhousie*, but they met with no real success. For a while the mission stayed at the British Consulate. What would the Prime Minister have thought of it, the aristocrat Lord Palmerston at his grand house in Piccadilly, he who when Foreign Secretary had authorised the opening of a British Consulate at Massawa? Not fit for a stable, recorded Rassam, and the heat almost unbearable in the summer; mercifully the upper rooms

– it was one of the very few houses with an upper storey – were kept clean by the Armenian in charge.

The British mission was eager to find out as much as possible, and gain as many friends as they could. To this end they sailed to the island of Dissee, and later to the ruins of the ancient port of Adulis. Hormuzd Rassam looked on these ruins with an experienced eye, for though he made no claim to being an authority on ancient Greek and Egyptian edifices, he enjoyed well-deserved prestige as an archaeologist.

A quarter of a century earlier when Austen Henry Layard had worked on the excavation of the ancient city of Nineveh, he had been assisted by a young man he had recruited from Mosul: Hormuzd Rassam. So impressed was Layard with Rassam's intelligence that he had later enabled him to go to Oxford to study.

Now, with Layard as Parliamentary Under-Secretary of State at the Foreign Office, their old association in the ancient capital of the Assyrians caused Rassam to be chosen to head the British mission to seek the liberation of the captives. A man of Nineveh was thus bearer of a royal message to the Ethiopian King of Kings.

16

ONLY CHAINS FOR YOUR PAINS

(1864–5)

By mid-October 1864 Rassam's anxieties began to increase. There was still no news of his messengers who had set off over two months before. Should he wait no longer, and go up himself, to hand Theodore the Queen's letter which was to secure the release of the captives? Rassam consulted the few Europeans and two or three of the people of the country whom he trusted. All agreed that the Emperor's governor of Tigré had strict orders not to let any foreigners pass through the country without permission; and there would be the greatest difficulty in getting through parts of the country held by rebels.

Rassam therefore decided to send a second letter to the Emperor. Written once more in Arabic, on 17 October, it declared:

> Be it known to your Majesty that it is now nearly three months since I arrived here, bearing a letter to your address from her august Majesty, our British Queen; and the day after my arrival I dispatched a letter to you by two messengers . . . but up to this time I have received no answer thereto. I hope that the cause is propitious.
>
> Different reports reach me daily regarding this delay, and a rumour has been current that the messengers did not succeed in reaching you, owing to some people on the road having intimidated them against approaching you. It is also suggested that perhaps the letter was handed to some individual who failed to deliver it to you. For this reason, I now write to you again, and enclose herewith a copy of my former communication, which may not have reached you . . .
>
> I beg you to honour me with an answer soon, and to let me know what are your intentions regarding the duty on which I have been sent by our English Government.

The Naib of Arkiko found two trustworthy messengers, who set off with this second letter.

At the end of October, the weather became cooler, but for Rassam and Blanc the frustrating wait continued. They passed the time as best they could, gathering as much information as possible, a task not helped by continuing rumours and reports, many false, which they had to sift from the possibly true. One report proving true was that the Mohammedans of Barka had again raided the Christians of Bogos, carrying off 120 children as slaves. Rassam noted:

> These raids are of frequent occurrence, the Mohammedans and Christians assuming the offensive by turns; the latter, I am sorry to learn, being as ready to engage in them as the former. Foreign interference, instead of quenching the old enmity between these rival tribes, has only embittered it, and their annual conflicts are reported to be more bloody and merciless.

So much for Plowden's and Cameron's noble endeavours.

The north-west monsoon set in, and with those winds no local boat would venture south beyond the Bab-el-Mandeb, so the *Dalhousie* had to sail to Aden for provisions, and Dr Blanc, who had been suffering from the climate, sailed away for a change of air. Some ten days later the ship was back, not only with the good doctor but also with his charming wife, who intended to stay with him until he started on the expected journey. The mission now took up residence at Monculo, Dr Blanc and his wife in Plowden's old grounds and Rassam on the hill opposite in the house of the Swiss Mr. Munzinger, French Vice-Consul at Massawa.

On the night of 14–15 December, heavy rain fell, the first since the mission's arrival in Massawa at the end of July. And three days after the first rains Rassam and Blanc heard the name which was to be imprinted on their minds for the rest of their lives: Magdala. This was the *amba* in the Wollo country which Theodore had captured after returning from Shoa in 1855.

Rassam had been at pains not to attempt to send messages to Consul Cameron by the bearers of his two letters to the Emperor, lest he should prejudice himself or them in the Emperor's eyes. But he had subsequently sent two separate messengers to Gondar some six weeks since to communicate with the prisoners, to take them some provisions and to find out what had happened to his first messengers. One of these last messengers returned to Massawa three days after the rains. He had reached Gondar in 13 days, only to find that the Emperor had departed for Debra Tabor, taking the prisoners with him; the messenger went to Debra Tabor, but from there the Emperor had gone to Zabeet. The messenger went on to that place, where he learnt that Theodore had gone down to Shoa to subdue a rebellion, leaving Cameron and other prisoners at Magdala. Being told that he would have no chance of communicating with the prisoners at Magdala, where too close a watch was kept, the messenger returned to Debra Tabor and stayed two days with the missionary Flad at Gafat, a hill some two miles away. After leaving Gafat the messenger was arrested by a local governor and imprisoned for about 14 days, but on the approach of rebels was set free, and being now penniless begged the rest of his way back to Massawa. Rassam was always cautious of spoken messages, but he placed some reliance in this man, and thus learnt something about the captives, and he sent the news, such as it was, in a report to London where it arrived some two months later.

The end of December was approaching and the mission prepared as best they could to celebrate Christmas and see the New Year in. On Christmas morning Rassam picked up a little more information. A respected merchant of Derita, south of Gondar, called and said he was at the court when the first messengers arrived and they had been well treated; he had seen the prisoners several times, they were chained, but otherwise well. He said Theodore was of variable temperament; he might never reply to Rassam's letter, or might suddenly release the prisoners. From this discourse Rassam tried to find some comfort.

Mrs Blanc did her best for Christmas, and invited round the few Europeans, but even the appreciative Rassam recorded 'a dreary Christmas'. He was always thinking how to take a fresh step to liberate the captives; he was at least acquiring more information, which should help. He now knew that there were two men among the Europeans at Gafat, Mr Flad and Mr Schimper, who had befriended the captives, and he wrote, always hoping his letters would reach their destination, asking what was the cause of Theodore's displeasure, what might be his reason for not answering him, and what did they think the best way to release the captives. Off went the letter, and again the thought of a long wait before any advice would come back. The mission spent 1 January 1865 at Monculo, and Rassam recorded: 'The dullest New-Year day in my life, despite the social gathering at Mr Blanc's hospitable house.'

If there were few at Massawa to speak favourably of Theodore, he had one sturdy champion whom Rassam met during one of his excursions. On a trip to a hot spring at Ailat, Lieutenant Carpendale took with him an Ethiopian sportsman who brought along his son Desta. The youth, who was about 14, impressed Rassam by his intelligence. He entertained Rassam with stories of the mighty Theodore. When asked if he did not think Theodore's power was declining the lad made answer:

> Master, don't believe either our common enemies, the Mussulmans, or the depraved Abyssinians who would make you think so. Despite his dementation, he is a great sovereign . . . As to his soldiers deserting him, and that the rebels are getting the upper hand, he has only to move against them and they will be scattered to the winds like this breath

– giving a hearty puff as he ended his comment. He joined Rassam's service and with his knowledge of Arabic, Amharic, Tigré and his mother tongue, Tigrinya, for he was a native of Adowa, the boy soon rose to a higher rank than that of muleteer.

The first few months of 1865 Rassam spent debating with himself and his colleagues what to do next. He also kept in touch with Colonel Merewether at Aden, his channel of communication with the Foreign Office. Early in January HMS *Pantaloon* called at Massawa from Aden for news: the *Victoria* (which had by then replaced the *Dalhousie*) took the opportunity to go to Aden for supplies and Rassam went aboard to consult Merewether, among other things on what presents to take to Theodore when the monarch at last sent the awaited permission to go up to him.

A week after the *Pantaloon* had sailed for Aden, two messengers returned to Massawa, bringing letters from Flad and Schimper. The Europeans repeated what Cameron had long before written in his pencilled note, that the captives would not be released until the arrival of a civil answer from the Queen. 'This stale announcement,' lamented Rassam, 'did not better my position in the least.' There were poor Cameron and the others held prisoner in remote Magdala, in the heart of Ethiopia, while he, Rassam, down on the coast, held the letter which would liberate them. Rassam was pinned down in Massawa, merely, it would seem, because of the neglect, obstinacy or whim of Theodore. Schimper did indeed say that Rassam should go up to the Emperor, even without permission, because 12 years earlier Theodore had proclaimed that anybody was free to enter Ethiopia without authorisation, but that seemed a long way back to count on the word of a monarch who seemed inclined to change his mind unexpectedly; moreover, Schimper's letter seemed to indicate that he too was a prisoner, so his advice was not too convincing.

Replying to Rassam's enquiry about the cause of the Emperor's displeasure, Flad and Schimper recited, each in his own way, the sorry story of the past 14 months; how the Emperor was angered by the alleged disparagement of him by words written or spoken by Stern and Rosenthal; and the King's offence at not receiving any reply to his letter to Queen Victoria and anger on learning of Consul Cameron's recall to Massawa. Flad ended his letter, which he wrote in his native language, German:

> I have to request that you will on no account mention my name to the Abyssinian spies by whom you are surrounded, nor to the Emperor. If it were suspected that I corresponded with you, I with my wife and children would be instantly hanged. I am always at your service, but please write to me in German. The German language is the safest here.

In his account of the imprisonments, Schimper stressed the lack of understanding between the British Government and the Emperor of one another's customs and procedures; he considered this the underlying cause of all the unhappy events.

At long last, towards the end of February, Rassam received what he had for so long been hoping for, messages from some of the captives, from Cameron and Stern, but they only said that the prisoners were well and had received the provisions, and gave no advice about proceeding to the court of the Emperor. Later one of the resourceful messengers he had sent up with provisions returned with two brief letters from Cameron, and letters for forwarding from Stern and Mrs Rosenthal. Cameron's messages confirmed that the Emperor had received Rassam's two letters. One of the Consul's epistles, dated Magdala, 17 January said: 'Your two letters have reached. We thought that the second had obtained an answer. We are all well, thank God.'

The Ethiopian messenger who had reached the imprisoned Consul was a scamp called Walde Mariam who brought back the verbal message for Rassam: 'Take care not to go up into Abyssinia before you receive an answer from the King, or wait for a more propitious time.' Walde Mariam also gave Rassam a description of this place called Magdala. The mountain on which the prisoners were placed was about five miles in circumference, and very high.

It would take a good walker at least an hour and a half to clamber to the top. There was only one narrow way up. There were 3,000 men garrisoning the fort. There was abundance of good water, but all food had to be obtained from below. Walde Mariam concluded his report in words which Rassam recorded as follows: 'In consequence of the general insecurity of the road just now all over Abyssinia, travellers have to use every precaution to guard against being made prisoners by the King's followers, or plundered by the rebels.'

Even now Rassam was not much wiser as what to do next. On the strength of what he had learnt, he sent more provisions to Magdala, and also wrote to Flad to continue supplying money to Cameron. But the question still remained: what to do next?

Early in March, Rassam despatched the *Victoria* to Aden with his latest information and a statement of his own views for the information of Merewether and the Foreign Secretary, Lord Russell. When the vessel returned she brought a packet of letters and newspapers for himself and the prisoners, and a new instruction for Rassam's mission. Lord Russell now judged that it might conduce to its success if an English officer were associated with it. Accordingly Colonel Merewether asked Rassam whom he would like for this purpose; Rassam preferred to leave the choice to his chief. The *Victoria* sailed for Aden with this intimation. At the end of March *Victoria* returned to Massawa, bringing Lieutenant W. F. Prideaux, Third Assistant Resident at Aden, to make the British mission, so far consisting of an Ottoman and a Frenchman, more British in nationality if not in patronymics. Rassam was delighted with the appointment.

By now, however, Rassam had been in Massawa, with the Queen's letter, more than eight months, and had little worthwhile to show for his pains; he began to wonder whether his mission had not reached the limit of its usefulness. And what would they be thinking in England of his producing no results? It would be difficult for Parliament and people in England to realise what an impenetrable barrier were those high defiant Ethiopian mountains which he could see towering up some 20 miles inland. Rassam was confronted by the baffling question of the inexplicable behaviour of Theodore, who had shown no displeasure towards him, had treated his messengers well, yet took no step towards remedying the injury of which he complained, or releasing the prisoners from their suffering.

Pondering over these things Rassam at last decided to address a third and final letter to the Emperor, and if there were no reply he would relinquish his mission and return to Aden. At this juncture two Muslims of the neighbouring Shoho tribe came to see him. One of them, called Ibrahim, said he was a relative of the Emperor's Steward, Samuel, and came to tell Rassam that there were many people in Ethiopia who were enemies of the English and sought to poison the Emperor's mind against them. Ibrahim also gave his reason why Theodore did not write to Rassam. He said that because of the rebellion Theodore could only get the mission up by providing it with a very powerful escort, and such an armed force he could not spare because of his constant wars; but Theodore was too proud to disclose his weakness, and did not wish to see another English representative killed as Mr Plowden had been.

Rassam now availed himself of Ibrahim to deliver a letter for the Emperor to Samuel, with a request that he should use his influence to induce the Emperor to reply. Ibrahim said there were a number of people at the court who could translate a letter in English to the Emperor, so this time, on 30 March, Rassam wrote in English, saying:

> Most Gracious Sovereign,
>
> I hope your Majesty will pardon the liberty which I am taking in addressing you this third time upon a matter which has given me much anxiety.
>
> More than eight months ago, I wrote and informed your Majesty that I had been sent here by the British Government as the bearer of a letter for you from our Queen. After having waited about three months for a reply, I was compelled to write to you again, through the Nâyib of Harkîko, as I feared that the first two messengers had not delivered my letter safely to you.
>
> Neither to the first nor to the second letter have I as yet received an answer, and the very thought of knowing that the two letters have reached you long since makes me the more anxious to learn the cause of your silence.
>
> I beg to inform your Majesty that the sole duty on which I have been sent is to convey to you our Queen's letter. I have nothing else to do but to deliver it to you, and to assure you of the sincere wishes which our Sovereign entertains for the welfare and prosperity of the great country which the Almighty has placed under your rule.
>
> It is rumoured that some evil-disposed persons, who do not wish to see England and Abyssinia on the best terms, have misrepresented the

object of my mission to you. I can confidently assure you that the British Government takes a sincere interest in the welfare of your empire, and would greatly deplore any unfriendly feeling taking place between the two countries through a mere misunderstanding.

The delay makes me feel this painful suspense the more, because I am at a loss what explanation to give to my Government as to its cause. Moreover, the rainy season is now fast approaching, and, if your Majesty will not honour me with an answer soon, I shall be obliged to return to my duties at Aden.

The messengers said that if the Emperor did not detain them they would be back in 40 days. Rassam decided therefore that he would wait until the end of May, and if then there was no reply, he would leave for Aden; but after the messengers had gone he heard that because of rebellion in Tigré they could not get through that province for nearly a month, so that far from his leaving Massawa, if he was to do so, by the end of May, it would be June before the messengers even reached the Emperor. There was always something.

Once again Rassam settled down to a long wait, and a few days after the messengers' departure he recorded: 'The hot weather has fairly set in again, and the bare idea of spending another such season as the last in this place is unsupportable.' Dr and Mrs Blanc, who had both been suffering, were then in Aden on a visit for their health's sake, and Munzinger went up to Kassala on business. At Monculo the day temperature in the coolest part of the Consulate was 170°F. Left on their own, on 1 May Rassam and Prideaux, with servants and escort, set off into the foothills in search of milder temperatures. They found places cool enough at sunrise, about 67°F, but still terrifically hot by noon. Messengers came up to Rassam during his few days' excursion into the hills, and on his return to Monculo he found another messenger there. He now had letters from Cameron and three missionaries, and those from Magdala struck one new note. Cameron wrote:

I speak advisedly, dear Rassam, and with the free consent and approval of our party . . . when I say, that the only way of settling this matter is to write strongly, and act, if further writing is of no use. Of course, we have no wish to press the Government in saying this: the interests of England and the good of the country must be always the first consideration, and will be with us; but it may remove a difficulty to know what we all feel. If Government acts energetically, and it entails suffering on us, we are prepared, as it must come to that sooner or later.

Then, after referring to a setback Theodore had received on his Shoa campaign, Cameron continued:

> He would like matters settled, but does not see how. But, for God's sake, do not come up here; he will cage you as sure as a gun, as he thinks that while he has us in his hands he is safe from attack, and, of course, with a swell like yourself in addition, matters would only be the better for him, according to his view.

The messengers related that Theodore had been badly defeated in Shoa and Wollo and his army was so suffering from death, desertion and hunger, that he dared not return to Debra Tabor. Also, that the rebel Tissoo Gobazie controlled more of the territory north of Lake Tana and had captured Gondar, while to the east the other great rebel Wagshum Gobazie had also extended his power. It seemed likely that one of them, outwitting the other, would soon march north and conquer Tigré.

The letters from Flad and Schimper advised that it would be dangerous to go up to the Emperor without a safe-conduct from him: Schimper suggested, therefore, sending up the Queen's letter by messenger, then annoyingly contradicted this advice by saying that 'the present perils of the road render it inadvisable to risk the future of this highly important document'.

A second letter from Cameron, brought down by the messenger from Flad, said: 'For God's sake, don't think of coming up here either with or without a safe-conduct. You will only get chains for your pains.' He added: 'If, instead of your third letter [to the Emperor] the letter in your hands [the Queen's letter] had been sent with a polite ultimatum accompanying it, it might have got us out, or brought matters to a crisis either one way or the other.'

Once again people who knew the Emperor and the country were giving conflicting advice and, Rassam recorded:

> There can be no doubt that the captives were sick at heart, and would gladly have encountered any dangers rather than endure further suspense; nevertheless, knowing that I was not warranted in assuming so grave a responsibility, I decided to refer the matter to superior authority.

The *Victoria* now arrived again in Massawa, bringing back Dr Blanc, not Mrs Blanc, and Rassam sent it back the next morning with copies of the letters he had received from the interior.

Rassam continued from time to time to send up money and provisions to the prisoners, sometimes direct to Magdala and sometimes to Flad at Gafat. Rassam had now made sufficient friends among the notability and merchants in and around Massawa that he had no longer any difficulty in finding trustworthy messengers. At one time he had seven messengers on the road between Massawa, Gafat and Magdala. Their journeys were always hazardous. Flad on one occasion sent his letter by a leper, feeling sure no one would lay hands on him. Despite the risks they continually faced, these messengers, some young, some old, proved remarkably resourceful and dependable.

With Rassam established at Massawa and sending up his messengers the prisoners now had a means of communicating with the outside world. When he received letters from them he sent on those addressed to their friends and relatives, those addressed to himself he copied and sent the copies to the Foreign Secretary. All this correspondence went by the *Victoria* to Aden and then on to London. Besides the messages from the Europeans, Rassam was always getting other news, some true some false, and when true never encouraging. The state of Ethiopia gave him increasing anxiety; the rebels were continuing to advance, thus making the mission's hoped for journey appear increasingly difficult, perhaps impossible. All the same Rassam continued to get money and provisions through to the captives, and the messengers brought back messages written or by word of mouth.

Towards the end of June Rassam recorded: 'More letters from the captives, all very desponding in tone, without a gleam of light to indicate how their liberation can best be accomplished.' Cameron's letters often included requests like that dated 29 May:

> Money, money, dear Rassam, again send us money; also chocolate, preserved fish, or meat, or vegetables, and simple medicines for eye disease or stomach complaints . . . also opium, ammonia, camphor, and anything good for rheumatism and bruises.

and in another letter of the same date the Consul wrote:

> What can you do for us you ask? Send up money; . . . send three messengers by Tigré, each with 100 dollars; unless you do this we may die of starvation. We are threatened with both siege and famine; we have only 180 dollars in hand, so for God's sake look sharp about this.

By mid June the messengers who had gone up with Rassam's letter, saying they would be back in 40 days, were nearly two months over their promised time. Slowly and sadly Rassam was coming to the conclusion that his third letter would receive the fate of the first two and remain unanswered; but he knew the dangers and troubles his messengers had to encounter, and he decided, even though unhopefully, to give them a little longer.

Once again the members of the mission decided to fill in the anxious waiting time by another excursion, and at the end of July, Rassam, Blanc and Prideaux set off from Monculo in a northwesterly direction, accompanied by an escort of irregular troops provided by the Governor of Massawa. Several days' travel took them up into pleasant hill country. And of their camp at 2,500 feet above sea level he wrote: 'So cool was the night that I felt comfortable under a blanket.' Early in August the party began the return journey and on the night of the seventh they camped at Kaafar, only 30 miles from Monculo. The next day the heat was so intense that they wrapped their heads 'in wet towels . . . During the afternoon there was a mist of impalpable dust, so dense that objects were almost invisible ten feet off . . . '

That 8 August turned out a day to be remembered. The Europeans were incongruously turbaned with their wet towels, and the strange sand mist was beginning to rise when, wrote Rassam:

> A little before noon, while seated in the tent, we heard a voice exclaiming, '*el-Bashârah! el-Bashârah!*' (good tidings!) On rising to see what it meant, I was accosted by Ahmed, one of the Nâyib's nephews, who had ridden hard from Massowah to report that Consul Cameron had been released, and that Theodore had written to invite me to go up; that the letter had not actually arrived at Massowah, as the messengers, Ibrahîm and Mohammed Sihâway, were too tired to bring it on, but they had despatched another man to announce the intelligence. I was so delighted with the news that I could have hugged Ahmed there and then, for the alleged release of the Consul was to me the most hopeful sign that all our difficulties with the King would be speedily and satisfactorily adjusted . . .
>
> We left Kánfar at 3.45 p.m. . . .

17

NEW HOPE: ABDUL-MELAK AND PALGRAVE

(1865)

By the beginning of 1865 Rassam and Dr Blanc had been at Massawa almost six months, but were apparently no nearer to delivering Queen Victoria's letter or to liberating the European captives than the day they landed. To many people outside Ethiopia the delay seemed strange indeed. Understandably some people interested in the liberation of the captives were now having doubts about any possible success of Rassam's mission and some began to doubt whether Rassam was the right person to head it.

That there should be such doubts in England, and held especially by Dr Beke, was to be expected, but apprehension was now being expressed as far away as Bombay. On 3 January 1865, the *Bombay Gazette* carried an article which said of Theodore, very truly, that he must be 'a man of great personal force of character', and then went on to suggest that Rassam and Blanc should therefore be replaced by persons of higher rank.

Rassam himself had no evidence that Theodore wanted a higher ranking mission. In addition to his official correspondence, he also kept up a private correspondence and later that month gave an indication of reasons why he thought Theodore was not inviting him up to his court – wherever it might be, for it was so often on the move. To his friend Henry Layard, he wrote that the Emperor's delay in writing was not intentional; and to another friend, Mr Badger, he wrote that he did not expect Theodore would be able to quell the rebellion. In London, Sir William Coghlan and Mr Badger were still taking a more optimistic view of the outcome of affairs, and they had both asked his views about establishing a regular British diplomatic mission in Ethiopia, to which Rassam had replied, yes, but after the prisoners' release.

In Aden, Colonel Merewether, while retaining confidence in

Rassam, was also beginning to wonder whether anything was to be achieved by the mission, so on 21 January he wrote instructions to Rassam to send one more letter to Theodore, to tell the monarch that unless a reply arrived within a certain time he and his mission should return to Aden. However, on 25 January (before receiving this instruction), Rassam sailed to Aden to consult, and returned to Massawa on 4 February. Rassam did not send the suggested letter; perhaps he had agreed with Merewether on a further delay.

In Egypt, Consul-General Colquhoun was also becoming anxious about the delay at Massawa, and he was dutifully alert to consider any new means of reaching Theodore, and prompt to advise the Foreign Secretary of any possibility that might present iself. On 27 January, he reported a visit he had that day received from a traveller who claimed to know Ethiopia, the Emperor, and the Ethiopian language. This was a Chevalier de Heuglin, who had heard of the imprisonment of Cameron, and he was willing to go and see the Emperor to try to liberate the Consul. De Heuglin had a high opinion of Theodore, reporting him to be 'a remarkable man', possessing to an extraordinary degree the 'coup d'oeil juste'. But this experienced traveller soon showed himself unable or unwilling to revisit Ethiopia.

In London, early in February, doubts about Rassam's mission were formally brought to the Foreign Secretary's attention in the memorandum which Brigadier Sir William Coghlan was asked to prepare. In this document, dated 8 February, to which he gave the matter-of-fact title 'On the Abyssinian Difficulty, and how best to get out of it', Sir William made some 20 observations or proposals. He began by observing that the Difficulty was how 'to open communication with one who has so grossly violated the rules of civilisation and international law as to seize and torture British subjects, one of whom is a British Consul'. Sir William was perhaps somewhat pedantic in assuming the Emperor to be familiar with international law, but in accusing him of violating rules of civilisation, he at least maintained some logic when in another paragraph he stated: 'Theodore is a *parvenu*, a powerful despot, of high aspirations, and a strong will, but is not a savage.'

Sir William ranged over policy, tactics and some details. Of the Queen's letter to Theodore (not knowing apparently that the text had already been agreed) he suggested that it 'should be indited in Oriental phraseology, highly emblazoned and sealed (the King will consider nothing valid which is not sealed)'; also 'some excuse should be made for the delay in replying to the King's Letter and his proposed mission should be accepted'.

Trying to assess the reasons for the Emperor's changed attitude to the English, Sir William wrote:

> There are probably several causes for his altered demeanour towards the British Consul; . . . the chief of them . . . is the long delay in replying to the letter which he addressed to Her Majesty . . .
>
> It is understood that his dignity is grievously wounded . . . there is reason to believe the King refuses Rassam's mission as one which is not of sufficient dignity . . .
>
> If any further effort is to be made to release captives, it must be by means of an Embassy headed by an officer of rank, who should be supported by a suite as would give dignity to his mission, a secretary (a military officer), two or three officers of the scientific corps, or departments, and a medical officer . . .
>
> Theodorus is known to attach great importance to military rank and scientific men; on that account, therefore, a liberal display of them will be expedient.
>
> A supply of presents should be provided, to be delivered or not according to circumstances.

Sir William gave no indication as to where he obtained his information concerning Theodore, or to what the Emperor did or did not attach importance. Although the memorandum gave no such supporting evidence, it specifically argued that it would be well to replace Rassam by a person of higher rank, supported by a larger mission.

Lord Russell did not act upon this suggestion, but he did take note of two others. On Tuesday, 14 February, a letter went from the Foreign Office to the India Office to say that he was of the opinion that if a British officer were attached to Mr Rassam it might conduce to the success of his mission, so could such an officer be spared from the Aden garrison. The India Office agreed. Noting also Sir William Coghlan's suggestion of presents, the Foreign Office wrote to the War Office requesting 500 muskets to serve as such a present.

Just at this time the Foreign Office learnt that the Government of India intended to withdraw its steamer *Victoria* from Aden. A letter was accordingly despatched, on 17 February, stating that Lord Russell requested that the vessel should remain under orders of Colonel Merewether.

The same day the Foreign Office sent to the India Office an

amended version of Queen Victoria's letter to Emperor Theodore, with the request that it be transmitted to the Governor of Aden for 'despatch to Massowah with the least possible delay', and that the earlier text should be returned.

The new version, which, unlike the old addressed the Emperor as 'Our Good Friend Theodore, King of Abyssinia', embodied several significant changes. The section in the earlier text opposing the despatch of an Ethiopian Embassy was suppressed, as was the supporting argument about the 'great' distance between the two countries. Also omitted was the passage stating that Theodore had subjected Cameron, 'and many others' in whom the Queen felt an interest, to treatment 'inconsistent with the Emperor's professions of friendship'. This was replaced by a new clause, designed as a possible face-saving formula for Theodore, stating that 'false representations about his withdrawal of favour' from Cameron might have emanated from ill-disposed persons who might 'desire to produce an alteration of our feeling towards you'.

Since the letter was to be taken by Rassam a new conclusion was added which expressly accepted the principle of an Ethiopian Embassy which had earlier been rejected. This part of the letter stated that:

> With the view of renewing to you the expression of our friendship, and of explaining to you our wishes respecting our servant Cameron, we have directed our servant Hormuzd Rassam, First Assistant to the Political Resident at Aden, to proceed to your residence, and to deliver to you this our royal letter. We have instructed him to inform your Majesty that if, notwithstanding the long distance which separates our dominions from those of your Majesty, you should, after having permitted Our servant Cameron and the other Europeans to take their leave and depart, desire to send an Embassy to this country, that Embassy will be very well received by Us. And so, not doubting that you will receive Our servant Rassam in a favourable manner, and give entire credit to all that he shall say to you on Our part, as well as comply with the requests which he is instructed to make to you, We recommend you to the protection of the Almighty.

The letter was signed: 'Your good friend, Victoria R.'

The Foreign Secretary's three special requests – that an Army officer should join Rassam, that muskets should be made available as presents, and that the *Victoria* should remain based at Aden – were all in due course granted. Lord Russell was certainly setting the machinery of government to work. He was also giving his full and active support to his representative in Massawa. The doubters about Rassam, however, continued to hold to their apprehensions.

While Lord Russell was taking steps to strengthen Rassam's hand one of the doubters quite unexpectedly learnt of a new possible way of reaching the remote Emperor. At the beginning of February Consul-General Colquhoun received a letter, dated 28 January, from his consul at Jeddah stating that there was a Sudanese Copt called Abdul-Melak who knew Ethiopia well, and might serve as a messenger. The man was duly sent up to Cairo where the Consul-General passed him on to his Arabic expert, Mr Ayrton, who duly cross-examined him.

Fairly satisfied with the apparent genuineness of Abdul-Melak, Consul-General Colquhoun conceived the idea that the latter could carry to the Abun in Ethiopia a plea to intercede with Theodore, and urged this suggestion on Lord Russell. Colquhoun continued nevertheless to make painstaking enquiries about Abdul-Melak, but does not appear to have enquired of Rassam whether he knew him. This was perhaps understandable as the idea was to by-pass Rassam.

Russell, while continuing to support Rassam's mission, was at the same time ready to consider any seemingly useful plan to bring about the liberation of the captives. He thus gave his approval to employ Abdul-Melak and send him on a separate mission. The hopeful Colquhoun duly had the message to the Abun beautifully written, in English with an Arabic translation. Addressed to His Eminence the Most Revered The Archbishop Metropolitan of Abyssinia, the Consul-General in Egypt asked him to 'inform the Sultan that my Royal Mistress the Queen does not desire to make any demands upon his Majesty or act otherwise than in accordance with the most friendly dispositions towards him'. The letter bore the large seal of the Consulate-General and also a list of presents Abdul-Melak was to carry. On 21 March Colquhoun sent Russell a copy of the English version of the letter, and in an accompanying despatch he provided additional observations about the intended messenger, based on further enquiries, claiming that 'the Copt's story is true and consistent'.

Although the Italian missionary Stella had left Egypt before the British Consul-General could personally seek his opinion of Abdul-Melak, an enquiry eventually caught up with him in Europe; he replied in Italian from Paris on 11 April, and Colquhoun sent Russell a translation of the letter. This no doubt helped some members of the Foreign Office more than Russell, who could read Italian very well. In his letter, addressed to a friend in Cairo, the somewhat verbose missionary gave some of his more general views. He wrote:

> The matter on which you write is involved in obscurity. That Abdul-Melak wishes to deceive you I cannot aver, for I have always known him for an honest man . . .
>
> As so many European prisoners are concerned it behoves everyone, if there be a ray of hope, not to lose sight of it. Since it appears that the Europeans are in Magdala, perhaps the Abun is in Magdala also; in this case I should doubt the success of Abdul's mission, but if the Abun is not in arrest we may hope . . .

So, with the letter, the translation and presents for Emperor and Abun, Abdul-Melak was sent on his way by Consul-General Colquhoun, who hoped the humble messenger would achieve what Rassam had spent so long failing to do.

In a subsequent letter to Lord Russell, dated Alexandria 13 May, Colquhoun had a further word to say: 'I expect before very long to hear what results attend the arrival of the Copt Abdul-Melak at Debra Tabor. He found a vessel leaving Jeddah for Souakin and availed himself of it very prudently.' When this despatch reached the Foreign Office the following notes were written at the foot of it: 'For the Queen.' 'Let Mr Layard see this.' And that seems to be the last Foreign Office record of Abdul-Melak. Whatever could have happened after he 'very prudently' sailed from Jeddah?

Rassam recalled: 'I discovered subsequently that the Abun had no knowledge whatever of this impostor; and his opinion was, that if he had ever been in Abyssinia, it must have been in the suite of the Coptic Patriarch, who visited Theodore about nine years previously.' As Father Stella might have said: 'The matter was involved in obscurity.'

Lord Russell meanwhile continued to pin his faith on the success of Rassam's mission. On 6 June he rejected a suggestion for military intervention, writing at the foot of an inter-departmental letter:

> I cannot think it would be wise to send a military expedition to attack the King of Abyssinia – I know not how we could reach him in that way.
>
> But Mr Rassam and Lieutenant Prideaux with the Queen's letter

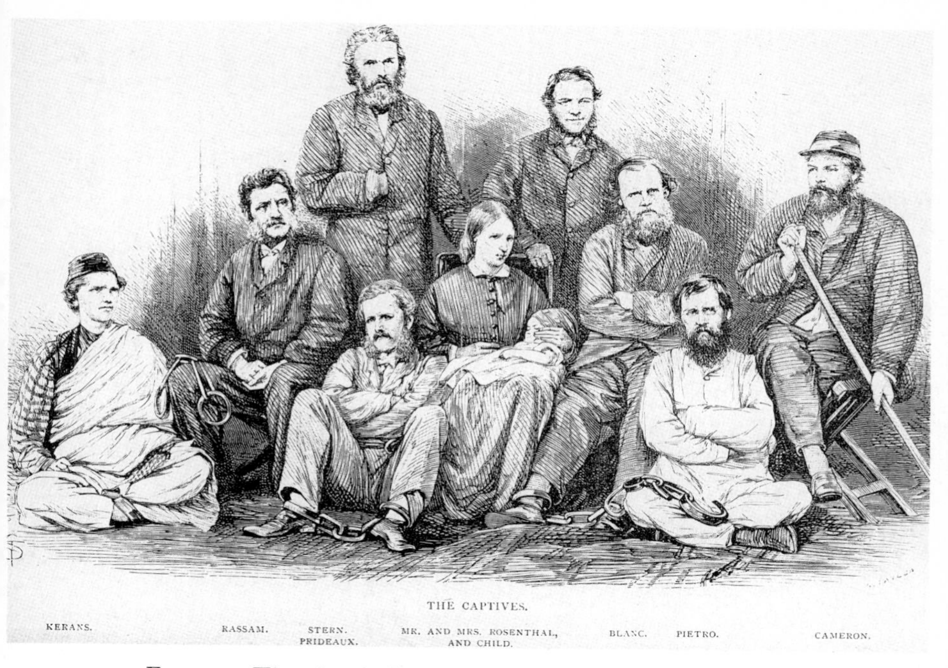

Emperor Theodore's European captives; from H.A. Stern, *The Captive Missionary*, (1868)

Emperor Theodore surrounded by his royal lions; from *L'Année Illustrée*, (1868)

The fortress of Magdala showing the Emperor's Palace at the top of the cliff; from R. Acton, *The Abyssinian Expedition*, (1870)

The huts at Magdala in which Theodore's European captives were detained; from R. Acton, *The Abyssinian Expedition*, (1870)

Transporting Theodore's great mortar Sebastapol to Magdala; from Hormuzd Rassam, *Narrative of the British Mission to Theodore*, (1869)

The port of Zulla showing the immense build-up of supplies for Napier's expeditionary force; from R. Acton, *The Abyssinian Expedition*, (1870)

Some of the elephants from India which transported British canons and other equipment for the assault on Magdala, and later carried back hundreds of large manuscripts and other articles of loot; from R. Acton, *The Abyssinian Expedition*, (1870)

Magdala in flames, burnt down by British sappers as a sign of their country's 'anger' at Theodore's 'ill-treatment' of his European captives; from R. Acton, *The Abyssinian Expedition*, (1870)

might procure a good effect and if they are willing to go, I should be disposed to send them.

I should send them with ten or twelve servants as escort with few presents and no threats . . .

The captives, on the other hand, were pressing for succour and action, and on 3 April Cameron wrote to Rassam:

It is impossible to suggest anything in regard to getting us out, but I fear unless the Government tells the King plainly that the retention of a single prisoner will be followed by war, Stern, Rosenthal and Macraire may be detained, as the King has a particular hatred of these three. I only tell you this on behalf of these poor people. The Government however will, I feel sure, act rightly as well as considerately, and we are prepared to acquiesce in everything.

The Foreign Office was now having second thoughts about making the present of 500 muskets to Theodore, so, compromising, on 14 July James Murray wrote to the India Office to say that if the 500 muskets had reached Massawa, Rassam should send back 450 to Aden and keep only 50 to use as he might think best.

One person preparing to give up his share of responsibility for liberating the captives was Mr Colquhoun, who was about to retire. In July 1865, Colonel Edward Stanton, then in England, was nominated to succeed him as British Consul-General in Egypt. Pending his appointment Colonel Stanton studied affairs relating to his new duty, including that of the captives. The retiring Consul-General had placed his hope on the Sudanese Abdul-Melak. The newly appointed Consul-General in his turn also attached hope in another newcomer, the well-known British traveller William Gifford Palgrave.

The son of English historian Sir Francis Palgrave, and brother of Francis Turner Palgrave, Professor of Poetry at Oxford and compiler of the anthology *The Golden Treasury of English Songs and Lyrics*, William Palgrave was a seasoned traveller, hardened in the two strangely different roles of soldier and missionary. After studying at Trinity College, Oxford, he had gone to India to become a Lieutenant in the 8th Bombay Regiment, but had been converted to Catholicism, and, after being ordained as a priest, served as a Jesuit missionary in India; he then visited Rome and afterwards went as a missionary to Syria, and later to Arabia. But he had now forsaken the priesthood, and found himself free to volunteer for a special mission into Ethiopia.

Lord Russell, who continued to give official support to Rassam's mission, did not close his eyes to engaging other persons to reach the elusive monarch. He therefore approved the employment of Palgrave, and on 21 July he therefore wrote to the latter, observing:

> As I have decided upon availing myself of your offer to proceed to the Court of King Theodore of Abyssinia, with a view to obtaining, if possible, the liberation of Mr Consul Cameron, and other British subjects . . . I have to instruct you to proceed at your earliest convenience to Egypt, and to place yourself on your arrival under the orders of Her Majesty's Consul-General, Colonel Stanton . . . In conclusion, I have only to urge upon you the greatest caution and prudence in carrying through this important and delicate mission.

When Lord Russell had approved that Abdul-Melak should take a letter to Abuna Salama it was assumed that the Sudanese's errand would in no way hinder or diminish the importance of Rassam's mission, until such time as Abdul-Melak achieved what Rassam had so far failed to achieve. The appointment of Palgrave, however, was quite another matter: Rassam's task was virtually being transferred to him – except that Palgrave was not being asked to carry the Queen's letter, which was still in Rassam's hands.

On the same day Russell also wrote a lengthy letter of instruction to Colonel Stanton, who was still in London, observing:

> You will endeavour to ascertain, on your arrival in Egypt, whether it would be most desirable for Mr Palgrave to attempt to reach the head-quarters of the King of Abyssinia through the Egyptian provinces on the Upper Nile, or through Massowah or some other port on the Red Sea.
>
> From the information recently received by Her Majesty's Government, it would appear that formidable rebellions have broken out in the territories of King Theodore, that his capital has fallen into the hands of his enemies, and that the districts between the Turkish province, now under Egyptian jurisdiction, on the borders of the Red Sea and the interior of Abyssinia are no longer in his power.
>
> It will consequently require much prudence and caution on your part in determining the route by which Mr Palgrave should proceed . . . If you should think it desirable to do so, you may request the Viceroy or the officer in charge of the Egyptian Government to furnish Mr Palgrave with a letter directed to King Theodore on behalf of the captives, but it is evident, considering the relations which exist between the King and the Egyptian Government, that such a letter, if furnished, should be used with the greatest caution . . .

It may also be advisable to procure for Mr Palgrave letters of recommendation from the Coptic Patriarch to the Aboona and clergy of Abyssinia.

Should Mr Palgrave proceed to Abyssinia through the Turkish territories now under the jurisdiction of the Pasha of Egypt on the Red Sea, you will instruct him to go in the first instance to Massowah, and to place himself in communication with Mr Rassam. That gentleman will be able to furnish him with the latest information that can be obtained with regard to the present state of Abyssinia, and as to the best course to be pursued in making an attempt to reach King Theodore. You will explain distinctly to Mr Palgrave that his mission is in no way connected with Mr Rassam, who will be instructed by the Secretary of State for India to return to Aden with the Queen's letter as soon as Mr Palgrave shall have departed for the interior.

If on your arrival in Egypt you should find that Mr Rassam has left Massowah for the Court of King Theodore, or if Mr Palgrave on his arrival at Massowah should find that Mr Rassam has already left for Abyssinia, or has made arrangements for doing so, Mr Palgrave should not proceed with his mission. He will in this case either remain in or return to Egypt, as the case may be, until I can furnish you with further instructions . . . The object of Mr Palgrave's mission is to procure the liberation of Consul Cameron and the other prisoners. On his arrival at the Court of King Theodore, he will if necessary deliver to His Majesty himself, or, if unable to do so, he will place in the hands of his principal Minister a copy of the inclosed Memorandum, with which I have furnished Mr Palgrave, inviting King Theodore, if he wishes to be friendly to the British Crown, to release Consul Cameron and the other British subjects, and informing him that he must not expect friendly conduct from the Government of Her Majesty the Queen, if he refuses to do so. Should Mr Palgrave, however, have reason to believe that he can obtain the liberation of the captives without making use of the Memorandum, which might have the effect of further irritating the King, he is at liberty to use his discretion in the matter.

Should Mr Palgrave succeed in liberating the prisoners, or should he find it impossible to accomplish the object of his mission, he will at once return to Egypt and await such further Instructions as I may consider it advisable to give him through you.

You will give Mr Palgrave clearly to understand that his mission is limited to a specific object – the liberation of the prisoners. He may give general assurances to King Theodore, that it is the desire of Her Majesty's Government to maintain friendly intercourse with Abyssinia, and to extend the commercial relations of the two countries. He may also say that when the prisoners are released Her Majesty's Government will point out the mode in which commerce between Great Britain and Abyssinia may be promoted. But he is not authorized to enter into any formal arrangements with the King on any subject whatever, nor to hold out any hopes to him of assistance from the British Government in any war or expedition against his neighbour. Mr Palgrave, however, is at liberty to state to the King, in the event of his thinking it expedient, that if his Majesty should at once release the captives and permit them and other British subjects in Abyssinia to depart freely from his territories with their property, Her Majesty's Government will on this occasion request no reparation or indemnity for their imprisonment, and will be willing to overlook what has occurred. But Mr Palgrave may at the same time take an opportunity of representing to the King the violation of international law and the great disrespect to the Queen's Government of which he has been guilty in detaining against their will, imprisoning, and maltreating Her Majesty's Consul and other subjects of Her Majesty.

You will further inform Mr Palgrave that he is to abstain from mixing himself up with political affairs of the country, from taking part in any struggle for power which may be going on in Abyssinia, and from giving any encouragement or hopes of assistance to any person in rebellion against King Theodore.

If, after the liberation of the prisoners, King Theodore should ask whether Her Majesty's Government would receive a mission to be sent by him to this country, Mr Palgrave will inform His Majesty that he will represent his wishes to Colonel Stanton.

Russell's memorandum for Palgrave, of which a copy was to be given to King Theodore, if Palgrave thought fit, was dated 21 July. It stated:

If His Majesty the Emperor of Abyssinia desires to be on friendly terms with the British Crown he must release Captain Cameron, Her Majesty's Consul at Massowah, and all other British subjects now kept in confinement in Abyssinia. He may then expect the most friendly conduct and most friendly intercourse on the part of the British Government and Her Majesty the Queen.

Should His Majesty the Emperor of Abyssinia refuse to release Captain Cameron and the other prisoners, His Majesty must not expect friendly conduct on the part of the Government of Her Majesty.

The Government of Her Majesty the Queen wish for friendly intercourse and peaceful commerce with Abyssinia.

Palgrave's mission had been set out comprehensively enough by Russell. The object was to liberate the captives. But that was precisely what Rassam was in Massawa to do. If Palgrave did indeed succeed in entering Ethiopia up the Nile, or if he were to arrive in Massawa, with intention to proceed into Ethiopia, what would Rassam – who had for so long been trying to do just that – think of it all and of Palgrave? If Palgrave were to go by way of Massawa, where, Lord Russell seemed to think, Rassam, who had failed to enter Ethiopia, would kindly tell him how to do so, it would certainly be a strange encounter between the two men.

Even allowing for the last-minute miracle for which allowance was indeed made in his letter of instruction, Lord Russell at no time took any step to inform Rassam why it was Palgrave and no longer he who was now to proceed into Ethiopia. Meanwhile in Massawa Rassam himself, as also his colleagues, Blanc and young Prideaux, were in complete ignorance of these machinations – or new hopes – in London.

One person who was not satisfied with this manner of displacing Rassam, was Palgrave himself. On the same day that the Foreign Secretary signed his instructions, Palgrave wrote to Lord Russell, and it being a Friday he anticipated that he might be at Richmond Lodge:

> After conversation with Colonel Stanton and Mr Layard and perusal of the documents relative to the Abyssinian affair at the Foreign Office, I find that there are some points of importance requiring *special* and *confidential* information.
>
> I could give it in writing to your Lordship, but I think that it would be clearer, and involve less loss of time if conveyed by word of mouth. Might I then beg your Lordship to allow me a few minutes' interview, either at the Lodge, or wherever else might best suit your Lordship's convenience, before my departure which is fixed for the middle of next week?

His Lordship acceded to the request. At the foot of Palgrave's letter a Foreign Office note records: 'Mr Palgrave saw Lord Russell on 24 July.' That was Monday, so little time was lost, and it was to be a busy day at the Foreign Office, with much to do before Palgrave set off for Egypt later that week.

On this same day, 24 July, Layard wrote to the India Office, giving the gist of the letters of instruction of 21 July to Palgrave and Colonel Stanton, as well as the memorandum that Palgrave would show Theodore, if he thought advisable. But in yet another letter of that day, addressed to the India Office, Layard in the final paragraph significantly altered the purport of one of the letters of instruction.

As a result of Palgrave's visit to Lord Russell, it was decided that the envoy's intended journey should not be up the Nile, but by the more usual route by way of Massawa. This meant that the problem of two Foreign Office envoys, in large measure competing envoys, needed resolving. That Monday Layard accordingly wrote to the India Office, reflecting these considerations. Alas poor Rassam, the letter showed that Russell was placing his hopes of liberating the captives, not so much now on the joint-excavator of Nineveh, but on the new-found traveller of Arabia. Layard's letter enclosed a memorandum, signed by Lord Russell on 21 July, 'to be presented to King Theodore, or his Chief Minister, by Mr W. Gifford Palgrave'. Similar in tenor to that earlier written, it stated: 'This Memorandum will be presented to His Majesty the Emperor, or His Majesty's Principal Minister, by Mr William Gifford Palgrave, who, as the Agent of the Government of Her Majesty the Queen, has been instructed to deliver it to His Majesty.' New people were thus to address themselves to the baffling task of liberating the captives.

So, Colonel Stanton and William Palgrave set out together for Egypt, both fairly confident that between them they could do a lot better than Hormuzd Rassam had so far done in 12 months. They reached Alexandria in August, and on arrival found interesting communications from Colonel Merewether, the Resident at Aden.

18

LORDS
(1865)

Early in 1865 Queen Victoria received a letter from a private citizen. It came from Captain Desborough, Consul Cameron's brother-in-law. The captives' friends and relatives were painfully conscious that the prisoners' sufferings had been endured for more than a year, and nothing done by Government had brought about their liberty. Could not more effective measures be applied? Captain Desborough now made a direct appeal to the Queen. In his letter he gave an account of Captain Cameron's distinguished military record, and concluded with a special justification for writing because of the anxiety of Cameron's old mother, aged 78, wondering if she would ever again see her only surviving son. Quite a good letter for a gallant Captain to write to a Queen and a mother who held in affection and pride her dear, ever brave soldiers and her own ever-loving family. Courteously and dutifully, as also wisely, Desborough sent the Foreign Secretary a copy of his letter. The Queen took notice of the letter from Consul Cameron's brother-in-law, but other matters now required Lord Russell's attention. So, when Parliament next met on 7 February 1865, no mention was made of the captive Consul or other Europeans in Ethiopia, nor was the question referred to in the ensuing parliamentary debates in either House. After Mr Seymour's first question in June 1864 had come the long recess and even with the reassembly of Parliament in February 1865 more than nine months passed without a word about them having been said in Parliament.

During these months, however, the Press did make some mention of the captives, but not very much. It was through the Press that such of the public as might be interested had learned that a certain Mr Rassam, whose appointment had never been officially announced, had gone to the port of Massawa, which it seemed was the port of entry to Ethiopia, and had carried a letter from the Queen to the Emperor.

By early 1865, more individuals, although not as yet the general public, were becoming concerned, or at least interested, in these matters. Not until April was the subject at last raised again in Parliament, and this time in both Houses. Clearly, behind the scenes persons interested in the captives had been active, for questions in Parliament do not as a rule arise by chance.

Up to the beginning of 1865, Rassam's appointment had never been communicated to Parliament or officially announced in England, but his presence in Massawa on an official errand was known to a number of persons, including those connected with the missionary societies, and of course the restless Dr Beke. To those who followed the matter it was also all too well known that Rassam, bearer of the Queen's letter, had been in Massawa since April of the previous year, apparently fruitlessly. So when another Member of Parliament who had become interested in the captives raised the subject, he asked about Rassam's seemingly unrewarding errand. On 24 April, Mr E. Warner, Member for Norwich, asked:

> What is the present state of the negotiations with respect to the British captives in Abyssinia, whether the Government have reason to expect a successful issue to the mission of Mr Rassam, and what steps they are prepared to take in the event of their not receiving good account from him?

Once again it was Layard who replied. He said that he 'could not give the Honourable Member much information . . . not that he wished to conceal anything, but that he considered it would be very unadvisable, considering the position of the prisoners, that anything should be said that might lead to greater complications'. He took this opportunity, therefore, of 'deprecating any mention in the press of what took place in the House or elsewhere with regard to those prisoners, as he had reason to believe that all these things were sent out to Abyssinia and got much exaggerated, and might lead to serious conequences'. He nevertheless claimed that 'every means had been taken by Her Majesty's Government to obtain their release', and added that the Government had lately heard from a reliable source that Captain Cameron and the missionaries, although in prison, were in good health, and letters received from Rassam but a few hours earlier held out hope that ere long the prisoners would obtain their release. This was a rather smooth and not very enlightening parliamentary answer, and the Under-Secretary advanced no solid evidence to support his, or

Rassam's, apparent implied optimism. The truth was that Layard had indeed very little information, and had he been more explicit he could only truthfully have said that Rassam's mission did not appear to be producing any worthwhile results.

As for the seemingly paranoid anxiety of Layard and his Foreign Office colleagues about publishing anything that might displease Theodore, and so possibly harm the prisoners, there was some slight justification for these fears for, strange as it may seem, what passed in England could, however belatedly, reach the court of the Ethiopian monarch.

But Layard was going rather far when he let his fears lead him to suggest that newspapers should not publish what passed in Parliament, and he was over-optimistic if he thought he could impose a censorship on the reporting of Parliament; Layard, a former Press correspondent in Constantinople, should have known better.

Of course, the next day the Press reported Layard's answer but treated it as of no special importance.

Then, before that week was out, there suddenly began an awakening of wider interest in the captives. Mr Warner had asked his question in the Commons on Monday. On Thursday an old and skilled politician appeared as a champion to espouse the captives' cause in Parliament. By one speech he stimulated the Press, enlightened the public, and stirred an interest in the fate of captives who had been in chains for well over a year, seemingly forgotten. He placed the Government on their mettle, and within a month a case not worth a Press comment suddenly became worth leading articles.

The sudden change in public interest was brought about when an Opposition peer raised the matter for the first time in the House of Lords. He was the Tory peer, Lord Chelmsford. He saw he had a good story to tell and a good stick to beat the Whig Government – the story of suffering British subjects in the hands of a barbarous and cruel captor, and the reproach that Lord Palmerston's Government, and his Foreign Secretary, Lord Russell, had for over a year shown themselves incapable of rescuing or bringing any relief to those suffering captives. So armed, the Tory peer set out to belabour the Whig Foreign Secretary and his Government, and he did not lose the fine occasion of making a noble cause a political duel.

While Lord Chelmsford was the first peer to bring the subject before the House of Lords, he was also the first of his family to take a close interest in Ethiopia. He could hardly foresee that he was not to be the last. The family connection, stretching over several generations, began with anxiety and conflict, but later associations in the twentieth century were to be ones of peace.

The first Baron Chelmsford was born Frederick Thesiger in London in 1794. His paternal family had come from Dresden, in Saxony. Thesiger, a handsome man with a fine presence, had begun his career in the British Navy, but had later turned with considerable success to law and politics. Called to the bar at Lincoln's Inn, he became a Queen's Counsel in 1834, was thrice elected as a Tory to the House of Commons and while there became successively Solicitor-General and Attorney-General. When Lord Derby became Prime Minister for the second time, Sir Frederick was raised to the peerage as Baron Chelmsford, and was Lord Chancellor in the new Tory Government. In 1865 Chelmsford was therefore an experienced parliamentarian, with the added authority and dignity of a former Lord Chancellor; he was a personage whom the Press could hardly ignore; in him the Government had a formidable critic, and the captives a redoubtable champion.

On 27 April then, the House of Lords heard what the Parliamentary Report referred to as a 'Question' by Lord Chelmsford, but which in fact proved to be quite a speech. The noble Lord explained that he wished to call attention to the imprisonment and severe treatment to which a British Consul and other British subjects had been exposed by the Emperor of Ethiopia, and to ask the Secretary of State for Foreign Affairs what steps had been taken to relieve their fellow-countrymen from the severities to which they had been subjected, and to which they were still subjected. Lord Chelmsford took the opportunity to tell the House both how great the suffering of the captives had been, and to indicate who was responsible that it had ever come about. He told the Peers: 'Several of our fellow-countrymen had been kept in imprisonment at Gondar, exposed to the most cruel sufferings, and a general impression prevailed that these sufferings were attributable to the want of prompt and judicious measures on the part of the English Foreign Office.'

Lord Chelmsford then gave the House a short history of events, in so far as they were known to him. How 'Mr Plowden, the British Consul at Massowah' had been succeeded by Captain Cameron, who 'met with a flattering reception at the hands of the [Abyssinian] Sovereign, who expressed a desire that negotiations for a treaty between the Government of Abyssinia and this country, which had fallen through in 1849, should be renewed'. How the Emperor in November 1862 had despatched a letter to the Queen, and how Captain Cameron having 'ceased to exert himself in favour of the Abyssinian Emperor, that Sovereign felt himself much aggrieved, especially as he had received no reply to his autograph letter'.

Lord Chelmsford then related how Stern had been beaten and then imprisoned, and how Cameron and other missionaries were later also imprisoned. Lord Chelmsford went on:

> As if to complicate matters, just at this time a letter arrived from England, which, instead of being a reply to the Emperor's letter, simply directed Captain Cameron to return to his post and not to interfere further in the Egyptian dispute.
>
> In consequence of this neglect of Her Majesty's Government to reply to the Emperor's letter, Captain Cameron was loaded with heavier fetters, and was treated with far greater severity, and the whole of the prisoners were chained night and day to a Native soldier.

Continuing his narrative, Lord Chelmsford said that 'subsequently Captain Cameron was able to send out a note to England' – and here Lord Chelmsford read out Cameron's first pencilled note written at Gondar containing the sentence, 'No release until a civil answer to King's letter arrives.'

Having stated the facts as he knew them, Lord Chelmsford then began to drive home his criticisms. He pointed out that the letter from the Emperor, which arrived in England 'in February 1863, remained unnoticed until June 1864, and then what the Government did amounted to a condemnation of their own conduct. In that month a letter was prepared to be sent to the Emperor of Abyssinia; but if it was right to send a letter in June 1864, much more necessary was it to have sent a letter shortly after the month of February, 1863.'

Lord Chelmsford now introduced into his speech a racial prejudice (perhaps inspired by Dr Beke's own personal interest in the matter) that was for long to bedevil public discussion. He observed that the person selected to deliver the Queen's letter:

> was Mr Rassam, an Asiatic gentleman, Assistant Superintendent to the Political Agent at Aden; a man of great experience and ability, but just the sort of person who ought not to have been selected for the purpose,

> and the consequences which occurred were just such as might have been expected.

And, continuing to examine the steps necessary for liberating the captives, Lord Chelmsford advanced a view that was to be in the minds of many English gentlemen: 'There could be no doubt that if a letter had been sent with the presents and conveyed by an Englishman of some rank, the release of these unfortunate prisoners would have taken place.' In Lord Chelmsford's choice of words one almost hears an echo of Dr Beke: if only the Government would do what I say the release of these prisoners would no doubt have taken place.

In concluding his account Lord Chelmsford, as *Hansard* records, declared:

> Let their Lordships then consider the situation of these unhappy persons during the whole of the present year. Under those circumstances he thought that he was fairly entitled to ask why the autograph letter of the Emperor of Abyssinia, which arrived in February 1863, was utterly disregarded until the month of June 1864, because the omission to answer that letter might have occasioned, or, at least, considerably aggravated the sufferings of the prisoners.

Lord Chelmsford thus spent half-an-hour in putting his question about the captives, or rather in presenting a criticism of the Government's handling of the problem of their release.

Lord Russell, on rising to reply, began by expressing the apprehension to which Layard had referred a few days before in the House of Commons. He said he felt a great difficulty in speaking on the subject lest anything 'might give offence to the King of Abyssinia and expose Consul Cameron and the other prisoners to greater hardships'. He then entered upon the history of the case and for the first time publicly disclosed something of British policy in this matter, or, more precisely, he (now in 1865) gave his interpretation of Theodore's letter of 1862 and his interpretation of what the Foreign Office's attitude was to that letter in 1863. Judiciously skirting over his own minute of May 1864 when he had asked 'Is there a letter from the King of Abyssinia unanswered?' he declared emphatically:

> The noble and learned Lord [Lord Chelmsford] seemed to think that when the King had written an autograph letter to the Queen it would have been a very simple matter to answer it civilly at once, and to send out some person to deliver the reply.

> But many difficulties stood in the way. The letter of the King of Abyssinia asked permission to send an Embassy to this country. The state of Abyssinia was unsettled at the time, and it had become more unsettled since.
>
> The King complained that the Turks and Egyptians encroached on his territory, and he wanted the English and the French to interfere and take part in his wars – a course which Her Majesty's Government thought by no means desirable.
>
> It became, therefore, matter for consideration what answer should be given; and the question being one of Eastern policy, the Secretary of State for India had to be consulted before any answer was returned.
>
> It appeared that in the meantime the King of Abyssinia had taken great offence at the conduct of some missionaries. On this fact being officially communicated to Her Majesty's Government, Her Majesty was advised to forward a letter to the King, replying to certain complaints made, and expressing regret at the occasion of them.
>
> The noble and learned Lord seemed to think that Mr Rassam was not a proper person to be charged with this duty. But Mr Rassam was a man of considerable experience and importance in the service; and when he [Russell] found that he held the office of first Assistant Secretary to the Political Resident at Aden, he thought no better person could be selected to execute this mission.

Russell went on to declare that Theodore's real grievance was that no aid had been given to him by England while he was engaged in the wars to which he, Russell, had alluded. The matter had been fully considered by the Foreign Office, but he had no further explanation to offer.

This ended the day's business in the Lords. The House, which had met at 5 p.m., adjourned at 6.15 p.m. But the story of the captives was good news for the morrow's newspapers. Lord Chelmsford's long 'question' and Lord Russell's fairly long reply, were well reported on the following day.

In giving the history of events, both noble lords had told it as they knew it or as they saw it. The public now had, from Press reports, a fairly good idea of the history of the imprisonment of the Consul and two missionaries, and some idea of the steps being taken to bring about their liberation. At long last the question of the captives had become a matter of public interest.

Clearly, Lord Russell had skated over a number of Foreign Office omissions and failings, as also the fact that Rassam's mission was seemingly far from achieving any results. But Lord Chelmsford was not going to leave the Foreign Secretary in any peace for long.

And although there was to be a pause in parliamentary activity, the merry month of May was drawing near, and once again a May meeting would remind the many members and friends of one missionary society, at least, of the continuing martyrdom of their two brethren in Ethiopia.

And then, on 23 May, the case of the captives was again debated in the Lords on a motion by Lord Chelmsford for the publication of official correspondence relating to the captives. While espousing their cause the noble Lord did not lose the opportunity of castigating Mr Rassam for not being an Englishman, and Her Majesty's Government for being careless. Lord Russell replied by suggesting that Lord Chelmsford's speech was not purely inspired with a desire to help the captives, but was politically motivated. Coming to the request for the publication of official papers, Lord Russell said that he did not think that the publication of any particular document would aggravate the lot of the prisoners, but 'the publication of all or the whole of them, accompanied, as it would be, by comments in this country, unfavourable, no doubt, to the conduct of the Sovereign of Abyssinia, would probably cause these unfortunate prisoners to be treated with greater severity'.

Having concluded his speech, Lord Russell resumed his seat. No one rose to continue the debate. As on the previous occasion the matter of the captives remained a duel between Lords Russell and Chelmsford.

Their Lordships then voted on the motion, and there occurred a comedy, although it was not so funny for the Government. Their Lordships having passed through the lobbies to indicate their vote and having returned to the House and being again seated, a member of the Government, Lord Granville, wearing his top hat (necessary then, to raise a point of order) remained seated. He spoke up to say that one noble Baron, Lord Ravensworth, was not in the House when the question had been put, and he (Lord Granville) therefore moved that the noble Lord's vote be disallowed. Though the formalities now indulged in were not without an amusing appearance, Lord Granville's point was important, for the voting had obviously been a close thing.

Lord Derby, the Leader of the Opposition, then rose to play his card. He said that he thought the objection was hardly one to be pressed, but he would give Lord Granville the advantage of it. But Lord Derby was not being as magnanimous as might appear, for he then drew attention to another irregularity, as he alleged.

A noble Peer, Lord Colchester (a Tory), had informed him that the Tellers had left the Bar before he could register his vote. Lord Bessborough, who had acted as Teller for the Whigs, said the Tellers had waited for a moment or two, and if Lord Colchester chose to remain behind it was not their duty to wait for him. Lord Granville now in his turn graciously conceded to the Tory Leader's request, and agreed that Lord Colchester's vote should be allowed. So, Lord Colchester's vote against the Government was included.

These procedural matters being settled, the result of the vote was then declared as follows:

Content (with Lord Chelmsford's motion)	43
Not content	42
Majority for Lord Chelmsford's motion	1

The Government had been defeated by one vote. The result was greeted with much cheering and laughter from the Opposition benches.

Thus, thanks to Lord Chelmsford, and his friends behind the scenes, the British public learnt from newspaper reports the next day much more than they had hitherto known about the captives and the Government's attitude to the problem, and, furthermore, the papers relating to it, which Lord Russell had been so eager should not see the light of day, were to be published. They were in due course widely reproduced by the British Press, and the printed copies of the papers, in book form, went to adorn many libraries, with the title: *Papers relating to the Imprisonment of British Subjects in Abyssinia. Presented to the House of Lords by Command of Her Majesty in pursuance of their Address dated May 23, 1865*. It was the first of the Blue Books on the captives, but not the last.

19

THE THUNDERER AND THE HERALD

(1865)

The House of Lords debate of 23 May 1865 was extensively reported in the Press the following day. The ample newspaper reports could hardly escape the notice of even the casual reader, and the principal papers gave the debate full coverage on their parliamentary page, as well as some mention in their news pages. Thus *The Times*, in an editorial of nearly a column and a half, thundered:

> The wrongs of the captives in Abyssinia must surely be now avenged. If they have suffered grievously, their cry for redress has sounded in the august precincts of the House of Lords, and has awakened an echo there. The Government has even been put in a minority of one on the subject of their woes . . . It is true that three British subjects have been imprisoned, and that one of them has been scourged; it is true that they have been deprived of necessary food, have been unable to take needful rest, and, in two instances at least, have been linked by chains only four feet long . . . All this seems certain, but consolation, though slow, has at length arrived. Lord Chelmsford has moved for papers relative to their case, and has beaten the Ministers of the Crown on his motion.

The article then devoted some lines to the procedural events in the House, after which it plunged into the vexed history of the captives.

> The question may still be asked, how it happens that British subjects have found themselves in such an evil case. The question is, unfortunately, more easily asked than answered. The story of their wrongs is, for very sufficient reasons, extremely obscure . . . If we narrate the alleged facts historically, it must be understood that a cloud of doubt, more or less dense, hangs over them all.

Then the article referred to Theodore, and observed:

> The Emperor of Ethiopia is a man of a type sufficiently well-known to us. He has assumed the supreme power, setting aside even the titular Emperor, under the claim that he, too, is descended from the All-wise Solomon. He has *Idées Theodorieuses*. He believes it to be his destiny to restore the Abyssinian Empire to its old limits, if not to extend it still further. His fatalism is, however, tempered by the conviction that Providence is on the side of the strongest battalions. Like all Eastern potentates, he has no other notion of government than that of a pure autocracy, and in spite of a certain sentimental element in his character, he crushes everything and everybody standing in the way of his designs. With all this, he is eagerly desirous of cultivating the English alliance, because he sees in it a help to the accomplishment of his aims . . . Theodore is the cause of the sufferings of the Englishmen whose case Lord Chelmsford brought before the House of Lords . . . They have had the misfortune to thwart some of his plans, or, at least to stand in the way of them.

The Times described Stern's unfortunate encounter with the Emperor, and the imprisonment of Captain Cameron and other Britons, and declared:

> That British subjects should be treated in the way we have described, on such slight provocation, must be acknowledged by all to be very deplorable, and Lord Chelmsford exercised the proper function of a member of the Opposition in inquiring what steps the Government had taken to redress such grievous wrongs.

Then, unaware how inaccurate was its knowledge of some of the facts, *The Times* weighed the action of the Government:

> The reply of Lord Russell must be deemed sufficient to clear the Ministers of the Crown of any negligence or unconcern in the matter. It is clear that, as far as Messrs. Stern and Rosenthal are concerned, they must be held to have voluntarily run the risk of the consequences of what they had written in England; and, however generous may have been the motive of Captain Cameron, he ought not to have quitted his post at Massowah.
>
> The case is one for very strong remonstrance, but had the circumstances been more flagrant than they are no other step could have been recommended at the outset. No one would suggest that a force should be immediately marched into the centre of Abyssinia. The Government took the proper course of despatching Mr Rassam, the Assistant Resident at Aden, to Massowah, whence he has sent messenger after messenger to the Emperor . . .

> When milder measures fail a more forcible method must be adopted, and a military officer has been recently despatched from Aden to Massowah in the hope that his efforts may be attended with better success. Time has not allowed us to hear the result of his mission, which every one must hope will be successful. Should it also fail, it may be proper to adopt another course of action; but so far the country will be of opinion that the Government, in the management of a difficult matter, has not been deficient in zeal or prudence. The vote of the House can only be regarded as an expression of sympathy for the sufferers, and as an assurance that they shall not be neglected.

Several inaccuracies notwithstanding, *The Times* had given a comprehensive account of the main events concerning the captives, and had played a considerable part in bringing their case into public prominence and in ensuring that they should be neither forgotten nor neglected.

Another London paper to devote a long and forthright leading article to the debate was not one to hide its light, and daily along with its title gave the following information to its readers:

> The *Morning Herald*. (First-class Conservative Journal, established 1780). It contains the best Fashionable Intelligence.

The first-class Conservative newspaper did not miss this excellent opportunity to flay the Whig Government and its Foreign Secretary Lord Russell in particular. Contriving to make the most of the Government's defeat by one solitary vote, and elevating a Consul to the diplomatic rank of Minister, the paper's leading article went straight to the attack. In its disparagement of Rassam and praise of Dr Beke, the article could have been written by Dr Beke himself (and he may well have had a hand in it). It declared that the vote for Lord Chelmsford's motion was 'a heavy blow at the credit of Lord Palmerston's Government', and added:

> It amounted to a vote of censure, of the most direct and severest kind, of the foreign policy of Lord Russell. When we remember that our legislators in either House of Parliament are always most indulgent to Ministers in questions of this kind, that even in the ranks of the Opposition there are seldom many who are inclined to press for the publication of diplomatic papers when it is pleaded that it is advisable to withhold them for a time on the ground of the public safety, or in the interest of British subjects, the grave importance of this vote will be at once appreciated. It is felt on all hands that this Abyssinian business has been miserably and shamefully mismanaged, that Lord Russell has been guilty of sins of omission and commission which

could hardly be forgiven in the merest tyro in statecraft, that he is directly and solely responsible for the fact that for eighteen months past a British Minister, with several of his fellow subjects, has been held a prisoner and tortured in an Abyssinian dungeon. Loaded with chains, and fastened to a native captive, Captain Cameron has been rotting out his life, unaided and uncared for. His companions in misfortune have been even worse treated than he . . . All this because Lord Russell, having received a letter addressed to Her Majesty the Queen by the Emperor Theodorus, contemptuously refused to answer it for more than eighteen months. When this bald and damning fact is alleged against him, Lord Russell feebly pleads that he was placed in a dilemma by the supposed desire on the part of the Emperor of Abyssinia to engage this country on his side in a contemplated war with the Egyptians and the Turks. This excuse will certainly not avail him, as, on his own showing, the letter of the Emperor merely proffered friendship and alliance, and made no mention of such a war. Lord Russell not only gave just cause of offence by refusing to answer it, he added the further insult to the susceptibility of the Oriental potentate of authorising a despatch in which Captain Cameron, then actually representing the British Court at Gondar, was curtly remanded to the Turkish port at Massowah. If it was possible under the circumstances to add to this list of blunders the chance of doing it was not lost sight of by our Foreign Minister. He refused to enlist the services of Dr Beke, the man in all the world the best acquainted with Abyssinia . . . and sent over to Massowah an Armenian, a former assistant of Mr Layard at Nineveh, who, having no European prestige or standing, made nothing of his mission. The Emperor, who had imprisoned a British Minister, and beaten British subjects, was now approached in an abject manner with presents and propitiatory letters. Lord Russell's politeness was a good many months too late.

Turning to Theodore's letter the paper observed:

no answer whatever was made to it before June 1864. In every interview which the Consul had with the Emperor indignant reference was made to this despised letter, and we can hardly be surprised to hear that the relations, at first so friendly, between the Emperor and the British representative, grew colder and colder as this injurious delay grew longer.

A little further on the article stated that:

Just at this unfortunate time arrived the luckless despatch, sent through the Consul General in Egypt, directing Captain Cameron to return to his post at Massowah, and interfere no more in the affairs of Abyssinia. It was twelve months after the receipt of the Emperor's letter, of which,

> however, it took no notice whatever. We cannot wonder that the sable monarch, who stands upon his dignity, as Eastern potentates do, should have been incensed at this contemptuous disregard of his offers of friendship. He ordered Captain Cameron to be loaded with heavier chains, he aggravated as far as he could the rigour of his imprisonment, and had him chained to a native night and day. The unfortunate Englishman contrived at last to send a letter to his Government by way of Massowah. He stated that there was no chance of his release unless a formal answer were first sent to the Emperor.

Here the *Morning Herald* launched a frontal attack on the Whig Government. The paper maintained that the story of the captives redounded to the 'eternal disgrace of Lord Russell's Administration', and that for four months a British Minister, with two British missionaries, were deliberately left by our Government to languish in prison, exposed to the foulest indignities, and to a daily and nightly torture most horrible to contemplate, and it added:

> After this – as if Lord Russell, indifferent to the safety of English subjects, utterly careless of the vindication of our honour . . . had been carefully studying the art of 'how not to do it' – instead of sending Dr Beke or Mr Coghlan, men of station and influence, who might have procured the release of the captives, sent to Massowah a friend of Mr Layard's, with presents for the Emperor, and the long expected letter with the Queen's sign manual. Mr Rassam was not suffered to leave Massowah, and his mission has been a failure.

Nor could the *Morning Herald* lose this excellent opportunity to point out to its readers what sort of a Whig Foreign Secretary they were having to put up with:

> Who is there that, after reading this narrative, does not agree with Lord Chelmsford, that 'this country has been placed in a painful and humiliating position, not merely in the eyes of Europe and America, but in the eyes of Africa also'? We give Lord Russell such credit as is due to his consistency. His policy towards the African potentate is of a piece with that which he has pursued towards Germany and the United States. His rule of conduct is simple enough. When a difference of opinion arises between Great Britain and any foreign country he first insults it and adopts a high tone which he is either unwilling or unable to sustain. When the estrangement is complete he truckles down with tears of penitence in his eyes, and endeavours, too late, to appease the Sovereign or the people whom he has outraged. Having taken no notice of his letter for eighteen months, Lord Russell sends the Emperor of Abyssinia 500 stand of arms. Upon a system of foreign

policy so mean and so paltry as this, the verdict of the country will be the same as the verdict of the Lords. Do the Government mean to liberate the captives in Abyssinia, or is the question of their liberation to be postponed to the hustings of July?

On the following day, 25 May, the *Pall Mall Gazette* published a rather startling report about the captives, based on a letter from Flad at Gafat, dated 16 March, from which it appeared that Theodore had ordered 'a change for the worse' in the captives' treatment. The letter also contained the following extract from a note from Mr Stern: 'As it appears that they have quite forgotten us in Europe, nothing remains for us but to prepare ourselves for the worst – a miserable death.'

This letter caused Lord Chelmsford to question Lord Russell again in the Lords, on 30 May. Quoting the *Pall Mall Gazette*, he asked the Foreign Secretary what was the date of the latest intelligence he had received from Ethiopia; whether Rassam was still at Massawa; and whether any steps had been taken to send any other mission to the Emperor and if so whether it would be accompanied by presents.

Lord Russell immediately replied, but it was one of those occasions when the frail little man was scarcely audible, and *Hansard* reported that he 'was understood to say' that the Government's latest accounts from Ethiopia were dated 28 April, when Mr Rassam reported that he had sent several messengers to the Emperor, and that rumours of additional hardships imposed upon the prisoners did not appear well founded. At that date Mr Rassam was still waiting to fulfil his mission.

The Lords, as well as the readers of the *Pall Mall Gazette*, now had an idea of how abandoned the distant prisoners felt. And it was clear that Lord Chelmsford, who had now raised the question of the captives three times in the House of Lords, was not going to let the subject, or Lord Russell, rest.

20

NEVER MEANT TO REPLY
(1865)

A mistake by the Foreign Secretary in the House of Lords debate of 23 May provided an opportunity for Lord Chelmsford to raise the matter of the captives again, on 13 June 1865. In the earlier debate Lord Russell had said that in a memorandum to the Foreign Office, Sir William Coghlan had expressed the opinion that a British mission should not be sent to Theodore until *after* the captives had been liberated. When Sir William read this statement he saw he had been misrepresented, and this he pointed out to certain people. The Foreign Secretary's error was duly brought to the notice of Lord Chelmsford, who challenged Lord Russell about it.

Lord Chelmsford told the House that a gallant friend of his had received a letter, dated 3 June, from Sir William which he proceeded to read out, with little apparent concern that he was disclosing details of a memorandum which might reasonably have been considered confidential. Sir William said that although he had kept no copy of his memorandum he was fairly sure what he had said, and in any case intended to say:

> that a mission of some dignity should be sent with an answer to the King's letter, and, as there would be an awkwardness in Her Majesty's recognising the fact of the captivity of her subjects, it would be expedient to make no mention of it in the answer, but leave the Envoy to find it out, and, by the exercise of the large discretion to be accorded to him, to effect their release before he proceeded to the complimentary part of his mission, as he could not make any presents and pay compliments while the captives were kept.
>
> But since the subject had been largely and publicly discussed . . . the Queen's letter must now recognise the fact, and the Envoy should be empowered to obtain their release by any means which may appear to him most suitable.

Having thus disclosed the tactics which had been recommended to the Foreign Office, Lord Chelmsford said that there was a further passage in the letter which he felt the writer had not intended to make public. This said, Lord Chelmsford proceeded to do so by reading it out to their Lordships: 'Mr Rassam's efforts appear to have failed . . . There is no disguising the fact that the long delay has added to the difficulty, but that difficulty must be encountered and overcome.' Lord Chelmsford thus also cast doubts on the emissary whom the Foreign Secretary had appointed. He had certainly made use of the letter, and extracted enough and more than enough for his purpose.

Lord Russell immediately rose to reply. He admitted that it would appear that he was mistaken in his earlier understanding of Sir William's memorandum. But, he added, it appeared:

> a very extraordinary proceeding to send out an English mission to go humbly before the King and ask him to receive presents while our Consul and other Europeans are still in custody . . . The subject is attended with considerable difficulty; but I shall be ready to adopt any means that may appear feasible for the liberation of the captives.

With this assurance Lord Russell concluded his reply. But this was not the end of the discussion.

All the exchanges on the captives that had taken place so far in the House of Lords had been exclusively between Lords Chelmsford and Russell, but now another noble Lord entered into the discussion. He was the Earl of Malmesbury, who had been Foreign Secretary in Lord Derby's first Government, and had exchanged despatches with Consul Plowden, some four or five years previously. Lord Malmesbury was still a prominent member of the Tory Party. The suffering captives in Ethiopia, who felt themselves so much abandoned, were in fact finding powerful friends in England – though little did they know it. Lord Malmesbury asked the Foreign Secretary whether the report was true, which he had heard on what he believed to be good authority, that:

> the unfortunate mistake through which the letter of the King was detained for some months did not arise in the Foreign Office, but in the India Office. If this is the fact I think the public ought to know it; for as respects the dignity of this country, this imprisonment of the Consul is one of the most important events which I remember to have occurred in our diplomatic history.
>
> It is true that a Consul does not stand in the same rank as an Ambassador, but he occupies an official position to which he is

> appointed by the Crown, and his person is always considered as sacred as that of an Ambassador.
>
> I do not say the noble Earl [Lord Russell] has been remiss in this matter; but I do not think he has been as prompt in vindicating the rights of a British subject as the case demands . . .
>
> I do not know whether the Noble Earl is of opinion that his arm is not long enough to reach Abyssinia. But if so it comes to this, that the Queen cannot be advised to send her servants to places too far away to be reached by the arm of England, because if Ambassadors or Consuls are sent to such places, disgrace may fall upon this country, to say nothing of the cruelties which may be perpetrated upon individuals.

Lord Russell then rose a second time to reply to Opposition criticism, but he dealt only with the impracticability of sending an armed force into Ethiopia:

> As to inducing the King of Abyssinia by force to give up these captives, the noble Earl [Malmesbury] knows that the whole country is now disturbed by civil war; and there are three or four different pretenders in possession of different points endeavouring to force the King into a corner. Instead of sending one ship we should have to send three or four, with some three or four thousand men, who would have to march through a hot climate before they could reach the King. On the other hand, I believe it is the opinion of those best able to judge, that if we were to send any mission to the King of Abyssinia he would probably imprison the persons composing it, with a view to forcing us to take his part against his rivals.

So Russell replied to his critic, but he did not answer Lord Malmesbury's question whether Theodore's letter had lain at the India Office for 'some months'. Apparently none of the Peers, at least those outside the Government, knew that the letter had been detained at the India Office not merely some months, but over a year, which might have been a good point to belabour not one, but two Whig ministers, the head of the India Office as well as the head of the Foreign Office; but the point was not pressed, and the Lords passed to the consideration of a Government Bill for closing public-houses at night.

The next day, 14 June, the parliamentary reports in the Press included the discussion about the captives. But within a few days the public were to learn a good deal more. The papers the Lords had asked for, on the initiative of Lord Chelmsford, were published as a Command Paper on 26 June.

The first document was Russell's own original letter of instruction to 'Captain Cameron, British Consul at Massowah, upon his proceeding to his Consulate', dated 2 February 1861, and the last a long memorandum from Dr Beke, dated 19 May 1865. In his memorandum, the doctor gave some interesting economic statements, for example that the cotton plant which had 'suddenly caused the wealth of Egypt was introduced into that country from Upper Ethiopia only forty years ago', and suggestions, such as laying a telegraph line from Khartoum through Ethiopia to the Red Sea and Aden. But the memorandum had one main purpose. After telling Lord Russell the proper way to persuade Theodore, Dr Beke came to the point, saying, 'I once more beg leave most respectfully to tender my humble service to Her Majesty's Government.' If it was objected that he did not occupy any official position, he took the liberty of reminding his Lordship 'that the late Richard Cobden, though holding no official post, was not thereby disqualified from acting as mediator between the two most powerful nations in the world, (England and France); and if Theodore attached importance to uniforms, 'I have for many years held the Commission, and I am consequently entitled to wear the uniform of a Deputy-Lieutenant, which (if I mistake not) gives me a rank equivalent to a Lieutenant-Colonel in the Army.' The Command Paper also included the *Memorandum by Brigadier-General* [Sir William] *Coghlan on the Abyssinian Difficulty, and how best to get out of it*, which urged up-grading the British mission to Emperor Theodore, in connection with which he offered his services.

If Dr Beke and Sir William had different ideas about the composition of a new mission, they agreed in opposing the use of force. Beke said, 'It is not to be expected that the British government will go to war with the Emperor of Abyssinia for the purpose of compelling him to set the captives free'; Coghlan wrote: 'The existing difficulty is one which cannot be surmounted by force.'

There was another valuable document, the by then much referred to letter of King Theodore to Queen Victoria, which was thus made public for the first time, as well as a long report of 1854 by Consul Plowden, which was almost encyclopaedic in its information about Ethiopia and the Ethiopians.

The Command Paper thus made public not only facts relevant to the freeing of the captives, its immediate concern, but also more information about Ethiopia than had been published for many years. In regard to its prime purpose, however, there was a serious omission. Lord Chelmsford, and indeed the Lords' Address to the

Queen, had specifically asked for a 'Copy of Report made by Captain Cameron from Bogos on or about March 1863, and of the Orders in consequence of such Report sent to him by the Consul-General in Egypt or from the Foreign Office'.

Since all despatches exchanged between a Consul and the Foreign Office would be confidential, it is interesting that Lord Chelmsford should have been able to name despatches so accurately. Be that as it may, Consul Cameron's specified despatch was not included among the papers published; indeed no letters at all from Captain Cameron were included, although the critical despatches from the Foreign Secretary and Mr Murray telling him that Her Majesty's Government did not approve of his proceedings, and telling him to return to Massawa, and stay there, were published.

On 27 June, the Command Paper was extensively reproduced in the newspapers so that the public was at last able to read Theodore's letter to Queen Victoria in the English translation that had accompanied it, as well as documents bearing on the captivity of their Consul in Ethiopia.

It was now almost the end of June 1865, and the parliamentary session was drawing to a close, but that summer was of special significance, for the life of Parliament was also drawing to a close. Electioneering was already in the air, and the Press and public, and not least MPs, were thinking of a General Election soon to come.

If the cause of the captives was to be further voiced in Parliament that year, if the Government was to be castigated in Parliament for not having secured their freedom, there was little time left. But a new champion was to hand, this time in the Commons, and he was fortunate in securing a debate shortly after the publication of the official papers about the captives. He thus had the advantage of having information which other speakers, outside the Government, had not hitherto enjoyed. The documents were published on a Tuesday and the debate was on the Friday.

The new spokesman for the captives was another Tory lawyer and a leading member of the Opposition, Sir Hugh Cairns, an Irishman, Member for Belfast, who had been Solicitor-General and later Attorney-General in Lord Derby's Governments. As in the Lords, so in the Commons, the captives now had a spokesman who was a leading Parliamentarian.

On 30 June Sir Hugh opened the debate by saying: 'I rise to call attention to a matter of great interest to a considerable number of families, which would be a subject of interest to the whole country if the circumstances were generally known.' He reminded the House that Consul Cameron and the other prisoners had been confined for 18 or 19 months. In this statement, Sir Hugh, lawyer though he was, fell into the oft-recurring confusion regarding Cameron's accreditation, for he referred to him as 'the English Consul accredited by Her Majesty to Abyssinia', overlooking Murray's letter to Cameron, published only a few days before, reminding him that 'you hold no representative character in Abyssinia'.

Sir Hugh gave an account of the prisoners' conditions, and commented: 'The House will allow that this is a strange and startling state of circumstances to have occurred in reference to an English Consul and a number of English subjects.' He then embarked on a review of Ethiopian history, in which he referred to the Ras Ali treaty, pointed out that it provided for the reception and protection of one another's envoys by Her Britannic Majesty and the Emperor of Ethiopia, and asked, 'What was the origin of the Emperor's change of feeling' towards England? This brought him to Theodore's letter to Queen Victoria, 'written in very intelligible style, but of course presenting all the pecularities which you would expect to find in an autograph communication proceeding from an Oriental Sovereign'. Having read out most of the letter, he pointed out that the Emperor proposed to send an envoy or ambassador to Queen Victoria. He would not presume to offer an opinion as to whether the Emperor's proposal ought to have been accepted or not – except that he found in the treaty:

> a positive stipulation on our part to receive and give every protection to any ambassador or envoy whom the Sovereign of Abyssinia might see fit to appoint. Yet one thing was, I think, incumbent on Her Majesty's Government, and the omission of which, I fear, has led to serious consequences. King Theodore, I should have thought, was entitled to an answer in some shape or form.

Sir Hugh observed that the answer to the Emperor was in fact sent on 26 May 1864, after a delay of more than 15 months.

The Tory Member then began a criticism of Rassam's appointment which was to be the beginning of a sustained attack on that envoy's mission, an attack in which Dr Beke played no small part. Sir Hugh declared that when the answer was at last despatched:

> it was not sent through any British Consul in Egypt, but through Mr Rassam, our assistant resident at Aden, himself a subject of Turkey –

> the very Power towards which, if the Emperor of Abyssinia was not actually at war with it, he at all events entertained feelings of considerable hostility.

Sir Hugh contended that it was Theodore's sense of injury at not receiving a reply from Queen Victoria, and Britain's apparent change of feelings towards him, that caused him to arrest Cameron and the others. In justifying this contention, Sir Hugh quoted from Sir William Coghlan's memorandum, which had just been published in the Command Paper. He also quoted from a letter which he said came from Egypt (but without saying from whom): 'Theodore is reported to have expressed himself very indignantly that the Queen's Government should have sent an Asiatic – a mere subordinate – on a mission to him and does not intend to take the least notice of him.' Sir Hugh said that in fact: 'He has not taken the least notice of him. The Emperor has refused to receive him and has even treated it as an aggravation of the first offence he supposed he had received.' Summing up his criticism Sir Hugh said that even admitting that 'the acts of the King of Abyssinia were a flagrant outrage of International Law', nevertheless Britain could 'confess that there had been a certain amount of neglect, a certain degree of indecorous treatment of a Sovereign with whom we had a treaty of alliance, in refusing to answer a despatch sent by him to the Sovereign of this country for a period of a year and a half'.

It was Sir Hugh's opinion, that, after making that admission, the Government should send out an Embassy of a nature acceptable to Theodore. At all events, said Sir Hugh in conclusion: 'some active and energetic steps should be taken to set these unfortunate people at liberty, and I do hope some announcement may be made which will relieve the anxiety which is felt by many throughout the country on this subject'.

Henry Layard rose to reply for the Government. He began by assuring the House that if he and the Foreign Secretary had hitherto abstained from entering into discussions about the captives the reason was 'simply this:- In the first place, we feared lest anything should be said which might have been conveyed – and it certainly would have been conveyed – to the Emperor of Abyssinia' which might have led to worse suffering for the captives or even death; and secondly, 'it would scarcely be fair to Consul Cameron, before receiving a full explanation from him, that statements should be made reflecting on his official character'. All of which was very fine and noble of Henry Layard, as might be expected of him, but before he ended his speech he had himself said a number of things that would have angered Theodore, had they been conveyed to him, and according to Layard they 'certainly would have been conveyed'; but the Under-Secretary, anticipating criticism on this score, placed the responsibility 'upon those who have forced the Government to make these explanations'.

What Layard may have meant by Government statements that might 'reflect' on Cameron's character is not clear. In so far as Cameron's official conduct was concerned, Lord Russell, and following him, *The Times*, had already expressed criticism, without much show on the part of the Minister to defend his Consul pending receiving a full explanation. The Command Paper had also published official criticisms, without publishing Cameron's explanation.

Entering upon his main theme, Layard then said: 'I do not wish to go into a history of Abyssinia. I refer members to two articles in *Revue des Deux Mondes*, by Mr Lejean, who was French Consul in Abyssinia at the same time that Mr Cameron was there.' What expectation Layard had of honourable members proceeding to lay hands on the French periodical and studying the relevant articles is not now very apparent. However, having by this device spared the House much history, he felt able quickly to refer to the Ras Ali treaty and tell the House where the Honourable and Learned Gentleman (Sir Hugh Cairns) was wrong. There was now no treaty between England and Ethiopia, he claimed, for on coming to the throne, the first thing Theodore did was to 'refuse to recognise the treaty entered into by his predecessor'. Referring to Theodore's desire to send an Embassy to England, and to Britain's attitude to it, Layard told the House that:

> Before Mr Plowden's death it had become known to us [Her Majesty's Government] that the King of Abyssinia desired to send a mission to Europe, and this mission was heralded by letters written, not only to Her Majesty, but to the Emperor of Russia, the Emperor of the French and some of the German potentates, calling upon them to help him in a great war against the Mohammedans . . . Her Majesty's Government had of course no desire to engage in any undertaking of the kind, and accordingly wrote to Consul Plowden that they would receive no mission from King Theodore except he gave 'a distinct assurance that he renounced all ideas of conquest in Egypt and at Massowah'.

He further declared that 'Her Majesty's Government would subject themselves to grave suspicions if they received an Embassy from a Sovereign whose designs against the Sultan, Her Majesty's Ally, were previously known to them.'

Here Henry Seymour (who had put the first parliamentary question about the captives) interrupted, to ask whether Layard was reading from a despatch which had been laid on the table. The Under-Secretary replied that this despatch had not so far been published, but, if members so desired, it would be.

After referring to the Foreign Office instructions to Consul Plowden to leave Ethiopia and return to Massawa, to the death of Plowden before he could receive those orders, and to Theodore's subsequent slaughter of prisoners taken in battle, the Under-Secretary spoke words which would hardly have pleased the Ethiopian sovereign. Of that slaughter Layard said:

> All this in revenge for the death of Consul Plowden, who had no business at the place where he was killed, who had been warned against taking any part in the affairs of the country, and met his death mainly through neglecting his instructions. It is not a pleasant thing to reflect that 1,500 innocent persons, more or less, have been put to the sword to revenge the death of one British subject; it is not a thing one can think of without horror.

On coming to the appointment of Captain Cameron, Layard recalled that:

> He was directed most positively to refrain from interfering in any way whatever in the internal affairs of the country; to refrain from mixing himself up with intrigues or attaching himself to any party in the country; he was merely to go to the King to deliver the letter and the presents, and then return to Massowah, and there promote by every means in his power the trade of England with Abyssinia.

Layard here turned to the three missionary societies working in Ethiopia, the Swiss, the British and the French (and Italians) who, he was sorry to say, 'as usual', were 'intensely jealous of one another' and 'the King had no love for any of them'.

Returning to British affairs the Under-Secretary told the House how Consul Cameron was at first well received by Theodore, but was later given hints to get on his way; but instead of departing he began to open negotiations with the King. Layard said:

> To our great astonishment, we one day received at the Foreign Office a despatch from Captain Cameron informing us that he was entering

into formal and official negotiations with the King . . . Now, that was altogether contrary to the instructions he had received. So far was Consul Cameron from being instructed to propose an embassy to England from the King, that he was distinctly told that Her Majesty's Government would not entertain the idea of a mission unless he gave up all idea of conquering the Turks and invading Turkish territory. So Consul Cameron was not justified in making such a proposal . . .

It is one of those things you do not like to state in a person's absence, but I have reasons to think that this letter was suggested by Consul Cameron, who wished to come to this country with the embassy. I am quite under that impression . . . and the letter bears that construction.

The King, after writing this letter, ordered Consul Cameron to leave Gondar at once, and to go to Massowah. In spite of this warning Consul Cameron remained – most imprudently remained – in the country.

Shortly afterwards we received a despatch from him, stating that he had gone . . . to the Egyptian frontier, and had extended the protection of the British flag to the tribes on that boundary.

All this was so contrary to his instructions and so alarming that we wrote out without delay to desire him to refrain from all interference in Abyssinian affairs, to confine himself to his duty of promoting commercial relations with this country, and to return at once to his post at Massowah.

As for Theodore's letter, Layard declared:

A great deal has been said as to no answer having been sent to the letter from the King. I will ask any impartial person whether – having Consul Cameron's despatches such as I have described them before us – knowing that that letter originated after a distinct understanding with the King that Her Majesty's Government would not receive a mission until he had given up all idea of conquest upon Turkey – after the King had rejected the treaty which authorised him to send a mission to Europe – whether, under such circumstances, we were under any obligation to answer that letter at all?

I can only say that even now, after what has passed, if the letter were put into my hands I should say it did not require an answer. The first letter of the King had been answered, and we did not wish that Consul Cameron should come home with a mission from the King.

Having no wish to answer that letter, we sent it to the India Office to know whether they wished to answer it, because it must be remembered, our relations with Abyssinia have been at all times more an Indian than an Imperial question. The India Office had, it appears, no

> wish to do so. They did not think it necessary that a mission should be sent to this country, the object of which was to get us to go to war with Turkey.

Turning to the question of Rassam, Layard remarked that the envoy's 'character and position' had been 'much misunderstood'. Though a 'native of Mossul' he had been brought up in Britain, had been educated at Oxford, and was in 'manners, dress and appearance like an English gentleman'. Adding a personal note Layard continued: 'He was with me during the whole of my explorations in Assyria, and without Mr Rassam's assistance this country would not, perhaps, now be in possession of that valuable collection of Assyrian antiquities which are deposited in the British Museum.' Little did Layard know that the Rassam affair would later further greatly enrich that museum.

If Cameron had been unfairly treated by the Under-Secretary of State for Foreign Affairs in the debate in the Commons, the imprisoned Consul had a ready friend in Lord Chelmsford who now was armed with the information contained in the documents which he had forced the Government to publish. Only four days after Layard spoke critically of Cameron in the Commons, the ex-Chancellor came to the latter's defence in the Lords.

The rules of procedure then prevailing permitted a Peer to discuss in the Lords things said in the Commons, even though he might not specifically name that 'other place'. Thus on 4 July, Lord Chelmsford rose to launch an attack on Layard for what he had said about Consul Cameron, with a few thrusts at Lord Russell and the Foreign Office thrown in. Lord Chelmsford asserted that:

> a discussion had taken place elsewhere in which great injustice had been done to Consul Cameron. In that debate circumstances were so jumbled together, facts were so misplaced, and such a mist was cast over all these transactions, that it was impossible to obtain a clear view of the circumstances; and that had been done for the purpose of exculpating the Foreign Office from the blame which attached to them, and of loading Captain Cameron with the obloquy, if he might so call it, of having been the author of his own sufferings.

Lord Chelmsford then delved into that early and constant cause of confusion: was Captain Cameron British Consul at Massawa, or in Abyssinia? Had Layard been correct in asserting that, being Consul at Massawa, Cameron had no justification at all in staying on in Abyssinia once he had delivered the letters and presents to

Theodore? Lord Chelmsford's plain retort was: 'The real fact was that he was accredited Consul in Abyssinia, as Mr Plowden had been before him, and this was clearly established by the Treaty of 1849.'

Of the documents recently published, the first was Lord Russell's letter of instruction to Cameron just before he left England. This the noble Lord read out in full to enlighten their Lordships, if they could take it all in, but also with the result that it appeared in *Hansard*, taking up more than a column in small print, and where it was more likely to be widely read than in the White Paper. In this somewhat diffuse letter Lord Russell indicated certain things which the Consul should or should not do. His first duty on arriving at Massawa was to make himself 'acquainted with the general state of political affairs in Abyssinia', but he was 'to abstain from any course of proceedings by which a preference for either party [in the recent civil war] should be imputable' to him. He was to 'engage in the promotion of amicable arrangements between the rival candidates for power', while avoiding involvement in religious rivalries. He was also instructed that it was his 'duty closely to watch any proceedings which may tend to alter the state of possession either on the sea coast or in the interior of the country', and had to keep Her Majesty's Government 'fully informed', and was told that 'in addition to matters of a political and commercial nature', he should 'pay particular attention to any traffic in slaves', 'report fully upon the same', and 'impress upon any native rulers who may directly or indirectly encourage or permit such a traffic, the abhorrence in which it is held by the British Government'. Lord Chelmsford asked his fellow peers: 'How would it have been possible for Consul Cameron to have acted up to those instructions if he had been constantly resident at Massowah, which was 400 miles from Gondar, the capital of Abyssinia?'

He made a further telling point. He informed their Lordships that Cameron, before leaving England, had been shown all the official correspondence of his predecessor, who, said Lord Chelmsford, 'had been continually in Abyssinia', and had 'received an allowance during the last twelve years of his life for travelling expenses in that country. Captain Cameron, therefore, naturally thought he was following the footsteps of his predecessor, and acting under his instructions, remained in Abyssinia.' Lord Chelmsford also read from another of Consul Cameron's now published despatches, in which the Consul said that (soon after his arrival at the royal camp) he had told the Emperor he was deputed to discuss with him '(1) a treaty; and (2) sending an embassy to England. I offered to take these up where Mr Plowden had left them.'

Lord Chelmsford next quoted Mr Layard's critical observation that Cameron's action was 'altogether contrary to the instructions he had received', and that the Consul had been 'distinctly told that Her Majesty's Government would not entertain the idea of a mission unless he gave up all ideas of conquering the Turks and invading Turkish territory'. Lord Chelmsford challenged this, pertinently asking: 'If such instructions were ever given to Captain Cameron, why had they not been laid upon the table?'

The noble Lord then came to the vexed question of the long delay in answering the Emperor's letter. He reminded their Lordships that the letter reached England in February 1863, but was answered in May 1864. He then quoted Layard's defence that the letter 'originated after a distinct understanding with the King that Her Majesty's Government would not receive a mission until he had given up all idea of conquest upon Turkey – after rejecting a treaty which authorised him to send a mission to Europe' – and 'whether any person would have thought it necessary to answer that letter at all'.

Lord Chelmsford quoted these statements to challenge them, and to say that he would 'like to know when it had been formally communicated to the King that we would not go to war with Turkey. When had a treaty been negotiated which authorised him to send a mission to Europe?' He would also like to know 'when an understanding had been come to with the King that a mission from him would not be received by Her Majesty's Government till he had given up all idea of conquest upon Turkey'. He added that 'he did not find any suggestion to that effect in the papers before their Lordships'.

Lord Chelmsford then challenged Lord Russell directly. Having quoted his Under-Secretary's statement in the Commons, that even now if the letter were put in his hands he would say it 'did not require an answer', he asked the Foreign Secretary, sitting opposite him in the Lords: 'Did the noble Earl agree with him, and say that even now, after what had passed, if the letter were put into his hands, he should say it did not require an answer?' Despite Layard's insistence that Cameron had brought all this trouble upon himself, it was still Lord Chelmsford's belief 'that the greater part of the misery and mischief endured by the captives had been brought about in consequence of the King's letter not having been answered'.

Lord Chelmsford then turned to measures for the rescue of the captives. From the beginning he had maintained, he said, that it was the duty of the Government to send out at the earliest possible time a mission, headed by an Englishman, with suitable presents to the Emperor, to procure their release, but 'unfortunately, Mr Rassam was appointed to this delicate mission'. And Lord Chelmsford again asserted his belief that the appointment of Rassam, 'being an Asiatic, and not a European', destroyed any hope of success, 'and he thought results so far had confirmed this view'. So, he returned to his recommendation of 'persons of experience and knowledge of the country . . . and who entertained sanguine prospects of success', and he named Sir William Coghlan and, inevitably, Dr Beke.

Then Lord Chelmsford came to the muskets – which the Foreign Office had been careful to instruct should go in cases so marked as not to reveal their contents, lest this should offend the Egyptians who were unfriendly to Theodore, if not to Ethiopia. He pointedly observed that on a previous occasion Lord Russell had said that it would not do to send presents to Theodore because it would lead to a belief on his part that they were to be procured by ill-using foreigners, but now he understood that the noble Earl had sent out 500 stand of arms as a present to the Emperor. Therefore everything that originally ought not to have been done had since been done.

He concluded by saying:

> It was an insult not to answer the letter of the King of Abyssinia for fifteen months, and the only reparation was by sending a mission, and thus endeavouring to release the captives. It was a reproach to England to allow these persons to languish in prison without using our utmost endeavours, and those pointed out by proper and experienced persons, to endeavour at least, though late, to relieve them from that misery which was mainly attributable to the noble Earl's conduct.

Lord Russell immediately rose to reply to these criticisms, and began by challenging Lord Chelmsford's motives, saying:

> My Lords, the noble and learned Lord has to-night, as on a former occasion, shown himself to be entirely regardless of the safety of Consul Cameron and other persons imprisoned by the Emperor of Abyssinia,

> in his solicitude that the blame on this subject should be attributed to the conduct of the Government.

Then he came to the Foreign Office's standing grievance against Cameron, with this accusation: 'It was obvious . . . from the facts already made known that Consul Cameron had not executed the instructions which he had received from Her Majesty's Government.' To substantiate this charge he recalled the then recent history of Anglo-Ethiopian relations. He began with the Ras Ali Treaty of 1849, admitting that 'it was part of that treaty that a mission should be sent from Abyssinia to this country'. However, he pointed out 'that on November 27, 1855, Lord Clarendon [the then Foreign Secretary] wrote to say that, though the establishment of friendly relations between the two countries would be of great advantage, and, though the Queen would have much pleasure in receiving a mission from the Emperor, yet it was solely on the condition that His Majesty should give a distinct assurance that he "renounced all idea of conquest in Egypt and at Massowah" '. Lord Russell continued: 'as Mr Plowden received that despatch in 1856, and as he lived there until 1860, there is every reason to believe that it was communicated to the Emperor'.

Lord Russell then turned to the question of Dr Beke, who was always being put forward by the Opposition as one of the best men to send out, and as Lord Russell only too well knew, was also always putting himself forward as the very best person for the task. To counter these proposals Lord Russell adroitly quoted Dr Beke as having written about Theodore's 'hypocrisy, treachery, and also cruelty'. Lord Russell then pointed out that Stern had been imprisoned for writing 'a similar account' of the King. 'And yet the noble and learned Lord recommended that I should accept the generous and courageous offer of Dr Beke, and send out a man who is almost certain to be imprisoned by the King', for Dr Beke's writings were 'certain to be made known to the King by the enemies of this country'.

Lord Russell was not accurate in the sequence of events of how Stern was made to suffer for what he had written about Theodore, but he was near enough to the truth to have a valid argument. Moreover, it was a good apparent justification for not sending Dr Beke, although in fact it was unlikely that the Foreign Office would have sent the pushful Dr Beke at any price. But Lord Russell had scored a point.

He now stated his Government's attitude, or what he maintained it was, to the Emperor's letter. Recalling that Lord Clarendon had told Consul Plowden in 1855 that the British Government would not sanction any proceedings by the King of Abyssinia against Egypt and the Turks, Lord Russell quoted from the final passage of Theodore's letter. The King had said of the Turks: 'I have told them to leave the land of my ancestors. They refuse. I am now going to wrestle with them.' That is, Lord Russell said, 'he meant to go to war'.

He next quoted the earlier passage in the letter in which Theodore had referred to the death of Plowden, 'and my late Grand Chamberlain, the Englishman Bell', and had gone on to say: 'my enemies, thinking to injure me, killed these my friends. But by the power of God I have exterminated those enemies not leaving one alive, though they were of my own family, that I may get, by the power of God, your friendship.' Lord Russell commented:

> These persons . . . were massacred in cold blood after they had been defeated in battle and had surrendered to the King. Now, was Her Majesty to be advised that putting to death persons in this manner was the way in which to gain Her Majesty's friendship? It was impossible for us to take any such course. I cannot imagine that the simple delay of a letter would, without other causes, account for the King's anger . . . we all know that the Abyssinians are most arbitrary in their notions of government; there is, therefore, no saying upon what slight grounds they may have taken offence, and Her Majesty's Government plainly cannot be responsible for causes which may induce the Government of that country to imprison a British Consul. But what we do know and what we are quite certain is that Consul Cameron, having had special directions not to interfere in the rivalries of parties in that country, did go to Gondar, and did interfere in local affairs. He says himself that he saved many lives there. But he did this by making himself a partisan, thereby disobeying the orders he had received . . . We did what we considered best under the circumstances. Consul Cameron himself points out that Mr Rassam was a person of great importance in the place from which he came, next in position to the Governor, and therefore likely to be acceptable to the King of Abyssinia.

At this point Lord Chelmsford interrupted, and the following exchanges took place:

> Lord Chelmsford: May I ask the noble Earl where the statement that he is now making is to be found?

Lord Russell: If the noble and learned Lord wishes for detailed information as to all the sources of information possessed by the Foreign Office as to the character, position and qualifications of the messengers whom they think proper to employ, the inquiry, I am afraid, will be a wide one.
Lord Chelmsford: I only asked for information in the particular case.

But Lord Russell brushed this aside: 'The information that we received satisfied us that the position of Mr Rassam was what I have already stated.' He then passed on to the delay Rassam was encountering at Massawa, by attributing this to several possible causes, 'one of these being that the King was unable to guarantee the safety of the persons conveying the letter, nearly the whole of the country about Massowah being occupied by forces in insurrection against his authority'.

Then Lord Russell expressed a curious speculation of the Foreign Office:

> Another explanation, and the one we are inclined to adopt, is that he may have wished to get a large British force into his power in order that he might threaten to put them to death in case the Queen did not comply with his wish to take part in operations directed against Turkey. To carry on that war was avowed originally to have been his object; it was so stated in his own letter. And what would the noble and learned Lord, anxious to lay blame on Her Majesty's Government, have said if we had actually sent a large mission to the King of Abyssinia, if the members of that mission had been imprisoned, and if, in an unwholesome country, we had been obliged to undertake warlike measures with a view to accomplish their release? How powerful would then have been the declamations of the noble and learned Lord . . . I trust that a better and safer way of establishing relations with the King of Abyssinia has been adopted by Her Majesty's Government.

Lord Russell next offered a somewhat naïve British view of Ethiopian affairs when he quoted and concurred in an opinion he had received from Sir William Coghlan that taking into account the state of civil war in Ethiopia: 'The probability was that either King Theodore or his enemies would be completely defeated, and in either event negotiations might be entered upon more advantageously than they could be now.'

Referring to presents for the Emperor the Foreign Secretary stated: 'We have pursued a cautious policy. If, without any ransom being required, we hear that the captives have been set free, we shall doubtless think it right to make the King some suitable acknowledgment.' He added: 'We are not, at all events, going to undertake a war on behalf of the King of Abyssinia, nor on behalf of a Consul who did not follow his instructions.'

This, however, was not the end of the debate. The captive Consul did not lack friends, at least in the Lords. When the Foreign Secretary resumed his seat another peer, also on the Government side, rose to defend the gallant Captain. This new champion was Lord Houghton, wealthy, well-connected, of a literary disposition, and one of the minor poets of his day.

Lord Houghton had sat in the House of Commons as the Liberal Member for Pontefract for some 25 years until 1863 when he was elevated to the peerage as the first Baron Houghton. He entered into the debate by observing that he was 'personally acquainted with Consul Cameron', was full of admiration for him, and he felt that he had interfered in the affairs of the country with the best possible intentions. Lord Houghton was also captivated by Dr Beke, and trusted that the Foreign Secretary would not refuse the latter's proposed involvement in Ethiopian affairs.

The final speaker was the former Tory Foreign Secretary, the Earl of Malmesbury, who maintained that 'it was most important to the interest and honour of this country that the captives should be released'. He therefore now joined in pressing that Dr Beke should be employed to establish communication with Theodore. Lord Malmesbury had known Dr Beke for 20 years, and could state that he was a most intelligent man, and possessed the advantage of being on excellent terms with the Emperor.

In Lord Malmesbury's ensuing remarks, which could not have surprised Lord Russell, it was clear that the ever pushful Dr Beke had not been allowing the grass to grow under his feet anywhere. Lord Malmesbury said that:

> Dr Beke has placed in my hands a paper, in which he states that he has not the slightest doubt that he should be able to obtain the liberation of the captives, as well as to convince the Emperor of Abyssinia of the wisdom of cultivating the arts of peace in preference to those of war, and developing the immense resources of his dominion. Earl Russell has no more right to refuse to aid Dr Beke in embarking on so noble a mission than a commanding officer would have to prevent a brave soldier from leading a forlorn hope.

Here the former Foreign Secretary introduced the interesting, if questionable argument: 'It was the duty of the Government to protect British subjects abroad by the arm of England, and we had no right to employ men in such places that that arm could not reach them.'

The Opposition peer concluded with a reference to the fast approaching end of that Parliament, by expressing the hope that the Foreign Secretary would 'earnestly direct his attention during the leisure time which he was about to enjoy to the liberation of the men in question'.

So that debate ended.

21

WILLING HELPERS
(1865)

The members of the London Society for Promoting Christianity amongst the Jews were from time to time reminded of the captives and their uncertain fate. Through its monthly publication, *Jewish Intelligence*, the Society continued to give its members and friends such information as it had about the imprisoned missionaries, and this came mainly from Mr Flad. The news was usually scant, and by the time it reached England, and found its way into print, it was at least three and sometimes even five, months old.

Thus in April 1865 the journal reported that up to the middle of January the prisoners were all well, and that in November of the previous year 'the European prisoners, and 150 native prisoners were conducted in chains to Amba Magdala'. In May the periodical gave a fairly full version of a letter from Mr Flad, in Gafat, dated 16 November 1864, stating: 'Since I last wrote in June this year our circumstances have in no way improved' – for the prisoners were still in the King's camp, but might be sent to a fort, perhaps Magdala. Flad also said that when the Emperor was at Gafat 'our German brethren besought him on their knees three times to liberate the captives, but in vain'. The missionary was meanwhile continuing with his work, and stated that he had lately 'translated three tracts into Amharic'.

May 1865 brought round another Annual Meeting of the Society. It began on the 4th, with the customary annual service again held at St Marylebone Church, on which occasion the sermon was preached by the Archbishop of York. On the following day there was the usual breakfast, and later the Annual Meeting at which the Earl of Shaftesbury again presided. He made little mention of the captives, but left it to others to speak of them. The meeting then considered the far-flung activities of the Society, in Europe and the Middle East, and Ethiopia was only one of its many stations. The question of the captives was nevertheless covered by a special Resolution, which began:

> That this meeting would record its deep sympathy with the captives in Abyssinia. For their sustained faith, and for the preservation of their health, notwithstanding the severity of their captivity, it would fervently thank God, and for their deliverance, it would earnestly ask the continued intercession of the Christian Church . . .

The motion was seconded by the Rev. W. R. Freemantle, who saw in the question of the captives the working of a Divine Will, for he declared, 'There can be no question but that there is a wise and merciful purpose in this sudden reverse in our prospect of evangelising Abyssinia.' He then gave a glowing description of Henry Stern's fine appearance and finer qualities. Aware that the Committee had decided to leave to the British Government all positive action for the release of the captives he concluded: 'We honour and prize the help of diplomatic interference, but let us not trust to that alone. We know that our Noble Chairman [Lord Shaftesbury] will do all that can be done to obtain this interference.' So, seeing the working of a Divine Will in the captivity of their missionaries, but nevertheless hoping for their liberation, and placing faith in prayer, the members of the Society passed on to other business.

Meanwhile the ever-active Dr Beke had made another contribution of his own towards making the case of the captives known to the British public. He wrote a lively pamphlet entitled *The British Captives in Abyssinia*, which was published by Longman, Green, one of London's leading publishers, at the price of 2*s.* 6*d.* It was dated Bekesbourne, 2 February 1865. In this work Dr Beke showed himself remarkably well informed on what was going on in Ethiopia; and he also wrote to the Foreign Secretary offering to help rescue the captives.

In consequence of this letter Dr Beke saw Lord Russell at the Foreign Office on 8 May, and some days later in a letter confirmed what he had said at the interview. He noted that Lord Russell still intended to leave the question of the captives to Rassam, but should the latter fail, he, Dr Beke, would put forward alternative proposals.

There was no restraining Dr Beke. On 7 July he wrote to the Foreign Secretary to say that he was prepared to travel to Ethiopia on his own account. At the foot of this letter, as a guidance for the reply, Lord Russell noted:

> H.M.G. cannot stop him, but he must clearly understand that in Abyssinia he would in no way be acting with the authority of H.M.G.
> Warn him that H.M.G. has private information about the cruel and merciless character of the King which almost leads to the conclusion that he is not in his right mind.
> Make the letter sufficiently civil but clear and to the point.

This note by Lord Russell would seem to be the first suggestion by the British Government that the Emperor might be mad. Her Majesty's Government's 'private information' must almost certainly refer to the letters from the captives Cameron and Stern and from the missionary Flad. But Lord Russell was not quite certain whether Theodore was mad or not, and in his note he committed himself only to saying that his information about the King might *almost* lead to that conclusion. Layard, on 13 July, wrote to Dr Beke on the lines indicated in Lord Russell's note, making it clear that if Dr Beke went to Ethiopia he would be doing so as a private individual, and with no government authority.

Knowing now that he could count on no support or assistance from the Government, Dr Beke addressed a letter to the London Society, on 20 July, telling them that he had decided to proceed to Ethiopia on his own account, and expressing his confidence that the Society would not refuse to help him. The Society's Committee for its part was very conscious how little it could do to secure the release of the captives, whose plight was constantly in its thoughts, and on 21 July it held a special meeting at 16 Lincoln's Inn Fields for prayer on their behalf.

On that same day, Dr Beke, in no prayerful mood, acknowledged direct to Lord Russell the Foreign Office notice that he could expect no Government support. He wrote that he took 'due note' of His 'Lordship's desires', but:

> would beg leave to represent that, so desirous am I, for my own sake, not to be considered as an organ of Her Majesty's Government, that I would hope to be excused for not even offering to be the bearer of despatches from your Lordship to Consul Cameron, on account of the extreme ill-feeling which unhappily exists between the British Government and the Abyssinian monarch.

Beke added that Layard had spoken of 'the cruel and merciless character' of the Emperor 'which almost leads to the conclusion that he is not in his right senses', but Theodore, according to one of the captives, '"considers the members of Her Britannic Majesty's Government" – I trust you will forgive me for daring to repeat the words now lying written before me – "the greatest miscreants that ever breathed" '.

Meanwhile, as time went by with still no progress in the Government's endeavours, certain other people, of whom little was heard but who were closely concerned, became increasingly anxious. These were the captives' relatives. One person not unmindful of their feelings was Dr Beke, who now communicated with several of them. He warmed to his task as self-appointed knight-errant, and a week after his letter to the London Society he followed it with a more specific communication, on 27 July, stating his determination to proceed to Ethiopia as soon as possible 'without counting the risk and regardless of remuneration', but looking to the Christian public to help him defray the cost of his journey and of the presents it would be necessary to take to the Emperor.

By now, towards the end of July 1865, there were three different expeditions officially charged with the task of penetrating into Ethiopia, and a fourth person eager to set off on his own chivalrous journey. First, there was Rassam, bearer of Queen Victoria's letter (amended version), in Massawa with his Aden colleagues, Dr Blanc and young Lieutenant Prideaux. Second, there was Abdul-Melak, bearer of an official letter to the Abun, and supposedly prudently pushing on, somewhere beyond Suakin. Third, William Gifford Palgrave, distinguished traveller of Arabia, so far bearer of no letter, but now, in company with Consul-General Stanton, on his way to Alexandria. Then, fourth, still in England, the restless Dr Beke, scheming his own mission that would – how could it be doubted? – really mollify Theodore and cause him to release his prisoners. The captives were certainly not being forgotten.

The machinations of Dr Beke were seemingly working well, for on 27 July Mr Purday, Mrs Stern's father, called on the Committee of the London Society and showed them a letter which he proposed that relatives of the captives should sign and send to the Foreign Secretary. The Committee saw no harm in this, and Mr Purday proceeded to collect the signatures.

Thus, just about the time that Consul-General Stanton and Mr Palgrave were on their journey to Alexandria – and while Rassam was languishing at Massawa – the Foreign Secretary received a letter, dated 30 July, saying:

We, the friends of these unfortunate people, wrote to Dr Beke to ask him for an interview on the subject of the offer he made to Her Majesty's Government to go out to that country on his own personal responsibility; and in consequence of the great uncertainty in which we have so long been left as to their fate, we have been induced to treat with him respecting his kind offer . . . such a proceeding is not at all intended to interfere with any action which Her Majesty's Government may be taking in the matter, but only to subserve that action, if needful, by additional influence, the object of which arises purely from a strong desire to rescue these our unfortunate friends and relatives from the painful captivity and suffering which they have endured . . .

(Signed)

Charlotte Stern	Wife
Charles Henry Purday	Father-in-law
Charlotte E. Stern }	Daughters
Louisa M. Stern }	
Aletta Cameron	Mother
M. Desborough	Sister to Capt. Cameron
L. Desborough	Brother-in-law
E. Blackall	Sister to Capt. Cameron
A. Blackall	Brother-in-law
L. C. Desborough	Nephew to Capt. Cameron
Mary Ann Purday	Mother-in-law to Mr Stern

And five other in-laws of Rev. Stern.

Lord Russell wrote at the foot of the letter: 'Advise them not to insert articles in the newspapers which may prove injurious to Mr Stern.'

The relatives' letter presumably reached the Foreign Office on 31 July, and if Lord Russell wrote his comment a couple of days later, it may well have been prompted by an article in the *Pall Mall Gazette* of 1 August, which contained the text of a letter from Mr Stern stating that Cameron, his European servants, and 'all the missionaries', had been put in fetters, and were 'confined in one common prison within the royal enclosure'. The article also contained sarcastic remarks about Lord Russell and Mr Layard who could be expected in the summer to 'unbend from the high official indifference' which they had 'shown to the sufferings of our countrymen'.

Layard replied to several of the relatives who had written the joint letter. To Cameron's brother-in-law, he wrote that there was no more news about the captives, but that he trusted 'the captivity may not be much further delayed'. He also confirmed that 'Mr Palgrave is about to proceed to Abyssinia – but not to replace Mr Rassam', but did not reveal that the Foreign Office had already requested that Rassam should leave Massawa and return to Aden.

Mrs Stern's father was not favourably impressed by Layard's reply to his daughter, and writing to the Parliamentary Under-Secretary, he observed on 17 August:

> it appears that all his Lordship can advise is not to insert herself, nor if possible to allow others to insert in the newspapers, letters from her husband, or relating to the captives, which may find their way to Abyssinia and prove injurious to Mr Stern and the other British subjects.
>
> Whilst thanking His Lordship for his advice, I cannot but express the regret which the distressed relatives of the unhappy prisoners feel that the principle was not acted upon by some members of Her Majesty's Government in the debate on this subject in Parliament.

At the Foreign Office the following observation was written at the foot of this letter: 'This is an impudent letter. It is the publication of these statements in the newspapers which compelled us to state the truth in Parliament.' This indignant observation is followed by a comment in Lord Russell's squiggly handwriting: 'To be sure Dr Beke possibly caused the mischief.' Up to then, it was mainly Stern's relatives who had corresponded with the Foreign Office, but on 30 July, a brother of Mr Rosenthal wrote supporting Dr Beke's projected journey.

Dr Beke, meanwhile, continued to be the most persistent private agitator, and he pursued his objective unswervingly. On 4 August he called on the Committee of the London Society to explain his project more fully. The last thing Lord Russell would have wanted was for Dr Beke to go to Ethiopia, but, making the most of what the Foreign Office had said, or left unsaid, Dr Beke assured the Committee that he had every reason to believe that the Government would not be unfavourable to his proposed visit.

The Committee adopted three resolutions on a matter on which the Society was always sensitive, namely that the Government might release only Her Majesty's Consul and not the missionaries. The resolutions laid down (1) That the Government's intention should be learned as to the character of Mr Palgrave's mission, and whether it was concerned with the case of the missionaries as well as of other captives; (2) That the result of the enquiry be reported to the Committee as soon as possible; (3) That the assistance that might be afforded to Dr Beke should then be determined, it being understood that his proposed journey, if undertaken, would involve the Society in no responsibility.

Meanwhile, early in 1865, more letters began to reach the Foreign Office from anxious relatives and friends, and also from people unconnected with the captives, asking either for news of them or offering to help in their release. In April Lord Russell received a letter from Captain Frederick de Dobse, of Peckham, in South London, stating that he was a naturalised British subject who had served as a British Army Captain in the Crimean War and was now offering to take charge of a mission to Ethiopia. And in June there was a letter from Archdeacon Tatham of Romford, offering to intercede with the Coptic Patriarch in Alexandria, on the suggestion of Mr George Manle of Ampthill Rectory, Bedfordshire, who had seen such a suggestion made in *The Times* by Mr Gardner Wilkinson of Tenby, Pembrokeshire, Wales. It would appear that among the clergy the captives were certainly not being forgotten. Then came a letter from the City of London. The writer, Thomas Gibson of Moorgate, had a secret plan, and all he needed was £5,000 from Her Majesty's Government. And even from as far away as the Windward Islands came offers of help.

While the Foreign Office and a number of individuals were concerning themselves with the captives the attention of the country was taken up with the General Election which followed the dissolution of Parliament on 6 July. Notwithstanding the dissolution, Her Majesty's ministers continued in their offices. At the Foreign Office the Secretary of State, being a Peer, had no electioneering worries; the Parliamentary Under-Secretary, Henry Layard, again contested Southwark, but with the advantage that it lay only across the river Thames from Whitehall. Other ministers had less convenient electioneering, although many held safe seats. Lord Palmerston had to go down to Devon to hold his pocket borough of Tiverton, which he did with relish despite his wife's age of 80 years. Although those near to him remarked that he was now, at long last, really showing signs of his age, he held his seat comfortably. All the House of Commons ministers of Lord Palmerston's Cabinet and most of the junior ministers were duly re-elected, Layard among them; and nearly all ministers, of both Houses, retained their same offices.

In fact it was Lord Palmerston who had won. Despite all his

Tory critics in Parliament, Press and the Constituencies, the unchanging old Pam was still the grand representative Englishman, his liberalism not too much for the average Conservative, his conservatism not too much for the average Liberal. Under, or at least during his Prime Ministership, England was at peace and prosperous; he was the nation's darling; and since it was taken for granted that he would live for ever he gave the country a sense of stability, which the English venerate and is indeed their only justification for their occasional revolutions.

The election over, everyone who had offered the Foreign Secretary help in the matter of the captives was thanked and politely told that his Lordship could not avail himself of the offers. The relatives who made enquiries were informed there was no fresh news, and were in some cases told that it was hoped the captivity would 'not be much more protracted'.

Meanwhile on 1 August 1865, Mr Colquhoun, the old Consul-General, left Alexandria for England, and later that month Colonel Stanton, the new Consul-General, and Mr Palgrave reached Alexandria. On his arrival the new Consul-General at once began his task of getting Mr Palgrave on his journey to Theodore; without loss of time he explained this project to the Egyptian Government and asked for their help in carrying it out; the Egyptians showed themselves co-operative, and Palgrave set about preparing for his journey up the Nile.

These hopeful negotiations and preparations lasted into early September. Egyptian help, relatively small though it was, was all the more gratifying, for it was the Consul-General's duty to oppose as far as he could the opening of the Suez Canal, of which the Egyptian Government so much approved. Encouraged by the co-operation of the Egyptian Government Consul-General Stanton and seasoned traveller Palgrave, both new to the long-drawn-out business of liberating the captives, were hopeful of success.

These happenings were watched with interest by the London Society, always anxious that the British Government in its endeavour to free the British Consul should not neglect to free the missionaries as well. The Society accordingly wrote to Lord Russell to enquire into the purpose of Palgrave's mission. But before the Society's Committee could be summoned to consider his reply a dramatic change of affairs became public knowledge.

22

DRAMATIC CHANGE
(1865)

The three members of the British mission had hurried down from the hills on learning the exciting news on 8 August 1865, that there was a reply from Emperor Theodore. They reached Monculo late, and being tired, spent the night there. The next day Blanc and Prideaux went to their camping ground by the mainland, while Rassam took a ferry-boat over to Massawa in quest of news.

The island was then gripped by famine, recorded Rassam, with the result that the bazaar was empty. 'The starving multitudes had even exhausted the shell-fish on the beach.' In the hot, depressed town Rassam found no comfort – his messengers had not yet reached the island, and so there was more waiting, and lurking doubts. Three days later Rassam was on the mainland having dinner when word came that the messengers had arrived at the Consulate with Theodore's letter. Rassam ferried over to the island and found to his surprise not two, but all six messengers who had taken up his three successive letters; but the Emperor had entrusted his reply to the two who had taken up the third letter, and very proud of it they were.

It was no little thing to be the bearer of a letter from the mighty Emperor to the representative of the Queen of England – and such an important and so much awaited letter, as everybody in Massawa was well aware. Ibrahim and Mohammed were conscious of their own importance as Rassam entered the room. It was now 12 August, nearly ten months since Rassam had first landed in Massawa. He was impatient to read the reply which had at last arrived, but had to control his impatience. First there was a ritual. In accordance with Ethiopian custom, as the two messengers soon told him, their first duty was to tell him the spoken message from the monarch. It was this: His Majesty was angry with Consul Cameron for having gone to the country of the Egyptians, instead of doing as he had requested, namely, to take to Massawa his, the

King's, letter, addressed to the English Queen, and forward it thence to England; to wait an answer and bring it up to him. Having thus spoken, they handed Rassam the letter he had been awaiting for almost ten months. It was written in Amharic and in Arabic.

Rassam opened the letter. Even before reading it he saw, to his chagrin, that it bore neither Theodore's seal nor his signature. This seemed an obvious discourtesy, as the letter itself made plain, and immediately cast doubt in Rassam's mind on the earnestness of anything the letter might contain; and might there not be an Ethiopian custom that whatever was in a letter unsigned need not be honoured? With these disheartening misgivings Rassam read the letter for which he had waited so long:

> In the name of the Father, and of the Son, and of the Holy Ghost, one God, to whom be praise for ever. Amen.
>
> The reason I do not write to you my name, because Abûna Salâma, the so-called Kokab [Stern], the Jew, and the one you called Consul, named Cameron (who was sent by you). I treated them with honour and friendship in my city. When I thus befriended them, on account of my anxiety to cultivate the friendship of the English Queen, they reviled me.
>
> Plowden and Yohannes [John Bell], who were called Englishmen, who were killed in my country, whose death, by the power of God, I avenged on those who killed them. On that account they [Abûna Salâma, the Rev. Mr Stern and Captain Cameron] abused me and denounced me as a murderer.
>
> Cameron, who is called Consul, represented to me that he was a servant of the Queen. I invested him with a robe of honour of my country, and supplied him with provisions for the journey. I asked him to make me a friend of the Queen.
>
> When he was sent on this mission, he went and stayed some time with the Turks and returned to me.
>
> I spoke to him about the letter I sent through him to the Queen. He said that up to that time he had not received any intelligence concerning it. 'What have I done,' said I, 'that they should hate me and treat me with animosity?' By the power of the Lord, my Creator, I kept silent.
>
> Be it known to Hormuzd Rassam that there exists just now a rebellion in Tigré. By the power of God, come round by way of Matámma. When you reach Matámma, send me a messenger, and, by the power of God, I will send people to receive you.
>
> Written on Wednesday, 29th of Sannê [5 July 1865].

Rassam found the letter unencouraging and lacking in any pledge for his safe-conduct. On the other hand, the messengers assured him that Theodore's attitude had been friendly, and they were so sure that this mission would succeed that they were all eager to go with him to the Emperor's court; also Theodore's Arabic scribe and his steward Samuel had both written to friends in Massawa recommending that the English mission should come up. It would also be difficult now, and perhaps disastrous, to refuse the Emperor's invitation. But there was still Cameron's advice not to go with or without a safe conduct. For the time being, however, it would not be possible to travel by way of Matemma until the end of the rainy season, which was also a time of malaria and would last another six weeks into October. The *Victoria* was not at Massawa at this time, but Rassam prepared despatches for Colonel Merewether and the Foreign Office explaining his doubts and difficulties and asking for further instructions; he resolved also that when the *Victoria* arrived he would proceed by her to Egypt to be in closer touch with London for the receipt of instructions. As news of the arrival of the Emperor's letter spread through Massawa, merchants and other friends of Rassam came up to congratulate him, although one or two still expressed concern about the risk of placing any faith in the Ethiopian monarch. As patiently as he could Rassam waited for the *Victoria*, which arrived on 23 August and brought him a shock.

Rassam was presented with a despatch from Lord Russell instructing him to return to Aden with the Queen's letter, and there to await further instructions; for a Mr William Gifford Palgrave had been appointed by Lord Russell to open communications with the Emperor for the prisoners' release. Was Rassam being dismissed from his mission? The despatch did not say so. He had now at long last been invited by Theodore to come and see him; was he to reject this invitation and tell the Emperor, so easy to take offence, that someone quite different would come instead? Here was a fine pickle. Rassam decided there was now all the more reason for going to Egypt for instructions. He wrote to Merewether to advise him accordingly, and to Theodore, the 'Most Gracious Sovereign', to acknowledge his letter and inform him that the road by way of Matemma would be unhealthy for another two months, and also that he would need to obtain permission of the Viceroy of Egypt for his mission to pass through Egyptian territory on the way to Matamma, but he would acquaint him as to the start of the journey.

Rassam wrote his letter to the Emperor on 24 August, and on the following afternoon, with Blanc and Prideaux, sailed for Suez which he reached ten days later after coaling, with exasperating slowness, at Jeddah. The British Party left Suez by train at 9.30 p.m. and arrived at Cairo soon after midnight where they were met by Consul Reade and Mr Palgrave. Could Rassam's long frustrated endeavours be at last on the way to success?

It was in the evening of 5 September that a telegram in cypher reached the Foreign Office from Alexandria: 'Rassam just arrived at Suez telegraphs Consul Cameron released. Will report further by telegram after seeing him. Palgrave still at Cairo.'

Russell was not then at the Foreign Office, but the Parliamentary Under-Secretary, Henry Layard, was, and he lost no time in spreading the good news, not forgetting Captain Cameron's mother and relatives. This was wonderful news indeed for an anxious old mother of 80. Layard also wrote without delay to Captain Cameron's brother-in-law at Reading, Mr Desborough, who replied next day thanking Layard for the 'gratifying intelligence'.

Henry Layard did, however, more than write to the Cameron relatives. At the beginning of the affair of the captives and long afterwards the Foreign Office had pursued a policy of reticence, but their sad plight was now a matter of public knowledge, and much had been said about the Government's failure to liberate them; most that had been said had been critical of the Government: and the Government had been able only to explain their own position, but never had they been able to give any good news. Moreover, many doubts had been expressed about the suitability of Rassam, Layard's friend. In all the discussions about the captives it was always the critics who had got in first; the Government had always been on the defensive. Now at long last Layard had good news, and it was from his trusty friend Rassam. Parliament, prorogued since July, was still not in session and so Layard could make no statement there, but he was not one to dawdle, and he gave the glad tidings to the Press. Worthy ex-newspaper correspondent, he caught the editions going to the printing presses that night for the morrow's morning papers, and acted quickly because some newspapers began printing as early as seven in the evening.

Thus London newspapers of the next day, 6 September, published Layard's good news; the item was brief, but most newspapers gave it some pride of place, as, for example, the *Daily Telegraph* (price one penny), which reported:

> *Release of Consul Cameron*
> We have much pleasure in stating that the long imprisonment of Consul Cameron in Abyssinia has terminated . . .

Other newspapers, *The Times* among them, published the bare news with the introductory phrase 'Information has been received at the Foreign Office'.

The next day the *Daily News* devoted its first leading article to the affair, and, based partly on the mistaken belief that Rassam had now completed his mission, observed: 'The brief announcement we published yesterday of the release of Consul Cameron, and the return of Mr Rassam, Assistant Resident at Aden, from his special mission to the Court of Emperor Theodore, by no means exhausts the Abyssinian question.' The article went on to say that the news was satisfactory as far as it went, but then proceeded to criticise the Foreign Office. Consul Cameron's instructions, the paper argued, had been too vague, and left it open for the Consul to get into trouble. The leader then praised Rassam, but pointed out that other prisoners besides Cameron were still awaiting release. The article also praised Dr Beke's courageous offer to go to Ethiopia, and declared that this offer should be welcomed. Nor did the *Daily News* overlook Palgrave, for it gave its opinion that he too should proceed with his mission and could not reach Theodore's court too soon. Finally, said the *Daily News*, it was understandable that the Emperor should have been offended at not receiving an answer to his letter. Newspapers outside London published Layard's 'glad news' two days later.

Within twenty-four hours the gladness was taken out of Layard's eager communications, for on Wednesday night another cypher telegram from Colonel Stanton arrived at the Foreign Office. It revealed that Cameron had been 'unshackled' – but not released. In sending his new telegram Colonel Stanton's main concern was to state the relative position of the two existing missions, that of Rassam, against which he was prejudiced, and that of Palgrave which he favoured, and he referred to Cameron almost incidentally.

In Massawa, Rassam had been without any means of communicating with London except by mail, at least as far as Egypt, whence telegrams could be sent to London. Thus it came about that the news which had so excited him at Massawa reached the Foreign Office in a telegram from Colonel Stanton which arrived in Downing Street at 9.30 p.m. The telegram decyphered was as follows:

> Rassam states on receipt of his third letter the King had Cameron unshackled and wrote him word to come via Matemma on account of rebellion in Tigré. Letter makes no mention of Queen's Letter and is neither sealed nor signed . . .
>
> Though released it is doubtful whether Cameron can leave the country. Rassam fears further complications by delay and wishes to return to Massowah immediately to prepare. He is also afraid that if Palgrave goes it will spoil all. I am myself of opinion that Palgrave should proceed at once.

The British officials in Alexandria that Wednesday had no idea that on that same day the London Press was publishing information that Consul Cameron had been 'released', and so Colonel Stanton's telegram contained no specific, but only an implicit, contradiction of that false information, which was to persist in provincial papers on the following day. The less happy facts about Cameron were, however, immediately appreciated at the Foreign Office.

An hour after this telegram arrived, yet another from Alexandria reached the Foreign Office, at 10.30 p.m. In this message Colonel Stanton stated that he had just received information from Cairo that 'steamboat, letters and other arrangements for Palgrave's journey' were 'ready and that the Egyptian Viceroy would defray expenses as far as Matemma'. He therefore enquired, 'Should not Palgrave proceed at once?' and added, 'Queen's letter might be entrusted to him. Rassam to return to Aden.'

Colonel Stanton had never made any secret that he regarded Palgrave as a better man than Rassam to secure the liberation of the captives. His recommendation was therefore almost to be expected; but a special consideration may also have been in Colonel Stanton's mind. He was already involved in discussions with the Egyptian Canal Company aimed at curbing, if no longer completely frustrating, the designs of the company which the British Government and Lord Palmerston in particular regarded as a French project endangering British interests. Colonel Stanton was much concerned to retain the goodwill of the Egyptian Government. He had successfully secured its co-operation, which was almost indispensable, in facilitating Palgrave's proposed journey to Matemma. If Palgrave did not proceed, it might well appear that Britain disdained Egypt's help and the Egyptian Government would be offended – which was the last thing Colonel Stanton wanted.

The Foreign Office was loth to enter upon any more hasty decisions, and the next morning the following telegram was therefore sent to Colonel Stanton: 'Do not take any steps until you hear further from Lord Russell. Keep Rassam and do not let Palgrave go.'

Meanwhile Layard had to undo the mischief into which Stanton's earlier telegram and his own impetuousness had led him. On 8 September he wrote letters in very similar terms to Mrs Cameron and Mr Desborough stating it would appear from further information 'that Captain Cameron had been released from his shackles, but has not left Abyssinia and that King Theodore has invited Mr Rassam to proceed to his Court'. And poor Mrs Cameron and Mr Desborough had to take what little comfort they could from this disappointing, and yet not entirely pessimistic, communication.

Layard had also to deal with the Press – and because of the press, the public – whom he had misled, and he acted without delay, with a courtesy that no longer characterises Press handouts. In consequence London newspapers of 9 September carried an announcement, with an opening phrase, such as appeared in *The Times*: 'Mr Layard presents his compliments to the Editor of *The Times* and begs to inform him' – followed with the information that Consul Cameron had been released from his chains, but not from Ethiopia.

Most newspapers were content merely to give the correction, but not so two of the London papers. Without loss of time the Liberal *Daily News* on 9 September published a leading article critical of the Government which it normally supported. And on 11 September the Conservative *Daily Telegraph* published a leading article defending the Government which it generally opposed. The leader opened: 'Seldom has a very simple and straightforward story been enveloped in more needless mystery than that of the Abyssinian captives, about which some of our contemporaries have indulged in a great deal of irrelevant verbiage and ignorant assertions.' The article went on to say that Captain Cameron had brought trouble on himself, and that it was not the business of England to save missionaries everywhere. The leader then declared:

> Nobody out of Bedlam has ever yet proposed that we should send an army, Heaven only knows where, in search of King Theodore and his Court.
>
> There are only two ways of dealing with semi-civilized countries. Either leave them alone, or add them to our dominion.
>
> If the censors of the Foreign Office have a better plan, it would be welcome; otherwise they might as well inveigh against Lord Russell and Mr Layard for not entering into negotiations with the man in the moon.

The Foreign Office now lost little time in deciding upon the relative advantages of the Rassam and Palgrave missions. Rassam clearly had an advantage; he had, at long last, a written invitation from Theodore, whatever doubts there might be about the significance of its letter being neither signed nor sealed. On the other hand, Theodore did not even know of the existence of Palgrave, and to thrust the letter upon him now might lead to disturbing complications. It was therefore decided not to accept Stanton's suggestion that Palgrave should proceed to Ethiopia and the following cypher telegram was accordingly despatched to him on 9 September:

> Rassam should go at once to King Theodore by way of Matemma, taking with him the Queen's Letter but not the muskets. You will ask the Egyptian Government to give him all the facilities prepared for Palgrave. He should be accompanied if possible by the officers who were with him in Massowah. Palgrave must not accompany Rassam whatever happens, but must remain with you in Egypt.

The London Society meanwhile continued to be anxious lest Rassam should be commissioned only to secure the release of Her Majesty's Consul. Accordingly, on 9 September, the Society's Secretary wrote again to the Foreign Secretary: 'most respectfully to solicit the continuance of your Lordship's kind efforts on behalf of the captive missionaries, and to instruct Mr Rassam to use every endeavour to procure their total release'.

So far, the Foreign Office had only received the news of Rassam and the developments which he reported, but on Sunday there arrived a despatch from Colonel Stanton, written on 6 September which stated:

> I have just seen Mr Rassam, and learned from him the actual state of affairs in Abyssinia, which appears to me most unsatisfactory. There is no assurance that Captain Cameron is free; his fetters were struck off in the presence of Mr Rassam's messengers, but the latter were

then hurried off and . . . we have no guarantee that after their departure he was not imprisoned again.

The letter of King Theodore to Mr Rassam appears also unsatisfactory and equivocal . . . and although he expresses himself ready to receive Mr Rassam, the letter being without seal or signature, its promises may easily be evaded . . . Mr Rassam's answer to it by making difficulties, is also not, in my opinion, calculated to improve the situation.

Mr Rassam awaits further instructions . . . he wishes to return to Massowah at once, to be able to inform the King of his having started on his journey to Matemma, and dreads the consequences of delay. He appears to think that the prisoners would now be released were he to proceed to the King's headquarters. I confess . . . I myself feel no such conviction, and think that better results may be obtained through Mr Palgrave's means, than by Mr Rassam's now proceeding after the slighting manner in which he, as bearer of a letter from Her Majesty, has been treated. I think, moreover, that Mr Palgrave is personally more likely to succeed . . . and, although it may seem invidious to the latter to allow another agent to proceed in his stead, I believe the public service would be benefited by the change.

I beg, therefore, to submit, with all deference, that Mr Rassam should be ordered to return to Aden . . . in order that he may not interfere with Mr Palgrave's mission . . . and that, should Her Majesty's Government still desire the letter from Her Majesty to be presented to King Theodore, the letter should be entrusted to Mr Palgrave . . .

I have received intelligence . . . that the steamer and letters and other arrangements of the Egyptian Government for Mr Palgrave's journey are ready and that the Viceroy himself will defray all expenses . . . this appears to me a further reason for Mr Palgrave's journey not being abandoned . . .

There appears, also . . . another urgent reason for no delay in this matter, and that is the projected journey of Dr Beke to Abyssinia; as I fear that any person not recognized by Her Majesty's Government, arriving in that country . . . could not . . . fail to endanger the chances of ultimate success.

The Consul-General's despatch seemed a little weighted in favour of William Palgrave. But ministers and officials at the Foreign Office were not exactly new to the duty of considering advice and then making up their own minds. The following telegram was therefore sent to the Consul-General on 11 September:

Rassam should go off as soon as possible. He should ask, but only as a favour, that the missionaries should be released . . . If the King wishes

> to send an Embassy to England, Rassam may say we will endeavour to obtain a passage for it through Egypt . . .
>
> Rassam may inform the King that the present Consul at Jerusalem will be told that he is to give the Abyssinians similar good office as was afforded by previous Consul.

So now, in mid-1865, the Foreign Office had moved a long way in its position since February 1863 when it regarded Theodore's letter to Queen Victoria as a dangerous proposal for an involvement which would condone the Emperor's possible aggression against Egypt and Turkey. Then the Foreign Office had decided to ignore Theodore's letter altogether; now the same ministry was willing to receive an Embassy. Had Theodore hit upon the right way of dealing with the British Government? The tide seemed to be turning in his favour – but would he be able to play his cards successfully?

While these developments were taking place, one person who was not at all pleased was Dr Beke. What was to happen now to his scheme for going himself to see Theodore?

Dr Beke gave vent to his feelings in a long letter to *The Times* on 14 September. Referring to Rassam's arrival in Egypt he wrote:

> It is not to be imagined that Mr Rassam has undertaken a journey all the way from Massowah to Alexandria, and thence back to Metamma, or Kalabat, a distance of 2,000 miles, simply for the purpose of crossing the Abyssinian frontier at the latter point, which is distant little more than 300 miles from Massowah.

Arguing that there was a 'special motive' for Rassam's visit to Egypt he argued that Cameron was not imprisoned because of 'any misconduct on his part', but on account of a 'radical change which (intentionally or otherwise)' had 'taken place in the policy of the British Government towards Abyssinia'. And he most pertinently added:

> By this new line of policy Abyssinia is virtually treated as a vassal province of Turkey, after having been dealt with as an independent kingdom for many years, and especially since the conclusion of the treaty between England and Abyssinia in 1849 . . .

After belabouring this and other points Beke conjectured that if the various questions at issue could be solved in Egypt Mr Rassam would 'then be in a position (but not otherwise) to avail himself of his Abyssinian Majesty's precious invitation'. However, Beke concluded:

The conditions on which the invitation has been given have first to be complied with; and whether they are or not must depend on the instructions given by the Foreign Office . . . and the power which [it] may possess over the Sultan and Viceroy of Egypt.

The Captives' Liberation Committee was now concerned about Dr Beke's proposal to go to Ethiopia, and met on the question on 15 September. Both Dr Beke and Mr Purday had written to ask the Society what they had decided. After consideration its Committee informed Dr Beke that in view of Theodore's invitation to Rassam, and the Government's assurance that they would 'do all in their power to obtain the release of the Missionaries', the Society felt it would be 'inexpedient' to 'promote any separate action'. That rather left Dr Beke out on his own: not that that would daunt him.

The Foreign Office for its part continued to give attention to the matter of their agents gathered in Alexandria, and Lord Russell accordingly replied more fully to Colonel Stanton's despatch by a cypher telegram sent on 19 September, as follows: 'I am confirmed in my opinion that Rassam who was invited ought to go to King, and that Palgrave should wait in Egypt. Rassam's delay may do some harm and he ought to go now as soon as possible.' Lord Russell could not forget what he considered the origin of all the trouble, so the telegram continued: 'Rassam can explain to the King that Cameron had no orders to interfere between him and the Egyptians or in the internal affairs of Abyssinia.'

Palgrave, whatever his personal disappointment, accepted the situation with good grace. He wrote to Lord Russell that he would obey the instructions sent to Colonel Stanton and hand over to Rassam. Stanton, of course, also acted on the Foreign Secretary's instructions, but he was obviously not happy about the arrangement. In a despatch of 11 September he complained that the plan for Rassam to go 'besides causing delay, upsets arrangements made by the Egyptian Government who have taken up the matter strongly at my request and will be annoyed at change'. In a longer despatch, of 14 September, he proposed that Palgrave should carry out a survey of the Sudan then under consideration, and go up the Nile to Khartoum, and added:

at Khartoum, Mr Palgrave would . . . be in a favourable position for carrying his journey as far as Abyssinia, should Mr Rassam fail to obtain permission to enter that country; and I am bound to state to

> your Lordship that this contingency is looked upon by many persons here as far from impossible, as it is stated that the King considers his dignity slighted by the fact of the Queen's letter to him being entrusted for delivery to an Asiatic instead of an Englishman, and that this has been the real cause of the delay in replying to the letters sent by Mr Rassam.

The doubts of the British Consul-General and others as to Rassam's ability were not shared by the envoy's two colleagues, Blanc and Prideaux, who were with him in Egypt. As for Rassam himself he seemed fully confident, and proceeded with the immediate task of buying presents for the Emperor and equipment for the journey, and on 16 September he left Cairo by rail for Suez, there to sail down the Red Sea to Aden and Massawa.

Rassam left Cairo a happier man than when he had arrived, but he left behind him two somewhat disappointed men: Colonel Stanton, not at all pleased with the frustrating of his own plans, and poor William Palgrave, at a loss how to employ himself. On 21 September, Palgrave wrote to the Consul-General requesting him to ask the British Government to clarify his role and status in Egypt, and also to enquire about his expenses. The next day the Consul-General sent a telegram to Lord Russell, notifying him that Rassam had sailed from Suez, but prefaced this information with matters in which he felt more closely involved. He stated that he had explained to the Egyptian Government why Rassam and not Palgrave was proceeding, and His Excellency Cherif Pasha, 'appeared perfectly to understand', but Rassam had 'refused to take the letter from the Vice Roy to Theodore which had been prepared for Palgrave'. And that concluded the Rassam-Palgrave episode.

While speculations about the fate of the prisoners and the prospect of Rassam reaching them continued, the latter was in fact continuing his journey as planned. By 27 September he had arrived in Aden whence he wrote to Layard:

> You will be glad to learn that Cameron has now changed his mind with regard to my going up to the King of Abyssinia and wants me to proceed up with Her Majesty's letter. It is premised that once I meet Theodorus with the Royal Letter he would release all the prisoners. I hope and trust that this will be the case.

Meanwhile, a French ship of war, the *Surcouf*, had visited Massawa and brought back several messages from the captives which were duly forwarded to London by the Consul-General in Egypt who, in a covering letter of 30 September 1865, wrote: 'The prisoners are in a critical situation . . . We can only hope that Rassam will now succeed in his journey, and that no further delay will take place.' On arrival at the Foreign Office, this bundle of letters was marked *The Queen*, so that they should go to her for perusal.

Despite Rassam's steady pursuit of his plans, doubts about the envoy's fitness for his task continued, and even increased. From the start of his mission fifteen months previously, Rassam had received the loyal support of his chief at Aden, Colonel Merewether, but in a letter reporting Rassam's final departure, the latter wrote on 6 October: 'Rassam left yesterday evening for Massowah. I pressed on him perpetually while he was here, the necessity of energetic action, but I confess I have an unpleasant conviction that little will be done.' When this letter reached the Foreign Office, Earl Russell wrote on it: 'Mr Rassam should hurry on with all speed as the only chance of releasing the captives.'

Colonel Stanton, of course, continued to have his own special doubts about Rassam. In a despatch of 13 October, he declared that the lives of the captives were 'now, more than ever, in danger', that the 'only hope' of obtaining their release apparently depended upon 'the energy of Mr Rassam in trying to reach King Theodore', but he confessed to 'suspicions' about the 'seriousness of Mr Rassam's resolution', and added: 'Mr Rassam . . . is . . . perplexed and troubled by the stories he has heard at Massowah of disturbances in Bogos and between that district and Kassala, and I have very serious apprehensions that he will find such difficulties on the road as to induce him to abandon the attempt to reach Metemmah.'

It must have been somewhat consoling to Colonel Stanton, therefore, when a little later he received the following despatch from the Foreign Secretary, dated 7 October: 'Lord Russell's intention of retaining Mr Palgrave in Egypt is that he should be that far on the road to Abyssinia if Rassam's own mission is halted.'

While such speculations continued to be exchanged in telegrams and despatches Rassam had left for Massawa. He sailed with his colleagues Blanc and Prideaux, on the evening of 5 October, but a good three weeks were to pass before this hopeful intelligence reached Alexandria, and then London.

23

RASSAM'S HISTORIC JOURNEY BEGINS

(1865)

By 7 October 1865, Rassam was back in Massawa, having been away six weeks. If only it were as easy to reach the capital of the Emperor of Ethiopia as it had been to reach that of the Khedive of Egypt, how different things might have been! At the port he found that added to the deaths due to the recent famine there were now deaths from cholera; everywhere there was mourning and wailing. This distress notwithstanding, the British mission prepared for their important journey. Ethiopian merchants offered to help them and even asked to come with them; surprised at this change in attitude, Rassam enquired the reason, and was told that while Theodore remained silent they had kept aloof from the British, but now that he had written they could safely associate with them. Rassam was glad they did not know that the Emperor's letter bore neither his signature nor his seal.

October was a fit time to go into the hot Sudan. Rassam was eager to set off. It took him just over a week of intensive activity to complete the necessary arrangements. He sent more provisions, medicines and money to Cameron, and arranged for Flad to receive money to send on to the prisoners. With the approval of Colonel Merewether, he appointed the Swiss Mr Munzinger, French Vice-Consul at Massawa, to be British Vice-Consul also, at a salary of 200 rupees per month. He also wrote to the Emperor, as promised, telling him he was leaving for Matemma. Finally, he left a sum of money for further contingencies with Kershotum and Bainaux, a merchant firm trading at the port.

The mission's departure, first from the island and then on the mainland, was hampered by the cholera; some of those who were meant to help were still suffering from the disease, while others were occupied in nursing the sick or burying the dead. On more than one occasion caravan people dropped dead only a few yards from him. The final preparations were made at Monculo, but that village was also seriously afflicted with the dread disease.

So at Monculo there was bustle and confusion with the gathering of porters and drivers, riding mules and baggage camels, with loading and fussing and shouting, and the champing of the armed escort as a representative of the British Queen prepared to go up into the interior with a letter and presents for a ruler of Ethiopia.

At last, on 16 October, Rassam set off. At 4 p.m., he, Blanc, Prideaux and an Italian merchant, Signor Marcopoli, having business in Matemma, mounted on their mules, and with their array of 46 loaded camels and porters, interpreters, cooks and servants, and a mounted escort of 15 men, lumbered away towards the towering mountains of Ethiopia.

One night they found locusts had eaten almost every edible plant and this was the beginning of trouble in feeding the camels. During that day's journey to Ain, on 18 October, the travellers encountered the insects in flight in their myriads, so dense were they that they cast the ground beneath them into deep shadow.

Plowden, and after him Cameron, had set off due west to climb onto the plateau whereupon each in turn had headed towards the south-west to follow the age-old caravan route into Tigré and then down to the south; not so Rassam. Soon after leaving Monculo his caravan turned north-west, to go up into the region of Bogos. His caravan came onto the plateau nine days after leaving Monculo, all well, except that three or four camels, footsore and weak, were abandoned to the hyenas.

Rassam had originally expected his meeting with the Emperor to be somewhere near Lake Tana, but on reaching the plateau he turned his back towards his ultimate objective and proceeded in almost the opposite direction through Bogos to reach the Sudan frontier to the north. Now Rassam descended from the cool Ethiopian highlands into the hot Sudan and then, over to the west, re-entered Ethiopia by way of Matemma.

On leaving Bogos a hoped-for Egyptian escort did not appear owing to the disruption caused by an army mutiny in the Sudan and its cruel suppression, with the rotting bodies of mutineers still to be seen in the streets. So the escort from Massawa stayed on as far as Kassala, the capital of that part of the Sudan. After some days' stay and re-provisioning, Rassam's party resumed their journey – now, at last, southwards, towards Matemma, the last important halt before the Ethiopian frontier. They arrived on 21 November, 36 days after leaving Massawa, and Rassam sent a letter to the Emperor, announcing his arrival.

In making this long loop out of and then into Ethiopia again Rassam was taking the longest way from Massawa to the imperial capital of Gondar. But, as he and Theodore knew, it would have been impossible to have travelled by the usual and more direct route through Tigré, for that province was in rebel hands. What had happened to Theodore's grand scheme, and Plowden's high hopes, of a unified and peaceful Ethiopia in which the long-troubled peasantry would live in peace and prosperity and enjoy untainted justice? Ten years after his accession, so widely welcomed, Theodore had not brought the promised peace and unity to Ethiopia. Had he prophesied before his time? Was he, or were perhaps his countrymen, to blame? Would anyone, could anyone, unify Ethiopia and give real meaning to its proud name? Could Theodore still succeed? If he failed, was there any man living who could succeed in that seemingly hopeless task? There was.

Indeed two young men then lived who would in turn lead Ethiopia forward to unity. They would not achieve as much as Theodore dreamed, but they would exceed what he achieved. First, Kassa, later Emperor Yohannes, a prince of the north, and after him Menilek, a prince of the south. But then who could foresee all this, except perhaps a gifted soothsayer, and certainly not the British officials, or Hormuzd Rassam, who was not greatly concerned, or Duncan Cameron in captivity; perhaps, among the English, had he lived, only Plowden would still have dared to hope.

It was nearly two months before the first news of Rassam's start, contained in a despatch from Colonel Merewether, reached England, where friends and sceptics alike knew nothing of the envoy's progress. But there was also something Rassam then did not, could not, know.

For on 18 October, a shadow of a different kind was cast over Britain. It was the shadow of one man, whom *The Times* a day later described as 'one of the most popular statesmen, one of the kindliest gentlemen, and one of the truest Englishmen that ever filled the office of Premier'. On 18 October 1865, Lord Palmerston died.

He was a few days short of his eighty-first birthday. Those near had noticed his infirmities increasing, and his death might have been no great surprise; yet now it seemed incredible that that strong, ageless man could really be dead, and at the news of it the whole nation was shocked. The death of Palmerston was not merely the death of a statesman; his passing was for Britain the end of a chapter of its history.

As the news spread it was received by democrats with sorrow, and by reactionaries with relief. In some countries the news was published the next day, but it was some months before Rassam and his colleagues learnt of the death of the Minister who had appointed the first British Consul to the ruler of Ethiopia, so hopefully, 19 years earlier.

24

THE QUEEN CAN TURN TO NO OTHER

(1865–6)

It was Lord Russell who succeeded to the Premiership on the death of Palmerston. Little Johnny was thus Prime Minister again, at the age of 73. This succession was almost a foregone conclusion. Who else could have headed a Palmerstonian Whig Government?

The Queen was in Scotland, at Balmoral. On the night of 18 October she learned by telegraph that her suddenly ailing, aged Prime Minister, had died that morning; but over the past few days she had already decided what to do. Without delay she wrote to her Foreign Secretary, Lord Russell, thus:

> The melancholy news of Lord Palmerston's death reached the Queen last night. This is another link with the past which is broken, and the Queen feels deeply, in her desolate and isolated condition, how one by one those tried servants and advisers are removed from her . . .
>
> The Queen can turn to no other but to Lord Russell, an old and tried friend of hers, to undertake the arduous duties of Prime Minister.

Because of the business of government-forming she felt obliged to leave her beloved Balmoral and go to Windsor earlier than planned; so at Windsor on the mid-morning of 29 October Lord Russell kissed hands as her Prime Minister. The Queen wrote: 'He seemed much impressed with the weight of the task he had undertaken, saying it was different to do so at 73, not 54; but that if he had been in the House of Commons, he could not have undertaken it at all.'

Lord Russell made up his Cabinet with few changes. Of the old group of 15 members, 12 retained their offices. The most important change was that Lord Clarendon became Foreign Secretary, for the second time. Most of the ministers who had to deal with the question of the captives were the same. The new Prime Minister, as Foreign Secretary, had personally dealt with the matter continuously since March 1864, and Sir Charles Wood was still at the India Office.

It was Lord Clarendon who had thus to pick up the threads of the elusive Ethiopian problem. But he was not new to dealing with Ethiopia, for he had already served as Foreign Secretary in Palmerston's first Cabinet, and it was while holding that office that he had exchanged despatches with Consul Plowden, including one of July 1854, in which he had approved of Plowden's action in going to protect the Christians being raided from the Sudan.

While Lord Palmerston's death, the pomp of his funeral in Westminster Abbey, and the formation of the new Government engaged the attention of Press and public, the matter of the captives nevertheless still received some popular attention. Those already concerned about the captives had not desisted from their own activities, least of all Dr Beke. On 18 October, the day Lord Palmerston died, a letter from Beke reached the Foreign Office. This time Beke's letter was from a private hotel in London's Pall Mall. Explaining his intention of approaching Theodore as 'a suppliant in the names of the distressed relatives of the captives', he stated, 'even should it happen that my endeavours were crowned with success, and Mr Rassam be thereby deprived of a position of the merit to which he might otherwise be entitled, it surely is time for personal considerations of every kind to be set aside'. Beke then referred to the Resolution of the London Society's Committee, and enclosed a copy of it, as if to show that it supported his proposed journey.

Lord Shaftesbury, who was at his country place, meanwhile sought guidance regarding Beke's proposed venture: he wrote to Lord Russell, on 14 October, stating that 'friends of Stern want to send Dr Beke to Ethiopia', and enquired: 'What is the position regarding Mr Rassam?'

On 16 October, Lord Russell replied from his home at Pembroke Lodge: 'As King Theodore invited Rassam to his court, we have ordered him to go there . . . You will, of course, exercise your own discretion as to the course you will advise the Jewish Society to pursue.' Writing on the same day, Lord Russell gave similar advice, somewhat more formally, to Dr Beke.

Thus matters stood when it fell to Lord Clarendon to concern himself with the question of the captives, but he had hardly taken up office, when there was one other important and more public event, calculated to help him.

Russell had little sympathy with the *Times*, and its editor Delane in particular; but, like other Cabinet Ministers, then and since, was quite ready to use the Press when it suited him. Possibly to counter Beke's letters he now took the unusual step of causing the Government's official weekly, the *London Gazette*, of 31 October, to publish the text of one of his despatches of 5 October, setting out 'the policy of the British Government regarding Abyssinia'. As was to be expected, the next day *The Times* and other newspapers reproduced the despatch, either in full or in part.

Apart from the unfortunate mistaken report in September of the release of Captain Cameron, there had been no Government statement on the captives since the debates in Parliament in July. Now at last the public had an official statement of British policy. The despatch, which took up six columns of the *Gazette*, began with an historical summary of Anglo-Ethiopian relations. Coming to British policy after the signing of the Anglo-Ethiopian Treaty of 1849 it declared:

> It may be argued that the British Government ought to have insisted on the validity of the Treaty on the one hand, and to have protected the Emperor of Abyssinia from the Turks on the other.
>
> But considering the short tenure of power of the Abyssinian Kings, whatever their title, the difficulty of reaching with a regular British force their seat of empire ... the risk of failure and the certainty of expense, it has seemed to the British Government a preferable course to withdraw as much as possible from Abyssinian engagements, Abyssinian Alliances, and British interference in Abyssinia.

Turning to the criticism which this policy had evoked, and conveniently omitting any reference to Theodore's unanswered letter to the Queen, Lord Russell considered the argument that the Emperor had seized Consul Cameron 'as a hostage for the recognition by England ... of the independence of Abyssinia, for the suppression of Egyptian aggressions along the frontier, and for the restitution of the church and convent at Jerusalem, torn from him and his people by the Copts, Armenians and Turks'.

To refute this view the despatch argued that England had asked Theodore to recognise the 1849 Treaty, but that the Emperor had refused. England, nevertheless, had never withdrawn her recognition of Ethiopian independence. As for the suppression of Egyptian aggression, England had used her influence to prevent such aggression, but would not agree to guarantee Ethiopian territorial integrity. 'Such a guarantee would be, in the opinion of Her Majesty's Government, an unwise engagement, impractical to execute.'

Lord Russell then dealt with the Ethiopian Church and Convent in Jerusalem. He pointed out that the British Foreign Secretary, Lord Malmesbury, had stated in 1852 that while the Government could not 'undertake to protect officially natives of Abyssinia' the British Consul would 'be instructed to use his good offices for them in case of need, as members of a Christian Church in spiritual communion with the Established Church in the Country'. Lord Russell, as Foreign Secretary, had referred the British Consul to those instructions, in 1852, but had enjoined him 'to act upon them with control and prudence'. Lord Russell now added: 'Those instructions remain still in force.' He then turned to the more immediate problem of the imprisonment of Cameron:

> It appears from the papers presented to Parliament, that after he had conveyed the Queen's letter and some few presents to the Emperor of Abyssinia, he went to the country of Bogos . . . It appears further that the chief cause of the Emperor's anger with Consul Cameron was this journey to Bogos, coupled with the Emperor's suspicion that Consul Cameron had intrigued to set the Turks and Egyptians on the frontier against him.

To this Lord Russell added the disingenuous admission that Theodore's suspicion had been 'aggravated in some degree' by the return of Consul Cameron to Gondar without any answer to his, the Emperor's, letter to the Queen.

Recognising that there were persons who wished Her Majesty's Government 'to interfere in behalf of Abyssinia as a Christian country against Turkey and Egypt as Mahommedan countries', Lord Russell insisted:

> This policy has never been adopted by the British Government, and, I trust never will be.
>
> If we were to make ourselves the Protectors of the Emperor Theodore against the Sultan and his Viceroy of Egypt, we should become responsible for his acts, and be entangled in his quarrels with all his neighbours and rivals.
>
> The obligations of the British Government are various enough, and heavy enough without undertaking so costly, hazardous, and unprofitable a Protectorate.

As a result of this despatch Lord Clarendon, on taking up the matter of the captives, had a fairly clear statement of British policy. This gave him a good start. So did the fact that a draft of this statement was marked 'Seen by Lord Palmerston. Seen by the Queen.' Lord Clarendon was further aided by a leading article in *The Times* on 2 November, which stated that, 'Lord Russell has bequeathed to Lord Clarendon a sensible Memorandum on Abyssinian affairs . . . ' Then, returning to its policy on Ethiopia, the leader continued: 'First get Consul Cameron safely out. Secondly, let Britain have as little as possible to do with Abyssinia.'

When the Russell despatch and the approving *Times* leader were published, the London Society was preparing for a Committee meeting which took place on 3 November, with Lord Shaftesbury presiding. It instructed its secretaries to prepare a statement on the efforts made to procure the captives' liberation. This statement reiterated the Society's view that while the Government was endeavouring to liberate the captives, it would be 'unwise' to aid any independent mission, which, however unintentionally, might interfere with the efforts being made by the Government, 'and perhaps prove fatal to the lives of the captives'. The statement also affirmed:

> It is in the power of the never-failing providence of God to help us in our difficulty: and, while your Committee will watch anxiously for any opportunity for further effort, they most earnestly intreat the persevering and more abundant intercessions of all the members of the Society, and of the Christian Church at large.

On 4 November a brief cypher telegram reached the Foreign Office at 9.30 a.m. that could well have given the new Foreign Secretary even greater satisfaction than the approval of British policy by *The Times* or the London Society. The telegram was from Colonel Stanton, and said: 'Information just arrived from Aden that Rassam left Massowah for Matemma on October fifteenth.' So now, 16 months after his appointment to his task, news reached England that Rassam was at last on his way. It was, however, only some six weeks later that the news appeared in the British Press; and then it came from foreign sources, in a *Times* report from Egypt.

Lord Clarendon was now immersing himself in the matter of the captives, and, needing for his guidance a history of the case, he asked the Chief Librarian of the Foreign Office, the knowledgeable

Edward Hertslet, to prepare one. So, on 3 January 1866, the latter presented the Foreign Secretary with a long 'Private and Confidential' memorandum: 'Imprisonment of Consul Cameron in Abyssinia', the opening of which stated, 'The following is a short account of what I consider to be the most important Points connected with the Case'.

Hertslet, who had always felt that Lord Russell and the Foreign Office had not been quite fair to Consul Cameron, began by pointing out that the 'general complaint of H.M.'s Govt. against Captain Cameron' was that he had 'interfered in the Political affairs of Abyssinia'.

Hertslet's memorandum dealt in some detail with a 'Proposed Mission from the King of Abyssinia to this Country'. It recalled that the question had first arisen during the Consularship of Mr Plowden, but that 'nothing was settled during Consul Plowden's lifetime'. Subsequently 'Captain Cameron, upon being appointed to succeed Consul Plowden, was told officially that no instructions could be given to him respecting the contemplated Mission *until* Lord Russell was in possession of further information on the subject. Captain Cameron, who was then still in London, replied in writing assuring his Lordship that he would lose no time, after his arrival in Abyssinia, in obtaining information respecting the proposed Mission.' However, 'Lord Russell made no reply to this communication from Captain Cameron who later departed for Abyssinia', as Hertslet put it: 'under the full conviction that it was his *duty* to speak, or write, to the King on the subject of the Mission.'

When Cameron eventually met Theodore, 'His Majesty spoke much of his goodwill towards England and his desire to send an Embassy to cultivate that friendship.' This Cameron reported to the Foreign Office in his despatch of 31 October 1862, together with the Emperor's letter to Queen Victoria, which reached the Foreign Office on 12 February 1863. Hertslet continued: 'but no reply has ever been returned to it; further than that Captain Cameron was told on the 22nd April following not to meddle in Abyssinian affairs, but to return to his Post at Massowah'.

The question of Theodore's mission, Hertslet explained, was in part related to supposed designs of Theodore on Egyptian territory. Even Consul Plowden had been informed that England could receive no Embassy from Theodore *unless* he gave an assurance that he renounced all ideas of conquest in Egypt and at Massawa which, observed Hertslet, 'implied that if he gave such an assurance his Embassy would be received'. Consequently, on meeting the Emperor, Cameron spoke to him about this, and the King *did* assure him that he would *not* undertake a war, until he had made an appeal to all Christendom. Consul Cameron thereupon told the Emperor that he would write to his Government to that effect. Cameron did so write; but at the Foreign Office no notice was taken of the matter, 'on the contrary . . . it was decided by H.M.'s Government not to receive the proposed Embassy, not to take any notice either of the King's letter to the Queen, or of the proposals made by Captain Cameron . . . for the conclusion of a new Treaty'.

Coming to the question of 'a new Treaty with Abyssinia', Hertslet began:

> It has, I believe, been considered an improper act on Captain Cameron's part . . . that he should also have talked to the King on the subject of a New Treaty; but when the King, during Consul Plowden's lifetime, objected to the Treaty made with Ras Ali in 1849 . . . instructions were sent to Mr Plowden to remind the King . . . that if he objected to any of its provisions he should propose modifications.

Captain Cameron accordingly felt it to be his *duty* (as he had no previous instructions to the contrary) to speak to the King on that subject; and he reported home that he had taken up the question where Consul Plowden had left it; and felt sure that there would be no objection on the part of the King to the conclusion of a new Treaty. No answer was returned to this Letter, nor any notice taken of the King's proposals, further than that Cameron was told not to meddle in Ethiopian affairs, but to return to his post at Massawa, and that as H.M.'s Consul there he had no 'representative character whatever' in Ethiopia, although 'he had a formal Letter of Introduction from Lord Russell to the King'.

Hertslet then came to another aspect of the question by declaring, 'It has been thought by many that the non-receipt by King Theodore of any Reply to his letter to the Queen has had but little or nothing to do with Captain Cameron's imprisonment . . . ' In using the words 'thought by many' – was the Chief Librarian being tactful in regard to his departmental superiors, when what he really had in mind was: it was thought by Lord Russell and the two or three senior Foreign Office officials?

Be that as it may, Hertslet recalled that when information reached Her Majesty's Government of Theodore's detention of the captives all of them wrote that there was 'no hope of release until a civil answer was returned to the King's letter'. There could therefore 'hardly be any doubt now of the fact that the non-reply to that letter was the *original* cause of Consul Cameron's detention (although other causes have been since assigned)'. Cameron himself had written to him from Magdala, in January and July 1865, saying: 'The King chained me because the Government has sent him no answer to his letter', and 'He chained me because I had not obtained him a letter.'

The memorandum then dealt with the employment of Mr Rassam. Hertslet began with this ruthless sentence:

> I have spoken to some persons who knew Mr Rassam well, and I have received myself, or I have seen, letters from others, who also knew him, and they, one and all, concur in the opinion that he does not possess the necessary courage to undertake such a Mission.

He went on to declare that all these critics agreed that Rassam was 'a most valuable public servant', but that he lacked 'pluck'. Such for example was the view, Hertslet declared, of a now better remembered Consul: Captain Richard Burton, the famous Orientalist, who had told him that 'he knew Mr Rassam too well to believe that he would ever go up to Gondar'. Similarly there was Sir William Coghlan, who had 'stated officially that he fears the King of Abyssinia will hardly be satisfied with such a Mission, but will regard Mr Rassam as a mere Messenger and not an Envoy'.

Hertslet had still not damned Rassam enough, so he continued:

> Mr Rassam is an *Ottoman* (although a Naturalized British subject, I believe) and it is publicly stated that he is an Armenian; now it was the Armenians who persecuted the Abyssinian Christians at Jerusalem, and the Turks are King Theodore's deadly Enemies.

It seems strange that Hertslet did not, apparently, consult the Parliamentary Under-Secretary, Layard, who had first met and employed Rassam at Nineveh and could have told him whether Rassam was an Armenian and whether a naturalized British subject or not.

The next section concerned the 'Visit of Consul Cameron to Bogos'. It began by noting that Cameron had stated in October 1862 that he proposed proceeding to Bogos, whose inhabitants had 'long been under the special protection of Great Britain', and 'did not feel justified, without further Instructions, to relinquish an influence which had already done much good'. Hertslet then recalled:

> It is quite true that Consul Plowden did interfere on the occasion of outrages being committed by the Bey of Taka upon the Christian Community of Bogos, and that his conduct . . . was *approved* by Her Majesty's Govt., and no instructions were ever given to him or to Captain Cameron not to interfere in their behalf, although a Despatch was addressed to Consul Plowden . . . in which he was told . . . that Her Majesty's Government did not consider that any special advantage was derived from his repeated visits into the interior . . . and that he was to return to Massowah, and not to leave it, unless under very exceptional circumstances without orders or permission from the Secretary of State.

Was Hertslet again being tactful in not mentioning the two Secretaries of State who had sent these instructions? Lord Clarendon was one of them.

Then Hertslet added: 'Captain Cameron, however, was *sent* by Her Majesty's Government into the Interior.' Also:

> It has been said that he ought not to have gone up again to Gondar when he had once returned to Massowah, but he never did return to Massowah after his first visit to the King, although he endeavoured to do so.

Hertslet then came out with a highly significant conclusion, namely, that even if the Queen's Letter, which Rassam carried, were delivered, it was 'hardly such a one as the King would *now* expect to receive, as it was written nearly two years ago'. The letter thus alluded to rumours that Cameron and others were in captivity. But surely after Rassam's letters and messengers to the King, the British Government could hardly go on pretending that they did not know what had happened about this.

Hertslet then drew attention to the fact that Dr Beke was also at that time on his way to Ethiopia and might even reach Theodore first, and would be asked for the reply from the Queen, and would not have it. Alternatively, Rassam might arrive first and present the letter ('supposing he ever delivered it') – but the text would not meet the case. So all appeared for the worse: Beke with no letter, or Rassam with an entirely out of date and inappropriate one.

This led Hertslet to conclude that it might be advisable:

> to send out direct from England (and not from Aden . . .) an English

> Gentleman with another Letter from the Queen, bearing upon the facts of the case as they at present stand, and so worded as to assure His Majesty that the British Government fully recognise him as an Independent Sovereign and are ready to receive an Embassy from him, and to conclude a new Treaty.

Hertslet, it will be recalled, had been asked by Lord Clarendon to prepare a memorandum on the imprisonment of Consul Cameron. In so doing, the Librarian had been at pains, and maybe with justice, to defend Cameron's actions, and it is on this note that he ended:

> I trust from what has now been stated that it will be admitted that Capt. Cameron was led to believe, before he left England, that it was his *duty* to sound the King about his proposed Mission, and not less so, about the conclusion of a new Treaty or a revision of the old one made with King Theodore's predecessor, and this naturally gave his 'Mission' a Political aspect, and placed him in a most embarrassing position.

25

AROUND LAKE TANA
(1865–6)

As 1865 was drawing to a close the British mission was coming to the end of its journey through the Sudan. On 28 December Rassam wrote:

> As we shall be starting this afternoon for Abyssinia, I must close this journal . . . Next month will be one of great importance for me, and of no little anxiety; for not only will the release of the prisoners depend on my diplomacy and the temper of the King, but also my own safety and that of my companions . . .

After a night of little sleep because of the cold, the party early next morning resumed its journey, and on the evening of 29 December came to the frontier river, the Gondawa, separating Egyptian-occupied Gallabat from Ethiopia. They forded the river, with the water up to the mules' knees. Rassam and his party were now in Ethiopia. They travelled on through the cold until midnight before making camp. The next day they went on through densely wooded country and crossed 30 streams to reach Wahni, the first Christian village, where they were well received by the chief and the Emperor's deputy. But of the chiefs whom Theodore had sent to meet the mission there was no sign. They had gone off to disperse rebels, but sent word that the British should go on to the next village, Balwaha, which had better camping ground, and they would meet them there in about five days. The Sudanese muleteers protested at the idea of going further up to the steep and dangerous roads of Ethiopia, but after hours of parley, cajolery and threats, they were persuaded to continue their journey. At Balwaha, Rassam camped and there saw the New Year in, hopefully. Three days later, on 4 January 1866, the chiefs duly arrived with their armed escort.

6 January being Christmas Eve, as observed by the Ethiopian Church, Rassam had two cows slaughtered which his Christian

followers enjoyed raw, a sight which somewhat amused the foreign visitors because it was new to them. Rassam also entertained a number of village children; the novelty, which at first overawed some, but which they later all enjoyed, was a swing which the British erected for them. That Ethiopian Christmas Day, Britons and Ethiopian children learned new customs. Meanwhile Rassam and the chiefs were mustering mules and porters, for the last stage of the journey to the fateful meeting.

On the following afternoon the party set off on the last stage of the journey which might take another fortnight. On two occasions messengers arrived from Flad and from the prisoners. It was lucky that on the first occasion the messengers were not intercepted because the letters were not complimentary to the Emperor; Desta, Rassam's bright young interpreter, got the men into the camp under the pretext that they were servants from Massawa who had come to join the mission, and only under cover of darkness did they hand over their letters. As the party advanced on to the plateau the nights became colder and the scenery more beautiful, and presently they came in sight of spectacular Sar Amba, one of the strongest natural fortresses in the country. The road at one time became so steep and difficult that the party had often to alight to get their mules round dangerous corners.

The mission was now in the country of the Qamant people whose religion was a mystery; they practised a kind of Christianity combined with strange Judaic and animist rituals and worship; the Qamants were most loyal to Theodore. Near Sar Amba the caravan was joined by the mother of two of Theodore's chiefs and others were joined by their wives. Rassam sent a trusted messenger to Massawa with despatches and letters for Aden and England. On this southerly journey the mission climbed a hill, and, looking east, had their first view of Gondar with Lake Tana in the distance. They kept well to the west of the town of Chilga with the intention of seeking the Emperor somewhere west of Lake Tana. As the caravan advanced the chiefs enlisted some 1,200 carriers, more for display than use; Rassam reckoned 200 would have been plenty.

For a number of days the grand caravan lumbered on its way, passing many villages and from time to time changing porters, the old ones returning to their villages. On 25 January the party descended into the valley of the Injabara, where Rassam gathered specimens of the colourful flora, under the illusion that he would soon be returning to England. The next day he had a moment of anxiety. About eight miles away he could see the smoke of the Emperor's camp rising, but his escort halted and would not advance, as they had received no imperial order to approach the camp.

By noon the next day, however, a kind message arrived from Theodore as a summons to his camp; but there was delay in getting the bearers assembled and a start was not made until noon the following day. On eventually arriving at the camp the visitors were conducted to Theodore's tent where they set eyes for the first time on the Emperor with whom they had to deal, and of whom they had heard such varying, and often unflattering, reports. There he was, sitting on a sofa, with his feet resting on the ground, while to his left stood his Ministers of State. Theodore wore over his other clothes a *shamma*, and, in keeping with Ethiopian custom, was covered with it up to his eyes, but after a while he allowed it to drop from his face. Dr Blanc has described the ruler whom he was now seeing for the first time:

> [He was] about forty-eight years of age. His complexion was darker than that of the majority of his countrymen, the nose slightly curved, the mouth large, the lips so small as hardly to be perceived. Of middle size, well knit, wiry rather than muscular, he excelled as a horseman, in the use of the spear, and on foot would tire his hardiest followers. The expression of his dark eyes, slightly depressed, was strange; if he was in good humour they were soft, with a kind of gazelle-like timidity about them that made one love him; but when angry the fierce and bloodshot eyes seemed to shed fire.

Immediately after they had exchanged salutations Rassam, who was dressed in a uniform of diplomatic blue, delivered Queen Victoria's by then hopelessly out of date and irrelevant letter, and then said briefly that His Majesty would find therein expression of goodwill. Theodore replied, 'I receive it with pleasure and I am glad to see you', and then invited the British officials to sit on his couch on his right side. Rassam then introduced his colleagues, Blanc and Prideaux, who wore coats of bright scarlet. All the exchanges were through an interpreter.

These exchanges completed, Theodore then launched into his grievances. All the misunderstandings between him and the British were due, he said, to the bad conduct of certain Europeans. He began, however, by a condemnation of Abuna Salama, who had intrigued in politics instead of attending to spiritual matters. Theodore then complained of Consul Cameron. Both Plowden and Cameron had told him that the British and their Queen had a great regard for him. So he wished to make them his permanent friends, and had accordingly written a friendly letter to the Queen. But Cameron, instead of taking the letter to Massawa and then returning with the reply, had sent it to Massawa by a messenger and had himself gone to Kassala to visit the Turks, the Emperor's enemies, and had reviled him in front of them. Theodore went on to assert that at a party given by the Turkish authorities, Cameron had made one of his servants imitate the war dance of the royal troops, at which the Turks had sneered and mocked the Emperor and his soldiers.

Regarding the Rev. Mr Stern, Theodore declared that the missionary had told him he had come to convert the Falashas to Christianity, and Theodore, because he believed in converting all the world to the Christian faith, welcomed him. But Stern had proved ungrateful, he had listened to the Abun's stories about the Emperor's mother being a woman of low degree who used to sell *kosso* – the flower taken for the cure of tapeworm.

Theodore then went on to complain bitterly of the Ethiopian people in general. When he was anointed Emperor he had intended to govern the country well, root out barbarous practices and other evils; he offered the chiefs who hitherto ruined the country by civil wars fixed stipends and attempted to bring administration under one ruler. But before he had been many years on the throne he found out that his compatriots did not appreciate good government, and preferred misrule. He was now determined to follow the rebels into every corner and send their bodies to the grave and their souls to hell. He went on to say that the Gallas had overrun the country of the Amharas, but he had brought them under his yoke. The Turks had unjustly taken Sennar and the Sudan, but he hoped before his death to drive them out. This said, the Emperor stopped and waited for the Representative of the English Queen to reply.

Rassam was immediately on his guard. He had no wish to be drawn into matters concerning the Abun or internal politics. He did not want to say anything which might appear to condemn the captives – lest they be further ill-treated; nor did he wish to oppose Theodore in opinions, lest he antagonise him at the outset. Rassam, then as always, kept uppermost in his mind the object of his mission – the captives' liberation. So, avoiding specific reference to any of the matters the Emperor had mentioned, he replied that he had not been sent to act as a judge or speak on things past. He suggested that Theodore should not be over-sensitive, but should be forbearing. Is not a king a father, and ought he not to be patient with his children? When the Emperor had read the Queen's letter he would forget the past, and try to establish friendly relations with England, and this he, Rassam, would endeavour to assist. Theodore appeared not displeased with this lecture, and smiled – but said a few more words about those whom he said had abused him. Before the audience ended, the Emperor appointed his steward Ato Samuel as interpreter to the mission, and also its *Baldaraba*, the official to help and guide them in matters concerning the court and the country. Samuel was a man of Senafé who had travelled widely, in India, Egypt and Syria.

Then the mission left the Emperor, and, accompanied by Ras Ingeda, the Prime Minister, went to their tents which had meanwhile been pitched. Soon after there arrived the Emperor's Amharic scribe with the Queen's letter and a request that Rassam with his own interpreters, Ato Samuel and the scribe, should translate the letter into Amharic. Rassam was reluctant to do this, and suggested that the Emperor's Arabic scribe could easily make the translation into Amharic, but the Emperor insisted, whereupon Rassam and the others set about making the translation.

Rassam learned that Theodore was pleased with the letter, and that his own first appearance at court had made a good impression. As a sign of favour the Emperor gave orders that the Ethiopians at the camp who had known Rassam in Massawa should be allowed to visit him. Several merchants from the port then called, with presents of honey and sheep; courtiers also called on the mission, introduced by Ato Samuel, and offered their service and friendship.

The next day brought glad tidings. Early in the morning the Emperor sent for Rassam, who came with Blanc and Prideaux. Theodore met them at the entrance of his tent, and, taking them inside, dismissed his attendants, only retaining Ras Ingeda, Ato Samuel, and the chief Amharic scribe, Aleka Ingeda. Theodore then invited them to be seated. Rassam had with him two of his own interpreters whom the Emperor questioned; one was from Shoa and he the Emperor said he could not trust because that province was in rebellion, and sent him back to his tent. The other interpreter, from Massawa, remained for the conference. The mission had not long to wait for the outcome.

To that small company Theodore said he could not sleep that night after what Rassam had said to him. He was glad to tell Rassam that for the sake of his friend, the British Queen, and in return for the trouble Rassam had taken in the matter of Cameron, he was pleased to pardon all the European captives. He said he had ordered their immediate release, and would make them over to Rassam to take out of Ethiopia.

The Emperor then ordered his scribe to read the draft of a letter in Amharic which he had written to the Queen, and told Samuel to translate it word by word into Arabic. The letter was as follows:

> To Her whom God has exalted above all Sovereigns, and glorified above all Princes and Peoples, and made the Defender of the Christian Faith, and the succour of the poor and oppressed, Victoria, the Queen of the United Kingdom of Great Britain and Ireland.
>
> Had the illustrious Hormuzd Rassam, whom your Majesty had mentioned to me in your letter, not been sent to me about the matter of Cameron and others, but the lowest of your servants, he would have been received graciously by me. I now send with Hormuzd Rassam, Cameron and all other Europeans about whom your Majesty has written. Your Majesty can learn from those who fear the Lord the ill-treatment and abuse which I have received at the hands of the above-mentioned Europeans, and the Copt who called himself Metropolitan, the Abûna Salàma.
>
> In my humble position I am not worthy to address your Majesty; but illustrious Princes and the deep ocean can bear everything. I, being an ignorant Ethiopian, hope that your Majesty will overlook my shortcomings and pardon my faults.
>
> The people, whom I have imprisoned for reviling and defaming me, did so because the Gallas had proved victorious over the royal Children of Israel and had humbled them [a reference to the usurpation of royal power by a Galla dynasty in Wollo]; but God has empowered me, the son of one of the humble women of Israel, to regain that which had been lost by my forefathers.
>
> Doubtless, your Majesty has learnt how ignorant and blind the people of Ethiopia are; wherefore I beg of your Majesty not to take amiss the mistakes I may make in my correspondence with you. Counsel me, but do not blame me, O Queen, whose majesty God has glorified, and to whom He has given abundance of wisdom.

As soon as the letter was read, Rassam thanked the Emperor, on behalf of the Queen and of the British nation, for the friendship he had shown that day. Theodore replied that he was as happy as

Rassam at the ending of the long-existing misunderstanding, and hoped that in future all would go well between the two countries.

That, however, was not quite the happy ending. The mission could hardly have wished for a better outcome, and so soon, to that morning's conference. But to Rassam's great disappointment Theodore then embarked on a long recitation of his grievances against Cameron and the missionaries: he, Theodore, had received the Consul with great pomp for the sake of his friend, the British Queen; he had heard that the best way to cultivate the friendship of a European Power was to send an Embassy to it; he had no ships and the Turks on the way were his enemies, so he had written to the Queen for a vessel to convey his Embassy; he made all necessary provision for Cameron to take the letter, but the Consul instead had gone to amuse himself among the Turks; Cameron returned without an answer, but he, Theodore, had allowed him to remain peacefully in the country; six months later Cameron sent him a letter which he had received from his country and requested to leave forthwith; he had summoned Cameron and asked why, if he wished to be at Massawa, had he returned to Gondar; when he could get no satisfactory explanation he had said to him, by the power of God, you shall be detained in prison until I find out whether you are the servant of the Queen or not.

In his record of this meeting Rassam wrote, 'I thought it prudent to give no answer to these complaints.' He told the Emperor he had brought presents with him which he hoped Theodore would accept, and the latter said he would let Rassam know about this later. During the day the Emperor sent word to Rassam that he would like him to translate the letter to the Queen into English and that he would sign it, even though he could not read the translation, to show his complete confidence in Rassam. A couple of days later the envoy was also given the Amharic version to send to England. Before accepting the presents (which were very modest, and far poorer than those despatched to King Sahle Selassie of Shoa a generation earlier) Theodore asked whether they were from Rassam or from the Queen, and on learning that although Rassam had himself purchased them, they were bought with British Government money, and he could accept them as from the Queen, he received them that same afternoon after the morning conference, in a field outside his tent, and seemed pleased with them. Rassam relates that when he said he had brought a mirror from the Queen, Theodore replied: 'Unhappily, since the death of my good Queen I have been leading an un-Christian and disreputable life; but I have a person now whom I intend to make Queen, and I will present it to her. I thank you very much for it.'

True enough, Theodore, after the death of his 'good Queen', Tewabetch, had married again, but not happily. After his defeat and imprisonment of Dejazmatch Wubie he had married the latter's daughter, Terunesh. Whereas Ali's daughter had loved and assisted Theodore, Wubie's despised him as an upstart, and, although she bore him an heir for whom Theodore showed great affection, the royal spouses had little time for one another. Theodore, deprived of the love of his first Queen, and receiving no love or companionship from his second Queen, turned to concubinage. In his reply to Rassam, he was probably referring to his beloved mistress, Yetemagnu.

On their third day at the royal camp the British mission received word that the Emperor wished them to go and stay at the village of Qorata on the eastern shore of Lake Tana, there to await the arrival of the captives from Magdala, his reason being that members of the mission were fond of the sea breezes and could amuse themselves fishing. Theodore also said he would escort the mission for a day or two on their way to the Lake.

At 7 a.m. the Emperor left his camp with his army, estimated at 45,000 men, followed by a like number of wives, children and male and female camp followers. Later in the morning the British mission moved off, and after about two hours reached the Emperor's new camp at Sakola. They found their red tent already erected next to the Emperor's white pavilion. The next day the army was on the move by 8 a.m. Leaving a little later, the mission caught up with it in the early afternoon, and found the court set up at Bifata on a hill overlooking Damot.

The following day, 1 February, the Emperor moved off early, and sent word that the mission should now ride with him. As Rassam relates:

> The King rode in front in a most graceful style, followed by two pages, one carrying his shield and the other a gun and a telescope. Next in order was Ras Ingeda, and then my companions and myself, Samuel riding at my side ready to translate . . . Behind us came the interpreters, the royal stud, and a number of courtiers; and behind them again the advancing multitude . . . The King and his immediage cortège pursued the regular path, but the bulk of the army had to make the best way they could over hill and dale, always managing, however, to reach the

> rendezvous in good time . . . The sight . . . was truly picturesque and grand.

On coming to a village, the Emperor chose to camp. By 8 a.m. the army was again on the move, and soon came to the Blue Nile. Theodore forded the river on foot and on reaching the far bank called out to Rassam and his companions not to dismount, and they forded the river on their mules, but the opposite bank proved slippery so here they dismounted and clambered up. Doing so, Rassam slipped and the Emperor ran and seized him, saving him from falling back into the river. Theodore stayed by the river to see his army, as well as the women and children, over safely. Rassam reflected: 'Theodore, when he chose, could be most condescending and kind, and few could excel him in the art of pleasing. But for the vicious temper with which these qualities were unfortunately associated, what a pattern man he would have been.' This day the Emperor camped early, and with his fighting men went off to disperse rebels, who, however, made off before he came in sight. Next day, deciding on a circuitous route, the Emperor led his army across the Blue Nile twice, but by better fords than the first.

On the march Theodore, through his interpreters, had a long talk with Rassam. He discussed European warfare, the civil war in the United States, British hostilities against the Ashantis in West Africa, and the Crimean War. Several of his questions were perhaps revealing. He wanted to know whether Czar Nicholas had died a natural death, or had been executed by the British. He also wanted to know 'how the French managed to have one of their own people as Prime Minister' in Madagascar. He wanted to know if there was a country called Dahomey, and was it true that its ruler 'annually sacrificed hundreds of human beings in some religious ceremony', and if so 'why the Christian Powers did not put a stop to such barbarity?' Then he spoke of Rassam's mission. Since the death of Plowden and Yohannes (John Bell), said Theodore, he had found the British and other Europeans 'wanting in sincerity, ill-mannered and ill-tempered'. And so he had delayed Rassam at Massawa to test him; his patient wait there had convinced him of his worth; now he wished to cultivate friendship with Britain – his object ever since he had come to the throne.

On entering the province of Agowmeder the Emperor made camp. It was now 3 February, five days since he had said he would release Consul Cameron and his fellow captives. On several occasions Rassam had pressed Ato Samuel on this matter, but it seemed that the Emperor had done nothing further about it. That day, however, at their camp in the district of Fagata, Theodore sent word to Rassam that he was sending an officer to Magdala to unfetter the prisoners and bring them to Rassam, and the Emperor requested him to write to Cameron to inform him of his release, and that of his fellow prisoners. He also requested the envoy to send one of his own followers with the officer to take care of the prisoners on their journey from Magdala. Delighted with this news, Rassam hastened to comply. The letter was written, and Rassam's follower and the Emperor's officer were ready to depart. Then orders came from the Emperor, countermanding his order for their immediate departure, as he had not decided where the prisoners should meet Rassam.

The next morning Theodore sent word that before Rassam left for the lake he wished to have a conversation with him. Rassam, with his two colleagues, found the Emperor waiting for them outside his tent. He ordered two carpets to be brought out; he then sat on one and the members of the mission on the other, facing him. When all were seated, Theodore began a recital of grievances, first against the missionaries, and then against Cameron. He had previously prepared presents for the Queen, and Mr Cameron had spoiled all that, but now he considered Rassam, Blanc and Prideaux like his brothers, and he would make presents of Ethiopian craftsmanship to Rassam, as a token of friendship. Then he embarked on his special grievance against Stern and also Mrs Flad and Rosenthal, all of whom had ridiculed and insulted him, and had not Mrs Flad been a woman he would have punished her too. 'The King', Rassam narrated, 'got so excited while repeating these different grievances . . . that I began to fear something disastrous was coming. His face grew ashy pale and his hands shook, especially when I tried to soothe him.' The envoy's answers, however, eventually pacified Theodore, who said he must not think of the past, but only of his friendship for the mission.

When Theodore's anger had somewhat abated he said he would like Rassam and his party to leave the camp the next morning, and that the envoy could choose whether to await the freed prisoners at Debra Tabor or at Qorata by the lake; but Rassam begged the Emperor to make the choice, and it was then agreed that the mission's resting place should be Qorata, with freedom to go to Debra Tabor and other places.

The Emperor then referred to the treaty Plowden haa made with Ras Ali, and how Plowden had wished to renew that treaty with him and hoist a British flag in Ethiopia, proposals which did not appeal to him, but he would now be willing to make a treaty with Mr Rassam. 'My answer to this,' the envoy relates, 'was that I was not sent by the British Government to make a treaty with his Majesty; that such a mission required authority and particular instructions; nevertheless, I felt convinced that when I returned to England, and represented to Her Majesty's Government how well-disposed he was towards it, due consideration would be given to all his Majesty's propositions.'

Thus in February 1866, at his camp in Agowmeder, Emperor Theodore proposed that he would make a treaty with the Head of the British mission; and the latter turned it aside as a proposal which he was not authorised to discuss. Walter Plowden lay at rest on the other side of the great lake. Did he turn in his grave? What would he not have given to have heard his friend Theodore utter those words. At Massawa, when first he was a Consul, though a sick man, he had travelled into the interior with his trade treaty to seek Ras Ali at Debra Tabor, and follow him on his campaign to Gojjam where at last he secured the Ras's signature to the treaty. Later he had asked Theodore to ratify that treaty, but in vain. All he had worked for, at risk of health and life, was in ruins: his successor as Consul was a prisoner in chains, and his much prized treaty, which Cameron had tried to revive, had suffered and more than suffered from Ras Ali's prediction: in the conditions of Ethiopia, the Ras had said, the treaty would be useless for ten years. Ten years had passed and the treaty had become a dead letter. Now 17 years later, Theodore, without even being asked, proposed to negotiate a treaty with England, a proposition which would have so delighted Plowden and vindicated his endeavours. What was in Theodore's mind? His dreams were in ruins, his Empire in chaos; there was rebellion in three great provinces, Tigré, Gojjam and Shoa, and some of the smaller provinces not in revolt he himself had ravaged. Could he have hoped that the great Queen of Britain might have become his ally to restore his power? But what value could Theodore's proposal now have?

In concluding this conference the Emperor, who may have recalled the presents earlier showered by an earlier British mission sent from India to King Sahle Selassie, said he considered the Queen too great a person for him to communicate with direct, but he had heard that she had a great number of Governors in India, and he would like her to appoint one of them to correspond with him: this would also be more convenient as India was nearer to his country than England. It was a strangely prophetic observation. Little did any of those who took part in that two-hour conference, in the growing heat of the climbing sun (so excited had been Theodore that he had forgotten his usual custom of calling for umbrellas), foresee that the British Government would soon give serious consideration to the fact that India was nearer to Ethiopia than England, and that the British Queen would send one of her great servants from India to communicate – in a different manner – with the strange Ethiopian monarch.

The conference over, Rassam asked the Emperor to appoint someone whom he trusted to be a messenger between them, and the Emperor said '*Ish-shi*; take Aito Samuel, because I both love and trust him.'

A little later the Emperor sent a letter to Rassam telling him he was making him a gift of one single-barrelled and four double-barrelled muskets and five single-barrelled pistols, and he was also arranging for him to be supplied with 5,000 Maria Theresa dollars on his way to Qorata. Like the two British Consuls before, Rassam was embarrassed by this gift, which was far more generous than the British presents for the monarch, and which British Service rules forbade him to accept, but, advised that the Emperor would take offence at a refusal, he did as those before him: he accepted the money and credited it to the British Government's account. The Emperor's parting letter concluded: 'When the men [prisoners] shall be delivered to you, if God permit, I will come and wish you farewell; but if I am not able to come to you in person, I will give orders to have you sent to the frontier in safety and in honour.'

Two days later the British mission made preparations to leave the camp the following morning and move off towards Lake Tana which lay some two days' march to the north, but they learned that the Emperor was in a dreadful mood. It was said officially that he was 'asleep', and when the morning for their departure arrived, the Emperor having 'over-slept', the mission did not get away until the afternoon. However, on Theodore's orders their old escort and other chiefs of the district accompanied the mission on its march to the Lake where the Emperor had arranged that they should take reed canoes to cross over to Qorata.

At the first halt, at Zugda, Rassam gave an Ethiopian merchant bound for Gondar a note for Colonel Merewether at Aden. After overnight stops the mission reached the south-westerly shores of Lake Tana at 2 p.m., their baggage catching up with them in the evening. The next day was spent at a lake-side village waiting for boats to arrive from the island of Daq and from Qorata. The British mission spent a pleasant day hunting hippopotami along the shore. Rassam secured one kill, to the delight of the local hunters who said the flesh would give food to 50 families for a week.

The next morning half the required canoes having arrived, Rassam and some of his party set off on the first part of their lake journey, as far as the island of Daq where they spent the night. The mules and horses, meanwhile, were being sent overland.

Embarking again on their strange craft early the next morning, the mission reached Qorata by noon. As ordered by the Emperor they were met at the shore by its leading merchants. The town was the nearest place the mission had yet reached to Magdala, which lay 200 miles farther to the east, and was a healthy and very pleasant spot in which to wait.

Waiting was still an anxious matter. Yet the mission had accomplished much: despite frustrations and difficulties they had secured the object of their errand, the liberation of the captives. And it was certainly better by far to be waiting at Qorata, within easy reach of the Emperor, than in Massawa. Now there would be only good news to send to Aden and to England. So it seemed.

26

FAREWELL TO LAKE TANA

(1866)

After some days the British mission moved out of Qorata to pitch their tents on ground near the lake. From their new position they could see across it the lofty Zagé promontory with a church on its high ground, and also the smoke rising from the Emperor's camp, though this itself lay hidden. Over the ensuing days reed canoes made frequent journeys as Rassam and Theodore exchanged many courteous messages.

Soon after making his new camp near the lake, Rassam received a letter from the Emperor saying he had previously acted towards the prisoners 'erroneously, through the devil, without consideration', but would make good any property they had lost 'not merely for the sake of my friendship for the great Queen, but for the friendship which I entertain for you three'. Then he went on to say: 'I apprehended that I had lost all hopes of your (the British) friendship; otherwise I would not have acted so badly.'

The captives were expected within four or five days, but owing to past sufferings they could not travel that fast, and the mission had to spend several more days of waiting, with some renewed anxiety. Meanwhile, on the morning of 28 February, the European artisans arrived from Gafat, in accordance with the Emperor's order, wearing silk shirts. They called on Rassam, and then pitched their tents. They were Messrs Moritz Hall, Saalmüller, Bender, Bourgaud and Dr Schimper. During the ensuing interview Schimper, speaking in Arabic, told Rassam of his experiences in Ethiopia, and warned him not to trust present appearances, however favourable they might be. 'Placing the palm of his hand upwards and then reversing it,' relates Rassam, 'Schimper said, "Abyssinia is like that; but I must say no more, as the walls have ears".' A little later the Emperor ordered the artisans to summon their wives.

A few days later a messenger, held up by a storm on the lake, arrived with a brief letter from the Emperor saying: 'The people [the prisoners] whom you want, may the Lord bring to you, and may He cause you to reach your country in safety. May the Lord plant my friendship and goodwill in your hearts, and may He cause you to open my eyes.' Rassam replied politely that he hoped the Emperor would before long grant him permission to leave Ethiopia, before the unhealthy season set in in the Sudan.

The first notes from the prisoners since leaving Magdala now reached Rassam. One was from Consul Cameron, the other from the Rev. Stern. They said they had been freed of their chains, but on account of their weakness had to travel slowly. Encouraged by receiving these letters the mission waited more hopefully, but a couple of days later a letter arrived from the Emperor to cause them some alarm. Theodore began with the words: 'When the people reach you, we will consult.'

Ever since the mission had entered Ethiopia, and ever since they had met Theodore, despite delays and anxieties, all had turned out well. Rassam had obtained from the Emperor permission to take out of Ethiopia not only the Queen's subjects, but all the Europeans who wished to leave; and the Emperor's order was well in course of fulfilment, most of the artisans were at Rassam's camp, and their wives were about to join them; the British and other prisoners were freed of their chains, and were half way to Qorata; their personal property was to be restored to them and compensation made for what could not be recovered; within a week all the Europeans should be under Rassam's control, and the season was still favourable for travel to the Sudan or Massawa as circumstances might require. And in all the exchanges with Rassam, whether written or oral, Theodore had always given the impression that once the Europeans were handed over to the envoy's care they could all leave Ethiopia in peace. What then did he now mean by 'we will consult'?

A few days later, on 8 March, one of Rassam's messengers arrived from Massawa with letters. One was from Munzinger, now the Acting British Consul at the port, and it gave very strange news: Dr Beke and his wife had arrived; and Beke was on a mission to Theodore to ask him to liberate the prisoners. The messenger had told Dr Beke that the captives would be released, and begged him not to let any news of his arrival reach the Emperor, lest harm might befall all the Europeans. Dr Beke's only reply was that Rassam had no chance of succeeding, and the only person who could succeed was Dr Beke.

The British Foreign Secretary, Lord Russell, had tried to persuade Dr Beke to give up his venture, which would most likely harm the Government's own mission; but Dr Beke knew best, and the British Government had no power to prevent his leaving England. In Egypt the British Consul had asked him not to go on, or at least to wait to hear more of Rassam's progress; but Dr Beke knew best, and went on to Aden; there Colonel Merewether repeated the arguments all over again, but Dr Beke remained convinced that only one person could liberate the captives, and that person was himself. So in January 1866 Dr Beke reached Massawa and he too was the bearer of a letter, or rather a plea, intended to bring about the liberation of the Europeans – a petition to the Emperor signed by the prisoners' relatives. News of Dr Beke's arrival did not gladden Rassam or his friends at Qorata, for they reflected that Theodore would have heard of the doctor's presence in Massawa before Rassam himself had learnt of it.

Amid these new perplexities Rassam received a favourable letter from the Emperor. It informed him that the prisoners had safely reached Debra Tabor, and gave permission for Dr Blanc to attend Consul Cameron who was ill, and concluded: 'When they reach you safely let me at once know . . . in order that we may have a chat together.' From these words, and from oral messages from the Emperor, it now appeared to Rassam that Theodore wanted to put Cameron and his companions again on trial. Rassam's great fear was that since the Emperor so hated the captives it would go ill with them if they appeared before him. The envoy therefore sent word to Theodore by Samuel that he should let the prisoners leave the country without more ado, but if he really wanted another trial it should be held at Qorata, without all the difficulty of getting the Europeans across the lake to Zagé.

On 10 March the wives of the artisans arrived at Qorata, all in Ethiopian attire, except a French lady, Madame Bourgaud, who was in European dress. They all assembled in the tent of Mr Waldmeier where Rassam went to welcome them. The ladies included two daughters of John Bell by his Ethiopian wife; they were now married, one to Waldmeier and the other to Mr Saalmüller. There were also two half-Ethiopian daughters of Dr Schimper, one the wife of Mr Bender; two other ladies were Gallas, the wives of Mr Mayer and Mr Zander; finally there was Mrs Moritz Hall, said to have been born of an Armenian father and an Ethiopian mother. Mrs Bourgaud spoke only French and the other ladies

Amharic, so Rassam addressed them through an interpreter. The next day there was good news in a letter from Cameron: he was better and reckoned that his party would arrive at Qorata on the morrow.

News of the captives' arrival reached the British mission in the afternoon of 12 March, a day to be remembered. The head of their escort was at first much concerned with etiquette, the order in which they should be brought in, and the method of counting the prisoners he was to hand over. Rassam managed to cut short some of these formalities. He was then able to welcome the people whose freedom it had for so long been his purpose to procure. They were Consul Cameron, and twelve other men from various countries, of whom five were missionaries, two women, wives of missionaries, and three Flad children.

The envoy had a few words for all of them, and then showed them where they were to stay. This was the great day for which Rassam had striven for over 18 months. Delighted as he was with this so longed-for outcome, his reception of the liberated prisoners was calculatedly formal; he had been warned that any great cordiality might prejudice him and them in the eyes of the proud monarch who still regarded them as enemies who had done him injury; Rassam must not appear to be siding with the Emperor's enemies. He felt it painful to suppress his feelings, especially in the case of Cameron and Stern; but he made sure his servants would supply them with all they needed.

The reception over, Rassam went to his tent and wrote to the Emperor, informing him of the arrival of Cameron and the others, thanking him for the consideration shown them on the road, and notifying him of the arrival of Flad and others from Gafat.

Rassam now waited to hear what the Emperor would do about any further trial. Theodore pondered for two days, and then sent his answer. The envoy himself was to hold one in his tent, on the Emperor's behalf, the charges against them should be read to them, and they were to be asked whether it was true or not that they had abused the Emperor. The purpose of this trial was to convince the mission that the accused had treated the Ethiopian monarch badly, and that he had acted justly in imprisoning them. If Rassam found this to be true, the Emperor required from the prisoners a *Feker-Kasa*, or friendly indemnity; on the other hand, if Rassam found the Emperor in the wrong, then the latter would indemnify the prisoners in any way the envoy thought fit.

Rassam considered what to do: should he refuse to hold the trial and perhaps provoke Theodore into sending them all back to Magdala, himself along with the others; or should he try to please the Emperor tactfully and hope for the best. Before taking any action, and before replying to the monarch Rassam consulted Flad, Waldmeier and Samuel, all of whom knew Theodore well. They strongly counselled him to fall in with the Emperor's wishes, the more so as Rassam was to spend a few days with Theodore and would have an opportunity of impressing on him the advantage of letting the Europeans depart in peace.

But Rassam's friends also gave their interpretation of the Emperor's letter, charges and intentions. They explained that a *Feker-Kasa* did not necessarily mean a light indemnity, and what Theodore desired was that Rassam should write to England for a 'scientific man' to come out to help and advise on plans for development of the country, and, moreover, it was the Emperor's intention to detain the Europeans as hostages until such a person or persons arrived.

Rassam acted on his friends' advice. The next morning, at 11 a.m., he held the trial in his tent, and at his command the charges were read out. They were presented in two parts, the first against Cameron and his sometime servant, Bardel, both of whom were specifically named.

The Emperor's case against Cameron was that he had been received in friendship and with honour, told that Theodore wished to send a mission to England, and given a friendly letter to the Queen, but this 'he abandoned, and went to the Turks, who do not love me, and before whom he insulted and lowered me. When Cameron returned, I asked him, "Where is the answer to the friendly letter I entrusted you with; what have you come for?" He said to me, "I do not know." So I said to him, "You are not the servant of my friend, the Queen, as you had represented yourself to be"; and by the power of my Creator, I imprisoned him. Ask him if he can deny this.'

The charge against Bardel was that he had told Theodore that he wished to put him in contact with the Emperor of the French, to whom Theodore had accordingly sent him. On his return to Ethiopia Bardel said Napoleon III had refused to see him, upon which Theodore observed, 'Never mind, I have my God.' Presently Bardel asked Theodore to release the Frenchman Macraire, and the Emperor said, 'For whose sake shall I release him?' and refused to do so. At this Bardel became offensive, whereupon, said Theodore, 'I was annoyed at this and, by the power of my Lord, I imprisoned him. Ask him if he can deny this.'

In the second part of the session the charges against the other prisoners were lumped together without any of the accused being named, not even Stern. The accusation read:

> The other prisoners have abused me . . . I used to love and honour them. A friend ought to be a shield to his friend, and they ought to have shielded me. Why did they not defend me? On this account I disliked them.
>
> Now, by the power of God, for the sake of the Queen and the British people and yourselves, I cannot continue my dislike towards them. I wish you to make between us a reconciliation from the heart. If I am in fault, do you tell me, and I will requite them; but if you find that I am wronged, I wish you to get them to requite me.

Everyone in the tent felt the trial was a farce; what they could not be sure about was the reason why Theodore wanted it enacted. The prisoners and their friends had been in Ethiopia long enough to know that it would be dangerous to dispute the Emperor's assertions. It was therefore agreed that the prisoners should all admit that they had done wrong, and beg his Majesty's forgiveness.

Rassam, by letter dated Qorata, 16 March, sent the Emperor a report of the trial held the previous day. He was at pains to avoid saying the prisoners pleaded 'Guilty', but stated that they had 'all confessed that they had done wrong, and hoped that as your Majesty had been good enough to release them for the sake of your friendship to our Queen, you would extend to them the forgiveness due from one Christian to another'. Regarding the scientific person desired by Theodore to teach the arts he said nothing would please him more than to be of service to the Emperor, and he could not do so better than by being on the spot to 'aid you in everything which my Queen can do for you; but if your Majesty desires otherwise, I shall be happy to comply with your wishes'.

Rassam further instructed the Emperor's officers to tell Theodore how dangerous it would be to detain him in Ethiopia until the arrival of the 'scientific man', for it would be construed in Europe that he was being detained as a hostage; far better that the Emperor should trust him and give up any idea that he would forget him once he had left the country.

Delayed by a storm, the officers set off across the lake a day later. The die would soon be cast. Despite the tact he had exercised Rassam reflected that the outcome would depend 'entirely on the whim of the royal gamester'. But would the Emperor act on a whim, as he so often seemed to do, or would he act, was he acting, however disguisedly, on a definite and settled, if ill-informed and misguided policy?

The trial held in his tent was not Rassam's only adventure of that day. A messenger arrived bringing a letter to the Emperor from Dr Beke, who had told him to take it straight to Theodore, but, being afraid to do so, had brought it instead to Rassam. (Beke had not thought fit to send any message to the latter.) Some of the Europeans urged Rassam to suppress the letter, but he refused to do so, and sent the letter on to the Emperor by one of his own messengers.

Two days later there was a favourable letter from the Emperor. He could not help saying again – it seemed ceaselessly to rankle – that he 'used to reckon' Cameron and other Europeans as his friends and had 'honoured them', but they had 'wronged' him. Nevertheless:

> For the sake of our Lord, and, below him, for the sake of the great Queen, my friend, Victoria, I have forgiven them. The contents of your letter have made me glad . . . I want you to come to me, in order that we may consult together.
>
> The relations of Cameron and his imprisoned companions have written to me in sorrow about them. By the power of God, and for the sake of my friend, the great Queen Victoria, I have been reconciled to them, and by the power of our Creator we will consult on all matters when we meet.

Theodore had given orders for release of the captives and had promised Rassam that he would hand them over to him to take out of Ethiopia, long before he had ever heard of Dr Beke's arrival at Massawa. Later, the Emperor sent Rassam Beke's letter and the relatives' petitions which contained such phrases as, 'humbly, at the feet of your Majesty, plead for mercy and pardon for the wretched Europeans'. Rassam reflected that Theodore, on reading such supplications, might well have thought that he had agreed to release the prisoners too cheaply, and that he might still exact greater satisfaction in some shape or other. Rassam believed that even after receiving the petitions Theodore still intended to consult with him about the captives' departure, but that on further reflection he began to see some plot or duplicity in the simultaneous presence of two British missions, and believed that the envoy, until now trusted, was a party to it.

Despite Rassam's growing misgivings optimism predominated in the European colony at Qorata. This was expressed in a letter, dated 20 March, written by Waldmeier, to Bishop Gobat, in which he said:

> Mr Rassam has so far perfectly succeeded . . . We expect that in about three weeks Mr Rassam will take his departure, together with the liberated Europeans . . .
>
> Three days ago the King received several petitions in favour of the captives . . . These petitions . . . deeply moved the heart of the King, though they were too late. The short answer of the King was: 'I have delivered all these persons to Mr Rassam out of friendship to the Queen; they are all free.' With respect to the presents about which Dr Beke has written to the King, his Majesty was most displeased, and expressed strongly his dissatisfaction that people should think that he loves presents, whilst friendship and love is all that he desires.

Theodore postponed the meeting with Rassam for some days to meet the ladies of his court, and inspect horses being brought from Debra Tabor. He nevertheless displayed his friendship for the mission. Some little while earlier he had sent goldsmiths to Rassam so that he might show them how to make the insignia of an order, called the Cross and Solomon's Seal, with which he proposed to honour Rassam and his colleagues; as the Ethiopian craftsmen did not make much progress in a fortnight Theodore commanded one of his European artisans, Mr Zander, to make the emblems. Theodore on two occasions also sent Rassam gifts of 5,000 Maria Theresa dollars, to pay for his expenses, and on the second occasion also sent 50 milch cows to enable the envoy to have milk for his now large party.

Anxious about the outcome of his next meeting with Theodore, Rassam despatched messengers with letters to be sent on to Europe. The men set off on 23 March, and the same day he received another friendly letter from Theodore summoning him to come to his camp. This said:

> With regard to myself, whether I dislike you or love you, oh English! you can discover from my conduct in the affair of Plowden and Yohannes [Mr Bell]. According to the rules of my country and my ability, I

> used to love and honour them [the English]. My love and honour towards them was for the purpose of obtaining the regard of the Queen and yourselves. That love of yours which I was longing for, I feel convinced I have obtained, and, by the power of God, it has given me joy.

Two days later, early in the morning, the members of the mission and the European artisans crossed over to Zagé. On reaching the shore, the members of the mission donned their uniforms. They were met by the Prime Minister, Ras Ingeda, and other chiefs, with richly decorated mules, and set off at a brisk trot to the royal encampment where tents had been prepared for them. A couple of hours later the Emperor visited them, a rare honour. After a cordial stay of about ten minutes he took Rassam by the hand, and said to him and his two colleagues, 'Come along, and let us have a chat.' He also summoned the artisans.

In the royal tent carpets had been laid out, and the mission sat near the Emperor, the artisans at some distance to the left. Theodore then alluded to his old grievances against the captives, but soon his eldest son, Ras Mashesha entered, whereupon the Europeans stood up, and the Emperor said: 'Mashesha, draw near, and shake hands with my English friends in the English fashion, as I want you to become one of them.' Theodore then said to Rassam: 'I wish this son of mine, and another at Magdala (his heir, Dejaj Alemajehu) to be adopted children of the English; and when you go back to your country, I want you to recommend them to your Queen, in order that, when I die, they may be looked after by the English, and not be allowed to govern badly.'

The ceremony over, the Emperor had his muskets and pistols, including the gift from Plowden, brought to him, and showed them to the mission, with suitable anecdotes and reminiscences. He made passing references to the Abun, Cameron and Stern, but even so the conversation, lasting two hours, was friendly; at their departure Theodore ordered his son and other officers to accompany the mission to their tent. So far so good, but when would Theodore come to the question of the departure of the mission and the former captives and others?

Early the following morning Rassam learned that the Emperor had summoned all his great chiefs then at the camp, some 85, and was consulting with them about the departure of the Europeans, and early in the conference he also summoned the European artisans to have their opinion. They all recommended that the

Europeans should depart, but the Emperor asked, 'What surety have I in hand?' Thereupon Herr Zander stepped forward. Queen Victoria's letter, which Rassam had brought, lay before the Emperor. The German picked it up, opened it, placed his hand on the royal signature and seal, and said: 'Trust to these, your Majesty; they are a true voucher to the word of the English Queen.' The Emperor told the Europeans to go and wait outside. He then turned to his chiefs, and again asked them whether he should let Rassam depart or retain him until some other evidence reached him to prove England's friendship. Not one dissenting, they again called out, 'Let Rassam go.' Theodore once more asked, 'What have I in my hands?' Then spoke up a mighty Ras saying, 'Let Rassam depart in peace; if he behaves falsely, let God be the judge between you and him,' and another chief added, 'If your Majesty does not trust the English, make Mr Rassam swear on the Bible, before you permit him to go, that he will not prove false to you.' The Emperor then dismissed his counsellors, and sent for Rassam. The three members of the mission went to the royal tent, after which Theodore called out for the artisans to re-enter, and all sat on the carpets. Addressing the mission, Theodore said he had consulted all those whom he trusted, Ethiopians and Europeans, and they had advised that Rassam and his party should go, so they would depart after Ethiopian Easter, but then Theodore added: 'How can I trust any European now after the ill-behaviour of those whom I have treated like brothers?'

Theodore concluded by saying that if other Europeans had treated him badly, how was he to know that Rassam would not do likewise. Rassam replied by begging the Emperor to trust him and judge him by his future conduct. Theodore said: 'Very well, I will try you; and may you reach your country safely.'

After the interview, which had lasted more than two hours, Theodore told Rassam to return to Qorata, and make preparations for his departure and that of his companions and the former captives; he also ordered that the messenger from Dr Beke should return with Rassam to Massawa, but he gave no letter for Dr Beke. The Emperor said he would see Rassam again as he wished him to come over and bid good-bye before leaving Ethiopia. Ras Ingeda then escorted Rassam and his companions to the shore, and taking to the reed canoes they reached Qorata at midnight.

Rassam and his companions waited for the coming of Ethiopian Easter which fell on 8 April, and in the interval hope and anxiety alternated. The artisans were making presents as well as insignias of the order, which the Emperor wanted to give to the members of the mission; and as far as Rassam was concerned they could not work too quickly, for the Emperor was not likely to let them depart without these honours.

Plans for the departure were now being made on the basis of orders by the Emperor. The released captives were to proceed overland to Gojja on the north-western corner of the lake, while the mission were to cross over to Zagé, with as little luggage as possible, take leave of the Emperor, and then go on to join the other Europeans.

On 5 April, Rassam received the following note from Theodore:

> I have been long fasting, and have abstained from eating meat, and I am anxious to see the light of Easter. Pray that I may see it in health. By the power of God, I will also offer up to Him the same supplication for you.

Samuel had been summoned to Zagé to receive further instructions regarding the departure and he left Qorata the next day, carrying a letter from Rassam to Theodore expressing Christian greetings for Easter. Two days later, Samuel brought back the Emperor's instructions and other information. Theodore's letter was brief. It opened with the words, 'May God grant me a meeting with you, my friend, after the light of Easter', thanked Rassam for a gift, and ended, 'I have ordered Lij Abita to take your mules through Dambea; and Kentiba Hailu and Aito Samuel to bring you to me.'

The letter made no mention of the other Europeans, but by an oral message the Emperor instructed Rassam to bring with him all the Europeans, released captives and artisans, and all the baggage; the mules were to be sent round the northern side of the lake, but there was now no mention of any meeting. The Emperor's officers told Rassam that a space had been reserved outside the Royal camp where the Europeans were to pitch their tents. This almost complete change of plans puzzled Rassam, and the Emperor's officers seemed as puzzled as he. Rassam was specially concerned that taking the released prisoners into Theodore's presence might mean that they might again be detained. So convinced was he of this that he asked two of the Emperor's officers to take a message from him asking the monarch's permission to allow the released prisoners to proceed on their way to Matemma, without coming to Zagé. To Rassam's delight, by messages which he received on 10 April, the Emperor approved this proposal, and gave additional instructions: the former captives were to proceed along the east shore of the lake, while Rassam with others were to proceed to Gojja, whence all were to set off for Matemma. Rassam was also told that the Emperor was preparing presents for him, and had named various high officers to escort him beyond Gojja, while his old escort, which had brought him into Ethiopia, were ordered to prepare to go with his party as far as Matemma.

Friday, 13 April was the great day of departure from Qorata. At 10 a.m. the cavalcade of released prisoners rode out northwards along the lakeside road, while Rassam, Blanc, Prideaux, the European artisans and their wives, and Ato Samuel and Hailu, set off by boat. The three members of the mission made a halt on the shore, some two miles before their destination, put on their uniforms, and resumed the canoe journey. At about 1 p.m. they landed on the shore at Zagé where they were met by the Prime Minister, Ras Ingeda, with mules for the ride to the Royal camp.

On reaching the Royal courtyard the party proceeded to the door of the Emperor's hall and saw it crowded with chiefs all in their silk shirts. This was unexpected, but Rassam presumed Theodore was continuing his Easter celebrations. Rassam followed the Prime Minister into the hall, and was followed in turn by his own two colleagues. Then began a strange performance.

On stepping into the hall Rassam made to move in the direction of the throne to salute the Emperor, but before he could take another step three chiefs seized him, two by the arms while the third took hold of the tail of his coat, and quickly searched him to see if he carried any arms. For a second Rassam thought he must accidentally have gone past the Emperor and the chiefs were holding him back, but at this moment the Prime Minister glanced at him and said, 'Do not fear', then Rassam thought something must be wrong and he looked round for Blanc and Prideaux, and saw that they too had been seized. All three were pushed to the front of the throne which they now observed was empty, and were held standing, to await the Emperor's orders. It was soon plain that Theodore was behind a door not more than ten yards away, listening to what was going on. Orders soon came from him that they were to have the seats of honour placed at the foot of the throne, with the Rases ranged on either side.

Soon a messenger, Kantiba Hailu, emerged from the door, and, speaking in Amharic, brought a question from the Emperor, which was translated to Rassam, and there thus began a long interrogation, with questions and answers carried to and fro by a messenger going and coming between the Emperor and the interpreters near the throne. Rassam spoke up loud and clear in Arabic, so that the Emperor might hear what he said, in addition to what the translation might be.

The first question was, 'Where are the European Magdala prisoners?' Rassam replied that the Emperor would know better than he where they were. The royal answer came back that the members of the mission should not fear, because the present was only a misunderstanding that would soon vanish. And Rassam with some acrimony answered: 'What have we to fear? Have we not come into this country depending upon the word of a King, and one who calls himself a Christian? And where are we now, but in the house of the very person who ought to afford us protection? But why this insult and disgrace? Is this the way to receive the messengers of a friendly Sovereign, who came for the sole purpose of establishing friendship?'

After delivering this message, Kantiba Hailu returned and told Rassam that the Chief Scribe would read out a list of charges against him, and he was to answer each one separately, and other scribes would put down his replies in writing. The Chief Scribe thereupon produced his document, and began to read. First he read out the Emperor's pedigree wherein he was described as the offspring of Solomon, the son of David, by the Queen of Sheba. When the Scribe paused, Rassam said he was delighted to learn that Theodore was descended from so wise a king. The Scribe then read out a brief history of Rassam's mission since their arrival in Massawa, and how they had come on the Emperor's invitation and how the Emperor had liberated the captives for Rassam's sake. Rassam observed that all this was a correct record, and the mission had already written to inform the world of their good reception. The real charges then began: Rassam had sent the captives towards Massawa without reconciling them to the Emperor. The envoy replied that everything he had done was with Theodore's knowledge and permission, and that Samuel, whom the Emperor had appointed as his *Baldabara*, had told him that the Emperor so hated the captives that he had no wish to see them. Samuel, who had been translating Rassam's statements, here became distressed, and asked permission to be seated. A native of Adowa was then appointed to translate, but soon gave up after becoming involved in what the scribes should write down as the translation; the latter were also becoming agitated and found difficulty in continuing. The Emperor soon sent word that Rassam's statements need no longer be written down, and that the translation should be brought to him orally. Rassam believed that the ensconced monarch was no doubt hearing and understanding what the envoy was saying in Arabic. At about this stage the European artisans came in; they had apparently until then been in the same room as the Emperor; they now sat down below the Rases. The next charge was that the envoy had sent letters to the coast without the Emperor's permission. Rassam replied that he did not know that it was the custom in Ethiopia to ask for this before writing to one's friends; but in any case he had sent all the letters openly with the assistance of the Governor of Qorata, and had informed the Emperor of this. Theodore replied that he did not remember any communication from Rassam about writing abroad, but Rassam pressed the Chief Scribe on the subject, and he, after some hesitation, confirmed that Rassam had done so.

The Emperor now sent word that the other charges, still not read out, were not to be proceeded with, and that he was sorry for the way he had behaved towards the mission, and hoped they would not take to heart what he had done. He then sent further word that he was vexed with the Europeans who had abused him, and could not allow them to leave the country until they had been tried before Rassam, and therefore had sent for them, and they would arrive in a day or two; and until then Rassam and his colleagues were to remain at the Emperor's camp and the European artisans were to act as their *Baldarabas*.

Theodore now sent an order dismissing the Ethiopian chiefs, but appointed two Rases to be responsible for the three members of the mission; and this duty the two Rases carried out with great civility. The Emperor now sent to Rassam for the keys to their baggage, which he wished to inspect personally, and the envoy thus learnt that the luggage he had sent on in advance had instead been brought to Zagé. The Emperor ordered the European artisans to attend its inspection, and take note of everything he kept, arms, money and trinkets. The members of the mission later learned that the Emperor's concern was mainly about any concealed arms, and not documents. After the members of the mission had their luggage returned they thought it wise to destroy their documents, lest evil-minded people might at some stage mis-translate them to the Emperor.

27

DETENTION FOR THE WINTER

(1866)

On Monday, 16 April 1866, the day after the European captives arrived at the Emperor's court at Zagé, they once again faced trial. Early in the morning Theodore summoned his Rases and other chiefs, and at about 8 a.m., all being ready, he summoned the mission, saying they should don their uniforms and come to him at once, as he wished to see them as friends, before he sent for the prisoners. He was seated on a couch, with some 1,000 of his officers and chiefs on either side of him, standing; the Rases were on the left below him, seated, with their backs towards him, and the European artisans some 20 feet away from him. When the mission arrived Theodore invited them to be seated in front of him, to his right. He then told them he was sorry for their treatment at the court two days before, if they were roughly handled it was against his wish and arose from a misunderstanding of his orders, due to the fact that they carried swords.

The sun now becoming hot, the Emperor ordered umbrellas for the mission. He assured them that he had only friendship for them, and they must not think he had any intention of treating them like the captives; and then for about an hour he spoke with Rassam on all manner of things before the prisoners appeared.

The captives came in chained in twos, and halted 20 yards in front of the Emperor. The mission were relieved to see that Mrs Flad and Mrs Rosenthal had not been brought along with the others. Cameron was unchained and told to sit with the members of the mission, the Emperor saying to Rassam, 'He is one of you, let him sit down with you.' Bardel was then unchained, and told to sit next to the mission. The Emperor, addressing Rassam, then began his charges against the prisoners, and started by complaining that some of the Europeans had abused him and said he was of low origin. He would, however, prove to Rassam that he was descended from noble families on both sides. A number of old men were called upon to say on oath that what he had said was true, and this they did. They swore that Theodore was descended from the King of Israel. Not content with this he also desired like evidence from the Emperor whom he had deposed, Hatsé Yohannes; but that poor man being sick, Rassam was asked to send a messenger to hear this testimony.

Satisfied that Rassam was convinced on this matter, Theodore proceeded with his more specific charges, and said all questions and answers were to be addressed to Rassam. The Emperor made his accusations or put his questions in Amharic, Samuel then translated them into Arabic, Rassam translated them into English, and Flad translated them into German for the benefit of those who only understood that language. Many of the captives understood Amharic, but being some distance from the Emperor did not hear what he said, and Rassam, to make sure that Flad and others heard what he said, raised his voice and sometimes repeated his questions.

Theodore's first charge was, why had the captives departed without first coming to see him? Rassam at once intervened to say that he could answer that question, but the Emperor told him to wait as he wanted to hear what Stern and the others would say. Flad replied for all that they had nothing to say, as they had been placed under Rassam's orders and had obeyed him; the Emperor replied that they should have begged the envoy to bring them to him. Rassam now said that he had made all the arrangements for the departure, and, if there was any blame, it should be his. Turning from this, Theodore began a long recital against the prisoners individually for having abused him, and for the first time included Flad in the accusations. Having vented himself on this old theme, he ordered the members of the mission to stand up before him. Rassam, Blanc and Prideaux accordingly rose, and Theodore then asked Rassam to answer certain questions. Why had he not taken the prisoners to him to beg pardon before they left? Rassam replied that the Emperor had never said that he wanted this; on the contrary he had heard Theodore say he never wished to see the prisoners again. The next question was similar: Why had Rassam allowed the released captives to leave Qorata, instead of bringing them with him to Zagé? Rassam replied that he had acted with the sanction of the Emperor and the concurrence of one of his officers. Theodore called that officer to come forward. The man confirmed what Rassam had said, and reminded the

Emperor that, on hearing that the envoy was sending the prisoners off without seeing them again, he approved and was pleased. Then looking at Rassam the Emperor said: 'Do you consider yourself a King?' The envoy replied that he did not, and asked why Theodore had asked such a question. The Emperor answered that Rassam had taken the captives off, without reconciling them to him, so that he could boast that he had taken them out of Ethiopia by his own power and skill. He added that if Rassam had brought the prisoners to him he would have given them mules and money; instead they were in chains.

This said, the Emperor asked the mission to be seated again in the place of honour. Then Theodore started a further speech, condemning the rebels in his country and his enemies the Turks. One day he would show Rassam how he would thrash those unbelievers. If only the British would help him, together they could build a wall round the province of Sennar, which the Egyptians now held. Having delivered himself of this tirade he asked 'Is this your friendship, Mr Rassam, that you wish to leave me and take away those that have abused me? Where I am there you shall be.' This said, he became all smiles, rose, and told the mission to go back to their tents. Rassam hoped that since he had taken all the blame for the prisoners' departure, they could be released of their chains, and this he asked the Emperor. But the imperial reply was: 'We have had enough for today; I will see to the rest tomorrow.' Rassam, Blanc and Prideaux then returned to their tent, and with the Emperor's permission Cameron went with them. Theodore on departing took Bardel with him. The rest of the captives and the artisans went off to their own tents.

The next morning the Emperor was up by dawn supervising the construction of a fence within the royal grounds. While this was going on he sent word to Rassam that for his sake he would release the prisoners from their chains, if the envoy became surety for them. Rassam replied that as some were neither servants of the British Government, nor indeed British subjects, he would have to consult with them first; whereupon the Emperor sent orders that the captives were to go to the mission's tent. They all agreed to Rassam standing surety for them, and their chains were accordingly struck off.

Later in the day the Europeans were again summoned to the Court as the Emperor wished to have a *chawata*, a chat, with them. In the audience hall the mission, and even Cameron, were invited to sit next to the Emperor, on his left hand, and the artisans were directed to his right. Then the released captives were called in, prostrated themselves, and were ordered to a place on the left of the mission. The Emperor was now in a different mood, and put on an appearance of humility. He asked one and all to forgive and forget. He bowed his head and said: 'For Christ's sake, forgive me.' Rassam and all the Europeans, following the Emperor's example, stooped, and remained so for some time, until one of the artisans called out to tell them his Majesty said they might sit up. Rassam did so, and all the others then raised their heads.

This ritual over, Theodore told Cameron that he had received a petition from relatives of his and of the other captives. He said the petition was touching, and ordered it to be given to Cameron to read out for the benefit of those who understood English; this done Theodore, looking towards Stern and those with him, said they ought to be very grateful to Rassam for all the trouble he had taken on their behalf. The petition had, of course, been sent to the Emperor with a covering letter from Dr Beke, but Theodore did not produce Beke's letter, nor did he make any mention of that gentleman.

The Emperor now dismissed all the Europeans except the members of the mission. At the meeting just ended he had shown himself no longer ill-disposed towards any of the Europeans. Rassam therefore expected to hear about the Emperor's plan for their departure from Ethiopia. All the other Europeans having left the hall, and being alone now with the members of the mission and his servants, the Emperor called the Chief Scribe and told him to write what he would dictate. Samuel was ordered to translate to Rassam, phrase by phrase, as the Emperor spoke. Amid a good deal of discussion about certain phrases and titles, Rassam understood that Theodore was dictating a letter to Queen Victoria. He and his companions listened attentively to Samuel's translation as the dictation proceeded. The letter eventually emerged as follows:

> In the name of the Father, Son and Holy Ghost – One God.
>
> From God's slave and His created being, the son of David, the son of Solomon, the King of Kings, Theodorus.
>
> To her whom God has exalted above all people, the Defender of the Christian Faith, the Protector of the poor and oppressed, the Queen of England, Victoria.
>
> Had not your servant Mr Hormuzd Rassam, whom you said that you had sent in the affair of Mr Cameron, come, but the lowest of

> your slaves, I would have welcomed him. By the power of God, I have released Mr Cameron and made him over to your servant, Mr Rassam; and, by the power of God, I have also released the other prisoners and all other Europeans who might wish to leave the country, and made them over to him; and I have kept your servant Mr Hormuzd Rassam for the sake of consulting together upon the extension of our friendship. We, the people of Ethiopia, are blind, and we beg of your Majesty that you would give light to our eyes, and so may you receive light in the kingdom of Heaven.

As the dictation proceeded the Emperor's intentions became apparent. Despite all the reservations the mission had kept in their minds, it was shattering to learn that Rassam, and presumably Blanc and Prideaux as well, were to be detained. The last passage in the letter meant that Theodore wanted the Queen to send him people possessed of skills which they could teach to his subjects; and Rassam interpreted the text as meaning that he was to be detained until such instructors arrived. He felt it would be worse than useless to protest against the Emperor's intention: to do so might bring only greater harshness upon himself and new torments upon the prisoners. The mission then sadly withdrew from the royal presence.

Soon after the mission reached their tent a letter was brought from Theodore, addressed 'to my friend and counsellor, the servant of the Queen of England, Aito Hormuzd Rassam'. It stated that 'My desire is that you should send to her Majesty, the Queen, and obtain for me a man who can make cannons and muskets, and one who can smelt iron; also an instructor in artillery. I want these people to come here with their implements and everything necessary for their work, and then they shall teach us and return. By the power of God, forward this my request to England.' The Emperor added that he would like to see the letter before it was despatched.

Rassam was in no mood to comply with the imperial request; in no circumstances would he have been pleased that he and his mission should be detained against their will, but he now thought he had been grossly deceived. Looking back over events, it appeared to him that up to about 8 April, when the mission had been in Qorata awaiting the arrival of the captives, the Emperor had genuinely intended to let him, the liberated prisoners and any other Europeans, leave Ethiopia. Then, it seemed something happened, and Theodore changed his mind; perhaps it may have been his own whim, perhaps other counsels had prevailed, or, quite likely, it was the information that another mission had arrived at Massawa, upon which event Theodore may well have had his faith in Rassam, and in the British Government, shaken; certainly signs of the Emperor's altered mood towards Rassam occurred just about the time that the news of Dr Beke's arrival would have reached him. On 8 April or thereabouts, Theodore, Rassam was now convinced, had decided to retain the mission, the prisoners and all other Europeans. His letters and orders that they might begin their journey, the subsequent accusations against Rassam on 13 April, and the retrial on 16 April, were all designed to give a semblance of legal justification to the Emperor's detention of the mission and the re-imprisonment of the captives.

Rassam now asked Ato Samuel to point out to Theodore the unfriendly line he was taking, and to advise him to let him leave the country with all the Europeans, and further, that once in Europe, he, Rassam, would attend to all the things the Emperor required. But Samuel's reply was that Rassam had now known Theodore long enough to know that once his mind was made up he would not change his decision. Rassam then sought the views of two of the lay missionaries in favour with the Emperor, who had known him for some eight years, Moritz Hall and Theophilus Waldmeier. They too thought it would be useless to try to persuade His Majesty to change his decision.

In the circumstances Rassam decided to write the requested letter, but, bearing in mind that the Emperor would have it translated to him, wrote it more for Theodore's eye than for the Foreign Office. It was months now since he had had any news from England, but he addressed the letter to Her Majesty's Principal Secretary of State for Foreign Affairs. He did not know who the British Foreign Secretary might be, but he felt he could hardly be wrong in opening his letter with 'My Lord', nor was he.

So the letter written to please Theodore, from the Emperor's court at Zagé, on 18 April 1866, stated that Rassam with his two companions had reached the Emperor's court on 28 January:

> His Majesty gave us a most magnificent reception, and treated us with great kindness and civility.
>
> He received her Majesty's letter graciously; in answer to which he wrote a very friendly and courteous reply.
>
> I had the first interview with his Majesty on the very afternoon of my arrival at his Court, when he related to me all his grievances with

> regard to Consul Cameron and the other European prisoners. Early the next morning he ordered the release of all the prisoners . . . All the released prisoners have been made over to me by his Majesty, and are now with me, enjoying good health.
>
> All the prisoners presented themselves before the Emperor . . . and after the charges were read to them, they all confessed that they were wrong in what they had written and spoken against his Majesty. The Emperor then forgave them for all that they had done, and said that he would be as friendly towards them henceforth as he is towards myself and my companions.

The letter went on to tell of several kindnesses and courtesies Theodore had shown towards the mission, and stated that he had 'in every respect been very kind and hospitable'. Mention was also made of the fact that the Emperor was about to create an Order with which he intended to invest the members of the mission. Rassam then came to the Emperor's long-held wish to have scientific men from England to teach his people how to smelt iron, make cannon and so on, and, continued Rassam, 'from his second letter to the Queen, which I inclose herewith, your Lordship will perceive that we are all detained in this country for the present, for friendship's sake'. The letter also asked for various fire-arms, and 'a boat, if practicable, for the use of his Majesty on the Lake and any other thing which Mr Flad, who is the bearer of this letter, may suggest'.

In his care to make his letter agreeable to His Majesty, had Rassam deceived Her Majesty's Foreign Secretary about the true state of the detention and probable danger in which he and all the Europeans now found themselves? Probably not. In the first place, in composing this letter Rassam kept in the forefront of his mind the main purpose of his mission – the liberation of the captives. Second, he had to write a letter which would not revive the anger of the capricious ruler in whose power they all were; and he had to produce a message which the latter would allow to go to England. Third, he placed his faith in Flad and the possibility of the latter reaching England, which he did not wish to prevent; indeed, all hope now rested on the success of Flad's mission. That same day the tents of the mission and of the captives were moved within the fence in the royal enclosure, and here they were now to stay, but for how long they did not know.

Later that day the Emperor sent for the two merchants of Qorata whom he had previously ordered to act as hosts to the mission,

Ato Kassa and Ato Wandé, and Ato Samuel was also summoned. All three were now accused of obtaining messengers for Rassam to take his letters to Massawa. They replied that they had received orders from the Emperor to attend to the requirements of the mission, and so when requested by Rassam, they had obtained him messengers. Ato Samuel added that he saw no harm in helping Rassam to send letters which told of his favourable reception by the Emperor and the liberation of the prisoners. Theodore then charged Kassa and Wandé with having supplied muskets to rebels in Gojjam. This the two men indignantly denied, but in vain. They were fined 20,000 dollars, and each was chained by the hand to a soldier.

When old Kantiba Hailu heard of the detention of the mission he sent word to the Emperor, urging him to release them and send them out of Ethiopia, but Theodore dismissed him, saying, 'You had better hold your tongue, you old fool, and go away.' In the evening Queen Yetemagnu sent a message to Rassam, advising him to put a cheerful face on his misfortunes for he would do himself no good by appearing gloomy, and added, 'the King really loves you'. Later Kantiba Hailu came to see Rassam and also advised him to maintain a cheerful appearance.

A few days later there was some manifestation of Theodore's friendly feelings; he sent Rassam the presents he had prepared to give him and his colleagues on their intended departure – Ethiopian saddles, arms and a fine mule for each of them; they were also invited to go out for a ride as, they were told, it would please the Emperor, and they rode out accompanied by the Master of the Horse and two other officers.

Flad's departure was set for 21 April. That morning Theodore made a display of friendship for Rassam and his mission; he sent back the arms, trinkets and part of the money which had been taken from them, and said he would present them with the new Order as soon as the decorations were completed. Money taken from the prisoners was also returned. Theodore visited Rassam in his tent, and, finding it bare, ordered carpets, and himself spread them on the ground. On leaving, the Emperor ordered the guard to be withdrawn. From that day for the rest of their stay at Zagé members of the mission were free to move as they pleased, but Rassam was always accompanied by one or more of the Emperor's officers, politely called a 'guard of honour'.

Flad and his caravan set out from Zagé. Since the early days of

Plowden's appointment as Consul, Theodore had spoken of his desire to send an Embassy to the British Queen and also to obtain Britons to teach his people skills. Now at long last, without any fuss, ceremonial, or glamour, a humble German missionary was leaving to obtain some craftsmen.

For the captives within the royal enclosure life became a little less restrained; and for the three members of the mission, much easier. Theodore became once again very friendly; he made Rassam a present of a fine thoroughbred horse, took him on several hippopotami-hunting expeditions, and from time to time made the envoy other gifts.

Rassam observed, however, that on some occasions when His Majesty held a trial, the Master of the Horse invited him to go out riding, and on his return Rassam heard of cruel punishment inflicted. Mrs Rosenthal was less fortunate – her tent was near the place of punishment, and she could hear each lash strike the agonised victim. Several chiefs were flogged to death only a few yards from her tent. These executions did not cheer the captives. One of them, Bardel, was soon freed, and again entered the Emperor's service, with the duty of translating for Theodore books and documents which had been seized from the captives; but the Frenchman promised Rassam he would not translate correctly any passages which might bring trouble to them. Two Irish prisoners previously employed by Cameron, Mr Kerans as secretary and Mr McKilvie as servant, both offered their services to the Emperor, who however declined them.

Cameron and the members of the mission were very discreet in their conversation. To safeguard themselves against adverse reports being carried to the Court, they adopted the device of speaking of Bardel as 'Shrimps' and Theodore as 'Bob'.

The detention at Zagé was enlivened on 24 May when, hearing that it was Queen Victoria's birthday, the Emperor commanded a celebration. There was much feasting. Learning of the European custom of firing salutes of honour on such occasions, Theodore requested Rassam to bring all the Europeans down to the lake, and at noon its waters and the hills around echoed to the sound of a 21-gun salute 'in honour of the birthday of the great Queen of England'.

Three days later messengers arrived at Zagé. They came from Dr Beke with a letter for the Emperor. The doctor, on coming up on to the Ethiopian plateau from Massawa, had not penetrated far.

He had reached the town of Halai, whence he had sent his letter in which he said that, having heard that His Majesty had graciously released the prisoners, he was on his way up to thank him for this clemency; but, on reaching Halai, rebels had imprisoned him, and would Theodore graciously send a ransom to release him so that he could come up to the Emperor. After reading the letter Theodore sent it to Rassam with a request that he should reply to it; but the envoy had not the slightest wish to become involved with the tiresome Dr Beke and declined to do so. Theodore then sent word to Rassam asking him to assist in translating an Amharic reply into English; not to vex Theodore, the envoy set Prideaux to this task. Theodore found no pleasure in Dr Beke's endeavour: he replied that he had no right to enter Ethiopia without permission, and ordered him back to Massawa to await further word from him.

Theodore stayed for a time at Zagé, but by about May the climate along the lakeshore ceased to be healthy, and he sent his female establishment, except Queen Yetemagnu, by water to Qorata. At the end of May cholera and typhus broke out among his soldiers, and soon 100 were dying daily. On 6 June he ordered his troops to march round the southern shore to Qorata, he and his Empress making the first stage by water. With an escort under Ras Ingeda, Rassam and the Europeans joined the march, and in two hours reached the place where they were to halt for the night. Sickness still raged in the army, and as many as 500 people died during the night. Cameron and Mrs Rosenthal had been ill for some weeks, but so far none of the Europeans was struck down.

The next morning Theodore, his army and the Europeans were on the move soon after sunrise, and at about 10 a.m. came to the river Abai which they forded, and at 11.30 halted to camp at Gadiro. The next day they arrived at Qorata. The Emperor made his camp near the lake, Rassam and his party on higher ground. In the night about 1,000 soldiers were attacked by cholera, some 300 died, and Theodore wrote to Rassam to seek his advice. Acting on this, the Emperor dispersed his troops on higher ground. Being now bent on an expedition against rebels beyond Debra Tabor, which might last some ten days, he summoned Samuel and several chiefs and told him that if during his absence Rassam should die he was to receive a proper and worthy burial.

News was, however, shortly afterwards received that the rebels had been defeated by one of the Emperor's chiefs. Changing his plan Theodore arranged to move all his troops to more mountainous ground at Debra Tabor. He commanded Rassam, Cameron and Rosenthal to accompany him; Mrs Rosenthal chose to come along with her husband, and the other Europeans followed soon after. So in June Rassam and the other captives, who only two months earlier had left Qorata hoping they were at long last on their way to Europe, set off, not northwards towards freedom, but eastwards to continued detention. They were on the road to Debra Tabor: but it was also the road to Magdala.

Two days' travel brought Rassam and his companions near to Debra Tabor; they were met by Theodore who rode with them to nearby Gafat. The Emperor allotted Waldmeier's house, one of the very few with two storeys, to Rassam, and, learning it was barely furnished, sent for carpets. While waiting Theodore carried on a lively conversation with Rassam with the help of the young interpreter Desta, the Emperor speaking sometimes Arabic and sometimes Desta's own language, Tigrinya. Rassam was drawn into a long explanation of the British income tax system.

Later Theodore had a number of Ethiopians turned out of their houses, and several Europeans moved into them. The artisans and others, including Mrs Flad, occupied their own houses. And so the European community settled down to spend the rainy season. According to custom at this time of year the Emperor dispersed a large part of his army to their homes. Nor were there any guards placed over the Europeans.

Theodore, who was then residing at Debra Tabor, three miles away, frequently visited Gafat. He came mainly to see the work of the artisans who were then making cannons and gun-carriages, the manufacture of which was the technological achievement of his reign. During his visits the Emperor usually met Rassam, and held long conversations with him on various subjects, including Ethiopian history, in which Theodore was well versed.

The members of the mission and the other Europeans resigned themselves, and settled down to make themselves as comfortable as they could, somewhat comforted by Theodore's recent good humour and friendliness towards Rassam. Then on 25 June the latter received a message from His Majesty to proceed as quickly as possible to Debra Tabor to attend a court he was about to hold, and to bring Cameron, the missionaries and any other gentlemen he had with him. Rassam immediately obeyed, and as his party passed by the houses of the European artisans the latter also decided to go with them. On arriving at Debra Tabor they were all taken into the Emperor's large black goat's-hair tent.

This tent was carpeted but empty. Rassam and his party took seats on one side; but the urgent summons and unostentatious reception predicted trouble, so the artisans went and sat on the other side of the tent, as far away as possible from Rassam's party, and the two lay missionaries, Staiger and Brandeis, thought it wisest to sit with the artisans. Presently the artisans were summoned to the Emperor, and Staiger and Brandeis elected to go along with them. Rassam and his party were left to speculate what was afoot, but not for long.

After about ten minutes their European friends returned with several Ethiopian chiefs. They brought a message from Theodore. He had been informed that a railroad had been built between Egypt and Kassala for the purpose of transporting Turkish, French and British troops to invade Ethiopia, and why had Rassam, who must have seen it, not informed His Majesty? Secondly, His Majesty had heard from Jerusalem that Rassam had been sent under false pretences, and once he had got the Europeans out of the country, Britain would launch an attack to avenge the imprisonment of her Consul.

Rassam replied that the story of the railway must be utterly false, for when he was at Kassala nine months previously no one had ever mentioned any such project. As for the story of the British intention to attack Ethiopia, that too would prove utterly false. Ato Samuel translated this to the chiefs, and declared emphatically that whoever had invented the report was a liar. M. Bardel, now in the Emperor's service, objected that this was not what Rassam had actually said, but the latter commented that Samuel's words would do very well and the chiefs could convey them to the Emperor. The chiefs departed, and a little later brought back a message from His Majesty that his friendship for the envoy was undiminished, but he felt that the British Government was not behaving well towards him. There then followed several exchanges between Rassam and Theodore, the chiefs going and coming between the black tent and the imperial residence nearby. Apparently accepting Rassam's explanation, the Emperor repeated his old charges against Cameron for having returned to him without bringing a reply from Queen Victoria, and against Rosenthal for having written ill about him. When Rassam had smoothed the matter out, Theodore wished to know if the envoy still stood surety for the captives and for Stern in particular; Rassam gave an affirmative reply, whereupon the Emperor replied that he accepted the renewed pledge, but, not being sure what the British Government intended to do, Rassam and all the ex-prisoners should remain at Debra Tabor, near to him, and should send to Gafat for their belongings. Stern had his tent pitched next to that of Rassam, but Samuel recommended that the missionary should never be far from the envoy, as only thus would he be safe.

Earlier Samuel had been one of those who advised that Rassam should remain aloof from the prisoners to avoid giving any impression that he was siding with the Emperor's enemies, but now he advised the envoy that since His Majesty 'has chosen to treat you so badly, you will do well to stand by all the late captives, for they will only be safe while in your company'. Accepting this advice Rassam had Stern live in the tent which had been erected for himself. A few days later Rassam obtained the Emperor's permission for Rosenthal to return to Gafat to rejoin his wife; on this occasion Theodore sent Rassam a message that he need not ask his permission for such matters; the prisoners were now in his charge, he could make whatever arrangements for them he liked, and he was free to visit Gafat if he wished.

Rassam now took the opportunity to send a message by Samuel to the Emperor to point out how unwise it was to treat the members of the mission in the unfriendly way which he had done for a second time, and that this would produce no goodwill in England where most likely the British Government was at that very time trying to meet His Majesty's wishes and arranging to send him the skilled people he wanted. The Emperor's reply, brought back by Samuel, was: 'There are customs in every country which only the natives of the place understand. You are a foreigner, and know not our rules, nor could you understand why I have acted in this way towards you. You follow your way and I mine, and you will see if I am not right in the end.' Samuel had tried to persuade the Emperor that Rassam was his friend, but was told to hold his tongue, and fell for a time into disfavour.

Rassam was now allowed greater freedom. He could go unguarded for walks and rides, frequently visited Gafat, and often received signs of friendship from the Emperor, polite messages and gifts. Theodore was also a frequent visitor to Gafat, to see the progress of the European artisans on the guns and cannon they were making.

For some four weeks the Europeans at Debra Tabor were left in peace, without any further alarms. It was known that the Emperor was planning to go on to Magdala to organise his expedition to punish rebels in Lasta, and on 28 June he sent a message to Rassam that he intended to set off, but so as not to weary Rassam and the Europeans by taking them around with him he intended that they should all go to Magdala and spend the rainy season there, and what did Rassam think of this plan? The envoy's reply was that His Majesty was the best judge. So it was to be Magdala. The ex-prisoners were to return to that scene of their earlier captivity, and the mission was also to go there.

On 3 July Theodore sent a kindly message to Rassam, by the young interpreter Desta, that he must go out more and not mope in his tent, and that Desta himself was to keep the Emperor informed of anything the envoy might need, even if it meant coming to him in the middle of the night. Rassam was somewhat reassured on receiving this considerate message, but in the afternoon Samuel ran into his tent to say that the Emperor, just back from Gafat, wanted him to come to him with the other gentlemen staying in his tent. What new matter could have arisen since the kind message a couple of hours earlier?

Rassam went over to the royal building and entered the hall accompanied by Cameron, Prideaux and Stern, and was shocked to find Dr Blanc standing like a prisoner before Theodore, and no less alarmed when a few minutes later Rosenthal was brought in by several soldiers. From the look on Theodore's face, Rassam thought the Emperor must have gone mad. Hardly was he in the royal presence when Theodore said Rassam hated him; on his enquiring what had happened to make the Emperor say that, the latter replied that he had four charges to make against him: first, Rassam had read Mr Stern's book, *Wanderings among the Falashas*; second, he, Theodore, had given Cameron a letter for Rassam's Queen, but the Consul had returned without an answer; third, Rassam had tried to send the prisoners out of Ethiopia without permission; fourth, the Turks had possession of Jerusalem, and the English and the French allowed them to keep it, and he, Theodore, demanded his patrimony, Jerusalem, and he wanted Europe to restore the Holy Land to him. This last claim was based, of course, on his claim to be descended from David and Solomon.

Rassam ignored the first two charges. Replying to the other two he said that in arranging for the prisoners to leave Qorata he had acted with the Emperor's permission. At this Lij Abitu, who had escorted the prisoners out of Qorata, was summoned. He supported what the envoy had said, and this Theodore appeared to accept. Rassam next replied that it was not the custom of European powers to interfere in such matters as the Turkish possession of their territories. Theodore then said abruptly: 'Are you not aware that India and half the world belongs to me?' This claim seemed not illogical to Theodore, at least in his then mood, for it was based on an Ethiopian legend that the Emperors were descended not only of Solomon, but also of Alexander the Great. To this Rassam acidly replied that he had not found it so stated in any books he had read, whereupon Theodore debated the matter with Stern. When these and other observations had trailed away the Emperor ordered the Europeans to be housed in the Treasury as a safer place of confinement.

Thus Rassam, Blanc, Prideaux and Cameron, with Stern and Rosenthal, were all placed in a small circular room only some 12 feet in diameter; later Kerans was sent in with them. At first 15 guards were also placed in the room, but fortunately the Emperor later relented, and ordered them to keep watch outside.

After nightfall there were exchanges of sometimes angry messages, the Emperor asking after Rassam's welfare, and Rassam reproaching him for his conduct. In one message Rassam said that His Majesty's enemies, on learning of his bad conduct towards his mission, would spread this ill-report all over the world. Theodore replied: 'Never mind your Government and my enemies, my friend. Your masters have already decided upon their treatment of me; and my foes would spread evil reports about me, even if I were to carry you on my head.' Whereupon Rassam sent word back that he had done his best to maintain friendship between the British Government and the Emperor, but from now on he washed his hands of all responsibility; His Majesty would only have himself to blame for the wrath of his Queen and her Government. Theodore's answer was: 'God be my witness, my brother and friend, and after to-day I shall not hold you responsible for the future action of your Government. I only want you to be happy, and as I hear from my attendants that you are not so, I must come and cheer you up; I only await your permission to do so.' Rassam told him not to bother, but Theodore, after replying that he could not sleep if his friend was not happy, came over to the Treasury, with a horn of potent arak and a bundle of wax candles to brighten the place. Taking a seat, Theodore poured some arak into a tumbler and gave it to Rassam, and after they had both drunk each other's health he filled glasses and handed them to Blanc and Prideaux. Then, turning to Stern who was standing by the wall, he said, 'How are you, Aito Kokab? Why are you standing in such a disconsolate mood and do not sit down?' Then he said laughingly to Rassam, 'Comfort Mr Stern, and tell him not to moan.'

Then, in serious mood, he said to Rassam: 'Do not regard my face, but trust to my heart, because I really love you. I would not say so before my people who are standing by if I did not mean it. It is true that I behaved ill to you this afternoon, but I have an object in what I do. I was obliged to put on a serious face on account of the bystanders, but I never meant to be angry with you. I used to hear that I was called a madman by my people for my acts, but I never believed it; now, however, after my conduct towards you this afternoon, I have come to the conclusion that I really am so; but as Christians, we ought always to be ready to forgive each other.' He then rose to leave. Rassam accompanied him to the door, where Samuel and the young interpreter were standing. The Emperor stopped and said, 'Mr Rassam, henceforward Desta shall be my child, and Samuel yours; good-bye.' Then, followed by his servants, he went out into the night. Although subsequently they were often to be near one another it was many months before the two men spoke to each other again.

Rassam and his colleagues were left to ponder on the Emperor's strange behaviour: his kind messages in the morning, his fury and accusations in the afternoon, the closer confinement in which he had placed them, and his friendliness in the evening. The puzzled head of the mission and his no less puzzled friends tried then, as later, to piece together some explanation of the strange man's strange conduct.

It would seem that on that ill-fated day, while the Emperor was on his way from Debra Tabor, he was given a letter which made him very angry. On reaching Gafat a beggar asked him for alms, saying he had previously received help from the European *Getotch*, or Masters; Theodore objected to his European artisans being referred to by this title (which was more applicable to himself), and was so angry that he ordered the unfortunate man to be beaten to death. Unfortunately, Rosenthal and Dr Blanc happened to be standing by at the time, and Theodore ordered the arrest of Rosenthal, whom he had always hated, and also had Dr Blanc arrested for good measure. But what was in the letter which earlier had so excited Theodore, Rassam never knew.

Shortly afterwards the Europeans received word one morning to prepare to leave in company with the Emperor, who was proceeding towards Magdala. By 1 p.m. Rassam and the Europeans, mounted on mules, left Debra Tabor, in the wake of the imperial party, uncertain whither the Emperor might be taking them, and knowing only that all were heading towards the mountain fortress of Magdala. As the actual destination was unknown, it was decided to leave Mrs Rosenthal, who was ill, at Debra Tabor with Mrs Flad to look after her.

Although Rassam and his party travelled with the army, and the Emperor from time to time sent complimentary messages, they had no opportunity to speak to him. On the third day of the journey, being all camped at Thankab, some 30 miles from Debra Tabor, the Emperor ordered Samuel to take Rassam and his official companions to see hailstones that had fallen on Mount Cuna nearby.

On 9 July came the dreaded but not unexpected order, that the Europeans were to be sent to Magdala. On that day, with a guard of about 100 men, the members of the mission and the Europeans previously imprisoned at Magdala, set out to travel the 50 miles to that *amba*. The Emperor wished them to reach that destination before the rise of the rivers, for which reason the party travelled light.

They reached the *amba* on the fourth day of the march in the afternoon. The authorities checked their number and wrote their names in a register, and then the commander of the garrison conducted them to their accommodation, a one-roomed house in the enclosure belonging to Ras Ingeda, an adjoining hut being allotted to the servants.

Four days later the chiefs who formed the administration of the fortress came to say that they were without definite instructions about the conditions of their imprisonment, so to be on the safe side the prisoners must be fettered. While the irons were being hammered on, the chiefs told them not to take this as any sign of ill-will, but they were merely doing what they thought the Emperor would wish. Rassam's turn was last, and one of the rings breaking while being hammered on, he was not chained until the next day.

So on 17 July 1866, almost exactly two years after landing at Massawa with the intention of bringing about the liberation of the captives, Rassam and his colleagues were in Magdala, themselves fettered along with the very people they had sought to unfetter. Rassam had got only chains for his pains.

28

MR FLAD COMES TO TOWN
(1866)

When Mr Gladstone, Chancellor of the Exchequer, introduced the Electoral Reform Bill on 12 March 1866, a bitter parliamentary battle was launched which was to last for some six weeks. The Cabinet all favoured the Bill, as did the Foreign Secretary, Lord Clarendon, aristocrat though he was, but there were many doubters among their Whig supporters.

While much concerned with electoral reform at home and with events in Europe, Clarendon received a telegram on 17 March on the relatively remote subject of the captives in Ethiopia. It was from Colonel Stanton, reporting from Cairo that he had heard from Aden that Rassam had reached a place about 50 miles west of Gondar, that he had received the kindest treatment from district chiefs, and that Theodore was believed to have sent an escort and means of transport for Rassam to reach his court. Taking this message as reliable Lord Clarendon promptly wrote to Captain Desborough and Mr Purday giving this encouraging news for them to pass on to their relatives. Lord Clarendon also issued the news to the Press.

So all was going well in Ethiopia. However, notwithstanding the favourable news, Lord Clarendon was not taking any chances. Palgrave was still in Egypt, and the Foreign Secretary decided to keep him there, in reserve, and authorised the Consul-General to continue paying him £100 per month. But news of Rassam, in fact, continued to be good.

On 26 March Lord Clarendon received a further despatch from Stanton, dated 8 March, enclosing a letter from Rassam, which confirmed the progress of his journey, for it was from Matemma, dated 27 December 1865, and it enclosed two letters from the Emperor in Amharic, with Rassam's translations. These letters augured well.

The next day, 27 March, a Reuters' express message appeared

in the London newspapers. It was replete with mis-spellings, apparently because someone could not read someone else's writing and in particular took *m* for *w*. As published in *The Times* the message stated that on arrival at 'Matawwa', Rassam wrote to the Emperor who sent an escort to conduct him to 'Debia Tebir', where, or at Korata on Lake Tana he was to await the Emperor's return from a campaign in 'Godjaw'. The Emperor had written to the German artisans at Gafat, ordering them to receive Rassam and treat him well. How did Reuters come to have a correspondent opportunely near Massawa? This was to become public a few days later.

On 19 March the Foreign Office received a telegram from Colonel Stanton containing even better news. He reported that the British Consul at Suez had received a letter from Dr Beke, dated Massawa, 12 February, saying that Rassam had met Theodore, had been well received by him, and that the Emperor had told him that he would have released Cameron long ago, but the Consul would not leave without the other prisoners. The Foreign Office gave this message to the Press, and the good report, on the authority of Dr Beke, appeared in the newspapers on 29 March.

With all the signs being so favourable for the success of Rassam's mission, a reserve man in Egypt seemed no longer required. So, at last, on 26 April, the Foreign Office informed Stanton that Palgrave's services were no longer required.

During the later days of March and throughout April good news continued to reach the Foreign Office, and was duly passed on to the relatives and to the Press. Stanton, once so critical of Rassam, observed that 'the complete success of Mr Rassam's mission can hardly any longer be a matter of doubt'. And when the long-awaited news came that the prisoners had been freed from their chains and were to join Rassam, another person who had doubted the latter's effectiveness, Captain Desborough, concluded a letter with the words, 'the release of Captain Cameron thanks to the patient exertions of Mr Rassam'.

While publishing such good news the Press was giving prominence to the great parliamentary questions of the day – the Reform Bill, and the proposals for revision of constituency boundaries to meet the greater agglomeration of voters in industrial areas which would result from an extension of the franchise.

One paper which concentrated on the question of the captives was, however, the *Jewish Intelligence*. Though unable to include news of the unchaining of the prisoners in its issue of 1 May it nevertheless reminded its readers of the missionary who still enjoyed some imperial favour, the good Mr Flad, for it published a letter from him which observed that he and his companions looked forward with 'mixed anxiety and hope' for the arrival of the British 'ambassador', who, it was reported, 'was on the road hither'.

If the *Jewish Intelligence* was perforce late with its information its readers had learned from other newspapers of the freeing of their brethren in Ethiopia, and a goodly number of members of the Society participated in communal rejoicing, for, it will be recalled, the merry month of May was the time for the Society's Annual Meeting. As in previous years, so in 1866, the Society kept to its well established procedures. On 3 May it held an evening service at St Marylebone Church, addressed by the Rev. E. Auriol, Rector of St Dunstan's-in-the-West, and on the following day friends of the Society breakfasted at Exeter Hall to hear an address by the Rev. E. Garbett, Incumbent of Christ Church, Surbiton Hill, Surrey. Then in the afternoon came the Annual Meeting, held in the large room at Exeter Hall, with Lord Shaftesbury once again presiding. The joint-secretary, Rev. C. J. Goodhart, read the Report for the year which spoke of the 'unfeigned joy' with which the Committee had:

> at length heard, just a week ago, that the long and deeply tried prisoners in Abyssinia were released from their chains on the 25th of February, and were about to proceed homewards.
>
> It has thus pleased God to answer the prayers of His people, for which we would express our fervent and devout thankfulness; and we would now further beseech Him, that He may speed their coming.

Lord Shaftesbury then gave his speech as chairman, and very soon said:

> The Report calls upon us to give thanks to Almighty God for the deliverance of the Abyssinian captives . . .
>
> Our congratulations are due in the first place to Mrs. Stern, for the near termination of all that she has endured, and for the great happiness which, under God's blessing, she will now experience . . .
>
> I hope that, in the course of the discussions of this day, nothing will be said in reference to that great African potentate, the Emperor of Abyssinia . . . A hasty word, incautiously spoken was the cause, as I believe, of all the trouble that was subsequently brought upon the missionaries; . . . and therefore I trust that nothing will be said on that subject. Strange as it may appear, it shows what is called the growing

> civilization of the world, that the remote Emperor of Abyssinia has as many agents in this country, to pick up and give him information, as the Emperor of Austria or the Emperor of Russia; and therefore our language should be discreet and our words wary and few.

In accordance with this injunction he then turned to safer ground – and proclaimed the Society's unfettered belief in prophecy. The Noble Chairman then brought the meeting to a close with an appeal for more money for the Society and an exhortation to its members 'to stick more closely to the study of prophecy'.

The *Jewish Intelligence* also published under the heading News from Missions Abroad: 'Abyssinia. Births: December 18 1865, the wife of Mr H. Rosenthal, a daughter. Deaths: March 25, 1866, the son of Mr H. Rosenthal, two and a half years old.'

More encouraging news meanwhile continued to reach Government Departments in England, some of it passed on to the Press. On 10 May *The Times* published a message which the India Office had received, from Bombay. It quoted a telegram of 8 May from Merewether at Aden reporting that 'Rassam and all released captives' were 'safe and well, and were preparing for journey to the coast'.

Merewether was then about to depart from Aden on leave. He began his homeward journey on the *Victoria* with a call at Massawa, reaching that port on 11 May, where he found letters from Rassam, dated up to 21 March. At the port he met another source of information, none other than the irrepressible Dr Beke, with his courageous wife, back from their brief excursion, and rebuff, on the fringe of the Ethiopian highlands. The Bekes joined him on the homeward journey.

The *Victoria* reached Suez on 21 May, and the Reuters man whom she carried was not slow, once ashore, to send a despatch to London. Thus on 23 May British newspapers published a telegram from Suez, stating – first things first – 'Dr and Mrs Beke have arrived here. The captives released by the Emperor Theodore are expected to arrive in Egypt shortly.'

On 22 May the Foreign Office had already received a telegram from Stanton at Alexandria, reporting that Rassam had gone across Lake Tana in mid-April to take leave of the King. The Foreign Office at once released the substance of this telegram and, on 24 May, the London papers accordingly published the good news that the prisoners had at long last begun their homeward journey. And the Foreign Office did not neglect to let the relatives of the captives have the news.

So May 1866 drew to a close, having brought nothing but glad tidings of the captives, while in the House of Commons the conflict over the Reform Bill continued to rage, with Mr Disraeli, the leader of the Tory Opposition, striving to overthrow the Whig Government.

On 5 June the Foreign Office received a letter from Consul Cameron, consisting of four pages of small paper. Dated Qorata, 16 March, it confirmed that the prisoners had been released from their chains, and had reached Qorata on 12 March. It added that on the morning of 16 March, the King had sent a letter restating all the charges against the prisoners, including those against Cameron himself, but nevertheless: 'We hope to leave soon, in company with the other prisoners who were at large at Gaffat – and Mr Rassam.'

By now the Foreign Office had received from Rassam the list of the released prisoners and had issued it to the Press, which, on 7 June, for the first time published the names of the much talked about 'Abyssinian Captives'. English people had heard about the captive Consul and some missionaries, but the length of the list may have come as a surprise.

So early June continued to bring glad tidings. But greater and no less anxious matters continued to confront the Foreign Office, and also cause deep anxiety to the Queen. There was great concern over Prussia's relations with the Austrian Empire. On 10 June the Queen wrote in her diary that the Foreign Secretary, Lord Clarendon, had told her 'there will be war'. The formal declaration took place on 18 June.

That same evening the Reform struggle in Britain reached its climax. In the Commons, a hostile motion by the young Whig Lord Dunkellin was carried in a crowded House, the voting being for 315, against 304 – a Government defeat by 11 votes. That the Government should have been defeated on a motion by one of their own party added to the tension, and on the declaration of the votes there was tremendous excitement. Only eight days earlier Lord Clarendon had assured the Queen that she could proceed to her beloved Balmoral without fear of a ministerial crisis, but he had reckoned wrongly, and the day after the crucial vote, the Prime Minister, Lord Russell, tendered his resignation. The Queen immediately wrote back to him, declaring that she declined it, and asked her ministers to think again. On 22 June the Prime Minister answered that the Cabinet had been unable to decide whether to persist in their resignation, and added a personal request, saying: 'It would be highly convenient . . . that your Majesty should come early on Tuesday to Buckingham Palace, instead of going to Windsor.' From Balmoral the Queen replied that she still hoped to retain the present Government, but as for it being convenient for her to go to London on Tuesday, the Prime Minister could jolly well come to Windsor if he wished to see her, and it would be 'quite impossible for her after her long night journey to go to London on Tuesday, but she will be willing to receive Lord Russell or any other of her Ministers . . . both that day and Wednesday at Windsor'. She added: 'The Queen will hope to see Lord Russell at one o'clock on Tuesday, or at half past twelve, if there is a train which arrives at that time.'

On 25 June, the Cabinet met, and decided to stick to its intention to resign. The next day the Prime Minister and the Chancellor of the Exchequer, Mr Gladstone, took the train to Windsor. The Queen expressed the hope that the Government would stay in office. The Ministers then returned to London, but at 6 p.m. Mr Gladstone announced in the House of Commons that the Government had resigned. Later that day the Queen received a telegram from her Prime Minister, informing her of her Ministers' resignation. She replied that she accepted this with much regret, but, by no means dilatory in operating the Constitution, ended by telling the out-going Prime Minister that she had written to Earl Derby to form a new Government. On the following day, Lord Derby received the Queen's invitation, and replied that although this would involve 'immense difficulties' he would 'go down to Windsor by the 2 p.m. train to-morrow – or any later hour or day the Queen may find more convenient'.

Mr Disraeli, of course, kept in close touch with these developments, and was already scheming. On the same day he wrote to his party chief, Lord Derby: 'What do you think of utilizing Lord Shaftesbury? . . . he would be a representative of Palmerstonian sympathies and influences; powerful with the religious middle classes . . . It is an adhesion that, I think, would bring strength at elections.'

Lord Derby acted quickly, and asked the great philanthropist to join his Government, so that he could refute the charge that the Conservatives were 'hostile to the working classes'. Shaftesbury, however, wrote to Derby, later the same day, wishing him success in the formation of his Government, but declined to join it, adding: 'While, however, I should bring but little aid to your Cabinet, I should in fact withdraw myself from the many and various pursuits which have occupied a very large portion of my life.'

Lord Derby again pressed Shaftesbury to join his Government, but the philanthropist refused, for, as he wrote in his diary, 'It would have been a self-sacrifice without any adequate result.' He was never again asked to make that sacrifice.

Another noble Lord who declined Derby's invitation was the outgoing Whig Foreign Secretary. Lord Clarendon wrote that he could not abandon his party allegiance, 'the only strong political feeling' he had. There was of course a former Foreign Secretary whom Lord Derby might have considered, the Earl of Malmesbury, but he was now not in sufficiently good health to take on that exacting office.

At the start of his search for ministers Lord Derby consulted members of his party. At 11 a.m. on 28 June, he assembled some 22 members of the Commons and the Lords; Mr Disraeli was among those who spoke, and his speech was greeted with cheers.

On that same day a London crowd gathered at Mr Gladstone's residence, in Carlton House Terrace, not five minutes' walk away, to cheer for Mr Gladstone and liberty. Partly under Disraeli's persuasion but without too much enthusiasm, Lord Derby selected his own son, Lord Stanley, as Foreign Secretary. Queen Victoria was even less inclined than Lord Derby to favour this choice and she wrote and told him so on 30 June.

While the public, press and politicians were engrossed in the ever-interesting subject of the formation of a new Government, neither politicians nor the Press, still less the general public, gave much thought to the captives. But Government Departments must continue with their work while the fates decide who is to be the minister at their head; and the turmoil of home affairs seldom gives much respite to the Foreign Office.

On the day Queen Victoria wrote that she did not favour Lord Stanley as head of the Foreign Office, a telegram arrived at that Office from Colonel Stanton in Alexandria announcing that the missionary Mr Flad had just arrived there with despatches from Abyssinia. Colonel Stanton's message continued: 'The Mission [of Rassam] and other Europeans are detained by the King who seems suspicious of ulterior proceedings against him and wants some guarantee of good disposition before allowing them to leave the country.' The Consul-General's message concluded: 'Flad leaves by French steam packet for England.'

Until now the Foreign Office and the Foreign Secretary had been expecting news that the Rassam mission and the other Europeans were on their way to Massawa – where Colonel Merewether had already planned to send the *Victoria* to embark them. But now it learnt that Rassam and his mission were being detained by the 'suspicious' king. This was indeed a strange turn of events. And what exactly was Mr Flad doing, visiting England? What had been happening in Ethiopia?

The captives were going to present new problems to the new Foreign Secretary – whoever he might be – and whether Queen Victoria liked him or not.

29

'... READY AND GLAD TO SEE MR FLAD'

(1866)

When the messenger arrived at Lord Derby's London house, in St James's Square, on 1 July 1866, with the letter from the Queen questioning the fitness of Lord Stanley to be her Foreign Secretary, he had to wait quite some time for an answer, because the Earl of Derby was at church.

When the Prime Minister-designate did get home and penned his reply to Her Majesty he told her that he too did not think the Foreign Office best suited for his son; however, since the former Foreign Secretary, the Earl of Malmesbury, was now too old, Lord Stanley was better suited than anyone else. And over the next few days Lord Derby went on with his Cabinet-making, and the Whig ministers completed their outgoing. On 6 July the Chancellor of the Exchequer, Mr Gladstone, went to Windsor to take leave of the Queen; he then came back to the Commons, taking his seat on the Opposition benches for the first time in 15 years.

While the important task of forming a new Government had been taking place there were some private people whose special concern was with the fate of the captives in Ethiopia. On 3 July Captain Desborough wrote to the Foreign Secretary that he had heard that the latter had received later news than was available in the Press, and 'would Lord Clarendon furnish us with the information, whatever it may be'. The next day Mrs Stern also wrote to Lord Clarendon, asking for any new information available. The Foreign Office replied promptly, but discreetly, to both in similar terms to say that 'Mr Flad is on his way and would doubtless explain how things stood. Seemingly the King was detaining the Europeans to procure assurances of good disposition.' That was the last time the matter of the captives was dealt with by Lord Clarendon, or in his name.

Despite Queen Victoria's misgiving, Lord Stanley moved into the Foreign Office that week, and one of his first tasks was to read a despatch from Mr Munzinger, from Massawa, which reached the Foreign Office on 7 July. It confirmed that Mr Flad had arrived at Massawa, and that all the other European prisoners were detained at Magdala. At the foot of this despatch a Foreign Office official observed: 'We must at all events await Mr Flad's arrival.' The new Foreign Secretary later added his comment: 'I agree. S.'

By 9 July the new turn of events had reached the Press. On that day *The Times* published a message dated Alexandria, 7 July, announcing that:

> The departure of the European captives has again been delayed. Their fate depends upon the mission of Mr Flad to the British Government, requesting on behalf of the Emperor, the assistance of England in the event of war between Egypt and Abyssinia.

On the same day the Foreign Office learnt a little more about the progress of Flad's mission, from two despatches. One, from the Assistant-Resident at Aden, dated 21 June, stated:

> In consequence of the strong head winds prevailing in the Red Sea at this season and the slow speed of the *Victoria*, in addition to the unsatisfactory state of her machinery, her Commander deemed it more advisable to return to Aden with Mr Flad . . . I considered it most prudent to send him on to Suez . . . by the French Mail Steamer which was signalled and arrived in harbour within an hour or so after the *Victoria* came to anchor.

The despatch added: 'Mr Flad is entirely without means and has no change of clothing.' And the Assistant-Resident accordingly gave him £50.

The story was continued in the other despatch. It was from Colonel Stanton, dated Alexandria, 29 June. 'Mr Flad, bearer of despatches from Mr Rassam, has just arrived at Alexandria . . . ' On it a Foreign Office official sagely noted: 'We must await to hear what Mr Flad says.'

The Foreign Office had not long to wait. On 10 July two long memoranda arrived, running to some 15 hand-written pages, headed *Report of the imprisonment of Mr Rassam and the English subjects of King Theodorus of Abyssinia*, and signed: F. M. Flad, Lay-Missionary of the London Jewish Society.

The first memorandum, which may have been written during the voyage, was addressed to Lord Clarendon, and ended with the words: 'Begging Your Lordship to make no public use of the above report, and as I am by birth a German and not well acquainted with the English language to pardon any mistakes I made.' Some idiomatic idiosyncrasies notwithstanding, Flad's letter was clear and to the point. He began: 'I deeply regret that I have to report, for Your Lordship's information, the melancholy events which Mr Rassam and his companions, together with the released prisoners, had to experience, just on the day appointed for their departure from Abyssinia.' He went on to give an account of the arrest of the Europeans at Zagé.

The second memorandum was probably written in London. In it Flad set out, first of all, what he considered to be at the root of the trouble:

> I have . . . to bring to Your Lordship's information that all the struggles by King Theodore, the misery and imprisonment of the English Consul Cameron, and all those who were under his protection, arose partly from the imprudent transaction of the Consul's business, and partly from the negligence of the Foreign Office, as also the conduct of some Europeans which caused the King's suspicion and distrust against the English nation.
>
> What I write now, I don't write it to bring accusations against persons; I merely write it down, to make Your Lordship more acquainted with the motives by which all these Collisions between the two Governments were produced.

Flad then listed the causes of the 'collisions'.

1 When Cameron first arrived in Ethiopia he brought with him a Frenchman, Bardel, as his secretary, 'a man of very equivocal character', commented Flad. Cameron and Bardel quarrelled and parted, and from then on Bardel became Cameron's constant enemy. Bardel then entered Theodore's service.

2 Bardel took to France the Emperor's letter to the French Government. After nine months he returned with an answer which the monarch did not like very much. Bardel told Theodore that he would never receive a reply from the British Government, because they preferred the Egyptians to him.

3 When Cameron first arrived he was well received and given presents by Theodore. The latter wanted Cameron himself to go to England, to take his letter to Queen Victoria, or else await the

reply at Massawa or Bogos, so that when the reply came he could bring it up to him.

4 It was against the Emperor's wish that Cameron travelled to Kassala. As he went by way of Bogos he parted from Ato Samuel, who had accompanied him as *Balderaba* (which Flad translated as introducer, escort, etc.). From Keren, Samuel wrote Theodore 'a very accusative letter' about Cameron.

5 Cameron, who then fell sick, returned to Ethiopia by way of Matemma and came to Gondar to get medicine in Flad's house there.

6 On Cameron's return Theodore was angry with him for going to the Turks, and also for not bringing an answer from the Queen, but still treated Cameron as his friend until 'the arrival of Mr Kerans, who brought a letter from the Foreign Office . . . in which the arrival of his despatches and the arrival of the King's letter at the Foreign Office was acknowledged'. But no further remark was made about the Emperor's letter, nor was there any hope that an answer would be sent to Theodore 'who for months had been anxiously waiting for an answer of Her Majesty the Queen'.

7 The Emperor now 'listened and believed all the calumniations of the Anti-Anglican Europeans and Abyssinians'. Some days after the arrival of the despatches brought by Kerans, 'Consul Cameron was ordered to leave his house at Gondar, and to take his abode in the King's Camp; that is to say: the Consul is a prisoner. This was in November 1863.'

8 Being 'out of good health' Cameron at once asked Theodore for permission to leave the Camp and go to Gondar. The King refused and said: 'Let him die, if they only cannot say that I have killed him. Where is the answer to my letter? Why does his Queen (abusing Her Majesty in a most vulgar manner) despise me?'

9 More than five weeks after receiving the Foreign Office letter Cameron asked permission to leave for Massawa. 'The following day he and all those who were under his protection were put in chains.'

10 'If Mr Kerans would have brought a letter for the King, whether good or bad, neither the Consul nor his subjects would have been imprisoned . . . Even Messrs. Stern and Rosenthal

would have been released, and, as it was reported to the natives, all of us, together with the Consul, would have been sent out of Abyssinia. But instead of sending an answer to the Emperor, the Government wrote to their Consul to leave immediately the Abyssinian territory, and to proceed to his post at Massowah . . . From all this the Emperor was fully convinced that the intention of the English Government is to have nothing to do with him any more. How could it be otherwise expected than that the Emperor would take revenge on the Consul and his subjects. When we were in prison the King sent us a message saying: "The Consul I have imprisoned because his Queen did not send me an answer. Personally, I have nothing against him. Messrs. Stern and Rosenthal I have imprisoned because they have abused me, and the rest (we were ten Europeans) I have imprisoned because I found that you white people are all bad."'

11 Flad then related how Stern was arrested, after which the Emperor treated him politely, but after his papers were found and translated a more severe imprisonment followed.

12 Flad next referred to a 'paper of recommendation' Cameron gave to Dejazmatch Merid, the ruler of Hamasen. Kerans appeared to have given a copy to Bardel, who, 'it seems to me', wrote Flad, 'made use of it, to the disadvantage of Mr Rassam's mission. There were also some Abyssinians, especially one, a former servant of the late Mr Baroni at Massowah, who advised the Emperor to keep Mr Rassam in his country "else the English Government would send him no artists", but might "send troops to take revenge".'

13 Flad went on to say that the Queen's letter brought by Rassam did not deal with the questions raised by the Emperor in his letter of 1862. Also, he believed the British Government had given Theodore some promises at the time of Plowden which they did not keep.

14 'From all these and many other things,' Flad wrote, 'the King sees himself deceived in his expectation from the English Government, and therefore he distrusts us and hates us.'

The report continued: 'I beg your Lordship to excuse my liberty in making here some additional remarks of my own', and he then made several observations and suggestions. He expressed the fear that the continued detention of Rassam and the prisoners might tempt many people in England to say 'send troops'. But he thought that this might lead to the torture or death of the prisoners. Far better, he suggested, to satisfy the claims of the Emperor. If the Government gave him, Flad, a man and money he would get the artisans Theodore wanted. Hitherto the Emperor had treated craftsmen well. He had also spent a lot of money, and given valuable gifts to Plowden, Cameron and Rassam. The latter, he urged, should be appointed Consul for Massawa and Ethiopia. This would show Britain had no hostile intentions towards the Emperor and his country.

There were 26 people connected with Rassam and 35 European workmen – the lives of 61 people in all were thus at stake. Flad concluded: 'It is most desirable to finish with this matter in peace.'

On the same day that the Foreign Secretary received Flad's memoranda he also received a despatch from Rassam, dated 18 April, enclosing two letters from Theodore in Amharic, with English translations. One, written on 18 April was addressed to 'the distressed relatives of the prisoners', and began in a customary manner: 'How are you? Thanks be to God, I am well. The petition which have sent to me,' etc. The second letter, which was addressed to Queen Victoria, and dated 29 January, contained the words: 'I have released Mr Cameron and made him over to your servant Mr Rassam . . . '

Flad, who had been in London some six days, saw Lord Stanley at the Foreign Office on 16 July. Colonel Merewether had now arrived in England, and on 18 July, he too saw Mr Flad. That day Flad wrote to Theodore. After reporting that he and the Emperor's letter had 'a kindly and friendly reception', he observed:

> Her Majesty's Governors take every day great trouble to find the artissants your Majesty want.
>
> I have received the promise to get my leave after a fourthnight. If God Allmighty keeps me in health I shall arrive at Massowah at the end of September . . .
>
> There is a great war in Germany. The King of Prussia united with the King of Italy are fighting the Emperor of Austria. In a great battle which was fought at Sadowa, the Emperor of Austria had a great loss, and was forced to retire.

When Parliament reassembled, the Commons was little interested in Flad and the captives, but very interested, as was all

Europe, in the matter Flad had thought worth mentioning in his letter: the 'great war in Germany' and the 'great battle' of Sadowa. While Bismarck had embarked upon, and won, a war which was to lead to the unification of Germany, and Piedmont had joined in that war seeking the unification of Italy, a brief report in *The Times* of 23 July gave news of a conflict for power in Ethiopia. Quoting *Il Commercio* of Cairo the paper stated that 'a tremendous battle' was 'imminent between Theodore II and Gubassie who aspires to the crown'. The paper also noted that the European prisoners were 'still in the King's power'. This gave the irrepressible Dr Beke an opportunity to wade in, and in a letter to *The Times* of 25 July he wrote to say that the report was 'quite in accordance with what I heard when recently in Abyssinia'.

Meanwhile Flad had something to learn of the British way of life. On 23 July there were disorders in Hyde Park, where a crowd, demonstrating in favour of the Reform Bill, angered at finding the gates closed, tore down the iron railings. Flad meanwhile had been 'writing home', and on 26 July, the Foreign Office despatched to Aden a batch of letters from him addressed to the Emperor, Munzinger, Rassam and also to Captain Goodfellow, the Assistant Resident at Aden.

At this time Palgrave, kicking his heels in London, sent the Foreign Secretary a statement regarding various things he had acquired for his intended journey, and suggested they might be useful to Flad. But James Murray at the Foreign Office said they would not be wanted, and it was agreed that they should be sold.

Flad himself continued to be in touch with the Foreign Office, and on 28 July Murray wrote a minute on a visit from the missionary on that day. Flad, he recorded, had received a note from Colonel Merewether, then in London, advising him to go to Germany, to visit his relatives, and then return to England before proceeding to Ethiopia. Murray also noted that he had told Flad that Her Majesty's Government had left entirely to him the responsibility of engaging the artisans who were to go and work in Abyssinia, but the missionary had refused this responsibility, and had said that Her Majesty's Government must do it themselves.

A few days later Murray was able to pen a more hopeful minute. On 1 August he noted that Merewether had called that day to report progress on his endeavours to engage a skilled workman, 'as

Mr Flad can do nothing, and will not undertake any responsibility – in fact he is useless'. Murray continued:

> Mr Flad's reports and letters he brought from Rassam have not yet been to the Queen, as it was thought of letting the Queen know at the same time of the proposed answer and steps taken for Mr Flad's return. But an answer to Theodore must wait until Col. Merewether can report on his endeavours about the artisans ...
>
> If Her Majesty's pleasure about seeing Mr Flad could be known, Mr Flad could make his plans for his return to Abyssinia.

At the foot of this minute the Foreign Secretary wrote: 'I agree in this generally. I will speak to you about it.'

The Permanent Secretary of the Foreign Office, Mr Hammond, also took an interest. On the same day he too produced a minute for the Foreign Secretary:

> Have you ever proposed to the Queen to see Mr Flad before he returns to Abyssinia? It is very important that Her Majesty should do so; and as she will only stay a night at Windsor ... Mr Flad might go down to Osborne, and if so the sooner the better; so that after having seen the Queen he may go and visit his relatives in Germany, and having done so return to England to make his final arrangements. He must leave for Egypt about the 10th of September.

On this minute Lord Stanley made the following observation: 'I have often spoken on this subject with Mr Murray. It must be done, I suppose.'

Now a Member of Parliament who had not previously shown interest in the captives asked a question about them. On 2 August Christopher Darby Griffith, the Liberal-Conservative member for Devizes, asked in the Commons whether it was not true that the two gentlemen who accompanied Mr Rassam on his mission had been detained. He also asked for publication of further official correspondence on the captives. Lord Stanley, the new Foreign Secretary, speaking on the subject for the first time, replied: 'It is unfortunately true that Mr Rassam and the other two gentlemen were still detained by the Emperor of Abyssinia. They were not in confinement, but were not allowed to leave the country.' He added that he had seen Flad, but there was no use the latter returning until after the rains in September. And, as *Hansard* reported, he concluded by stating that:

> He hoped the honourable member would not press for papers. All these transactions had taken place before he had anything to do with

> the Foreign Department; but he found that the general belief among those who were best acquainted with it, was that the publication of these papers would be much more likely to injure than to benefit the unfortunate prisoners.

The next day in the Lords, a member who had for some time shown an interest in the captives, also asked a question. Lord Houghton (Monckton Milnes) enquired about: 'those unhappy persons who are detained in captivity by the Emperor of Abyssinia. He had heard that a change had taken place in the disposition of the Abyssinian Monarch since the receipt of Mr Rassam's despatch.'

Lord Derby's new Government had no ministers of the Foreign Office in the Lords. Questions on foreign affairs were therefore taken by the Lord Privy Seal, Lord Malmesbury, the former Foreign Secretary, who replied:

> There is every hope of obtaining the release of those unfortunate men, but not so speedily as was at first expected.
>
> Mr Rassam has obtained their liberation from captivity, but the King has insisted on their attending him in his war with his rebellious chiefs, and they are now in the camp of the King.
>
> He has, however, sent one of their number, Mr Flad, over to this country with a letter to the Queen, in which he has made requests for different articles. Her Majesty's Government are now doing their best to obtain the things required by King Theodore, and although Mr Flad cannot return on account of the rainy season until September, we hope that when he does that His Majesty, having obtained what he requires, will then release the prisoners, who are said to be detained without any further restriction than is implied in keeping them in the country, and they are well treated.

Despite the Government's reluctance to publish official documents, the Commons resolved on 3 August that a humble address be presented to Her Majesty to lay before the House copies of all the relevant papers.

Arrangements were meanwhile being made for Flad to see the Queen, and on 7 August she wrote from Osborne to the Foreign Secretary to say she: 'would be quite ready and glad to see Mr Flad, if Lord Stanley would bring him here any day, before the 19th, in the hope of being able to put an end to this sad captivity, or at least detention, of these unfortunate people'. At the Foreign Office a note was made: 'Mr Flad to proceed to Osborne on Tuesday next by the 11 train to Southampton.'

On that same day the Foreign Office received a batch of letters from Cameron, some of them to be passed on to other people, including two MPs, Christopher Darby Griffith and Henry Seymour, who were later to ask parliamentary questions, and Hertslet, the Foreign Office Librarian – to be treated as private; and one to be passed on to the permanent head of the Foreign Office, Edmund Hammond – to be treated as official. In the letter for Hammond, Cameron starkly wrote on 24 May:

> My letter from Korata was written under circumstances in which it was difficult to express myself plainly, and my last letters to England forwarded by Mr Flad are so much waste paper. It would not have been honest to that gentleman to trust him with papers which, if he had been arrested on the road, might have brought him into trouble ...

The true fact was that the King in his letter had asked for 'pledges of friendship', but:

> This meant, in fact, artisans who were to take our place; and it was not His Majesty's intention to let us go until he obtained these. 'If I let them go,' said he, 'what shall I have in hand?' He is afraid, I believe, of reprisals; and ignorant as he is of European usages, wishes to have hostages in his hands, so as to prevent any aggressive movements on your part.

Cameron went on to urge the British Government that in its relations with Theodore it should:

> be firm, and let him know the truth. It should not be disguised from him that his course of proceeding is not one which the British Government approves; and if presents and a courteous letter are sent, they should be accompanied by strong remonstrance and a demonstration on the Abyssinian frontier. It would not be a bad thing if a strong-minded man, with courage and firmness before consequences, were sent with the next letter ...
>
> I don't believe that more presents will ever get Mr Rassam and his people out. They are looked on as valuable capital; and the King will work his new mine as far as he can.

The following day, a Mr George Eveleigh, who claimed to be a relative of Cameron, wrote to Lord Stanley offering to open up trade in Southern Ethiopia, with which he claimed to be familiar, and argued that this would help the captives' liberation. His offer was politely declined.

Cameron's friends in Parliament were not forgetting him. On the last day of the session, 10 August, in the Commons Mr Baillie

Cochrane and Mr Henry Seymour, the recipient of one of Cameron's letters, asked for news of the captives. Replying, Lord Stanley said he had nothing new to report but the Government were preparing to send Flad back and hoped that this would lead to the prisoners' release. Another member made a soldier's suggestion. Colonel Sykes, a scholarly officer interested in the East, suggested that a present of gunpowder and rifles to the Emperor would bring about the desired liberation.

But then official parliamentary interest in the subject of the captives went into abeyance, for Parliament was prorogued until 25 October. In the event it did not in fact reassemble until February of the following year, 1867.

The Queen's speech on the prorogation was read by the Lord Chancellor. It covered a wide range of matters, including the suspension of Habeas Corpus in Ireland, and the successful connection of Europe and America by means of an Electric Telegraph. But there was no mention of the captives.

30

MRS FLAD

(1866)

It was Mrs Flad, the humble and anxious German mother in Ethiopia, who caused the matter of the captives to be brought before the British Cabinet in September 1866. Soon after the arrival of her husband in England, and right up to mid-September, the Foreign Office had been concerned to find the artisans which Theodore had requested. The Foreign Office by then had few illusions about him, but they believed, as did Flad and Merewether, that if they could meet his request it was reasonable to hope that he would release the long-suffering captives. There was no certainty about such a deal, but it was a transaction that could not be neglected. So, Merewether, although it was not really part of his duty – he was in any case on leave from Aden – had spent a good deal of time trying to secure skilled men who would be willing to go out to work for the Emperor.

Merewether at last succeeded in finding one man willing to serve as foreman of the others still to be selected; but the Colonel's success was soon undone. This man read a letter in his newspaper of warfare in Ethiopia, and of continued detention of Europeans, and promptly informed Merewether that he no longer had any desire to go. And who wrote that letter, frustrating Merewether's endeavours – guess who? Who else but Dr Beke. So the search had to start all over again.

Eventually Merewether found another person willing to be foreman. So on 18 August 1866, a written agreement was signed by Colonel Merewether and Matthew E. Talbot, Esquire, who 'undertook to proceed to Abyssinia and enter the service with Emperor Theodorus for three years at a salary of One Thousand Pounds per annum to be paid by the Emperor'; and it was part of the agreement that Talbot should take with him certain artisans who would also enter into Theodore's service. The salary of these other artisans was to be £300 p.a. For the rest the agreement with them and with Talbot was essentially the same: the British Government was to pay all salaries up to the time they reached 'Massawah the Abyssinian port'. Talbot was to receive £100 and the others £30 each for their outfit. Provision was made for paying salaries and fares back to England for all in the event of their not entering the service of the Emperor, and for payments to their families should any of them through death or sickness be unable to continue their work.

However, news from Ethiopia that the captives had been abused by the King, deprived of all that they possessed and sent to Magdala, had made Flad come at last to the view that all these efforts to secure men and material were in vain, and that the Emperor would not in fact release the prisoners in return for the craftsmen. Flad was due to go to Leeds, but now he wrote to Merewether on 19 September. Referring to Theodore, his former master, he declared:

> As this madman is going on in his dishonourable way, once flattering, and a second time abusing and imprisoning those whom he had called his friends, I think it is no advantage to send him the required artisans, because the release of the prisoners would, I fear, not be obtained. Most likely he would go on requiring other things from the British Government, to which they never could surrender. And they, after having had a great expense, and given to that man six prisoners more, they would at last be forced to use their arms, if ever the Government wishes to release the poor sufferers. Therefore, I deem it advisable that Her Majesty's Government should at once use stronger terms, and I am sure if the last report is true, Mr Rassam and his companions will give the same advice.

Merewether realised that their efforts were a gamble, but he felt that it was still worthwhile, so he proceeded with the recruitment of the artisans. By mid-September the six men were enlisted and agreements signed, between him on the one part, and each by a separate agreement on the other part: George Carr, Richard Joy, John Charles Morris, Charles Bowers, William James Lewer and John Brampton, if that be the interpretation of their signatures, some less clear than others.

Of course, Theodore was pressurising the British Government to give him this aid in recruiting workpeople and obtaining certain material, not to mention courtesy presents. And he was not doing badly; at no cost to himself these men were being enrolled and transported to his doorstep. And even the fares and expenses of his emissary, Flad, were paid for by the British. Thus the British Government carried out the Emperor's request, and while those closely concerned were not without their doubts about the ultimate success, they proceeded with the task, painstakingly and not ungenerously, and not without some hope.

The arrival in London of Mrs Flad's letter was therefore a blow. Flad lost no time in translating his wife's letter from their native German, and sent it with a covering letter of his own, to James Murray at the Foreign Office, where it arrived on 22 September.

Mrs Flad's letter had been written at Gafat, the village where most of the European workpeople had been for some time, and was dated, 7 July. It began: 'My dear Martin, Only with a few words I venture to inform you of our last sad experiences, our present situation and gloomy future. Now as then I feel as if the seventh tribulation, in which we are at present, wishes to devour us utterly.' The country was suffering, she reported, from a serious cholera epidemic; the priests were 'day and night engaged in burying the dead', and wailing had been heard, 'day and night, in every house' until the Emperor had given orders to 'prohibit any more lamentation'. The captives' morale had further suffered when a 'fearful thunderstorm with hailstones came over us'. In the wake of these tribulations Theodore had summoned them all to Debra Tabor, where they were confronted by the Emperor, who had with him a copy of the *Fetha Nagast*, or legal code. The captives had then been subjected to a further 'judgement', Stern, Rosenthal and Makerer had been charged that they had 'calumniated the King before the English Government'. Rassam and the three accused had been detained at Debra Tabor, though the craftsmen had been permitted to return to Gafat. A few days later, on 3 July, Theodore had himself appeared at Gafat. He was in a 'bad humour'. On seeing Rosenthal, he said in a 'most violent' manner, 'Why didst thou abuse me?' and to Dr Blanc, 'quite raging', he asked, 'Why didst thou say that the Turks will come and take my country?' Both men had immediately been transported to Debra Tabor, and 'put, together with Mr Rassam, in one prison'. 'The Lord', Mrs Flad ended, 'gives me willingness to suffer, yea, even to die, for him; but my heart pains me, and bleeds for our dear children's sake.'

In his covering letter to Murray, dated 21 September, Flad wrote: 'God only knows what may be the consequence if there does not arise some way of putting a stop to these difficulties.' For his part he suggested that the Ethiopians should be restored their convent at Jerusalem. Were Theodore informed of this it would 'go a great way towards bringing the King to a satisfactory feeling towards the captives', but he added: 'If, after all this, the King should go on in this way, then, may the consequence be whatever it may, attack him at once with your arms.'

Murray passed the two Flad letters on to the Foreign Secretary the same day with the observation that he would be seeing Merewether on the following Monday, and would 'then learn his impression of Mr Flad's new views'. In returning the letters to Murray, Lord Stanley noted, 'I will speak to you on this.' On the Monday Merewether duly called at the Foreign Office, saw the Flad letters, and decided to reflect upon them. On the following day he sent his opinion to Murray by letter dated 25 September.

Merewether still thought the artisans should be sent out to Massawa, but he now decreed that they should only go to the Emperor's court after the prisoners had been released and come out of Ethiopian territory; but if Rassam and the others were not released, 'the question should be taken up vigorously' and 'the threat of punishment' should be 'strictly adhered to' – by the despatch of a force from India. So at last, two-and-a-half years after Cameron and Stern had been imprisoned, serious advisers who could influence the British Government were giving it as their opinion that the Government should now seriously think of using force.

With Mrs Flad's news before him, and the opinions of Flad and Merewether on it, the Foreign Secretary decided that these and other relevant documents should go before the Cabinet. Little time was lost. Only five days after Flad had received his wife's letter an official ten-page document was produced, headed: *Printed for use of the Cabinet. September 26, 1866. Confidential*. This pamphlet reproduced Flad's letter of 21 September, his translation of his wife's letter from Gafat, and Merewether's letter of 25 September, as well as Flad's earlier letter of 19 September saying he saw no advantage in sending artisans to Theodore. Little could the good Mrs Flad, harassed, worried and anxious for the safety of herself and her three young children, know that the letter she wrote at Gafat that July would be placed before the British Cabinet, and survive as a permanent record in the Foreign Office archives.

Merewether learned of the Cabinet Meeting when he called on

Murray two days later, after which he wrote to the latter on 1 October:

> I could see clearly the Cabinet had found it inexpedient, not to say impossible, to proceed to extremities with the King Theodorus. I regret this deeply, because as matters have now come to pass, I am confident the bold and firm attitude is the proper course, and the only one likely to bring affairs to a speedy issue. The having to put up with further insult from this barbarian tells terribly against us as a nation, both in Europe and in the East.

Merewether nevertheless suggested that Flad should go ahead to the Emperor with a letter from the Queen which should contain some opening of tangible advantage to Theodore provided he released the prisoners. Then Merewether himself would follow with the artificers. The Government eventually adopted this plan. The Colonel also offered to go himself on a mission to Theodore, provided he was 'supported by other people, to give dignity to his mission – which is what Rassam sadly lacked', but Lord Stanley did not take up this suggestion, being of opinion that there were already enough envoys, and the appointment of yet another would only cause confusion.

In due course Flad took with him a diplomatic, but admonishing, and very convoluted letter from the Queen,

> Victoria by the Grace of God . . . to Theodore, King of Abyssinia, sendeth greetings.
>
> Relying on the assurances contained in your Majesty's letter of 29th of January, which duly reached us, we were daily in expectation of the arrival in England of our servant Rassam, together with our servant Cameron, and the other Europeans, so long detained in your country, but whom your Majesty had announced that you had sent with our servant Rassam. When Flad arrived bringing your Majesty's further letter of the 17th of April, in which, while repeating that you had released and made over to our servant Rassam, our servant Cameron and the other Europeans, in order that they might leave the country, you stated that you had kept our servant Rassam for the sake of consulting together upon the extension of the friendship between us. We will not disguise from your Majesty that we found it difficult to reconcile your assurances with the obstacles which were still opposed to the departure of our servants and the other Europeans from your country; but we were willing to accept the desire expressed by you for the extension of friendship between us, and we accordingly admitted Flad to our presence, and having heard from him your Majesty's

wishes, we gave directions for the transmission to your Majesty, by the hands of Flad of such articles as we understood from Flad your Majesty desired to obtain, and we also gave our sanction to the engagement in your Majesty's service of skilled workmen such as you desired to employ in Abyssinia. These arrangements were made, and Flad was on the point of leaving England to rejoin your Majesty, when intelligence reached us that you had withdrawn from our servant Rassam the favour which you had hitherto shown him, and had consigned him, together with our servant Cameron and the other Europeans, to prison. We have received no explanation from your Majesty of the grounds of a proceeding so inconsistent with the assurances and professions formerly made by your Majesty, and we have, therefore, lost no time in allowing Flad to depart, and have given to him this letter for your Majesty, not allowing ourselves to doubt that immediately on its receipt you will redeem your promises, and give effect to your professions, by dismissing our servant Rassam, with our servant Cameron and the other Europeans . . .

Your Majesty must be aware that it is the sacred duty of Sovereigns scrupulously to fulfil engagements into which they may have entered; and that the persons of Ambassadors, such as our servant Rassam, and those by whom they are accompanied, are, among all nations, assuming to be civilized, invariably held sacred. We have, therefore, the more difficulty in accounting for your Majesty's hesitation, and we invite your Majesty to prove to the world that you rightly understand your position among Sovereigns, and do not desire to neglect the international duties which it is incumbent on all Sovereigns to fulfil. Your Majesty may be assured that we shall be disposed to attribute to misapprehension on your part, rather than ill-will towards us, the delay that has occurred in the return of Rassam, and those whom you had engaged to send with him; but in the uncertainty which we cannot but feel as to your Majesty's intentions, we cannot allow Flad to be the bearer of those tokens of good-will which we purposed that he should convey to your Majesty. But, in full confidence that the cloud which has darkened the friendship of our relations will pass away on the return of Flad, and desiring that you should as soon as possible thereafter receive the articles which we had proposed to send to your Majesty in token of our friendship, we have given orders that those articles should be forthwith sent to Massowah, to be delivered, for conveyance to your Majesty's Court, to the officers whom you may depute to conduct our servant Rassam, and our servant Cameron, and the other Europeans, so far on their way to our presence. And so we bid you heartily, farewell.

Your good Friend,
Victoria R.

Another letter, out of the blue, arrived at the Foreign Office on 4 October.

It was from one of the men most knowledgeable about Ethiopia then living, the old German missionary Dr Krapf – the same who had first reported seeing snow in Africa – on Mount Kilimanjaro; the letter was dated 1 October 1866, from Kornthal, near Stuttgart, Germany. In tendering advice on how now to deal with Theodore, missionaries seemed more ready than Colonel Merewether to use force. Dr Krapf for his part suggested that two British forces should be despatched, one to Massawa, and a flying division to the Bay of Tajoura, on the Gulf of Aden, whence they were to proceed to Magdala. Although suggesting stern measures Dr Krapf retained his affection for Ethiopia, and concluded that the country had everything 'except a good Ruler'.

By now the Foreign Office had come to its decisions. Flad was to go to the Emperor, tell him the artisans he desired had been recruited, and explain the conditions on which they would enter his service, while Merewether was to follow later to Massawa with the artisans. Flad was in a somewhat strange position. He was neither an Ethiopian nor a subject of the Emperor of Ethiopia, nor yet a British subject. He was in fact a citizen of the German State of Württemberg, but had left Ethiopia as an emissary of Theodore, and, after reaching Aden, his passage and expenses had been paid for by the British Government and would be so until he reached Massawa.

The Foreign Office now prepared a memorandum for Flad's guidance – it could not be called instructions, because he was not a servant of the British Government. Dated 8 October it began: 'The period having arrived at which you propose to return to Abyssinia, Her Majesty's Government have no wish that you should prolong your stay in this country', and went on:

> The King will naturally expect to hear from you what are the feelings of the British Government towards him.
>
> You will not disguise from him that the confidence which they were disposed to place in his promises and assurances was considerably weakened by his detention of Mr Rassam and the others, and has been nearly destroyed by the intelligence which has just reached England of his having placed Rassam, and those whom the King solemnly made over to him for conveyance out of his dominions in confinement.

The memorandum for Flad nevertheless conceded that 'evil-disposed persons' might have 'endeavoured to infuse suspicion' into the mind of the King, and added:

> The British Government has authorised you to say that nothing is further from their desire or intention in any way themselves voluntarily to seek to disturb, or encourage the Governor of Egypt to disturb, King Theodore in the peaceable possession of his dominions; but you will not disguise from his Majesty that, in return for such good-will, the British Government require substantial proof on his part that the same good-will is entertained by him, and that the first and immediate proof of its existence, which can now be given, is the release of Mr Rassam, Captain Cameron, and all other Europeans detained in Abyssinia . . . and their safe conduct beyond the frontiers of the King's dominions.

While the Foreign Office were making their final dispositions for the departure of first Flad and later Merewether it learned that it was unlikely to receive any more information about the captives for quite some time. In a postal despatch from Alexandria on 1 October 1866, Stanton reported:

> We cannot expect as yet any further intelligence, as the rains, judging from the unusually high state of the Nile, must have been very severe in the Abyssinian Mountains, and it is probable that the communications with the coast are suspended, in consequence of the flooded state of the rivers.

Flad was by this time well on his journey. On 18 October he arrived at Alexandria, but was unable to obtain Egyptian Government permission to stop over in Egypt. He went almost immediately to Suez, by the Quarantine Train. Stanton was able to see him for only a few moments while he was still aboard the ship in Alexandria. The missionary then sailed down the Red Sea and arrived at Aden on 25 October.

He wished to stay there until machinery he had purchased for Theodore should catch up with him, but Captain Goodfellow, the Acting-Resident, urged him to sail on to Massawa the following morning. Flad agreed. At about the same time Goodfellow forwarded a message from Munzinger reporting that rebels were in possession of nearly the whole of Ethiopia, with only three provinces remaining in the Emperor's possession.

Merewether meanwhile was still on leave in the United Kingdom, and on 27 October he wrote from Esgair, Machynlleth, North Wales, where he was with his family, to tell the permanent head of the Foreign Office, Mr Hammond, that all the workmen, and machinery would be embarked on a steamer at Southampton, due to sail the next day. Merewether himself proposed to follow, leaving London on 10 November, and to meet the artisans at Alexandria.

While a few people in England occupied themselves with the captives, public opinion was much taken up with the question of parliamentary reform. The Queen was still at Balmoral, but never out of touch with political events, and ever ready to tell her ministers what they should do. Writing on 28 October, she told her Prime Minister, Lord Derby, that she was convinced that, 'if the question of Reform' was 'not taken up in earnest' there might be 'very serious consequences'.

On 29 October the *Victoria* brought Flad to Massawa. At the port he received news of the captives, as well as a letter from his wife. Reporting this to Hertslet he added that there was no road open for him to go up into Ethiopia, for Tigré was in the hands of the rebel Wagshum Gobazie. He had nevertheless sent two different messengers to Theodore, with copies of the Queen's letter and an Amharic translation. He also wrote to the Emperor to say that the British Government would not take up the workmen before he sent down the prisoners.

Continuing to take a militant line Flad nevertheless declared:

> There is not the least hope that Her Majesty's letter will have its effect. There is only one way which the Government ought to take without delay. Capt. Cameron as I hear from Mr Munzinger, gives the advice to go to war at once. And this I think is the opinion of all. I doubt whether it will not also be the advice Mr Rassam gives.

On 28 November the Foreign Office received a number of despatches and letters, from which it learnt at last that the prisoners had been sent on to Magdala and were all in chains. If the news about the captives was causing anxiety to the Foreign Office, it was causing ever greater anxiety to the much-strained relatives. And Dr Beke, with his remarkable lines of communication, was at it again. On 29 November Purday wrote to Lord Stanley to say he had received a letter from Beke saying that as of 1 October the captives were still in chains at Magdala. A reply was sent to Purday that same day, to say that the Foreign Office could not but confirm this news.

Meanwhile, despite growing doubts of the Foreign Office and all concerned arrangements for providing Theodore with men and machines went ahead. Merewether left England at the end of November, reached Alexandria as planned, and made his way via Cairo to Suez whence he sailed to Massawa.

And then yet another idea was presented to the Foreign Secretary for liberating the European prisoners, this time from Russia. Lord Stanley received a telegram on 28 October from Sir A. Buchanan, the British Ambassador at St Petersburg: 'An Armenian here suggests that the Armenian Patriarch at Constantinople if applied to could obtain the release of the Abyssinian captives.' Lord Stanley lost no time in following up the suggestion. On the following day he caused a telegram to be sent to the British Ambassador in Constantinople, Lord Lyons. After explaining the proposal he commented: 'It would not be right to neglect this intimation and I have therefore to instruct your Excellency, if any convenient opportunity occurs, to place yourself in communication with the Patriarch, and to enlist his good offices in favour of the captives.'

31

THE TIME HAS THEREFORE ARRIVED

(1867)

The Queen's Speech at the Opening of Parliament on 5 February 1867, once again made no mention of Ethiopia. Her Majesty had come up from Windsor for the ceremony, and returned that same afternoon. If the Government thought the long-drawn-out affair of the captives not sufficiently important to be included in the Speech, or wisest not to refer to it, several Parliamentarians had not forgotten the matter. On 5 March Christopher Darby Griffith, one of those to whom Cameron had written, rose to ask the Foreign Secretary:

> whether the British artisans who have been or are about to be taken out by Colonel Merewether to Massawah are to be exchanged for the captives now detained in Abyssinia, or are to be sent into that country after the latter are released.

Lord Stanley replied:

> Strict orders have been given to Colonel Merewether that these artisans are under no circumstances to go into the interior, until all the prisoners now detained by the King of Abyssinia shall be released. They have gone by their own free choice and upon their own responsibility.

In fact, the artisans were just then toughening up in preparation for their journey, as Lord Stanley learnt from a despatch from Merewether which reached London some days later.

Merewether himself spent his time reconnoitring inland and along the coast. His despatch, written with the eye of a soldier, gave a report of roads – mere cattle tracks – but good enough for artillery – water supplies, and grazing grounds, and mentioned that the highest point he visited was only 989 feet above the sea, whence a road descends to the plain of Ailat where 'there is a spring of good water always running'. This, he added significantly, 'would be an excellent place to locate a large body of cavalry on first landing'. Merewether also described alternative routes up into Ethiopia, and gave an account of Theodore's position: his territory shrinking and rebels gaining ground everywhere. All this was information which Lord Stanley did not have – nor seek – any opportunity of imparting to the Commons, for the Government and Parliament were then far more concerned with the great domestic and party issue: Reform.

In those same days, however, notwithstanding the vexations of Reform, there was a happier duty for Lord Derby's Government and the Queen. There was then in London a delegation from Her Majesty's North American citizens come to discuss with the Colonial Secretary, Lord Caernarvon, various matters affecting their newly formed Confederation of the British provinces of North America. The Queen accepted the suggestion that these should be called Canada.

On the question of Reform the Derby Government made a bad start. They thought that since the Whig Opposition had not long before brought in a Reform Bill which had only narrowly been defeated, there would be no difficulty for a Tory Government to enact one. But in this Lord Derby and Mr Disraeli, though astute Parliamentarians, were wrong; many a battle royal lay before them. They also had to face opposition within their own party. In March Lord Cranborne, General Peel and Lord Caernarvon resigned. A Government reshuffle followed and their places were taken by Sir Stafford Northcote (India), Sir John Pakington (War), and the Duke of Buckingham (Colonies); in consequence, one newcomer brought into the Cabinet was Mr H. Lowry-Corry (Admiralty). All four were soon to come closely into contact with the Ethiopian question.

The Foreign Office was still confronted with the baffling problem of the captives. Towards the middle of April Lord Stanley decided that he must take preliminary steps in case Britain should have to use force. The first formal steps were taken on 20 April, when a well-documented letter went across from the Foreign Office to the War Office. At the top of the copy retained at the Foreign Office are the following words: 'Seen by Lord Derby and the Queen.' After recalling how Her Majesty's Consul, Cameron, and her special representative, Rassam, had been imprisoned, the letter stated:

The time has . . . arrived when it is needful for Her Majesty's Government to consider what further steps it may be at once possible and advisable to take in order to vindicate the Honour of the Crown, and to protect Her Majesty's subjects from further harm.

I am to state that Lord Stanley would be glad that this subject should engage the early and careful consideration of Sir John Pakington with a view to deciding upon the course to be adopted.

And even the tireless Dr Beke had to come into it, for the letter concluded: 'Since the above was written Lord Stanley has received a letter (copy enclosed) from Dr Beke, whose information as to routes in Abyssinia may be of value.'

A letter was also sent on the same day to the Under-Secretary of the India Office. Referring to the 'present position of affairs between this country and Abyssinia,' it said: 'I am directed by Lord Stanley to request that you will call his attention to the gravity of the circumstances, and to the necessity of considering what further steps should be taken with a view to procuring the release of the captives.' Explaining that 'the employment or co-operation of Her Majesty's Indian Forces would be necessary in carrying out operations', the letter stated that Lord Stanley was 'anxious to obtain the opinion of Sir Stafford Northcote', and continued:

You will perceive that Colonel Merewether is of opinion that force must be resorted to, and that Sir William Coghlan, who has hitherto deprecated the employment of force, has reluctantly come to the conclusion that it is inevitable. He seems, however, to think that the preliminary steps which would be necessary before troops could be despatched from India, and would, of course, reach King Theodore's ears, might have the effect of opening his eyes to the danger of persevering in a wrongful course, and might produce the release of the captives, in which case perhaps the employment of Troops might be avoided.

The probability of their being required must, however, be so far counted on, in the event of it being decided to employ force, so as to insure their services being available at the right season, which appears to be in October.

So by the end of April 1867 the great machinery of State was at last set to work to prepare for war against Theodore – if necessary. Yet even now the die was not yet cast, for the British Government felt no great urge to go to war against the Emperor, still less against that seemingly somewhat nebulous state Ethiopia. So one more endeavour to liberate the captives by peaceful means was made – but this time it included a first hint of an ultimatum.

This was sent to Colonel Merewether at Aden, for forwarding to Theodore.

With the ultimatum Lord Stanley sent a covering despatch, dated 20 April, to Merewether into which was written a statement of the British Government's position. It was perhaps strange that Lord Stanley thought fit to spell out to Merewether what the Government's policy was, as he knew it perfectly well and had played no small part in formulating it. However, as Merewether was the agent of the Government, there was no harm in giving him a clear policy statement. The Foreign Office file copy bears the words: 'Seen by Lord Derby and the Queen', and reads:

> I have received your several despatches . . . and have learned therefrom, with unfeigned concern, that all the efforts which have hitherto been made by Her Majesty's Government to effect, by reasonable means, the release of the prisoners . . . have been unsuccessful. Up to this time Her Majesty's Government have been willing to believe that King Theodore's intentions were pacific, and based upon a desire, however unusually indicated according to European notions, of introducing into his country the enlightened intelligence of other Christian nations; but the fact of the King having lost sight of the rule, observed throughout all ages, of considering the person of envoys sacred, and having imprisoned and detained in chains Mr Rassam and his companions . . . necessarily leads to the conclusion that peaceful relations are not the King's object, and the idea of entering into friendly relations with him must be abandoned.
>
> Under these circumstances it will be for Her Majesty's Government to consider carefully the course which they should adopt; being unwilling, at least in the first instance, to proceed to extremities, I have addressed to King Theodore, by Her Majesty's command, the accompanying letter, which you will forward to him; and if at the expiration of three months . . . the captives shall not have been set at liberty and have left Abyssinia, you will either send home, or sell the presents now in your charge, and hold the proceeds at my disposal.
>
> I have only to add that I am in communication with the India and War Offices, in regard to any further steps which circumstances may render necessary.

Merewether could be considered quite capable of understanding the significance of that last sentence.

With the despatch was a further note from the Foreign Office informing Merewether that Lord Stanley's letter to the Emperor was being sent in triplicate, plus a copy for Merewether, who was instructed to send each of the copies to Theodore by a separate messenger. The Foreign Office knew by now something of the problem of getting letters up from Massawa. The text of the ultimatum, which was dated 16 April, declared:

> I am commanded by the Queen, my Sovereign, to state to your Majesty that she had expected to hear by this time that the prisoners, respecting whom Her Majesty wrote to you on the 4th of October last, had been all released and had arrived at Massowah, and that the presents which were awaiting their arrival at Massowah, were already on their way to Abyssinia. The Queen regrets to find that, although you had become acquainted with the contents of her letter by the copy sent up by Mr Flad, you had hesitated to comply with Her Majesty's wishes for the release of the prisoners, and instead of sending them at once to Massowah to be exchanged against the presents, had looked still to obtain the presents on the faith of your own assurance that, on the receipt of them, you would release the captives. Looking to what has already passed, the Queen cannot again write to your Majesty, but she has desired me to write, and to say that her determination, as expressed in Her Majesty's letter, of which you know the contents, is unchanged and unchangeable; and that so far from being willing to allow the presents to go on before the prisoners have reached Massowah, the Queen has sent orders that the presents shall be returned to Europe, unless the British authorities at Massowah are satisfied within three months after the dispatch of this letter from that port, a copy of which is sent by three different messengers, that the prisoners are actually released and on their way to the coast. In that case the return of the presents may be deferred for such time as may suffice for the prisoners to perform the journey to Massowah, on their arrival at which place the presents will be made over to your Agents.
>
> The Queen has forbidden her Agents to enter into further correspondence on these matters. Her Majesty requires for the last time, by her Secretary of State, that the prisoners should be made over to her, and she trusts that your Majesty will be sufficiently well-advised to comply with her demand, rather than forfeit the friendship which, notwithstanding all that has happened, the Queen is still disposed to entertain for you.
>
> Having thus fulfilled the commands of the Queen my Sovereign, I bid your Majesty heartily farewell.
>
> Your sincere Friend,
> Stanley.

When this letter reached Magdala it was promptly destroyed by Rassam, who felt it would unduly annoy the Emperor.

Saturday, 20 April was the beginning of the Easter week-end, but despatches still arrived at the Foreign Office, and on Easter

Monday one arrived from N. T. Moore, the British Consul at Jerusalem. The suggestion that had originated in Moscow was bearing fruit, and the Armenian line of communication was being put into use. Moore reported that the Armenian Patriarch of Jerusalem had appointed his Vicar-General, Bishop Sahak, to be the bearer of a letter from the Armenian Patriarch of Constantinople to Theodore; apparently the Jerusalem Patriarch did not think the Constantinople Patriarch's letter would be much use, and therefore had written one of his own, properly illuminated, with an Amharic translation, and presents, for Bishop Sahak to take. He hoped all would be ready for his envoy to embark for Egypt 'by the next French steamer' on 14 April.

The Foreign Office instructed Consul Moore to express the Government's thanks to the Patriarch, and Lord Stanley followed this up with an instruction to the British Ambassador to express thanks 'for the service thus rendered not only to British interests, but to the general interests of humanity'. Bishop Sahak, accompanied by a priest, duly left Jerusalem on 13 April. So yet another envoy had set off on the liberation quest.

On 29 April a despatch dated 6 April from Merewether, still at Massawa, reached the Foreign Office. It contained nothing to cause Lord Stanley to change his mind about the need to be prepared to use force, but rather confirmed it. Merewether included an extract from a strongly worded letter from Dr Blanc, who said:

> We will never get out unless active measures are used . . . We are all getting grey, even Prideaux . . . Rassam's whiskers are almost white; Stern looks like a man of seventy . . . Cameron is very much worn out. We are weary, mentally and bodily, of this uncertain state of affairs.

Meanwhile, Lord Derby's Government was still in the throes of getting its Reform Bill through the Commons. The Queen, now in the Isle of Wight, closely following this parliamentary battle, wrote urging the Government to accept an amendment put forward by the Opposition, and 'not resign – as Lord Russell so unnecessarily did last year'.

The year's parliamentary session was by then well advanced, and there had been no further question or debate about the captives since Mr Darby Griffith's solitary question about the artisans in March. But on 14 May, Mr James Wyld asked the Foreign Secretary whether it was true that 'the King of Abyssinia has refused to comply with the Queen's request that he should liberate the captives', and what was happening about the English engineers engaged to enter Theodore's service, and what steps were being taken to release the captives. Lord Stanley gave an informative reply:

> I cannot say that the King has refused to liberate the prisoners, because we have at present received no answer from him on the subject; but we know, or believe, the Queen's letter must have reached him some time ago, and that the prisoners are still detained.

Lord Stanley went on to say he had agreed the engineers should return to England. Further, he, Stanley, had written to the Emperor on 16 April, expressing regret at the long detention of the prisoners, and stating that unless they were liberated immediately the presents which had been sent out would not be delivered. Thus the Foreign Secretary made public the position of the captives, and of the artisans, and the Government's action to date. What the Foreign Secretary did not tell Parliament was that the British Government was at long last giving consideration to the use of force.

32

NO GREATER ENEMY THAN HIMSELF

(1867)

The season of the May meetings had come round again, and in 1867 the London Society followed its usual procedure. On 2 May there was an evening service at St George's Church, Bloomsbury. On the following morning a breakfast, and in the afternoon the Annual Meeting at Exeter Hall, Lord Shaftesbury presiding. The Secretary, the Rev. C. J. Goodhart, read his report of the widespread activities of the Society.

The noble President then rose to address the meeting, and, as reported in the next issue of the *Jewish Intelligence*, 'was received with much cheering'. After dealing with other matters he ended with a word of advice to the meeting: 'I trust that the speakers today will touch as lightly as possible upon the subject of Abyssinia. The King, no doubt, has his friends, his agents, and his observers – not to use a sharper term – in this country, and depend upon it they will convey to him very speedily anything which may be said in disparagement of His Majesty, and therefore let your words be wary and few.'

Subsequent speakers ranged over the Society's many fields of activity far from Ethiopia, but one speaker, the Rev. J. H. Bruhl, a missionary from Baghdad, reminded the meeting of his 'dear predecessor', Mr Stern, who had 'laboured indefatigably in the cause, and whose name is always heard with very great gratitude and great love by many of my Jewish brethren'. A later speaker entreated prayers for the Society's missionaries and Jewish converts, 'and more especially for our captive brethren in Abyssinia, that they may still be sustained in faith and patience, continue to prove a signal blessing to those about them, and speedily, if it be the Lord's Will, be released from their captivity'.

In May 1867 the British Government and the Queen learned that Abdul Aziz, the Sultan of Turkey, together with Ismail Pasha, the Viceroy of Egypt, then in Paris for the great International Exhibition, proposed to visit London. They were expected in July, and the British Government and the Queen (with no great relish) set in hand plans to entertain the two Muslim visitors. As Lord Stanley explained on 22 May: 'English influence is at present greater than that of any other Power at Constantinople. To maintain it is important.' As had been pointed out by Lord Shaftesbury, and by several ministers in Parliament, what happened in England that concerned Theodore seemed to reach his ears. The Emperor had little love for Muslims, or Turks and still less for Egyptians, whom he saw as a menace to his frontiers; however, there does not appear to have been any significant British apprehension that the visit would have any effect on the British Government's efforts to persuade Theodore to liberate his European captives.

While attention was being given to the hospitality for the two Muslim rulers, the Foreign Secretary could not escape the concern for the bedevilled Christians in Ethiopia. In the House of Lords one of the captives' most persistent champions had been Lord Chelmsford, but he was now Lord Chancellor, and, whatever he might feel, was less free to speak on their behalf. But a new and formidable advocate appeared on the Government benches: none other than the once famous British Ambassador at Constantinople, Lord Stratford de Redcliffe. After giving up the Constantinople Embassy and retiring from the diplomatic service in 1858 (after the fall of Palmerston), Lord Stratford took little part in public life. In 1867 he had no special commitments, and was therefore free to take up the cause of the captives, which he now did with his natural persistence.

The question had been raised in the Commons twice that year, but not so far in the Lords. Then, on 21 June, Lord Stratford rose to call the attention of their Lordships to the case of the captives, whose position had remained unchanged since the previous session. The noble Lord read an extract from 'a work recently published by Dr Beke', and reminded their Lordships that Cameron and the missionaries had been in detention for three years, and that Her Majesty's representatives and several others had been subjected to great indignities and even torture. The former Ambassador, as quoted in *Hansard*, then went on to say:

> Not only was our common humanity interested in this case but our national honour and dignity were also at stake. There was a time when it used to be said that England, if she did no right to other nations, would suffer no wrong to be done to herself; but now the case seemed to be reversed, for at no previous period had so much sensitiveness been displayed with regard to the rights of other nations.

The Prime Minister, Lord Derby, considered the subject of sufficient importance to reply himself. He told the House that on the Emepror's assurance that the prisoners would be released, presents and artisans, as requested, had been sent out, but when it was learnt that Rassam and the others were still detained, instructions were given that neither were to proceed further than Massawa. Lord Derby stated that the letter written by the Queen to Theodore had been delivered, but no reply had been received. Consequently, the presents had been detained, and the artisans had returned to Britain. This news was greeted with cheers.

The Secretary of State further reported that he had written to the Emperor that if within three months all captives had not left Ethiopia, the presents would likewise be returned. No reply to that communication had been received, and until some further information was obtained, Her Majesty's Government was not prepared to state what course it would pursue. The Government, he concluded, was willing to lay any correspondence on the table, but in whatever course they adopted must be guided by considerations affecting the safety of the prisoners. It was well known that nothing passed in Parliament, or in this country, intelligence of which was not transmitted to Theodore, and it was at the greatest possible risk that any opinions were expressed, or any discussions held in public, lest these were detrimental to the very persons they sought to rescue. That old friend of the captives in the House of Lords, Lord Houghton, followed the Prime Minister. He had seen a letter, he said, from Consul Cameron, written in very bad spirits and containing the expressive phrase: 'perhaps the sooner the *mauvais quart d'heure* is over the better'.

These exchanges were fully reported in the Press. Lord Derby's reply provoked one person to write to *The Times* to complain at the Prime Minister's apparent apprehension regarding action by Theodore. The letter, published on 27 June and signed 'H.B.', said:

> If the Government is fully assured that King Theodore is possessed of the means of obtaining information of which Lord Derby gives him

> credit, it is deeply to be deplored for the sake of the lives of the prisoners, for the honour of the country, and for the maintenance of our position in the East, that far different language . . . does not come forth from the lips of the same Minister . . . It is far from being my opinion that a resort to force is always or the only way to such an end; but the impunity with which British subjects have been captured without an effort, except that of bribery, being made to procure their release is sure to be known throughout Arabia . . .

Such Press comment provoked Dr Beke on 29 June to write a long letter to the Foreign Secretary – not that he needed much provocation to do that. In the course of this letter he made reference to the 'bellicose tone' then recently 'assumed by many of the organs of public opinion' from which it might be 'inferred that hostile measures will ere long ensue'. Dr Beke expressed the hope that in the event of hostilities his suggestion to secure assistance of 'Waagshum Gobazze, the actual ruler of Northern Abyssinia, would not be disregarded'; and he thought that the whole cost of warlike operations should not be borne by the Imperial Treasury 'inasmuch as the Government of India is not less responsible than the Home Government for the breach between England and Abyssinia, if indeed it might not be contended that the mischief *originated* with the Indian authorities'. Some people at the Foreign Office were by then getting rather tired of Dr Beke. In passing his letter up to Lord Stanley, someone therefore wrote at the foot: 'Simply acknowledge? or Don't Answer.' Lord Stanley wrote in his instruction: 'Ack. July 3/67. S.'

But as the matter of the captives gained wider general interest, more people offered advice. Many quaint letters arrived, including one from the Reverend Ernest Reed who suggested that the cause of Theodore's displeasure might be found in the activities of the French, and that 'strenuous measures' were called for 'to vindicate the good name' which Great Britain had 'universally acquired for justice and honour'.

Meanwhile, the wheels of government that Lord Stanley had set in motion, were turning. On 2 July a batch of letters was sent from the War Office. One addressed to the Under-Secretary of State of the India Office, stated that Sir John Pakington, the Secretary of State for War, was 'decidedly of opinion that force, in the event of its being determined to send one, should be provided from India, and that the whole expedition should be organised at and proceed from Bombay'.

On 6 July, Lord Stanley received a long despatch from Colonel Merewether, dated Aden, 15 June. It reported that HMS *Dalhousie* had returned to Aden, bringing letters from Rassam and others dated 3 May. Once again the news from Magdala was that the prisoners were in continuing anxiety about their future. They were the more anxious because the temper of the Emperor had become more uncertain. He had now vented his displeasure on the European workmen living at Gafat, whom he had hitherto invariably treated well. Rassam said:

> Unless you come up and take us out, I fear there will be no chance of our ever leaving this country. Our friend the Emperor has no greater enemy than himself.
>
> For the past four years he has done nothing but destroy the foundation of the mansion he had so nobly reared. He has been going from bad to worse . . . and now there is scarcely a spot in the whole of Abyssinia where peace and safety prevail.

Up to this time, Flad (whose mission was soon to be overtaken by events) had not yet reached the Emperor, but on 16 April, a letter had arrived from him stating that he had reached Matemma. Rassam reported that the Lasta road was every day becoming safer for messengers as the chiefs of that district had thrown off their allegiance 'to our friend'. And Rassam hoped the British Government would act swiftly to liberate the prisoners – or let them know if they did not intend to do so.

In this despatch Merewether also dealt with matters concerning the use of force. He noted that the British Government's three months' notice to Theodore would end on 17 August, and therefore urged that officers be sent from Bombay to Aden to make arrangements for a force to proceed to Ethiopia – presumably to act in October.

Nor was Merewether letting grass grow under his feet. By his arrangement Munzinger had travelled on the *Dalhousie* southwards from Massawa to Amphilla Bay on 10 June, where he had landed to explore the country up to Lake Ashangi and if possible to Lake Haik.

Then Lord Stanley received from Mr John Petherwick of Henley-on-Thames a simple plan for coercing Theodore. In brief, Britain should land a force at Massawa and establish a blockade to stop the Ethiopians from obtaining salt (which Mr Petherwick wrongly assumed to be obtained at the coast – the country in fact relied on rock salt from the Afar plains). All the chiefs and people affected by the loss of this vital commodity, he suggested, would then work for the liberation of the captives in order to restore its supply. Lord Stanley wrote to Mr Petherwick that his ingenious plan would receive consideration.

On 8 July Mr Purday sent Lord Stanley a copy of yet another gloomy letter from Stern to his wife, dated 2 May 1867. On the following day, 9 July, the captives' new champion in the Lords, Viscount Stratford de Redcliffe, demonstrated his continued interest when he expressed his desire 'to know . . . if the Government have received any further information with respect to the Captives, and whether they intend to take any further steps'. Lord Derby replied that he would be obliged if the noble Lord would postpone the question 'as I have no communication to communicate'.

A momentous day in the Commons (or a momentous night) was 15 July. The day's proceedings began as usual with Questions. On the previous Tuesday Lord Stratford de Redcliffe had raised the matter of the captives in the Lords; now, only seven days later, it was discussed in the Commons. Colonel William Sykes asked the Secretary of State for India whether there was any foundation for a rumour circulating in Bombay that troops had been told off for an expedition to Ethiopia. Sir Stafford Northcote gave a carefully worded reply. First of all he stated categorically, but perhaps disingenuously: 'There was no truth in the rumour to which the honourable and gallant gentleman referred.' Then he added:

> No troops had been told off for an expedition to Abyssinia; but the Government were engaged in a correspondence which they hoped might lead to the release of the British subjects now detained in that country. No measures of force to accomplish that object were, however, at present contemplated. It was true that he had addressed private communications to his right honourable friend the Governor of Bombay requesting him confidentially to inform him what could be done in the event of any measure of force being resorted to; but no such instructions as the Question implied had been sent out to Bombay, and the correspondence had been of a most private character.

The Commons soon afterwards embarked on the business that made the evening memorable, and filled all the benches – the Third Reading of the Bill that had caused so much turmoil. That night Mr Disraeli, back in Downing Street, wrote to the Queen:

'The English Reform Bill passed . . . without a division. House full.' And Mr Gladstone wrote in his diary: 'A remarkable night.' The Bill had still to pass the Lords where it was given a first reading the next day; but the battle was in effect over.

The Queen was now staying in the Isle of Wight and preparing to receive the Sultan and the Khedive, and it was as well that she was a good sailor, for the reception on board the royal yacht *Victoria and Albert* on 17 July took place, as she noted in her diary, amid 'violent squalls and heavy rain'. A splendid ball for the Sultan was subsequently given at the India Office.

But in Parliament the captives were not forgotten by their friends, and on that same day Mr Baillie Cochrane, the Conservative member for Honiton, asked the Foreign Secretary whether he would publish any recent correspondence on the subject. Lord Stanley replied, 'Papers were now in course of preparation and would be laid upon the Table in a few days, and further, the House would very shortly have an opportunity of discussing the whole subject.' This debate took place on 26 July. It was opened by Mr Henry Seymour, the Liberal Member for Poole. He raised the subject, he said, not to discuss military intervention or non-intervention, but to publicise the lamentable position in which nearly 60 Europeans were placed. He dealt out, with some fairness, condemnation of Theodore for his errors and praise for his better qualities. Early in his speech, as quoted by *Hansard*, he said:

> By all Governments, civilized and even uncivilized, the person of one holding the position of Ambassador was regarded as sacred. Abyssinia appeared to be a solitary instance to the contrary, and the circumstances of the case demanded that some notice should be taken of her infraction of the usages of all countries.

Mr Seymour then dwelt on Theodore's abilities and original intentions. He also referred to the Egyptians, who, he said, had 10 years earlier obtained the release of the Coptic Patriarch whom the Emperor attempted to detain, and had done so by an ultimatum and the threat of force. Mr Seymour accordingly moved:

> That an humble address be presented to Her Majesty, that proper steps may be taken to procure the release of Her Majesty's Consul and other subjects of Her Majesty at present held prisoners by the King of Abyssinia, if necessary by force of arms.

Mr Seymour's motion was seconded by the gallant Liberal member for Frome, Sir Henry Rawlinson, who roundly asked:

'Why have we hesitated and still hesitate?' He offered three reasons: (1) Fear for the lives of the captives; (2) Danger of losing a war; (3) Expense. He then answered each of these objections. He observed that Britain had in the past released its captives both in China and Kabul, and added that he had collected information about Ethiopia: invasion would be hazardous, but was that a reason for flinching? And he drew a comparison with the Sitana campaign. He went on to give the Government two pieces of advice: (1) There should be no foreign entanglement; and (2) India should pay half the cost of the expedition, as in the case of the Persia Campaign and the China War.

The debate was also joined by one all too familiar with the problem from its beginning: Henry Layard, who now rose from the Opposition benches, and began: 'This is a question of no common difficulty. No question came before me during the time I had the honour to hold office that gave me greater anxiety; for, whatever way the matter was viewed, it was full of embarrassment.' Layard never had much love for the ever-interfering Dr Beke, and now he gave the house a piece of his mind, and spoke of the 'mischief' of Dr Beke's undertaking a mission of his own while Rassam was at Theodore's court. And then Layard, who had been a party to so many efforts to persuade Theodore, came down in favour of the use of force. He said that an expedition was the only course.

Lord Stanley then rose. He said:

> Almost from the first day that the present Government had succeeded to power, the question of what should be done for these unfortunate Abyssinian captives has occupied our most earnest attention . . .
>
> Since their detention being a pure act of caprice, the same caprice might at any moment lead to their being again released, without any effort on our part.

The Foreign Secretary recited to the House the course of events since the arrival of Flad in England, the engagement of the artisans and their arrival at Massawa, and his own letter to Theodore. He then gave his first indication to the House that the Government had at last considered the possibility of using force, but seemed to give the impression that this had been rejected, for in a phrase later to raise some eyebrows, he added, 'it would be madness to throw a British army into an unknown country, in a tropical climate, very far from the sea, very far from its reserves and supplies without a full previous investigation'. Ominously, however, he added:

> I have been in communication with the War Department and with the India Office as to the best mode of proceeding.
>
> The Secretary of State for India has telegraphed to the Indian Government to send over an officer or officers to meet Colonel Merewether at Aden and with him to examine minutely the points on which information is necessary.

Lord Stanley nevertheless still appeared cautious on the use of force, and concluded:

> I do not think we should be called upon even now to give any pledge on the part of the Government as to an expedition, unless it is found to be practicable with only a reasonable expenditure of men and means.

The prospect of the use of force brought the gallant Liberal member for Aberdeen appropriately into the debate at this point. Colonel Sykes, who had earlier drawn attention to rumours of military preparations at Bombay, began by recalling the happy days of Plowden and the episode of the Emperor's unanswered letter. He then examined the difficulties of conducting a campaign in Ethiopia, and dwelt at length on the climate while emphasising that 'the lives of the captives did not appear to be in danger'. He considered that an army of not less than 10,000 men would be required, and, after examining the cost, concluded by declaring that a military expedition would not be justified. This view was shared by another Liberal, Ralph Bornal Osborne, who urged that Ethiopian merchants trading between the coast and the interior 'would be better able to bring about a solution than any European diplomatist'.

The debate was brought to an end with a speech from the Opposition by one who had long taken an interest in the captives, Mr Ayrton. He too was opposed to a military expedition, and advocated the use of 'natives as ambassadors'. The next day, the Press gave a good coverage to the debate.

Parliament still had some time to run before the Summer recess, and Members who had taken up the captives' cause continued to be active. On 9 August Henry Seymour returned to the subject, and, referring to Munzinger, asked the Foreign Secretary whether he considered it would help: 'if there were an English gentleman, of position and experience to perform the duties of English Consul at Massowah, instead of a German gentleman who acts as agent both for the French and English Governments?'

Lord Stanley replied:

> Apart from this question of the prisoners there are really no consular duties to be performed at Massowah.
>
> The only object of having an agent there is to keep up communications with these unfortunate gentlemen . . .
>
> Affairs relating to their liberation have been left very much in the hands of Colonel Merewether, the Resident at Aden, and I believe he is perfectly satisfied with the qualifications of the present Consul . . .

The Foreign Secretary's reply was all too true; 'there are really no consular duties to be performed at Massowah'. Oh, Plowden! Oh, Palmerston!

On 13 August, a fortnight or so after the debate, the Cabinet finally decided on armed intervention, and on the following day Lt-General Sir Robert Napier was appointed commander of the unit to be despatched. Five days later Lord Stanley informed the Acting Consul in Alexandria that Her Majesty's Government, 'after having exhausted all peaceful efforts to induce King Theodore to release the European prisoners . . . have resolved, should it be necessary, to use force for that purpose'.

Parliament, however, was not informed of this important decision for another three days. This happened, on 21 August, not in a Ministerial Statement, which Members might have discussed, but, more conveniently for the Government, in the Act of Prorogation, which constitutionally ruled out any debate, at least within the current session. The Queen's Speech, delivered in Her Majesty's absence by the Lord Chancellor, contained the words:

> The Communications which I have made to the reigning Monarch of Abyssinia, with a view to obtain the Release of the British Subjects whom he detains in his Dominions, have, I regret to say, thus far proved ineffectual. I have therefore found it necessary to address to him a peremptory Demand for their immediate Liberation, and to take Measures for supporting that Demand, should it ultimately be found necessary to resort to Force.

The Government's Demand and threatened use of force was therefore never discussed in either House. The Mother of Parliaments was given no last opportunity for deliberation.

33

CONCLUSION: THE BATTLE AND ITS AFTERMATH

Having at last decided on intervention the British Government acted rapidly. A small advance party, consisting largely of British Indian troops, sailed from Bombay on 16 September 1867. A fortnight or so later, and well before it had landed, Lt-General Sir Robert Napier, who was still in Bombay, despatched two messages to Ethiopia. The first, a very emphatic letter, was addressed to 'Theodorus, King of Abyssinia' and declared:

> I am commanded by Her Majesty the Queen of England to demand that the prisoners whom your Majesty has wrongfully detained in captivity shall be immediately released and sent in safety to the British Camp.
>
> Should your Majesty fail to comply with this command, I am further commanded to enter your Majesty's country at the head of an army to enforce it, and nothing will arrest my progress until this object shall have been accomplished.
>
> My Sovereign has no desire to deprive you of any part of your dominions, nor to subvert your authority, although it is obvious that such would in all probability be the result of hostilities.
>
> Your Majesty might avert this danger by the immediate surrender of the prisoners.
>
> But should they not be delivered safely into my hands, should they suffer a continuance of ill-treatment, or should any injury befall them, your Majesty will be held personally responsible, and no hope of future condonation need be entertained.

The second message was a proclamation addressed to 'the Governors, the Religious Orders, and the People of Abyssinia'. It stated, no less emphatically:

> It is known to you that Theodorus, King of Abyssinia, detains in

captivity the British Consul Cameron, the British Envoy Rassam, and many others, in violation of the laws of all civilised nations.

All friendly persuasion having failed to obtain their release, my Sovereign has commanded me to lead an army to liberate them.

All who befriend the prisoners or who assist in their liberation shall be well rewarded, but those who may injure them shall be severely punished.

When the time shall arrive for the march of a British army through your country, bear in mind, People of Abyssinia, that the Queen of England has no unfriendly feelings towards you, and no design against your country or your liberty.

Your Religious establishments, your persons, and property shall be carefully protected.

All supplies required for my soldiers shall be paid for.

No peaceable inhabitant shall be molested.

The sole object for which the British Force has been sent to Abyssinia is the liberation of Her Majesty's subjects.

There is no intention to occupy permanently any portion of Abyssinian Territory, or to interfere with the government of the country.

The advance party duly landed at Mulkutto, also known as Zulla, at the end of the month, after which it made its way into the highlands of the then rebellious province of Tigré where it was met by an envoy of the local chief Dejazmatch Kassa. In the ensuing talks Kassa agreed to collaborate with the British – and to provide them with provisions – on condition that after the defeat of their common enemy Theodore, they would quickly leave the country, thus, if all went well, leaving him in a good position to seize Theodore's crown to which he had long aspired. Sir Robert Napier, who landed at Mulkutto on 2 January 1868, therefore found the political situation from the British point of view extremely satisfactory.

The British enjoyed moreover massive superiority in weapons. Napier thus had at his disposal over 16,000 men – British and Indians – armed with rifles, including many quick-firing Sniders, a new type of weapon never previously used in war, and terrifying rockets entirely unknown in Ethiopia, as well as six 9-pounder Armstrong guns, twelve small steel guns, and two 8-inch mortars. Theodore had scarcely more than 3,000 men armed with percussion muzzle-loaders, and 1,000 with antique matchlocks. Thanks to the skills of the missionary craftsmen at Gafat he also, it is true, had some 30 recently locally cast pieces of artillery – but these were still more or less untried, and his men had not learnt how to use them. The invaders, who imported no less than 4,530,000 Maria Theresa dollars to meet local expenses (and, unlike traditional Ethiopian soldiers, refrained from looting the peasantry), also had a much more efficient transport service than anything ever seen in the country. It was based on a 10½-mile railway across the torrid coastal lowlands, as well as the utilisation of 44 transport elephants imported from India, and no fewer than 11,000 mules, horses, camels and donkeys also brought in from abroad.

The outcome of the war was almost a foregone conclusion. Thanks to the co-operation of Dejazmatch Kassa and other chiefs, and the monetary payments for provisions received, Napier's men were able to advance right across northern Ethiopia to within sight of Theodore's fortress at Magdala without encountering any opposition.

On eventually reaching the Dalanta plateau, within easy access of Magdala, on 3 April, Napier despatched a further letter to Theodore, which the latter refused to accept. Differing from the earlier communication in that it for the first time demanded the release not only of the British, but of the 'other Europeans' it stated:

> By command of the Queen of England, I am approaching Magdala with an army, in order to recover from your hands Envoy Rassam, Consul Cameron, Dr Blanc, Lieutenant Prideaux, and the other Europeans now in your Majesty's power. I request your Majesty to send them to my camp, as soon as it is sufficient to admit of their coming in safety.

A few days later, on Good Friday, 10 April, Napier launched his first, all-decisive, attack on Theodore's army. The battle took place below Magdala, in the Arogé plain whither Theodore's warriors rushed down from the mountain, while the Emperor on the nearby Fala crest supervised the firing of his artillery. His forces were mowed down by British fire, and suffered predictably heavy casualties. Theodore himself was at one point almost killed when a rocket hissed within a foot of him, whereupon he is said to have exclaimed, 'Would that it had gone through my head!' Among the many chiefs struck down in the unequal conflict was the monarch's life-long friend and companion Fitawari Gebreyé.

Theodore at once realised, as Clement Markham, a contemporary British historian of the campaign, wrote, that 'no hope was left but in concession to an irresistible enemy'. Early on the following morning, 11 April, the monarch therefore despatched an embassy to the British with instructions to sue for peace. The envoys consisted of the Emperor's son-in-law Dejazmatch Alemé, one of the captives Lieutenant Prideaux, and the German craftsman missionary Martin Flad. Sir Robert Napier received the envoys, but sent them back with an Ultimatum. This demanded not only the release of the British captives, the originally stated object of the expedition, and the freeing of the other European prisoners, but also what was presumably of much greater concern to Theodore – his own unconditional surrender. This latter demand had never been formulated in Napier's written instructions – let alone disclosed to the House of Commons, but had by then become the Commander-in-Chief's discreetly unstated policy, for in a speech delivered at Westpool four months later he declared that his object, imparted to none but his Military and Political Secretaries, was 'to receive no negotiations from Theodore', but 'simply to take the prisoners, and then advance upon him and take himself'. This hitherto undeclared policy – which might have been a surprise to Theodore if he had followed the British Press as assiduously as was so often asserted in Parliament – found expression in the Ultimatum which declared:

> Your Majesty has fought like a brave man, and has been overcome by the superior power of the British army. It is my desire that no more blood be shed. If, therefore, your Majesty will submit to the Queen of England, and bring all the Europeans in your Majesty's hands, and deliver safely them this day in the British camp, I guarantee honourable treatment for yourself and for all members of your Majesty's family.

In explaining this Ultimatum, Sir Robert sternly informed Dejazmatch Alemé that 'not only all Europeans must at once be sent to the camp, but the Emperor must come in also and submit to the Queen of England'. He said that if Theodore 'complied he would be honourably treated, but that if any Europeans now in his hands were injured, he could expect no pity; and that had he [Napier] to remain for five years in the country, he would not leave until the last murderer was punished, had he even to buy him from his mother'.

To further underline this threat, Alemé was shown the expedition's mortars and elephants, and was told, with some evident exaggeration, that 'the arms used in the action of the previous evening . . . were mere playthings in comparison with these destructive machines'. The chief is said to have been duly terrorised, and said to Flad, 'There is no hope for us . . . we must surrender, or we shall be killed.' Prophetically, he added: 'I am sure the King will send down the captives, but I fear he won't go down himself.' Napier had originally demanded Theodore's surrender within 24 hours, but at Alemé's entreaty agreed to extend this to 48 hours.

The Ultimatum was then taken to Theodore. The envoys, who found him overlooking the British camp, and just beginning to dictate a letter to his secretary, were soon joined by the missionary Waldmeier. Together they delivered the Ultimatum into the royal hands. It was twice translated by Flad, with the assistance of Waldmeier, whereupon the Emperor at once asked, 'What do they mean by honourable treatment? Do they intend to treat me honourably as their prisoner, or do they intend to assist me in recovering my country from the rebels?' He thereupon ordered the envoys to move aside, while he continued his dictation.

His remarkable document, which was acquired over a century later by the Ethiopian Ministry of Culture, had apparently been intended as a testament to the Ethiopian people, but after the arrival of the envoys it was almost immediately turned into a message to the British who were then poised to attack. Theodore, most significantly, divested himself of his imperial name and title, and, referring to himself only by his original name, Kassa, began:

> In the name of the Father, of the Son, and of the Holy Ghost, one Lord. Kassa, he who believes in the Three in One, in Christ [thus speaks]: Well then, people of my country, will you not abandon the fight unless I, by the power of God descend [i.e. go down from the mountain to fight] for you?

At about this point, having received the Ultimatum, he turned to address the British, and continued:

> As it seemed to me that I had sway over all Christians, I brought them to the land of the heathens [i.e. to Magdala]. There are young women who have no men [i.e. husbands] and tomorrow there will be those whose [husbands] have died on them. Old men who have no children [to look after them], old women who have no children, there are many in my town for whom I provide. Grant them out of which God has given you . . . When they said that I had said to the people of my country that they should submit to the discipline of taxes, they refused and quarrelled with me.

Referring to the previous day's engagement he added:

> The men who loved me and followed me, fearing a single bullet, abandoned me and fled. When you attacked them, I was not with those men who ran away, when I strove with inadequate artillery, alas for me! The people of my country would give me ten reasons [for their retreat], saying that I had adopted the faith of the Franks and had become a Muslim. May God give them good out of what I had done to them! May it be as he wills! I had thought, if God granted it to me, to rule all. If God removed it [i.e. the power] from me, I should die; this was my thought. From when I was born till now, no man has seized hold of my hand. Whenever my men fled, I arose and had the habit of reassuring them. Darkness prevented me [yesterday]. You men who dwelt in happiness yesterday, may God make you like me. Let alone my Ethiopian enemies, it had seemed to me that I should march to Jerusalem and drive out the Turks. A man who has held other men, in his turn cannot be held.

On completing this testament Theodore had it folded into the cover of Napier's Ultimatum which was then handed to Prideaux and Flad to take back to the British camp, whither the distraught monarch insisted that they should immediately return.

After their departure the Emperor sat a long time in the open air without speaking. He then told his followers to move away from him, after which he said a prayer, bowed three times with his face to the ground, crossed himself, and drank some water. Then he drew a double-barrelled pistol from his belt, put it to his mouth, and pulled the trigger. The weapon, however, failed to go off. Ras Ingeda, the Prime Minister, thereupon rushed to him with a number of soldiers, and wrested the weapon from his mouth. The pistol at once fired, grazing the monarch's ear. Theodore struggled, and for a minute or two he and his men were rolling on the ground. However, he rapidly got up, composed himself, and declared that it was God's wish that he should not die at that time.

Having decided to live, he held a Council with his chiefs at which he became 'so excited', according to Dr Blanc, 'that it was with difficulty he was restrained from committing suicide'. All but one of his chiefs now advised him to kill the European prisoners, but, taking the more humanitarian line, he instead sent a message to Rassam saying, 'Go at once to your people: you can send for your property tomorrow.' Those freed also included Cameron and Blanc, as well as the missionaries Stern and Rosenthal, all of whom then descended to the British camp. The wives and children were to remain at Magdala, and be collected by their husbands on the morrow.

Flad and Prideaux had meanwhile taken the envelope containing Theodore's Testament, together with the Ultimatum, down to the British camp. Napier, infuriated by the return of his letter, and perhaps by the Emperor's failure to address him by name, took little interest in the communication Theodore had dictated. In a report penned three days later the British Commander-in-Chief dismissed it as an unsealed 'paper', which was 'not in the form of a letter', and subsequently complained that it was a 'rambling letter' which Theodore had left unsigned because he 'believed it beneath his dignity to hold such correspondence with me'. Napier, who was in a bellicose mood, and felt that 'the honour of England stood above all', immediately ordered Prideaux and Flad back to Magdala with the message that 'no terms would be accepted', other than those he had earlier demanded.

Theodore, by then, was desperately anxious to make peace. Swallowing his pride, he sent the British a further, much more conciliatory, letter, which was destined to be his last. Written in the early hours of Easter Sunday, a time when it was customary for Ethiopian Christians to slaughter cattle for the great post-Lenten fast, it was addressed to the Queen of England's servant, but was obviously intended for Napier, though the latter was not mentioned by name. In this conciliatory message the monarch reverted to his imperial name and title, and declared his intention of sending the British a peace offering. The text referred to the monarch's previous letter, his attempted suicide, and the subsequent release of Rassam, and declared:

> With regard to the letter that I sent yesterday to Mr Flad and his companions, I saw that the people of my country had departed from [my] command on account of my quarrel with you, my friends, and secondly as I have seen the discipline of your attack [and] of your men . . . I was full of resentment. Satan placed in me the thought that I should die by mine own gun. Oh! realising that I should not go and abandon the whole army without a provider, and that God would abominate me, hurriedly I sent [the letter], thinking that when I was dead, when there would be confusion, my words would fail to reach you. But after I had sent it to you, when I cocked the hammer of my gun and put into my mouth, though I kept on pulling [the trigger], it refused [to fire]. When people came running and pulled it out of my mouth, it fired. But since I have survived since God has told me that

> I should not die, thinking that your heart would yearn [for him] I sent Mr Rassam away . . .

Turning to his proposed peace offering, and apologising again for his previous letter, he continued: 'Today is Easter Sunday . . . so permit me to send heifers for you. In sending your letter back I had not thought we would meet on earth, but rather in heaven.'

He then referred to the death of Gebreyé, and, declaring that he had instructed that if he and Gebreyé were both killed they should be buried together, he begged, since he alone had survived, that the British should give him the chief's body, so that he could bury him as befitted a friend.

Finally, he affirmed that Waldmeier and all the other foreigners at his camp were free to leave, and begged the British commander not to abandon his friendship, for Theodore concluded: 'I am your friend, a lover of artifacts' – or, as we would now say, of technological progress.

This letter, duly sealed, was entrusted by Theodore to his secretary, Aleka Ingeda, and a German missionary craftsman, Mr Bender, who brought it down to the British camp soon after dawn. The text was at once translated in Napier's tent. The Emperor's secretary began by reading a passage in Amharic which Samuel translated into Arabic, whereupon Rassam rendered it into English. Though convoluted in style the main thrust, Napier at once saw, was an attempt to make peace. Describing the letter as 'an apology for the rude missive of the previous day', he observed that it showed that Theodore 'desired friendship' and was 'prepared to send down . . . every European, along with an offering of a few cows as it was the Easter feast'. The significance of the proposed gift was not lost on Dr Blanc who stated that 'according to Abyssinian custom' it implied 'a peace-offering, which once accepted, removed all apprehension of hostilities'.

Napier, however, had no desire for reconciliation, for he was determined on nothing short of Theodore's unconditional surrender, and indeed he went further, for two days later he wrote: 'It was essential for the vindication of our national honour . . . that he should be removed.' He therefore brushed aside Theodore's letter and deliberately ignored the proposed gift of cattle. He accordingly sent back the envoys, together with Dejazmatch Alemé and Ato Samuel, with only a verbal message, telling the Emperor to refer to his Ultimatum of the previous day, and again ordering him to send down the remaining Europeans without delay.

Samuel, however, took it on himself to ask what answer concerning the cattle they should take back. There was later much controversy about the ensuing conversation. The recollection of Rassam, from which he never departed, was that when asked about the cattle Sir Robert replied, 'I accept them', and that was the answer he therefore translated to Samuel. Merewether, who sought to exonerate the Commander-in-Chief from any suggestion of bad faith, claimed, on the other hand, that 'no words were uttered', and that Napier, 'without apparently giving the matter a thought, simply bowed his head'. Napier for his part was perhaps deliberately vague, and, without subscribing to either version, subsequently asserted that he had no idea of the size of the proposed gift, and that 'any assent, given by me . . . was under the impression that the question referred to the present of a few cows and sheep'. (The letter in fact specified neither the size of the gift nor the number of animals.)

Dejazmatch Alemé, Samuel and the missionaries then climbed up to Magdala fortress to arrange for the evacuation of the craftsmen's wives and children, as well as a few artisans who for one reason or another were still in the Emperor's camp. On reaching the summit the emissaries, who in response to the Emperor's letter took with them the remains of Fitawari Gebreyé, found the monarch in a tolerably good mood. He immediately turned to Samuel, and eagerly asked whether his gift had been accepted. The courtier bowed respectfully, and replied: 'The English Ras says to you, "I have accepted your present, may God give it back to you",' the last phrase being the customary Ethiopian expression of thanks. Theodore, on hearing this, drew a deep breath, as if relieved of great anxiety, for he assumed, as Markham explains, that 'peace was granted', and that 'the deadly peril was over'. Then, turning to the craftsmen, he said, 'Take your families and go', adding that 'now he was friends with the English' he could 'get as good workmen as they were'. He then bade them farewell in good spirits, for, Markham says, he was 'under the belief that peace was established. Never was a surrender, when once resolved upon, so freely and unreservedly made. Not a hostage, not a child, not a box was kept back. It was an act of a King, an act without cunning or treachery, how slight soever, to mar its fulness.' On hearing of the acceptance of his gift, Theodore ordered that livestock should immediately be sent down to the British camp. The present is said to have consisted of 1,000 cattle and 500 sheep, and is thought to have comprised virtually all the animals then in his possession.

Meanwhile the craftsmen and their families left Magdala, and arrived at the British camp just before sunset. Theodore for his part remained cheerful in the fond belief that peace with the British had at long last been established; he therefore took no further steps to improve his defences.

In Napier's camp, however, misgivings about the cattle had begun to be felt. Rassam questioned the morality of accepting a gift if it had been decided to attack its donor on the morrow, and Munzinger took a similar view, declaring that the English name would become 'a bye-word' for deceit. Colonel Fred Thesiger, a British officer who overheard these words, at once reported them to Robert Napier, who thereupon ordered that the cattle should not be allowed within his lines. News of this rejection of his peace offering reached Theodore shortly after the craftsmen's departure, when one of his men, Agafari Mashesha, reported that the livestock had been stopped by the first piquet guarding the British camp. Convinced, as Markham admits, that he had been deceived, he spent the greater part of the night walking dejectedly about his camp.

The next morning he addressed his followers saying, 'Warriors who love me, gird yourselves, leave all behind, take nothing but arms, and follow me. The time has come to seek another home.' Many of his men, however, refused, saying that they would never flee before an enemy again, and preferred to die at Magdala. He then reflected for a short time, after which he said, 'Be it so.' He then told those who were not prepared to share his fortunes, to seek their own safety. Most of the soldiers, shell-shocked from the earlier engagement, then disbanded, but some of his most loyal chiefs and followers decided to remain with him to the end.

Napier, meanwhile, had given orders for the assault. The attack began with a bombardment from all the artillery at the British disposal. One shell burst by the Emperor's treasury, two others in his courtyard, killing two servant girls. A third exploded a few feet above his head, while a fourth killed his faithful Prime Minister, Ras Ingeda. Not long after this, British troops, after climbing the steep heights, burst into the citadel. Theodore fought heroically to the last, but, realising that further resistance was impossible, dismissed his followers, saying, 'Flee. I release you from allegiance; as for me, I shall never fall into the hands of the enemy.' Then, turning to his valet, he added, 'It is finished! Sooner than fall into their hands, I will kill myself.' He then put his pistol to his mouth, fired, and fell dead; the bullet passed through the roof of his mouth and out of the back of his head. By that last act he earned a unique position in the annals of Ethiopian history.

On finally breaking into the citadel the British found a scene of carnage, with dead and wounded in all directions. Seeing the body of the dead monarch, Markham relates, they 'gave three cheers over it, as if it had been that of a dead fox, and then began to cut and tear the clothes to pieces until it was nearly naked'. The victorious troops then dispersed over the mountain in search of plunder. Most of the buildings, including the palace, the treasury and the storehouse of the principal church, that of Medhané Alem, the Saviour of the World, were soon rifled by the soldiers who thus acquired around a thousand costly manuscripts, many of them finely illustrated, as well as crowns, processional crosses, church paraphernalia and other items. The American journalist, H. M. Stanley, recalled that they covered 'the whole surface of the rocky citadel, the slopes of the hill, and the entire road to the [British] camp two miles off'. The loot was later collected by the British military authorities, and auctioned to provide 'prize money' for the troops. The lion's share of the booty was purchased for the British Museum, and can be seen there, and in its successor institution, the British Library, to this day.

The defeat and death of Theodore marked the end of a heroic, but disastrous era in Ethiopian history, as well as unhappy page in the story of Anglo-Ethiopian relations. The British Government, having no desire to remain longer in Ethiopia, honoured its pledge to withdraw from the country speedily. Finding no Ethiopian chief interested in taking over Magdala, British sappers burnt the settlement to the ground on 17 April, thus, as Napier declared, showing their country's 'anger' at the 'ill-treatment' of Theodore's European prisoners. The Emperor's artillery was at the same time demolished – though one of his mortars survived, and can still be seen at Magdala. Theodore's young son, Alemayehu, was taken back to Britain, where he was befriended by Queen Victoria, but died there at early age, without issue.

With the demise of Theodore the government he had built up with great pains almost immediately disintegrated, and most of his attempted reforms came to an end. Civil war, from which the country had so long suffered, intensified as a power struggle was waged to determine who should succeed him as King of Kings.

Theodore failed in his attempt to unify and modernise his age-old country, but his vision contributed to the achievements of his successors, first Yohannes and then Menelik, who, following in his footsteps, were destined to triumph where he had failed. Though condemned by many abroad for his imprisonment of the European captives, which contributed to his undoing, among his own compatriots the memory of a leader who preferred death to dishonour has over the last century and a quarter been increasingly revered.

BIBLIOGRAPHY

Contemporary letters and accounts

Abbadie, A. d', *L'Abyssinie et le roi Théodore*, Paris, 1868.
Acton, R., *The Abyssinian Expedition and the Life and Reign of King Theodore*, London, 1870.
Beke, C. T., *The British Captives in Abyssinia*, London, 1867.
Blanc, H., *A Narrative of Captivity in Abyssinia*, London, 1870.
Burette, H. A., *A Visit to King Theodore*, London, n.d.
Dimothéos Saprichian, *Deux ans de séjour en Abyssinie*, Jerusalem, 1871.
Dufton, H., *Narrative of a Journey through Abyssinia in 1862–3*, London, 1867.
Flad, J. M. *Zwölf Jahre in Abessinien, oder Geschichte des Konigs Theodorus II*, Basel, 1869.
Henty, G. A., *The March to Magdala*, London, 1869.
Holland, T. J. & Hozier, H. M., *Record of the Expedition to Abyssinia*, London, 1870.
House of Commons, *Correspondence respecting Abyssinia, 1846–1848*, London, 1868.
Hozier, H. M., *The British Expedition to Abyssinia*, London, 1869.
Isaacs, A. A., *The Life of the Rev. Henry Aaron Stern*, London, 1886.
Lejean, G., *Théodore II. Le nouvel empire d'Abyssinie et les intérêts françaises dans le sud de la Mer Rouge*, Paris, 1865.
Lindley, A. F., *The Abyssinian War from an Abyssinian Point of View*, London, 1868.
Markham, C., *A History of the Abyssinian Expedition*, London, 1869.
Napier, H. D., *Letters of Field-Marshal Lord Napier of Magdala*, Norwich and London, 1936.
Napier, R. J., *Theodore's Cattle*, Poona, 1869.
Noldeke, T., 'King Theodore of Abyssinia', in his *Sketches from Eastern History*, London, 1892.
Plowden, W. C., *Travels in Abyssinia and the Galla Country, with an Account of the Mission to Ras Ali in 1848*, London, 1869.
Rassam, H., *Narrative of the British Mission to King Theodore, King of Abyssinia*, London, 1869.

Shepherd, A. F., *The Campaign in Abyssinia*, Bombay, 1868.
Stanley, H. M., *Coomassie and Magdala*, London, 1869.
Stern, H. A., *Wanderings among the Falashas in Abyssinia*, London, 1862.
—*The Captive Missionary*, London, 1868.
Veitch, W. D., *Notes from the Journal of Martin Flad*, London, 1860.
Waldmeier, T., *Erlebnisse in Abessinien*, Basel, 1869.
—*The Autobiography of Theophilus Waldmeier*, London and Leominster, 1886.
Wilkins, H. St. C., *Reconnoitring Abyssinia*, London, 1870.

Ethiopian chronicles and letters

Appleyard, D. L. & Irvine, A. K., *Letters from Ethiopian Rulers (Early and Mid-Nineteenth Century)*, London, 1985.
Appleyard, D. L. & Pankhurst, R. K. P., 'The Last Two Letters of Emperor Téwodros II of Ethiopia (April 11 and 12, 1868)', *Journal of the Royal Asiatic Society*, 1987, I.
Fusella, L., 'La cronaca dell'Imperatore Teodoro II di Etiopia in un manoscritto amarico', *Annali dell'Istituto Universitario di Napoli*, 1954–6, VI.
—'Le lettere del dabtarā Assaggakakhañ', *Rassegna di Studi Etiopici*, 1961, 1963, XVII, XIX.
Girma-Selassie, Asfaw, Appleyard, D. L., & Ullendorff, E., *The Amharic Letters of Emperor Theodore of Ethiopia to Queen Victoria and her Special Envoy*, London, 1979.
Mondon-Vidailhet, F. M. C., *Chronique de Théodorus II, roi des rois d'Ethiopie (1853–1868)*, Paris, 1905.
Moreno, M. M., 'La cronaca di re Teodoro attributa al dabtarā Zaneb', *Rassegna di Studi Etiopici*, 1942, II.
Pankhurst, R. K. P., 'An Unpublished Letter of Emperor to Egégé, or Queen, Yätämäññu', *Ethiopian Journal of African Studies*, 1989, V.
—'An Unpublished Order of the King of Kings, Téwodros II, at the Institute of Ethiopian Studies', *Ethiopian Journal of African Studies*, 1988, V.
Pankhurst, R. K. P., & Girma-Selassie, Asfaw, 'An Amharic War-Song of Emperor Téwodros's Soldiers', *Journal of Ethiopian Studies*, 1985, XVIII.
—*Tax Records and Inventories of Emperor Téwodros of Ethiopia (1855–1868)*, London, 1978.
Ullendorff, E., 'A Letter from the Emperor Theodore to Queen Victoria', *Neue Afrikanische Studien herausgeben Johannes Lukas*, Hamburg, 1966.
Weld Blundell, H., 'History of King Theodore', *Journal of the African Society*, 1906–7, VI.

Recent writings

Amulree, Lord, 'Prince Alamayou of Ethiopia', *Ethiopia Observer*, 1970, XIII.
Chandler, D. G., 'The Expedition to Abyssinia, 1867–8' in Bond, B., *Victorian Military Campaigns*, London, 1967.
Chojnacki, S., 'William Simpson and His Journey to Ethiopia 1868', *Journal of Ethiopian Studies*, 1968.
Chojnacki, C. & Marshall, I., 'Colonel Milward's Abyssinian Journal', *Journal of Ethiopian Studies*, 1969, VII.
Crummey, D., 'Téwodros as Reformer', *Journal of African History*, 1969, X.
—'The Violence of Téwodros', *Journal of Ethiopian Studies*, 1971, IX.
Hooker, J. R., 'The Foreign Office and the Abyssinian Captives', *Journal of African History*, 1961, II.
Jesman, C., 'The Tragedy of Magdala', *Ethiopia Observer*, 1966, X.
Methodios of Aksum, Metropolitan, 'An Unpublished Document' [by Y. Kossika], *Abba Salama*, 1970, I.
Morgan, M., 'Continuities and Tradition in Ethiopian History: the Reign of Téwodros', *Ethiopia Observer*, 1969, X.
Myatt, F., *The March to Magdala*, London, 1970.
Pankhurst, R. J., 'The Library of Emperor Téwodros II at Maqdala (Magdala)', *Bulletin of the School of Oriental and African Studies*, 1973, XXXVI.
Pankhurst, R. K. P., *Economic History of Ethiopia 1800–1935*, Addis Ababa, 1968.
—'Indian Reactions to the Anglo-Indian Expedition against Emperor Téwodros of Ethiopia: the "Magdala Campaign" of 1867–8', *Africa* 1981, XXXVII.
—'The Napier Expedition and the Loot from Maqdala', *Présence Africaine*, 1985, CXXXIII–IV.
—'Popular Opposition in Britain to British Intervention against Emperor Téwodros of Ethiopia (1867–1868)', *Ethiopia Observer*, 1973, XVI.
—'Sir Robert Napier's Comments on Clement Markham's "History of the Abyssinian Expedition"', *Ethiopia Observer*, 1968, XII.
—'Téwodros as Depicted in European Engravings', *Journal of Ethiopian Studies*, 1987, XX.
—'Yohannes Kotzika, the Greeks and British Intervention against Emperor Téwodros in 1867–8', *Abba Salama*, 1972, III.
Pankhurst, R. K. P., & Ingrams, L., *Ethiopia Engraved*, London, 1988.
Rubenson, S., *King of Kings, Téwodros of Ethiopia*, Addis Ababa, 1865.
—*The Survival of Ethiopian Independence*, London, 1976.
Tadesse, Beyene, Pankhurst, R. K. P., and Shiferaw Bekele, *Kasa and Kasa. Studies of the Lives, Times and Images of Téwodros II and Yohannes IV (1855–1889)*, Addis Ababa, 1990.
Taye Assefa, 'Téwodros in Ethiopian Historical Fiction', *Journal of Ethiopian Studies*, 1983, XVI.

INDEX